PRAISE FO

'For those seeking deeper co   tine
crisis ... *Policy of Deceit* is the   , ran-minded
examination of the Hussein–McMahon correspondence that exposes
how the British government broke its promises to the people of Palestine
and concealed this betrayal from the British public.'

The Times Literary Supplement, Books of the Year

'In a dispassionate, meticulous account of the colliding promises Britain
made before the carve-up of the Ottoman Empire, and afterwards
denied, Shambrook nails the obfuscation, betrayal and imperialist
contempt that underlie the present catastrophe.'

Tablet, Best Books of the Year

'This superbly researched book grapples with the 100-year-old debate
over whether Palestine was included in the territories that the British
pledged to Hussein ibn Ali Sharif of Mecca, concluding that Palestine
was indeed a twice-promised land ... It is essential reading for anyone
interested in understanding the roots of the tension between the Arab
world and the West.'

Raja Shehadeh, author of *We Could Have Been Friends,*
My Father and I: A Palestinian Memoir

'Basing his narrative on painstaking archival research, Peter Shambrook
shows precisely how British policymakers dodged and weaved in order to
make the claim that Palestine was never included in the Hussein–McMahon
agreement. His forensic dissection of this particular "policy of deceit" is an
important contribution to the historiography of British rule in Palestine.'

Laila Parsons, Professor of Modern Middle
East History, McGill University

'Crisply, forensically and objectively, *Policy of Deceit* refutes once and for
all the contention that Britain excluded Palestine from the Arab lands to
which it pledged independence in the 1915–16 correspondence with the
Sharif of Mecca. The failure by successive British governments to face
the truth led to tragedy that endures to this day.'

John McHugo, author of *Syria: A Recent History*

PETER SHAMBROOK is an independent scholar and historical consultant to the Balfour Project, which works to advance equal rights for all in Palestine/Israel. He holds a PhD in modern Middle Eastern history from the University of Cambridge, and over the course of his career he has held a number of research positions, including at Durham University and at the Centre for Lebanese Studies in Oxford. He is the author of *French Imperialism in Syria, 1927–1936*. He lives in Durham.

POLICY OF DECEIT

Britain and Palestine, 1914–1939

Peter Shambrook

ONEWORLD
ACADEMIC

Oneworld Academic

An imprint of Oneworld Publications

First published by Oneworld Academic in 2023
This paperback edition published in 2024

ISBN 978-0-86154-949-8
eISBN 978-0-86154-633-6

ILLUSTRATION CREDITS

Sir Henry McMahon, Arnold Toynbee, Sir Hubert Young, Sir John Shuckburgh, Malcolm
MacDonald and Lord Maugham © National Portrait Gallery, London. Chaim Weizmann
© Sueddeutsche Zeitung Photo/Alamy. Ronald Storrs © Alpha Stock/Alamy. David Lloyd
George; Emir Abdullah with Sir Herbert Samuel and Winston Churchill; Lord Allenby,
Lord Balfour and Sir Herbert Samuel; and King Hussein in Amman, 1921, courtesy of the
Library of Congress, Prints & Photographs Division (LC-DIG-ggbain-33445, LC-DIG-
matpc-04380, LC-DIG-matpc-05811, LC-DIG-matpc-05807). Emir Feisal © Pictorial Press
Ltd/Alamy. George Antonius © Matteo Omied/Alamy. James Heyworth-Dunne, courtesy
of the Heyworth-Dunne family. McMahon's 24 October 1915 letter in English, courtesy of
the House of Commons Parliamentary Papers Online © 2006 ProQuest Information and
Learning Company/National Archives (FO371/23227). McMahon's 24 October 1915 letter in
Arabic, courtesy of the National Archives (FO371/23223). For map credits, see LIST OF MAPS.

Typeset by Geethik Technologies
Printed and bound in Great Britain by Clays Ltd, Elcograf S.p.A.

Oneworld Publications
10 Bloomsbury Street
London WC1B 3SR
England

MIX
Paper | Supporting
responsible forestry
FSC
www.fsc.org   FSC® C018072

Contents

To the memory of
James Roderick (Roddy) Evans (1923–2020)
Irish surgeon, scholar and peacemaker who courageously
acknowledged the shadow side of his community's past policies
veritas sine timore

List of Maps

Unthinking respect for authority is the greatest enemy of truth
Albert Einstein

Not everything that is faced can be changed;
but nothing can be changed until it is faced
James Baldwin

Introduction

In 1939, at the request of the Arab delegation to the London Conference on the future of Palestine, the British government finally agreed to the publication of the wartime Correspondence between Sir Henry McMahon, British High Commissioner in Cairo, and Sharif Hussein of Mecca, the Ottoman-appointed chief religious authority of Islam's holiest shrines. The Arabs and their supporters had consistently claimed since 1920 that in the Correspondence, McMahon, in return for the Sharif leading an Arab revolt against Ottoman forces, had included the Palestine region in the British government's offer of an extensive, independent Arab state. On the other hand, successive British governments since 1920 – and to this day – have argued that Palestine was excluded from the area promised to the Sharif.

Although publication of the Correspondence – ten letters exchanged between July 1915 and March 1916 – had been urged from all sides of both Houses of Parliament on no less than twenty-four occasions since 1920, successive British governments had always objected on the ground that it would be 'detrimental to the public interest'.[1] Moreover, throughout the 1920s and 1930s, Anglo-Arab relations were severely soured by such steadfast refusals. Only in February 1939, when Chamberlain's government wished to extinguish the Palestinian revolt, with war clouds gathering throughout Europe, and the need to 'secure Imperial routes to the East',[2] did the government agree to its publication.

At the same conference the government also agreed to establish an Anglo-Arab committee to investigate the Correspondence in detail.

---

1 Hansard, Lords, 1 March 1923, c232, statement by the Colonial Secretary.
2 FO 371/23225. Typewritten memorandum, unsigned (probably written by the Colonial Secretary), 27 February 1939.

Presided over by Frederic Maugham, the Lord Chancellor, the committee, following four lengthy meetings, ended in disagreement: in a joint report both sides held to their original positions, the Arabs maintaining Palestine was promised to the Sharif, and the Lord Chancellor arguing that 'on a proper construction of the correspondence, Palestine was in fact excluded.'[3] The Second World War then intervened, and the Correspondence disappeared from the political arena, never to be officially re-examined.

The evidence reviewed in this book reveals that the British case was untenable. A close and systematic study of the official records confirms that the Sharif was indeed entitled to consider Palestine included in the area promised for Arab independence. What is more surprising, in fact, shocking, is that all the senior officials involved on the committee, and in the cabinet, who were kept fully informed of the committee's proceedings, knew and acknowledged privately that the British case was seriously weak. The Lord Chancellor, having been briefed by Foreign Office officials and having read the relevant documents, was forced to produce 'out of the air' contentions in an attempt to bolster the British case, contentions which the government had never previously brought forward, and which he himself did not believe. He made this clear in a note to the Colonial Secretary, Malcolm MacDonald, who had appointed him to chair the committee and defend the government's position. His despair at having been handed such a poisoned chalice is revealed in the same note:

> ... how pleased I would be if I could hear of anyone in the Foreign Office or the Colonial Office or in the Government who could make one useful & helpful suggestion to assist in meeting or contesting the Arab claims.[4]

MacDonald, equally worried at the evident weakness of the British case, had also turned to the Attorney General, Sir Donald Somervell, for advice, but having read the relevant papers, Somervell's observations provided no comfort to the Colonial Secretary:

---

3 Anglo-Arab Committee Report (Cmd 5974), March 1939, 9.
4 CO 733/411/14, 45–46. Maugham to MacDonald, 28 February 1939. Underlined in the original.

It is, I think, very difficult to suggest that McMahon could have regarded Palestine as automatically excluded ... my own view [is] that the more we can avoid this issue the better, and that the more closely it is gone into, the greater I think our difficulties will appear to be.[5]

Thus, in 1939 the government's two most senior legal officials agreed that the British contentions were so weak that they would not stand scrutiny by an independent judicial inquiry, or by Parliament or public opinion. Yet, in a shrewd but dishonourable exercise, in what one scholar has termed 'sharp practice',[6] the Lord Chancellor publicly maintained the government's position in the report. For his part, the Colonial Secretary summed up the committee's conclusions by informing his colleagues, 'We have let the ball touch one stump without removing the bails.'[7]

MacDonald's cricket analogy was indeed apt: for a batsman to be 'out', at least one of the two bails needs to be removed from the top of the three stumps. The Lord Chancellor, batting, had been at the crease, defending his wicket, namely the government's red line (the exclusion of Palestine), while skilfully conceding, whenever expedient, some, but not all, of the Arab contentions bowled in his direction.

Since 1939, the truth of this matter has never been acknowledged by any British government. This book suggests it is time to do so: the evidence, both textual and contextual, is overwhelming. I hope this book will contribute to setting the record straight concerning Britain's multiple wartime promissory notes about Palestine and to the historiography of Britain's mandatory policies during the 1920s and 1930s, which led inevitably to the events of 1948 and whose legacy remains an 'open wound' for all who live between the River Jordan and the Mediterranean Sea, as well as for the millions of refugees beyond Palestine's borders.

Since the early 1970s, when I was first introduced to the study of nineteenth- and twentieth-century French and British involvement in the

5 FO 371/23226, E1572. Somervell to MacDonald, 27 February 1939.
6 Geoffrey Furlonge, *Palestine Is My Country. The Story of Musa Alami* (London, 1969), 226.
7 FO 371/23231, E2166, 319. Baggallay minute, 18 March 1939.

Near East,[8] Britain's wartime pledges between 1914 and 1918 have held my attention, perhaps because the region has not experienced peace since that particular global conflict. In particular, my curiosity about the Correspondence pledge deepened because of the wide range of opinions which had been offered over the decades by established, reputable historians and other writers, many of whom were explicitly non-committal on the subject. In 2009, I decided to dig further into this issue after reading the preamble to *Palestine. A Twice-Promised Land?* by Professor Isaiah Friedman,[9] in which he categorically states that 'The refusal to allow publication was due not to the weakness of the British government's case, as its critics suspected, but to considerations entirely unconnected with Palestine.'[10] His book is the most recent on the subject and uncritically supports the 100-year-old interpretation of the Correspondence by successive British governments, as does Elie Kedourie's *In the Anglo-Arab Labyrinth* (1976). However, on my desk was a photocopy of a six-page, handwritten minute of 16 May 1930 by the acknowledged Foreign Office expert on the Correspondence, William J. Childs, who unambiguously pointed to Palestine as the principal reason why the government would be unwise to publish. According to Childs, the Arab contentions that Palestine was included in the area promised to the Sharif were 'almost irrefutable'.[11] So where does the truth lie?

This book refutes both Friedman's and Kedourie's main claims. It grapples afresh with the undoubtedly labyrinthine complexities of this now 100-year-old debate – cover-up, cock-up, or neither – whose political and moral repercussions still resonate today. In the West, and in Western historiography generally, the Correspondence is not a major issue, but in the Arab world it remains as a symbol of *la perfide Albion* and as an essential foundation stone of the running sore of the unending Arab–Israeli conflict, a touchstone of current febrile relations between the West, the Arab world and the wider world of Islam. The key issue in the Correspondence debate

---

8 Up to the early twentieth century, the Near East referred to lands between Persia (Iran) and the Mediterranean Sea. Today the terms Middle East and Near East are often used interchangeably.

9 Isaiah Friedman, *Palestine. A Twice-Promised Land? The British, the Arabs & Zionism 1915–1920* (New Brunswick, 2000). Published in Hebrew as *The Myth of the Double Promise*.

10 Friedman, *Palestine. A Twice-Promised Land?*, xix.

11 FO 371/14495, 10–11.

is whether Palestine was included in the promise, that Britain and the pro-Zionist historians say it wasn't, and that this book demonstrates conclusively that it was – in other words Britain lied all along. This is relevant today: the Israeli–Palestinian conflict was made in Britain.

History should be written responsibly. Any proper understanding of the modern history of Palestine, indeed, of the Middle East, must be predicated on a non-defensive, frank appreciation of Britain's role during the First World War and its legacy. This book confirms that Palestine was twice (if not thrice) promised by successive British governments in 1915, 1916 and 1917. A century later, these wartime pledges are not merely a matter of academic interest. They sowed the seeds of a bitter conflict for the control of Palestine, and established the political, economic and military framework which has contributed significantly to the appalling, relentless and still unresolved hundred-year war for Palestine. Moreover, the failure to resolve the latter has contributed in no small manner to radicalisation within the Middle East, and between that region and the West in recent decades. Even now, the long-time diplomat Sir George Rendel's 1957 assessment can hardly be contested:

> I still believe that this issue [Palestine] – and particularly the eventual creation of the independent State of Israel – played a major part in altering the whole trend of our relations with the Arab and Moslem world, and that many of our Middle Eastern difficulties today are due to the inconsistencies of our Palestine policy during this critical period.[12]

Prior to the Second World War, two major studies – *The Arab Awakening* by George Antonius and *Palestine. The Reality* by J.M.N. Jeffries[13] – both concluded that the Arabs' interpretation of the Correspondence was correct. Neither author, of course, had access to the official records of the period, some of which were opened in the 1960s, and led to a plethora of publications on many aspects of Britain's role in Palestine and the creation of the State of Israel. However, relatively few provide a balanced synthesis of the history of the three main players involved,

---

12 George Rendel, *The Sword and the Olive. Recollections of Diplomacy and the Foreign Service, 1913–1954* (London, 1957), 124.
13 George Antonius, *The Arab Awakening* (Beirut, 1938), reprinted 1969; J.M.N. Jeffries, *Palestine. The Reality* (London, 1939), reprinted 2017.

many explicitly or implicitly supporting either the concept of *la sainte Albion* or *la perfide Albion*.

Since the 1960s, only three scholars have published detailed studies on the McMahon–Hussein Correspondence, namely Isaiah Friedman (*The Question of Palestine, 1914–1918*, 1973; *Palestine. A Twice-Promised Land?*, 2000), Elie Kedourie (*In the Anglo-Arab Labyrinth. The McMahon–Husayn Correspondence and Its Interpretations, 1914–1939*, 1976) and Abdul Latif Tibawi (*Anglo-Arab Relations and the Question of Palestine, 1914–1921*, 1977). According to Tibawi, a Palestinian scholar, whose detailed study was limited to the period 1914–1921, British governments acted dishonestly, Palestine was undoubtedly included in the area promised to the Sharif and the Arabs' case was sound, linguistically, politically and morally. In contrast, Friedman (an Israeli professor) and Kedourie (a British professor of Iraqi Jewish heritage), who both cover the period 1914–1939, come down decisively, but not uncritically, on the British governments' side of the debate. They both give Britain's two wartime governments a clean sheet, Friedman explicitly and Kedourie implicitly, arguing that all of Britain's wartime pledges were compatible, that in the Correspondence Palestine was excluded from the territories pledged to the Sharif, and exonerating successive British governments of almost any moral or political double-dealing. According to them, McMahon's letters, written in the heat of war, were merely a series of ambiguous, obscure statements of intention regarding future policy, and both suggest that the principal reasons why British governments between 1920 and 1939 refused to publish the Correspondence bore little or no relation to Palestine.

To my knowledge, this is the first comprehensive study of the subject since the appearance of Friedman's *Palestine. A Twice-Promised Land?* twenty years ago. Over the past decade, as I made my own extensive study of the relevant official records between 1914 and 1939, a distinctive counter-narrative, particularly to that of Kedourie and Friedman, began to emerge from the documents, which suggests that their interpretation of the Correspondence requires reappraisal. The following brief points concerning their theses which caught my attention are not exhaustive, but are nevertheless significant.

Friedman's thesis rests largely on the context in which the Correspondence was written, which is a plausible and relevant approach, rather than on the text. However, the analysis he does

provide of both the English and Arabic texts of the letters is unconvincing, and in part, quite unsound. In particular, his explanation of
the meaning of the word 'districts' (*wilāyāt* in Arabic) in the
Correspondence is, in my opinion, linguistically untenable. As the
reader will see in Chapter One, the debate concerning the meaning of
the word *wilāyāt* has played a significant role in the discordant
historiography of the Correspondence.

For his part, Kedourie also uses an extensive range of the relevant
documents to build his case. However, as I worked my way through the
official records, with Kedourie's *Labyrinth* in one hand and the documents
in the other, I became increasingly aware – and surprised – that he had
omitted to use a number of sources which appeared to me essential to an
understanding of the Correspondence itself, and of the reasons why its
publication was withheld until 1939. These significant omissions include:

- Any reference regarding Childs's minute to Lord Monteagle and Sir
  John Shuckburgh on 16 May 1930, warning them of the difficulty
  that any government spokesman would face in parliamentary debate
  concerning the Correspondence because of the Arabs' 'almost irrefutable' arguments.
- The British government's acknowledgement in 1937 that the Sharif
  of Mecca did not know in 1915 of French interests in Palestine.
- Colonel Vickery's 1919 (inaccurate) 'vilayets' translation of the
  Correspondence circulated by the government to the Arab delegates
  on 14 February 1939.
- Deputy Foreign Minister 'Rab' Butler's subsequent embarrassment
  in the Commons on 1 March 1939, when the question of an inaccurate British translation of the texts was raised.
- The Lord Chancellor's qualms concerning the strength of his own
  novel 'unique position of Palestine' contentions, which he employed
  in order to bolster the British case during the 1939 Anglo-Arab
  Committee's proceedings.
- The existence, role and findings of James Heyworth-Dunne, the
  independent scholar employed in 1939 by the Foreign Office to
  provide a definitive, accurate translation of the letters.

Moreover, Kedourie made almost no use of the extensive reports of the
four meetings of the Anglo-Arab Committee in February and March 1939,

the only committee (to date) ever appointed by a British government to investigate and officially report on the Correspondence. The reports of the four meetings, written by British officials, describe in forensic – and revealing – detail, for the first and only time, the official British and Arab contentions and counter-contentions, and are central to an understanding of the debate over the Correspondence. The overwhelming body of evidence presented in this book reveals that the resultant Anglo-Arab report can only be described as a government whitewash.

Chapter Eight provides a more detailed discussion of Kedourie's and Friedman's theses, as well as those of Antonius, Jeffries, Tibawi and Ernest Dawn.[14] The most recent academic debate – now fifty-two years ago – concerning the Correspondence was the appearance of two contrasting articles in the *Journal of Contemporary History* in 1970 by Friedman and Arnold Toynbee, who politely but robustly argued that specific aspects of each other's theses concerning the inclusion or exclusion of Palestine in the Correspondence were untenable.[15]

Although the Correspondence understandably disappeared from the British political scene in the summer of 1939, since the 1970s, scores of scholars, with increasing access to the official records of Britain, Israel, the United States, France, the League of Nations and other sources, have commented briefly on the Correspondence in their diverse surveys of modern Middle Eastern history. A majority, including established scholars such as Albert Hourani, Martin Gilbert, Jonathan Schneer, Benny Morris, Ian Black, Eugene Rogan and Sean McMeekin, have on the whole remained non-committal on the issue, commenting typically that the truth of the matter 'remains elusive' and is a 'matter of dispute'. However, some twenty years ago, in his magnum opus, *The Iron Wall*, Avi Shlaim wrote that 'Britain's public promise to the Jews could not be reconciled either with its earlier promise to Hussein, the sharif of Mecca, … or with the secret Sykes-Picot agreement of 1916',[16] and in a

---

14 C. Ernest Dawn, 'Hashimite Aims and Policy in the Light of Recent Scholarship on Anglo-Arab Relations during World War I', in *From Ottomanism to Arabism* (Urbana, 1973), 87–121.

15 Isaiah Friedman, 'The McMahon-Hussein Correspondence and the Question of Palestine', *Journal of Contemporary History*, vol. 5, no. 2 (1970), 83–122; Arnold Toynbee, 'The McMahon-Hussein Correspondence: Comments and a Reply', and Friedman's response, *Journal of Contemporary History*, vol. 5, no. 4 (1970), 185–201.

16 Avi Shlaim, *The Iron Wall. Israel and the Arab World* (London, 2000), 7.

recent study Rashid Khalidi maintained that 'for decades, British officials disingenuously but steadfastly maintained that Palestine had been excluded from wartime promises of Arab independence.'[17]

This divergence of interpretations by successive generations of scholars does suggest that there is no easy answer to the question. In a sense, there are not one but two fundamental and related questions to be investigated, and, if possible, answered: in the Correspondence, was Palestine included in the area assigned for Arab independence, and why did successive British governments consistently decline to publish the Correspondence until 1939?

My own research, a primary source-based study, has led me to the conclusion that the Sharif was indeed entitled to conclude from the Correspondence, and in particular from McMahon's letter of 24 October 1915, that the Palestine region was included by the latter as within the area assigned for Arab independence. As to the second question concerning non-publication, the official records reveal that the principal reason was that Foreign Office and Colonial Office officials, as well as successive cabinets, were almost always united in their conviction that the government could not effectively defend their interpretation of Palestine's exclusion from the area promised to Hussein, either in Parliament or in front of national and world opinion.

Chapters One to Seven describe events between 1920 and 1939, based primarily on the Foreign Office, Colonial Office, cabinet records and the parliamentary (Hansard) online records, as well as officials' memoirs, papers and other international primary and secondary sources, including the press. The Correspondence rarely found its way into the public arena during the interwar period, except when raised in parliamentary debate. Indeed, the events can only be adequately analysed by a close study of the primary sources. In the text I have endeavoured to let the personalities involved speak for themselves as much as possible by the use of extensive quotations, rather than allowing my own interpretation to come to the fore.

All writers of history have a primary responsibility to their readers, to interpret the sources at their disposal and to produce a coherent narrative which reflects the truth of the past to the extent that it can be

---

17 Rashid Khalidi, *The Hundred Years' War on Palestine. A History of Settler Colonial Conquest and Resistance* (London, 2020), 37.

discovered. On a subject such as this, any discerning reader will treat any writer's claim to impartiality with considerable caution, and rightly so. Nevertheless, every writer has their personal journey, assumptions and perspective. When I started to investigate this affair, I did not have a thesis upon which to build or to be proved. Since my introduction to studies of modern Middle Eastern history in the 1970s I had always considered the Correspondence to be a slightly obscure, unresolvable mystery incorporating the type of typically vague, non-binding, secret pledge that empires make when searching for allies in times of need. My interpretation gradually changed as my research of the primary documents progressed.

Chapter One provides an essential, brief description of the Ottoman region of Palestine, followed by a historical survey of nineteenth- and twentieth-century European relations, focused specifically on those events relevant to our story. It also provides the reader with some understanding of the political mindsets of the decision-makers in the corridors of power in London, Paris, St Petersburg, Vienna, Berlin and Constantinople (now Istanbul) during the First World War, as they searched for allies to give them a strategic edge over their enemies.

Key Figures

Abdullah ibn Hussein (1882–1951) Represented Mecca in the Ottoman parliament, 1909–1914. Became Emir of Transjordan in May 1921, and reigned as King of the independent state of Jordan, 1946–1951. A key figure in the Arab Revolt, alongside his younger brother Feisal. Assassinated in 1951 in Jerusalem.

Allenby, Sir Edmund (1861–1936) Commander-in-Chief of the British Third Army in France from October 1915; Commander-in-Chief of the Egyptian Expeditionary Force, 1917–1918; High Commissioner in Egypt, 1919–1925. Best known for capturing Jerusalem in December 1917.

Amery, Leo (1873–1955) Conservative politician and journalist. War cabinet secretary in Lloyd George's government. Lord Milner asked him to draft the Balfour Declaration. Under-Secretary of State for the Colonies, 1919–1921; First Lord of the Admiralty, 1922–1924; Colonial Secretary, 1924–1929; Secretary of State for India and Burma, 1940–1945.

Antonius, George (1891–1942) Lebanese-Egyptian author and diplomat, best known for his book *The Arab Awakening* (1938). Served as a civil servant in the Mandatory administration in Palestine during the 1920s; Secretary-General to the Arab Delegation at the London Conference in 1939.

Asquith, Herbert (1852–1928) Liberal Prime Minister, 1908–1916.

Baggallay, H. Lacy (1897–1943) Acting Head of the Eastern Department (Middle East), Foreign Office, 1939–1940.

Balfour, Arthur (1848–1930) Conservative Prime Minister, 1902–1905, whom Lloyd George brought back as Foreign Secretary in December 1916. Published the Balfour Declaration in November 1917. Resigned in 1922.

Baxter, Charles W. (1895–1969) Head of the Eastern Department (Middle East), Foreign Office, 1938–1939, 1940–1947.

Beckett, Sir W. Eric (1896–1966) Second Legal Advisor, Foreign Office, 1929–1945; Legal Advisor, Foreign Office, 1945–1953.

Bushe, Sir H. Grattan (1886–1961) Legal Advisor, Colonial and Dominions Offices, 1931–1941; Governor of Barbados, 1941–1946.

Cavendish, Victor C.W., ninth Duke of Devonshire (1868–1938) Conservative politician. Governor-General of Canada, 1916–1921; Secretary of State for the Colonies, 1922–1924.

Chamberlain, Neville (1869–1940) Prime Minister, 1937–1940.

Childs, William J. (*c.* 1869–1933) Traveller, member of the Intelligence Department (Admiralty) and Foreign Office official, mid 1920s–1931. Author of *Across Asia Minor on Foot* (1918), and of a significant memorandum on the Correspondence (May 1930).

Churchill, Winston (1874–1965) Secretary of State for the Colonies, 1921–1922, in Lloyd George's administration. Prime Minister, 1940–1945 and 1951–1955.

Clayton, Gilbert (1875–1929) Director of Military Intelligence at British Army Headquarters, 1914–1916; in charge of the Arab Bureau and Hijaz operations, 1916–1917; Chief Political Officer in Egyptian Expeditionary Force, 1917–1918; Military Governor, Palestine, 1917–1919; Chief Secretary to the Palestine administration, 1922–1925.

Cocks, F. Seymour (1882–1953) Labour MP, 1929–1953. Campaigned in Parliament for the publication of the Correspondence.

Colville, John Rupert (1915–1987) Foreign Office official and Secretary of the Anglo-Arab Committee, established in 1939 to investigate the Correspondence. Assistant Private Secretary to three Prime Ministers: Neville Chamberlain, 1939–1940, Winston Churchill, 1940–1941 and 1945, and Clement Attlee, 1945.

Crossley, Anthony (1903–1939) Conservative MP who campaigned in Parliament for publication of the Correspondence.

Djemal Pasha, Ahmed (1872–1922) Commander of the Ottoman Fourth Army and Military Governor of Syria from December 1914; recalled following the loss of Jerusalem, December 1917. Assassinated in Georgia by Armenians in July 1922 in retribution for his role in the Armenian genocide.

Downie, Harold (1889–1966) Head of the Middle East Department, Colonial Office, 1937–1943.

Feisal ibn Hussein (1885–1933) The third son of Hussein ibn Ali, the Sharif of Mecca. Elected in 1913 to the Ottoman parliament to represent Jedda. Took a leading role in commanding operations during the Arab Revolt of 1916–1918. King of Iraq, 1921–1933.

Friedman, Isaiah (1921–2012) Professor of History at Ben-Gurion University of the Negev, and author of, among many works, *Germany, Turkey and Zionism, 1897–1918* (1977) and *Palestine. A Twice-Promised Land?* (2000).

Grey, Sir Edward (1862–1933) Secretary of State for Foreign Affairs, 1905–1916; Ambassador to the USA, 1919–1920; Leader of the Liberal Party, House of Lords, 1923–1924.

Heyworth-Dunne, James (1902–1974) Orientalist who studied Arabic literature under H.A.R. Gibb. Was Senior Lecturer in Arabic, School of Oriental Studies, London University, when employed by the government to translate the Correspondence in 1939. Multilingual (Arabic, Turkish, Persian and Urdu); published and edited many books about the Islamic world.

Hogarth, David (1862–1927) Archaeologist and scholar; Keeper of the Ashmolean Museum, Oxford, 1909–1927. As Acting Director, Arab Bureau, 1916, he was instrumental in bringing T.E. Lawrence into intelligence work in Cairo. President, Royal Geographical Society, 1925–1927.

Howard-Bury, Colonel Kenneth (1881–1963) Soldier, explorer, botanist and Conservative MP, 1922–1924, 1926–1931. Led the 1921 British Mount Everest reconnaissance expedition; one of the few MPs who championed Palestinians' aspirations in the House of Commons, and campaigned for publication of the Correspondence.

Hussein ibn Ali (1853–1931) Appointed Emir of Mecca in 1908 by Sultan Abdul Hamid. Revolted against the Ottoman government in June 1916. Recognised as King of Hijaz in 1916. After Abdul Aziz ibn Saud overran the Hijaz in 1925, he spent the rest of his life in exile.

Husseini, Jamal (1894–1982) Secretary to the Executive Committee of the Palestine Arab Congress, 1921–1934, and to the Muslim Supreme Council. Leader of the Arab Delegation to the St James's Conference, 1939.

Ibn Saud, Abdul Aziz (1875–1953) Born in Riyadh; consolidated his control of Nejd by 1922; overran the Hijaz in 1925; King of Saudi Arabia, 1932–1953; presided over the discovery of petroleum in 1938.

Jeffries, J.M.N. (1880–1960) War Correspondent for the *Daily Mail*; visited Palestine in 1922 with Viscount Northcliffe, the paper's owner. A severe critic of British mandatory policy in Palestine, he is best known as author of *Palestine. The Reality* (1939, 2017).

Kedourie, Elie (1926–1992) Historian who taught at the London School of Economics between 1953 and 1990; the author of some nineteen books, many on the politics of the modern Middle East.

Kitchener, Herbert (1850–1916) Commander-in-Chief, Egyptian Army, 1892–1899; Consul-General in Egypt, 1911–1914; Secretary of State for War, 1914–1916. Drowned while on his way to Russia in June 1916.

Lawrence, Edward (T.E.) (1888–1935) Intelligence Officer in Egypt, December 1914–November 1916, then transferred to the Arab Bureau to work on Hijaz operations, where he worked closely with Emir Feisal. Renowned for his role in the Arab Revolt, 1916–1918.

Lloyd George, David (1863–1945) Minister of Munitions, May 1915–July 1916; Secretary of State for War, July–December 1916; Liberal Prime Minister, December 1916–October 1922.

MacDonald, Malcolm (1901–1981) Secretary of State for the Colonies, June–November 1935 and May 1938–May 1940; High Commissioner to Canada, 1941–1946.

MacDonald, Ramsay (1866–1937) Labour Prime Minister, Foreign Secretary and Leader of the House of Commons, January–November 1924; Prime Minister (National Government), 1929–1935.

Mackenzie, James Young (1914–1971) Foreign Office official who wrote an influential memorandum on the Correspondence in December 1938.

Maugham, Frederic (1866–1958) Barrister and judge; Lord Chancellor of England and Wales, 1938–1939.

McDonnell, Michael (1882–1956) Chief Justice of Palestine between 1927 and 1936. After Cambridge, where he studied medicine and law, he joined the Colonial Service in 1911 and served in British West Africa for sixteen years before being appointed to Palestine. An advocate of the Arab cause in Palestine.

McMahon, Sir Henry (1862–1949) British Indian Army officer; High Commissioner in Egypt, 1915–17.

Milner, Lord Alfred (1854–1925) High Commissioner for Southern Africa, 1897–1905. As Minister without Portfolio in Lloyd George's war cabinet, he played a key role in drafting the Balfour Declaration.

Monteagle of Brandon, Thomas, Third Lord (1883–1934) Head of the Eastern Department (Middle East), Foreign Office, 1928–1930.

Oliphant, Sir Lancelot (1881–1965) Head of the Eastern Department (Middle East), Foreign Office, 1920–1928; Assistant Under-Secretary of State for Foreign Affairs (Middle East), 1928–1936; Deputy Under-Secretary of State for Foreign Affairs (Middle East), 1936–1939.

Ormsby-Gore, William (1885–1964) Intelligence Officer, Arab Bureau, Cairo, 1916, attached to Sir Henry McMahon; Parliamentary Private Secretary to Lord Milner and Assistant Secretary in the war cabinet, 1917; British military liaison officer with the Zionist Commission in Palestine, March–August 1918; British representative to the Permanent Mandates Commission of the League of Nations, 1921–1922; Under-Secretary of State for the Colonies, 1922–1929 (with a brief interruption during 1924); Secretary of State for the Colonies, 1936–1938. Significant senior official in the development of Britain's pro-Zionist mandatory policy in the 1920s and 1930s.

Rendel, Sir George W. (1889–1979) Head of the Eastern Department (Middle East), Foreign Office, 1930–1938.

Rothschild, James (de) (1878–1957) A decorated army officer during the First World War. Liberal MP for the Isle of Ely, 1929–1945; President of the Palestine Jewish Colonization Association from 1924.

Rūhi, Husayn (c. 1885–1960) Occasional spy for the British; translator, poet and author; an Arabic-speaking Persian best known for translating into Arabic (with Ronald Storrs) McMahon's letters to Sharif Hussein in 1915–1916. Between 1920 and 1935 he worked as a school inspector in the Palestine Department of Education.

Al-Said, Nuri (1888–1958) Arab Ottoman Army officer who joined the Arab Revolt in July 1916. Followed Emir Feisal to Iraq after the war, and served fourteen terms as Iraqi Prime Minister between 1930 and 1958.

Samuel, Sir Herbert (1870–1963) The first High Commissioner for Palestine, 1920–1925; Leader of the Liberal Party, 1931–1935.

Shiels, Drummond (1881–1953) Labour politician. Under-Secretary of State for India, 1931; Under-Secretary of State for the Colonies, 1929–1931.

Shuckburgh, Sir John (1877–1953) Secretary, Political and Secret Department, India Office, 1917–1921; Assistant Under-Secretary of State for the Colonies (Head, Middle East Department), 1921–1931; Deputy Under-Secretary of State for the Colonies, 1931–1942.

Somervell, Sir Donald (1889–1960) Attorney General for England and Wales, 1936–1945.

Storrs, Ronald (1881–1955) Oriental Secretary, Cairo, 1909; member of the Arab Bureau, 1916–1920; Governor of Jerusalem, 1920–1926; Governor of Cyprus, 1926–1932; Governor of Northern Rhodesia, 1932–1934.

Sykes, Sir Mark (1879–1919) Traveller in the Middle East, Conservative politician and political advisor who negotiated the Sykes–Picot Agreement.

Thomas, James Henry (1874–1949) Trade unionist and Labour politician. Secretary of State for the Dominions, 1930–1935; Secretary of State for the Colonies briefly in 1924, 1931 and 1935–1936.

Tibawi, Abdul Latif (1910–1981) Palestinian historian and educationalist who taught at London University, Institute of Education, 1948–1977. Wrote extensively on many aspects of Middle Eastern history.

Toynbee, Arnold (1889–1975) Historian and author of numerous books, who taught for many years at the London School of Economics, and King's College London. A leading commentator and specialist on international affairs.

Wedgwood, Josiah (1872–1943) Conservative MP and committed Zionist.

Weizmann, Chaim (1874–1952) Russian-born chemist. Head of the Zionist Commission to Palestine, 1918; President of the World Zionist

Organisation, 1920–1931, 1935–1946; first President of Israel, 1949–1952.

Williams, Owen G.R. (1886–1954) Head, Middle East Department, Colonial Office, 1928–1937.

Wingate, Sir Reginald (1861–1953) Governor-General of the Sudan and Commander-in-Chief (*Sirdar*) of the Egyptian Army, 1899–1916. Succeeded Sir Henry McMahon as High Commissioner in Egypt, 1917–1919, and retired from the army in 1922.

Wood, Edward, third Earl of Halifax (1881–1959) Parliamentary Under-Secretary of State for the Colonies, 1921–1922; Viceroy and Governor of India, 1926–1931; Secretary of State for Foreign Affairs, 1938–1940.

Young, Sir Hubert (1885–1950) Assistant Political Officer and Logistics Officer in Mesopotamia, 1915–1918; Secretary to the Interdepartmental Conference on the Middle East, Foreign Office, 1919–1921; Assistant Secretary, Colonial Office (Middle East), 1921–1927.

West of the Line of the Four Towns

1915–1919

Palestine: A Brief Outline

A small region of Western Asia, Palestine owes it name – *Filastīn* in Arabic – to the Greeks and Romans, and before them to the biblical Philistines. Locally, Palestine was perceived for millennia as part of *Bilad al-Sham* (Greater Syria or *la Syrie intégrale* – roughly today's Syria, Lebanon, Israel/Palestine and Jordan). It is bordered in the north by today's Lebanon, to the east by the River Jordan and the Dead Sea, in the west by the Mediterranean Sea, and in the south, after a British–Ottoman agreement in 1906, by a marked frontier with Egypt which separates today's Israel from the Sinai Peninsula.

Although the Palestine region had been Arab in language, culture and collective historical memory since the Muslim Arabs seized it from Byzantium, the predecessor of the Ottomans, in 637 CE, its twentieth-century inhabitants were not merely the descendants of the seventh-century conquerors, but the cumulative populace that included all the races, including the Hebrews and pagan tribes, that had entered and settled in Palestine since the dawn of history. The region thus had a diverse and multicultural population and a multilayered identity deeply rooted in the ancient past.

The Ottoman Turks, who defeated the Byzantine Empire when they occupied Constantinople in 1453, took Palestine in 1516, and remained its masters until 1918. Politically, Palestine belonged, except for the interlude of the Crusades in the twelfth and thirteenth centuries, to whoever ruled in Baghdad, Cairo, Damascus and Constantinople, but culturally it remained an integral part of an Arabic-Islamic civilisation for some thirteen centuries. The cradle of Judaism, and later of Christianity, Palestine was for the Islamic world the home of Jerusalem's al-Aqsa mosque and the Dome of the Rock – the third most sacred site after Mecca and Medina – from where the Prophet Muhammad had ascended to heaven in 632 CE.

The Ottoman Empire was divided into distinct administrative units (in descending order): *vilayets* (provinces), *sanjaqs* and *nahiyas*. Palestine, however, had always been a geographical entity, never an officially defined administrative entity. In 1918, it roughly covered the Ottoman Sanjaqs of Acre, Nablus and the Independent Sanjaq of Jerusalem, which, in 1872, had been accorded this higher status, meaning its governor (*mutasarref*) enjoyed the prerogatives of a *vali* (provincial governor) so far as executive powers and direct reference to Constantinople went. (The Lebanon had been similarly elevated into an 'independent sanjaq' (*Mutasarrifate*) in 1861.[1]) Roughly one fifth the size of England, at 10,000 square miles, Palestine measures some 260 miles (north to south) and between 35 and 40 miles (east to west). It was only with the British Mandate that Palestine acquired defined political boundaries, for the first time in its history (Figure 2).

In 1914, Arabs constituted some 92 percent of the population, of whom 90 percent were Muslim and 8 percent Christian. The small Jewish population (some 7 percent of the total) was largely religious. They were not foreigners, nor were they Europeans or settlers; they were, saw themselves, and were seen as Jews who were part of the Muslim-majority society.[2] At that time, Jewish land ownership in Palestine comprised some 2 percent. According to Shlomo Ben-Ami, Israeli historian and former Foreign Minister, when David Gruen (later David Ben-Gurion) arrived in Palestine in 1906 from the Polish town of Płońsk, 'the country consisted of 700,000 inhabitants, 55,000 of whom were Jews, and only 550 could be defined as Zionist pioneers.'[3] In 1918, British authorities estimated that out of a total population of 639,000, some 80 percent (512,000) were Muslim Arabs, 10 percent

---

1 Between 1861 and 1920, this semi-autonomous region within Greater Syria was known in English as 'the Lebanon', in French as 'Mont Liban' and in Arabic as *jabal lubnān*. It did not include the city of Beirut.

2 Rashid Khalidi, *The Hundred Years' War on Palestine* (London, 2020), 19.

3 Shlomo Ben-Ami, *Scars of War, Wounds of Peace: The Israel-Arab Tragedy* (London, 2005), 2.

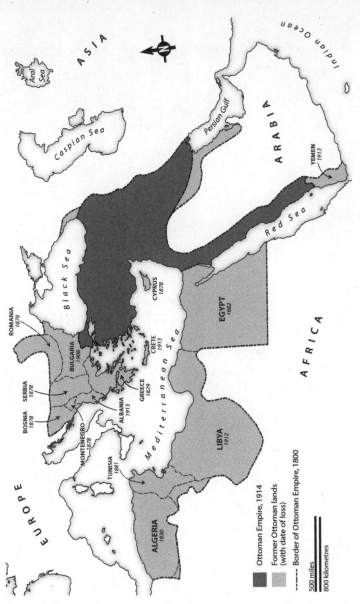

Figure 1: The Ottoman Empire, 1914

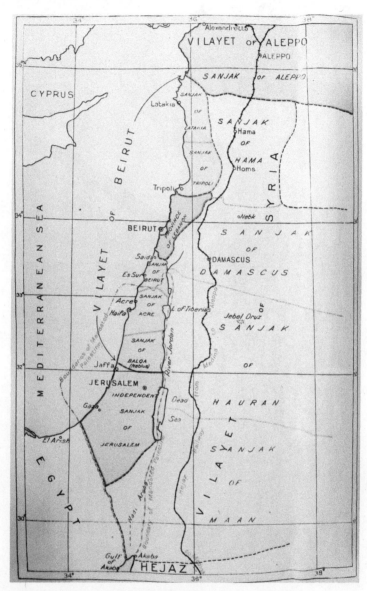

Figure 2: Ottoman administrative divisions in the Levant, 1915

(61,000) Christian Arabs, and 10 percent (66,000) Jews, of whom some 15,000 were European (mostly Russian and Polish) Jewish settlers who had arrived since the 1880s. Many of the latter lived in forty-five rural colonies (*moshavot*) and were quite distinct from the indigenous, Arabic-speaking Jewish community (*Yishuv*), the majority of whom lived in four towns, namely Jerusalem, Safed, Tiberias and Hebron.[4]

In common with other Arab regions of the Ottoman Empire, in 1914, Palestinian society was predominantly rural and pre-industrial, and led by a traditional and patrician urban elite. In principle, the governors, senior administrators and judges in the Ottoman Empire's provinces were sent from Constantinople and appointed for one year only, to prevent them from putting down roots and identifying themselves with the local community. In practice, however, a large share of political power passed into the hands of the local elite of Sheikhs, *ulama* (religious hierarchy) and landowners, and the region had sent representatives to the Ottoman parliament since it was created in the late nineteenth century. People generally conversed in Arabic, while all official correspondence was conducted in Ottoman Turkish; the upper 'notable' classes were bilingual. In a few towns soap was manufactured, as well as pottery, glass, lace, embroidery and clothes. Wheat, barley, olive oil and citrus fruit had been exported to Europe since the second half of the nineteenth century.

Between 1914 and 1916, Syria, including Palestine and Lebanon, suffered severe famine. Food, livestock and fuel were in short supply due to the requisitions of the Turkish military. Villages were ravaged by military drafts, and devastated by cholera, typhus and recurrent fever. The Jewish population was depleted by emigration and the deportation of enemy nationals, especially Russians, whose loyalty was suspect: some ten thousand were shipped to Alexandria. In the spring of 1915, all fifty thousand civilian inhabitants of Jaffa were expelled, for fear they might assist the British in any advance. In Jerusalem, as in Beirut and Damascus, Arab nationalists had been hanged by the Turkish authorities, who ruthlessly enforced conscription.[5]

---

4 Ian Black, *Enemies and Neighbours. Arabs and Jews in Palestine and Israel, 1917–2017* (London, 2017), 19.

5 Kristian Coates Ulrichsen, *The Logistics and Politics of the British Campaigns in the Middle East, 1914–22* (Basingstoke, 2011), 151.

When the British occupied Palestine in 1918, conditions were undoubtedly dire: starvation, disease and privation prevailed. Nevertheless, nearly
one third of Palestine was still cultivated (approximately 3,300 square
miles), another third was urban and the rest a mixture of desert, small
natural reservoirs and what had been flourishing forested areas before
they were erased by the Turkish war machine. The region was both popu-
lated and cultivated, neither empty nor desolate. It could not, by any
stretch of the imagination, be described as *terra nullius*, as some Zionists
sought to characterise it. As Sir Herbert Samuel, Britain's first High
Commissioner to Palestine, told the Permanent Mandates Commission in
1924, under the Ottomans there had been a system of government where
there were taxes, newspapers,[6] schools, a system of land registration,
political parties, a judicial system, hospitals and a railway.[7]

Cooperation, Rivalry and the Search for Allies

The purpose of this section is not to summarise in a few pages the
complex course of nineteenth- and early-twentieth-century international relations, but to direct attention to events and trends that illumi-
nate the 'broken promise' story to follow. Britain's policies during the
First World War, including its pledges regarding the future of the Near
East, can only be understood in the context of its relations with the
other Great Powers in the preceding decades, when 'trading' territories
and colonies, and dividing 'buffer' states into zones of influence was
normal Great Power diplomacy.[8]

During the nineteenth century, a major industrial and technological
expansion in Britain contributed to an accelerating growth of the

---

6 Thirty-two new newspapers were established in Palestine between 1908 and 1914,
with even more in the 1920s and 1930s. See Khalidi, *The Hundred Years' War on
Palestine*, 19.

7 Minutes of the Fifth Session at Geneva, 28 October 1924, pp. 59–94. Cited in
Victor Kattan, *From Coexistence to Conquest: International Law and the Origins of the
Arab-Israeli Conflict, 1891–1949* (London, 2009), 135.

8 Literature on the origins, process and legacy of the First World War is extensive.
For an excellent primer, see Norman Stone, *World War One. A Short History* (London,
2008). Two comprehensive studies are Hew Strachan, *The First World War* (London,
2003) and John Keegan, *The First World War* (London, 2014).

economy and pressure to seek new overseas markets. This resulted in unrelenting competition with other Great Powers, principally France and Russia, for the monopolisation of markets, control over valuable raw materials and domination of the lines of communication. A Great Power capable of controlling trade routes could also control a rival's access to the sources of raw materials and potential markets. But in forging ahead of France in Asia and the Pacific, and in crowning that achievement by conquering India, Britain stretched its lines of transport and communications so far that they could be cut at many points.

A major influence on eighteenth- and nineteenth-century British foreign policy was suspicion of Russia's designs on Constantinople, which was regarded as the 'key to India'. This was partly because of its proximity to the overland routes to the east and partly because it was feared that if Russia occupied Constantinople, it would be able to dominate the Near East. Russia longed for warm-water ports with access to the world's seas. Britain in turn bolstered an ailing Ottoman Empire to keep the Russians safely bottled up in the Black Sea. From 1830 onwards, Lord Palmerston and his successors feared that if Russia destroyed the Ottoman Empire, the scramble to pick up the pieces might lead to a major war between the European powers. Britain had little desire to control directly the Near East region during the nineteenth century, but did wish to keep any of its European rivals from doing so. The Crimean War of 1854–1856 was fought mainly to check Russian influence over Turkey; Queen Victoria put it clearly: it was, she said, 'a question of Russian or British supremacy in the world'.[9]

In 1882, Britain occupied Egypt to safeguard the Suez Canal (which had been opened in 1869), restore Egypt's political and financial stability, and prevent France from occupying it first. The country was not declared a colony but remained in theory an autonomous province of the Ottoman Empire ruled by a hereditary khedive. In reality, it was a veiled protectorate presided over with absolute authority in the areas that mattered by a series of British Consul-Generals: Evelyn Baring, later Lord Cromer (1883–1907), Sir Eldon Gorst (1907–1911) and Lord Kitchener (1911–1914).

---

9 David Fromkin, *A Peace to End All Peace: Creating the Modern Middle East, 1914–1922* (London, 1989), 27; G.D. Clayton, *Britain and the Eastern Question: Missolonghi to Gallipoli* (London, 1971), 139.

Meanwhile, to the west of Egypt, France had occupied Algeria in 1830, Tunisia in 1881 and most of Morocco by 1914. Further south, the partition of much of the rest of the continent by the Great Powers in the 'Scramble for Africa' was accomplished in about twenty years, roughly between 1880 and 1900. Equally striking was the sheer scale of the share-out. By 1900, only about one tenth of Africa had not fallen under European rule, whereas twenty years earlier only one tenth had been colonised.[10] To the existing colonial powers of Britain, France, Spain and Portugal were now added Germany, Italy and Belgium. Britain was involved in rivalry during this period with virtually all of these countries at one stage or another. This is not surprising since Britain had used its sea power to assert a sort of 'paramountcy' over most of Africa's coasts in the mid nineteenth century.

In the latter part of the nineteenth century, British governments perceived no necessity to contemplate changes that would give Egyptians or Indians a real measure of control over the defence and foreign policies pursued in their name. Indeed, across the whole span of imperial commitments, the absence of any serious colonial revolt (following the suppression of the Indian Mutiny in 1858) seemed to suggest to the policymakers in London that there was little if any need to envisage any substantial alteration in the methods by which British control was exerted. A not untypical example of a nineteenth-century imperial leader's mindset is that of Evelyn Baring (later Lord Cromer), a colonial administrator with several years' service in India (before moving to Egypt) who was convinced of the innate superiority of Western civilisation and who believed that all 'Orientals', including Egyptians and Indians, would require many, many more decades of enlightened tutelage before they absorbed and mastered the ways of the West. 'Let us,' he wrote, 'in Christian charity, make every possible allowance for the moral and intellectual shortcomings of the Egyptians, and do whatever can be done to rectify them.'[11] Cromer's distorted and self-serving model of Egyptian society would serve as a template for what the British chose to see in Palestine: a land composed of three

---

10 John Lowe, *Rivalry and Accord: International Relations 1870–1914* (London, 1988), 54.
11 Lord Cromer, *Modern Egypt* (London, 1908), vol. II, 538. A graduate of the Royal Military Academy, Woolwich, and a lover of the classics, Cromer (1841–1917) read and spoke Greek, Latin, Italian, French and Turkish. He never learned Arabic.

religious communities, only one of which, the Jews, had national rights and status.

For such decision-makers – they were all men – either in London or in the colonies, India 'belonged' in the British Empire, the Ottoman Turks were not really Europeans and 'Arab nationalism' was not part of their diplomatic lexicon. In the context of our story, concerning the decision-makers' mindsets, it is notable that almost all of Lloyd George's last cabinet had lived their formative years in the nineteenth century. Balfour was born in 1848, Milner in 1854, Bonar Law in 1858. Curzon was, in Lord D'Abernon's phrase, 'born grandiloquent' in 1859. All but Lloyd George (born 1863) and Churchill (born 1874) were in their forties when the twentieth century began.

In 1870, Prussia's incorporation of the southern German states, including Bavaria and Württemberg, into the new German Empire transformed the political situation in Central Europe. The subsequent Franco-Prussian war of 1871 was a disaster for France, which was outnumbered, outgunned and outmanoeuvred. It marked the end of an era in which France had been regarded as the great military power on the continent, alongside Russia. The victors demanded the cession of Alsace and Lorraine, two provinces with rich iron ore deposits, textile industries and good agricultural land. They also insisted upon an indemnity of 5,000 million francs, and until it was paid German troops occupied parts of France. A final humiliation was a victory march through Paris, and the Kaiser being proclaimed German Emperor in the palace of Versailles in January 1871. Instead of a relatively weak collection of states with powerful neighbours on each side, 'Germany' was now a major power, the product of 'blood and iron', as Bismarck aptly expressed it.[12]

Between 1871 and 1914, Germany became the greatest industrial power on the continent. Unification, creating a single internal market, contributed to its rapid economic expansion. By 1900, it had outstripped Britain, previously the leading industrial nation in Europe, and was second in the world only to the United States. The figures speak for themselves: between 1870 and 1913, the British gross national product (GDP) grew by 124 percent, while that of Germany grew by 229 percent. In 1880, Britain's share of world manufacturing production was 23

12 Lowe, *Rivalry and Accord*, 1–3.

percent, Germany's 8 percent; and in 1913, the figures were 14 and 15 percent, respectively.[13] The growth of the German economy intensified the competition among all industrial states for markets and raw materials. This, combined with population growth, increased the pressure on Germany's leaders to transform their country from a continental power into a global empire.

An agreement, commonly known as the Triple Alliance, was formed between the 'Central Powers' of Germany, Austria-Hungary and Italy in 1882, mostly at the behest of Germany, which perceived itself as surrounded, and under a rising threat from both an openly revengeful France, smarting under the loss of Alsace and Lorraine, and Russia, the Big Bear to its east. Socially conservative, France was, in spite of its intellectual vitality, deeply aware of its military inferiority. The events of 1870 had shown that the French could not on their own beat the German army. In an effort to guarantee its security against an increasingly powerful neighbour, France signed an agreement with Russia in 1894 that became the keystone of the former's foreign policy for the next decade.

In 1897, Germany embarked on a policy of *Weltpolitik* that was, by intent, a rejection of the restrained 'continental policy' of the Bismarck era. The emphasis was now on expansion, especially overseas, and the creation of a large navy that would demonstrate Germany's status as a world power. For its part, Britain's reliance on imported food and raw materials, and the need for markets for its manufactured goods, meant that the nation's lifeblood was dependent on the uninterrupted flow of seaborne trade. To ensure that the sea lanes remained open to merchant shipping, Britain considered that it had to maintain its global naval supremacy. Moreover, as the only European power that did not introduce conscription after 1871, Britain lacked the mass army of its continental rivals. Furthermore, much of the British Army was either deployed in the defence of India or was scattered throughout the rest of the Empire. By 1900, many British statesmen were becoming convinced that Britain's resources were overstretched and that it needed allies if it were to maintain its role as a world power. Hence, the settlement (*entente cordiale*) of long outstanding disputes between Britain and

---

13 Bernard Regan, *The Balfour Declaration* (London, 2017), 2; Niall Ferguson, *Empire. How Britain Made the Modern World* (London, 2003), 288.

France in 1904 – in essence an agreement about Africa, where France was to be given a free hand in Morocco in return for Great Britain having one in Egypt. In 1907, under pressure of mounting tension in Europe, a second alliance was formed when the British government, now a Liberal one under Sir Henry Campbell-Bannerman, agreed with Russia to divide Persia into three zones: a Russian zone adjacent to its frontier; a British zone to the south-east covering the Indian border; and a neutral zone separating the two. Their agreements on Tibet and Afghanistan also contributed to the security of India, long the key issue in Anglo-Russian antagonism. In effect, both sides agreed not to meddle, to the disadvantage of the other, in the internal affairs of these two 'buffer' states.[14]

Thus it was that by 1907 Europe was divided into two increasingly rival sets of 'power-alliances': on one side, the Triple Entente (Great Britain, France and Russia) and on the other, the Triple Alliance (Germany, Austria-Hungary and Italy). Germany's sense of insecurity was intensified by Britain's agreements with France and Russia, creating what the Germans called 'encirclement' but which Britain and its partners regarded as 'containment' of an unpredictable Germany.

The years 1905 to 1909 saw a great increase in international tension, precipitated in large measure by the Anglo-German naval race. From 1906, this became focused on the construction of a new class of battleship developed in Britain – the dreadnought. Britain won the contest – by 1914, it had commissioned twenty to Germany's fifteen – but the damage done to Anglo-German relations was immense. In German eyes, Britain's naval supremacy did not belong to it as some kind of 'divine right', but from London's perspective any threat to Britain's naval supremacy was considered a threat to both the nation and the Empire. Secretary of State for Foreign Affairs Sir Edward Grey insisted in 1913 that 'The Navy is our one and only means of defence and our life depends on it.'[15]

In 1907, the formation of the Triple Entente also raised the spectre of Great Power cooperation in dismembering the Ottoman Empire, whose leaders responded in two ways. They re-emphasised military

---

14 Lowe, *Rivalry and Accord*, 104–105.
15 Lowe, *Rivalry and Accord*, 108.

reform in the hope that they, like the Japanese, could ward off Europe by developing more effective European-style armed forces, and they strengthened the Empire's economic, military and diplomatic ties with Germany, a potential ally in any confrontation with the Triple Entente.

The Ottoman Empire thus became a major factor in Germany's imperial planning, not least because its capital, Constantinople, straddles the Bosphorus. In the age of naval power this was one of the world's strategic bottlenecks: it was through the Black Sea Straits that much of Russia's trade was conducted. In time of war, a hostile Turkey could menace not only the flow of supplies to Russia but also, as previously mentioned, Britain's imperial lines of communication with India. For these reasons, the Germans had worked hard to secure Turkey as an ally in the years before 1914. Kaiser Wilhelm II visited Constantinople twice, in 1889 and 1898. Since 1888, the Deutsche Bank had played a leading role in financing the so-called Berlin–Baghdad railway. From the early 1880s, German military officers helped to train and modernise the Ottoman Army; between 1883 and 1896, the German Field Marshal Colmar von der Goltz was employed by the Sultan to overhaul his forces, while another German, Otto Liman von Sanders, was appointed the army's Inspector General in 1913.[16]

Thus, by 1914, a European 'balance of power' which had kept the peace between great states for over forty years was distinctly fragile. Yet, on the eve of the conflict, many European statesmen were still finding it difficult to see why another conference of ambassadors or even a European congress (as in 1878) would not extricate them from their problems. Then came the assassination on 28 June 1914 of Archduke Franz Ferdinand, the heir to the throne of Austria-Hungary. On 30 July, even before the Turks had finally committed themselves to fighting alongside Germany, the Kaiser was planning the next move:

> Our consuls in Turkey, in India, agents ... must fire the whole Mohammedan world to fierce rebellion against the hated, lying, conscienceless nation of shopkeepers, for if we are to bleed to death, England shall at least lose India.[17]

---

16 Ferguson, *Empire*, 302.
17 Ferguson, *Empire*, 302.

By the end of the following week, Europe was at war. The Ottoman Empire joined forces with Germany in November. None of the powers involved expected to get bogged down in a muddy, bloody stalemate, especially on the Western Front. In fact, the benign word 'stalemate' hardly does justice to the scale of carnage and suffering on all sides. In the Franco-Prussian war of 1870, French casualties amounted to some 17,000, and the Prussians' to 10,000. In comparison, by the end of 1915, the French army had lost 300,000 dead, and in 1916 the battle before Verdun added another 315,000; the Germans lost 280,000. In 1916, the British suffered 420,000 casualties on the Somme and the Germans a similar number. The following year, some 400,000 died to gain five miles of mud at Passchendaele.[18] As the stalemate developed, Britain's search for allies became more acute.

This international relations background is the lens through which Britain's wartime agreements (secret and public) and declarations concerning the Ottoman Empire, including its Arab provinces, need to be considered. Such agreements, forged in the heat of war, marked a continuation of a tradition stretching back at least two hundred years, as each power strove to defeat their enemies, neutralise potential enemies and win new allies. If the war had been won, or lost, by the spring of 1915, there would have been no negotiations with the Sharif of Mecca, and a declaration in 1917 in favour of a Jewish national home in Palestine distinctly uncertain.

Wartime Agreements: Dividing Up the Bear's Skin

At the beginning of the war there was no unanimity among British policymakers concerning the future of Arabia or the Ottoman Empire's Arab provinces. Secretary of State for War Herbert Kitchener's plans for an Arabian Raj, essentially an Arabian Kingdom under the auspices of England,[19] were completely unacceptable to Arthur Hirtzel (Secretary, Political Department, the India Office), who saw the Persian Gulf, Aden and the Mesopotamian provinces as no more than adjuncts to India. The third competing view emanated

---

18 J.M. Roberts, *The New Penguin History of the World* (London, 2004), 893, 896.
19 See Elie Kedourie, *In the Anglo-Arab Labyrinth. The McMahon–Husayn Correspondence and Its Interpretations, 1914–1939* (Cambridge, 1976), 60–61.

from the Liberal Prime Minister Herbert Asquith himself, who became increasingly reluctant (and Foreign Minister Edward Grey more so) for the Empire to take on any more territory, this for material rather than sentimental or moral reasons. Asquith wrote later that when the cabinet discussed the opportunities that lay in the Ottoman Empire, 'their discussions had resembled that of a gang of buccaneers.'[20] But he then added that 'if we were to leave other nations to scramble for Turkey without taking anything ourselves, we should not be doing our duty.'[21]

As previously mentioned, it was standard eighteenth- and nine-teenth-century Great Power policy for allies to negotiate which victori-ous power would take which region(s) of their defeated foes' territories, and the First World War was no exception to this tradition. In spring 1915, the Triple Entente governments concluded the Constantinople Agreement: Russia would take Constantinople and the Straits; France would take Syria,[22] Cilicia and Alexandretta; the British reserved their right to (any) Ottoman territory 'in due course'. This was followed by the McMahon–Hussein Correspondence, conducted between July 1915 and March 1916, in which the British promised the Arabs an independ-ent Arab state if they rose against the Turks; the Sazonov–Sykes–Picot Agreement of May 1916, where the three Allies drew 'lines on a map', delineating their respective regions of postwar influence and control over the whole of the Middle East;[23] the Balfour Declaration of November 1917, in which Britain promised to facilitate the establish-ment of a Jewish national home in Palestine; and finally, the Anglo-French Declaration in November 1918, which affirmed the latter's war aims as 'the complete and final liberation of the peoples who have for so long been oppressed by the Turks, and the setting up of national

---

20 H.H. Asquith, *Letters to Venetia Stanley*, eds. Michael and Eleanor Brock (Oxford, 1982), 469.

21 Martin Gilbert, *Winston S. Churchill. Companion Volume III, Part 1: July 1914–April 1915* (Boston, 1973), 716.

22 Namely, *la Syrie intégrale*: Ottoman Syria, which stretched from the Taurus Mountains to Aqaba and included the region of Palestine.

23 On 7 January 1916, General Macdonogh, Director of the Intelligence Department at the War Office, remarked, 'We are rather in the position of the hunters who divided up the skin of the bear before they had killed it.' FO 371/2767.

governments and administrations deriving their authority from the free exercise of the initiative and choice of the indigenous populations'.[24]

How complementary, or contradictory, these pledges – 'expansionist bookings-in-advance'[25] – were has been a matter of acrimonious debate for a hundred years. Although there are other unresolved issues surrounding all the aforementioned promises, 'The Question of Palestine' has been at the heart of this debate. Was Palestine a twice-promised land, pledged by McMahon to be part of an Arab state, and subsequently to the Zionist Organisation as an eventual Jewish state? Given the prevailing political and military constraints (five empires at war), the Constantinople Agreement, McMahon–Hussein Correspondence and the Sazonov–Sykes–Picot Agreement were all conducted in strict secrecy: only the Balfour Declaration and the Anglo-French Declaration were made public immediately. None of the aforementioned were discussed in either the French or the UK parliaments, but merely privately arranged among the Allies without any consultation with the populations of the Middle East, as was standard eighteenth- and nineteenth-century European imperial practice.

However, in the five years or so after the war, as well as numerous internal discussions in the Foreign Office and the Colonial Office, there were vigorous debates concerning these wartime pledges and agreements in both Houses of Parliament and in the press. From 1929 onwards, mostly in response to unrest or rebellion in Palestine, parliamentary debates on Middle Eastern policy almost invariably included some (usually brief) discussion of the wartime pledges, including the Correspondence, but successive governments' refusals to publish the latter remained steadfast until 1939.

The Correspondence itself consisted of a series of ten letters, all written in Arabic, exchanged in the period from July 1915 to March 1916 between Sharif Hussein of Mecca and Sir Henry McMahon, the British High Commissioner in Cairo, representing the British government. The letters can only be understood in the context of the Allies' war against the Ottomans, otherwise their very existence just doesn't make sense. The British, before the war and after it, had little, if any,

---

24 FO 371/3384.

25 Elizabeth Monroe's apt phrase. Elizabeth Monroe, *Britain's Moment in the Middle East, 1914–1956* (London, 1963), 26.

desire whatever to promote Arab nationalism and, certainly before the war, had no particular desire to promote Jewish nationalism.

The strategic context to the genesis of the Correspondence in the historiography is uncontested. When the Ottomans declared war on the Allies in November 1914, the latter were confident the Turks, the 'sick man of Europe',[26] would buckle rapidly under the combined onslaught of Britain, France and Russia. The Allies' confidence was misplaced. In January 1915, Djemal Pasha, the Commander of the Ottoman Fourth Army, led a force of eighty thousand men across the Sinai Peninsula for a quick strike against the Suez Canal, but the campaign was poorly coordinated, and the Ottomans were driven back before they could cross the Canal. Nevertheless, alarmed by the near success of the Pasha's attack, the British began a massive build-up of troops in Egypt. At the same time, with stalemate on the Western Front, Winston Churchill (First Lord of the Admiralty) believed there was an opportunity to attack Germany 'through the back door'. But the Gallipoli campaign to take Constantinople, well documented elsewhere, was a total defeat and provoked a political crisis in Britain. According to Sean McMeekin, had the Russians delivered the troops they had promised to Kitchener during the Dardanelles and Gallipoli campaigns, the Ottoman war might have been over by spring 1915.[27]

Allied war planners' fear of jihad among colonial Muslims now became even more acute: 100 million Muslims lived under British rule, mostly in India and Egypt, including 400,000 Muslim men serving in the Indian Army. Whitehall feared that war with the Ottomans, the only independent Muslim power, and the Caliph of Islam might over-tax India's loyalty; there was, of course, another major British fear – the military threat to the Suez Canal at a time of need for the quick passage

---

26 According to Sean McMeekin, the phrase 'Sick Man' was first used by Tsar Nicholas I in conversation with the British Ambassador Sir George Hamilton Seymour in March 1853, the Tsar's idea being to broach plans for a general Ottoman partition. He did not say 'Sick Man *of Europe*'. Nevertheless, the phrase became popular in early-twentieth-century British historiography. Sean McMeekin, *The Ottoman Endgame: War, Revolution and the Making of the Modern Middle East, 1908–1923* (London, 2015), 288.

27 McMeekin, *Ottoman Endgame*, 289. For two excellent accounts, see Eugene Rogan, *The Fall of the Ottomans. The Great War in the Middle East 1914–1920* (London, 2015), 129–158; McMeekin, *Ottoman Endgame*, 163–221.

of Indian troops to France. The throttling of the Canal would not just embarrass England, but cripple its Empire communications. Land attacks on the Canal could only be made across territories inhabited by Arabs, and one way of reducing or even successfully warding off that threat would be to win the Arabs over to the Allied side.

Whitehall hoped that an alliance with the Sharif of Mecca, Hussein ibn Ali, would neutralise the appeal of the Sultan-Caliph's call to jihad, proclaimed in Constantinople in early November 1914, which had caused profound concern in Paris as well as London.[28] Even a partially successful jihad might prove a serious threat to the Allies. The British wanted, to quote one writer, 'to rob the call to Holy War of its principal thunderbolt', by striking an agreement with Sharif Hussein themselves.[29] Appointed by Sultan Abdul Hamid in 1908, the Sharif belonged to the Hashimite family and traced his lineage back forty-one generations to the Prophet Muhammad, who was born in Mecca and was himself a member of the house of Hāshim, a noble clan of the Quraysh tribe. The Sharif, cautious, single-minded, autocratic and ambitious, had devoted his first years in office to the construction of a network of tribal alliances that would enable him to obtain a greater degree of autonomy from Constantinople, whose centralising policies he opposed. He showed no desire to give up his quasi-independent status, his armed following, or his authority over the population of the Hijaz.

The distance between the imperial capital and the Hijaz, magnified by its primitive state of transportation and communications, had always lent it considerable autonomy. About 750 miles long and, at its widest, about 200 miles across, it precariously supported a population estimated at some 300,000, half Bedouin, half townsmen. Dates were the staple crop, but the main industry of the province was the annual pilgrimage: about seventy thousand pilgrims made the journey to Mecca each year. The imperial government, dominated as it was by the Committee of Union and Progress, was intent on extending the Hijaz railway from Medina to Mecca and to the port of Jedda, which would have threatened the camel-owning Hijazi Bedouin tribes and their lucrative control of the pilgrim routes to the Holy Places.

---

28 Rogan, *Fall of the Ottomans*, 184.

29 Antonius, *Awakening*, 140. The Hashimites established themselves as hereditary emirs of Mecca sometime before the Ottomans took control of the city in 1517.

Although the British hoped that a counter-declaration of jihad by the Sharif would turn the fledgling Arab nationalist movement against the Ottomans, they had little confidence that the Arabs would or could develop an effective military machine that would seriously endanger Germany's eastern ally. In fact, when the British first conceived the idea of encouraging an Arab revolt, they hardly expected it to break out much beyond the Hijaz. Moreover, as Ronald Storrs admitted years later, to encourage the transfer of the Caliphate from Constantinople to Hussein was attractive precisely because, in 'uniting the strongest religious with the weakest material power, it would be greatly to our interest'.[30]

Contacts between Britain and the Hashimites began, in fact, six months before the war broke out. In February 1914, Emir Abdullah, the Sharif's second son, travelled to Cairo to meet with Herbert Kitchener, the British Consul-General of Egypt. Abdullah then had two subsequent meetings with Ronald Storrs, the Oriental Secretary,[31] at the residency. The Emir, who had no particular admiration for the British, nevertheless wished to sound out the latter's attitude if there were to be a revolt in the Hijaz against the Turks. Since the Young Turk government's rise to power in 1908, its policies of Turkification and centralisation had increasingly alienated the Arab communities throughout the Ottoman Empire. The new constitution gave no weight to the principle of equality. Turkish was to replace Arabic in schools and official forums. Enver Pasha, the Ottoman Minister of War, withdrew Arab officers from their posts and excluded Arabs from military schools. These policies led some Arabs throughout Syria – students, writers, military men and local politicians – to create a number of underground 'Arab nationalist' movements for increased Arab autonomy and local self-governance within the Empire. Abdullah knew the Ottoman government had secretly decided to depose his father, who secretly hoped to create an

---

30 Ronald Storrs, *Orientations* (London, 1939), 160.

31 Storrs later recalled that 'Tradition within the Agency – that is of documents and archives – was (and is) preserved by the archivist; tradition without – political, diplomatic and social – by the Oriental Secretary, who must anyhow be the eyes, ears, interpretation and Intelligence (in the military sense) of his Chief, and might become much more. His influence extended with that of the British Agent, and in the zenith of British power in Egypt – that is from 1890 until the War – the post, usually filled from the Levant Consular Service, was one of the minor key positions in the Near East.' Storrs, *Orientations*, 62.

autonomous Hijaz, but Storrs was not encouraging – the British and Ottoman empires were publicly still on relatively friendly terms – and the conversations closed without issue. However, they did open the eyes of Kitchener and Storrs to the strength and depth of Turko-Arab animosity, and to the possibility of turning it to Britain's advantage.

In the last week of September 1914 – that is, following the outbreak of war between Britain, France and the Central Powers, but before the Ottomans had entered the war – Kitchener (newly appointed Minister of War by Asquith), concerned as he was for the strategic defence of the Empire, including the Canal and the Persian Gulf, directed Storrs to enquire of Abdullah whether, in the event of Turkey joining the Central Powers, his father would loyally support the latter or join Great Britain. Eventually, the Sharif replied that he was potentially willing to come to an understanding with the British, and hinted that it might be possible to lead his immediate followers in the Hijaz to revolt, provided Britain promised effective support and guarantees. In fact, Hussein discovered in January 1915, through intercepted letters, written evidence that the Ottoman government were planning to depose him at the end of the war – and indeed had postponed doing so only because of the conflict.[32] He was also acutely aware that the Arabs of the Hijaz, or indeed anywhere else in the Empire, were not sufficiently prepared – militarily, politically or economically – to rise up against the Ottomans. German officers had been training the Ottoman Army since the end of the nineteenth century and Hussein's few rifles would be no match for Turkish machine guns and artillery. For their part, the British considered that any Arab revolt against Ottoman authority would be helpful, but they had no expectation that it would do much apart from keeping some extra Turkish troops holed up fighting in the Hijaz, and peppering the Turkish armies with desertions. As it turned out, when the revolt occurred, not a single Arab unit of the Ottoman Army defected intact. Like the Ottoman holy war, Hussein's holy war failed to catalyse the Arabs to rebel en bloc, but nevertheless Hussein's forces were to play a not insignificant role in the campaign against the Turks between 1916 and 1918.

On 31 October 1914, just a week before the Ottomans declared war on Britain and France, Kitchener's second note promised the Sharif that if he and his followers were to side with the Entente powers, the

---

32 Fromkin, *A Peace to End All Peace*, 174.

British government would guarantee his retention of the dignity of Grand Sharif and defend the Hijaz against all external aggression. He held out a vague promise of support to the Arabs in general in their endeavours to secure freedom, on condition that they would ally themselves to Britain. The note, in Arabic, spoke of the 'Arab nation', the 'emancipation of the Arabs' and concluded with a hint that, in the event of the Sharif being proclaimed caliph, he could count on England's recognition. Ten months later, McMahon, equally unwisely, stated in his first letter to the Sharif: 'We now declare once more that the government of Great Britain would welcome the reversion of the caliphate to a true Arab born of the blessed stock of the Prophet.'[33]

On 16 November, Kitchener's message reached Abdullah, who replied in early December on behalf of his father, committing the latter to a secret alliance with England; he asked for time to prepare, to complete his enquiries among other Arab leaders and to muster his forces. Given the need to preserve secrecy – the Sharif and his sons were undoubtedly contemplating treason – this procedure took some eight months. Eventually, on 14 July 1915, the Sharif wrote to Sir Henry McMahon, this first letter reaching Cairo on some unknown date in August. Meanwhile, the Turks continued to press for the Sharif's endorsement of jihad and for his active support. Deluged as he was with letters and telegrams from Constantinople, his defence for not doing so publicly he put down to his fear of enemy reprisals: the British navy controlled the Red Sea, and the long seaboard of the Hijaz was entirely at its mercy.

In his letter the Sharif stated the Arab terms for intervention, and set out clearly the natural boundaries of the Arab countries for which he demanded independence:

On the north, by the line Mersin–Adana to parallel 37° N and thence along the line Birejik–Urfa–Mardin–Midiat–Jazirat (ibn 'Umar)–Amadia to the Persian frontier; on the east, by the Persian frontier down to the

---

33 McMahon to Sharif Hussein, 30 August 1915; *Correspondence between Sir Henry McMahon, His Majesty's High Commissioner at Cairo, and the Sherif Hussein of Mecca, July 1915–March 1916 [with a map]* (Cmd 5957), March 1939, 4. Copy in FO 371/23227, 356–365; reproduced here in Appendix I, it can also be found online at https:// palestinianmandate.files.wordpress.com/2014/04/cm-5957.pdf (accessed 30 September 2022; the map is missing from the final page). A (proof) original copy is in FO 371/ 23231, E2166, 16 March 1939, 4. See also Antonius, *Awakening*, 416.

Persian Gulf; on the south, by the Indian Ocean (with the exclusion of Aden whose status will remain as at present); on the west, by the Red Sea and the Mediterranean Sea back to Mersin.[34]

These borders were essentially those traced by the Damascus Protocol, a series of proposals for an independent Arab state stretching from Anatolia to the Gulf and Red Sea (Figure 3), which originated from a Greater Syria political project developed clandestinely by members of two Arab nationalist groups, *al-Fatat* (the Young Arab Society) and *al-'Ahd* (the Covenant Society).

Having originally approached Emir Feisal, the Sharif's third son, in secret in January 1915, later the same year, on 23 May in Damascus, these two groups formally presented him with the proposals, requesting that he present them to his father for approval. Feisal, who became a member of *al-Fatat* sometime during that period, returned to Mecca in June, the Protocol, 'written out in Lilliputian characters', sewn inside the lining of one of his retainers' boots.[35] With Abdullah's support, Feisal persuaded his father to support the document. According to Jonathan Schneer, the Protocol was 'the foundation document and lodestar of the Arab Revolt'.[36]

The Sharif's letter included other mutual stipulations: first, that Great Britain would agree to the proclamation of an Arab Caliphate for Islam; second, the Sharifian Arab government would grant Great Britain preference in all economic enterprises in the Arab countries; third, they would come to each other's assistance in the event of any foreign state attacking either of them – peace would be concluded only when both parties concurred; and fourth, Great Britain would agree to the abolition of the capitulations.[37] For prudence's sake, the letter bore no date

---

34 *Correspondence* (Cmd 5957), 3; Antonius, *Awakening*, 414.

35 Antonius, *Awakening*, 159.

36 Jonathan Schneer, *The Balfour Declaration. The Origins of the Arab-Israeli Conflict* (London, 2010), 54; Regan, *Balfour Declaration*, 94–96.

37 During the time of the Ottoman Empire's military hegemony, successive Sultans sought to encourage trade with the West by granting rights and privileges to the subjects of various Christian European nations who took up residence or conducted trade in Ottoman territories. These arrangements were known as capitulations. When Europe became militarily superior in the eighteenth and nineteenth centuries, the Ottomans went further, allowing the European powers to enjoy substantial economic and political advantages. For example, foreigners resident in the Ottoman Empire were subject not to local laws but those of their respective countries.

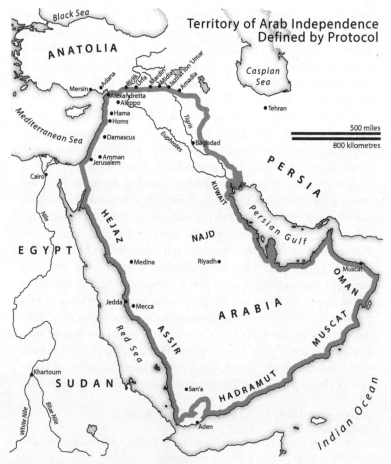

Figure 3: The Damascus Protocol, 1915

and no signature, and had been carried in the greatest secrecy by the Sharif's trusted emissary Sheikh Muhammad 'Aref ibn 'Uraifan from Mecca to Cairo, a long and exceedingly dangerous journey of at least eight hundred miles, depending on the route taken. It was enclosed in a letter from Abdullah addressed personally to Storrs, and dated 14 July 1915.

History has not revealed to us exactly where the Sheikh hid the letter on his journey. Somewhere in the inner folds of his garments, or perhaps sewn into the lining of his footwear? Storrs himself, a decade before this Correspondence saga, had been an Assistant Inspector of Customs at Alexandria, and had considerable experience of smugglers' talents. Hashish smugglers, for example, he wrote later, 'introduced their drug in chair-legs, piano-pedals, false calves, olives, as well as in unbelievable fastnesses of the human frame'.[38]

What we do know is that all ten letters arrived safely, a remarkable achievement in wartime. As for the mysterious route that the trusted Sheikh took between Mecca and Cairo, two alternatives come to mind. From Mecca to the coastal port of Jedda is some 45 miles, at that time a two-day trip by camel, followed by a voyage across the British-controlled Red Sea to Port Sudan (some 180 miles) by *sambuk*, a light, lateen-rigged Arab sailing vessel. The Sheikh would then have had a choice: the faster, simpler and probably safer route, perhaps taking a further week, would be by steamer northwards for 770 miles to the town of Suez, from where there was a rail link (85 miles) westwards to Cairo. Otherwise, from Port Sudan, the train 300 miles north-west to Abu Hamad (Northern Sudan), then by camel track for over 300 miles northwards to Aswan, the southern-most terminal of the Egyptian railway system, before a 550-mile rail journey north from Aswan to Cairo. This second route would have taken more than three weeks to complete.

When this letter reached Sir Henry McMahon, who had replaced Kitchener as High Commissioner in Egypt at the beginning of 1915, the British were still confident of defeating the Ottomans in Gallipoli and were not impressed by what they considered to be Hussein's pretentions. However, as the Allied position in the Dardanelles grew increasingly untenable, McMahon resumed negotiations with the Hashimites with a new sense of urgency: an agreement with Hussein became more

---

38 Storrs, *Orientations*, 44.

of a priority for the British, particularly from the perspective of officials in Cairo. And in London, Sir Edward Grey noted, 'What we want is Arab help <u>now</u> against the Turks.'[39]

The new High Commissioner was a long-serving officer of the Indian Political Service, whose last appointment in India had been that of Foreign Secretary. 'Slight, fair, very young for 52, quiet, friendly, agreeable, considerate and cautious' was Storrs's first impression.[40] McMahon was unacquainted with conditions in Egypt, and said so, and he knew neither Arabic nor French, which was spoken by most foreigners in Cairo. It was generally understood that he was only in Egypt to keep the chair warm for Lord Kitchener, who had moved to the War Office. Commenting on the appointment a few months later, Lord Hardinge, the Viceroy of India, informed Sir Arthur Nicolson, the Permanent Under-Secretary for Foreign Affairs, 'He is a nice man and I like him very much, but his ability is of a very ordinary type while his slowness of mind and ignorance of French must be serious drawbacks to him.'[41] According to Ronald Graham, Advisor to the Egyptian Ministry of the Interior, McMahon was 'quite the laziest man I have met'. His 'only visible enthusiasm was locusts', wrote Laurence Grafftey-Smith, a junior consular official. 'He had had some success with locust control in India, and would discuss his methods with all and sundry. Hence a nickname "Loki", which also became the combination of the Chancery safe (at the Cairo residency).'[42] By all accounts McMahon appears to have been content to leave Arab affairs in the hands of Clayton and Storrs, who were both Arabic speakers and between them had nearly three decades of experience in Egypt and Sudan.[43]

---

39 FO 371/2486, 166819. Underlined in the original.

40 Storrs, *Orientations*, 200.

41 FO 800/377 and 378, Nicolson Papers, Hardinge to Nicolson, 6 January and 25 May 1915. Cited in Kedourie, *Labyrinth*, 35.

42 Sir L. Grafftey-Smith, *Bright Levant* (London, 1970), 21.

43 According to Storrs, the High Commissioner and his wife, Mary, found themselves 'confronted with an unforeseen and unique situation set in an atmosphere and tradition entirely strange to their experience ... The British system in Egypt had been a mean between the *Hukum Hai* [It's an order] of direct Indian administration and the almost Byzantine technique [We suggest you ...] which European governments found necessary to maintain their prestige and privileges, their contracts and concessions, at the Sublime Porte.' Storrs, *Orientations*, 201.

Sir Henry McMahon, High Commissioner in Egypt, 1915–1917

McMahon's reply on 30 August was typically cautious and ambiguous. He declined to confirm the area of Arab independence as specified in the Sharif's first note, declaring it was inopportune to do so under the stress of war and because the Turks still occupied most Arab lands. He and his officials considered that the ambitious Sharif was speaking only for himself, and that he could be won over by a promise to recognise him as Caliph and by an undefined prospect of Arab independence. They had little if any idea in August 1915 of what lay behind the Sharif's proposal, namely the Damascus Protocol and its Arab nationalist proponents. In a lengthy reply on 9 September, the Sharif expressed his surprise at the High Commissioner's hesitation concerning the fixing of boundaries. He underlined that the success of their negotiations would depend solely upon 'whether you will reject or admit the proposed frontiers'.

In the interval, McMahon and his advisors had received further information concerning Arab affairs, through the appearance in Cairo of Muhammad Sharif al-Faruqi, a young Arab officer in the Ottoman Army (Aide-de-Camp to the Commander of the Ottoman Twelfth Army Corps), who turned out to be a member of *al-'Ahd*. The information he disclosed had a significant influence. He was not, in fact, a credited emissary of *al-'Ahd*, but he was well acquainted with the organisation and the aims of the society, and those of *al-Fatat*, its civilian sister, and came to be regarded by British officials not only as a well-intentioned informant, but also the authorised spokesman of both *al-'Ahd* and *al-Fatat*, which the British only later discovered he was not. His information was, nevertheless, deemed to be reliable. Thus, when the Sharif's second note arrived, McMahon and his advisors felt better acquainted with the background to the Sharif's demands.

This is the point in the saga when the interface between the uncontested 'facts' of history, and subsequent historiography, become blurred — where half a dozen or so 'competing narratives' really commence. McMahon realised that, in order to strike a deal, he would have to respond in some way to the Sharif's territorial claims. From the very start, McMahon had been under orders from London to be as vague as possible in his correspondence, in order to leave all options open until the end of hostilities. Such ambiguity was the standard default position for all trained imperial administrators, particularly when communicating with 'lesser powers'. However, by October 1915, the High Commissioner was informing London that unless the Arabs were given specific assurances, they might well throw in their lot with the Turks.[44]

McMahon began to urge the Foreign Office to make a quick decision. Around 20 October, London replied that McMahon could be 'more precise' if the situation warranted it.[45] With that, Foreign Minister Edward Grey essentially delegated McMahon the responsibility of coming to an arrangement with the Sharif. So, in his letter of 24 October 1915, the High Commissioner sought to square British and French interests in the Middle East with the Sharif's territorial ambitions. But who actually drafted the letter (the initial draft in English)? According to Sir Gilbert Clayton's biographer, Timothy Paris, Clayton may well have done so, or possibly Storrs.[46] In 1915, Clayton was Director of Intelligence in Cairo, having served in the Sudan and Egypt since the

---

44 See FO 371/2486. McMahon to Grey, 14 October 1915.

45 FO 371/2486, 155203.

46 Timothy J. Paris, *In Defence of Britain's Middle Eastern Empire. A Life of Sir Gilbert Clayton* (Eastbourne, 2016), 131.

turn of the century. Knowledgeable, discreet and with ears on the ground throughout the region, he spoke Arabic and would have been the obvious choice to draft the letter. And in 1923, in a note to Herbert Samuel, he claimed that he made the initial drafts of all the letters. The evidence is inconclusive. Be that as it may, the High Commissioner, on behalf of the government, took responsibility for all the letters. In this particular one, McMahon wrote that since the Sharif had represented the matter of frontiers as fundamental, the British government would be willing to offer certain assurances: His Majesty's Government pledged to recognise and uphold the independence of the Arabs in the area contained within the frontiers proposed by the Sharif in his first note, with certain reservations. McMahon defined the pledge and its accompanying reservations as follows:

> The districts of Mersin and Alexandretta, and portions of Syria lying to the west of the districts of Damascus, Homs, Hama and Aleppo, cannot be said to be purely Arab, and must on that account be excepted from the proposed delimitation.
>
> Subject to that modification, and without prejudice to the treaties concluded between us and certain Arab Chiefs, we accept that delimitation.
>
> As for the regions lying within the proposed frontiers, in which Great Britain is free to act without detriment to the interests of her ally, France, I am authorised to give you the following pledges on behalf of the Government of Great Britain, and to reply as follows to your note:
>
> That, subject to the modifications stated above, Great Britain is prepared to recognise and uphold the independence of the Arabs in all the regions lying within the frontiers proposed by the Sharif of Mecca.[47]

His letter contained four other stipulations: first, His Majesty's Government guaranteed that the Holy Places would be secured against external aggression; second, they would be ready to assist the Arabs in setting up suitable systems of administration in the area of future Arab independence; third, the Arabs would have recourse to Britain only for the recruitment of foreign advisors and officials; and

---

47 FO 371/2486, 278–280; Antonius, *Awakening*, Appendix A, 413–427. Note McMahon's use of the word 'treaties' in this letter to the Sharif.

fourth, in view of His Majesty's Government's special interest in Iraq, a particular form of unspecified administration would have to be devised for the provinces of Basra and Baghdad, which implied some measure of Anglo-Arab partnership in that part of the independent Arab State.

Finally, McMahon expressed his hope that his assurances would result in a lasting alliance between Great Britain and the Arabs, and that an early result of the alliance would be the expulsion of the Turks from the Arab countries and the liberation of the Arab peoples. He did not mention the question of the Caliphate, nor did he do so in his subsequent letters to the Sharif. According to George Antonius, the Arab historian and former Mandate official, this letter

> is by far the most important in the whole correspondence, and may perhaps be regarded as the most important international document in the history of the Arab national movement. It contains the pledges which brought the Arabs into the War, openly on the side of the Allies. In the years that followed the War, it became an outstanding bone of contention; and, down to the present day, is still invoked as the main piece of evidence on which Arabs accuse Great Britain of having broken faith with them.[48]

It is notable that throughout the Correspondence, and particularly in this letter, McMahon never defined in his own words the area of Arab independence. He merely accepted the frontiers proposed by the Sharif, save for two reservations: a specific 'districts' reservation and a much more general 'French interests' reservation.

A significant element of the subsequent century-long debate has hinged on the linguistic interpretation of the word 'districts', which was rendered by *wilāyāt* (singular: *wilāyah*) in the Arabic translation sent from the residency in Cairo to Hussein. In Arabic, *wilāyah* denotes a province (or region) or district without any specific administrative connotation; the word *vilayet* is the Turkish form, and it denotes a specified administrative division of the Ottoman Empire with precise limits and boundaries (somewhat equivalent to a large UK county). Thus, there existed a Vilayet of Beirut, a Vilayet of

---

48 Antonius, *Awakening*, 169.

Aleppo and a Vilayet of Syria (Figure 2). In this Correspondence, conducted wholly in Arabic, the word used throughout was the Arabic *wilāyah*, and its use only occasionally corresponded to a Turkish *vilayet*. For example, the text speaks of the *wilāyah* of Mersin, the *wilāyah* of Alexandretta, the *wilāyah* of Damascus, the *wilāyah* of Homs and the *wilāyah* of Hama, none of which was an Ottoman *vilayet*.

These phrases in McMahon's letter could only make sense linguistically if the word *wilāyah* was read in its proper Arab significance of region, or district, without any reference whatsoever to administrative boundaries. As mentioned previously, the Palestine region in 1918 consisted (roughly) of the *sanjaqs* (*vilayets* contained a number of *sanjaqs*) of Acre and Nablus, and the Independent Sanjaq of Jerusalem. The word 'Palestine' (*filastīn*), did not feature in either the English or Arabic version of the letter: although not an Ottoman administrative unit it was – like the English Lake District – a commonly used and understood name for a particular region.

However, as we shall see, between 1920 and 1939, successive British governments held that *wilāyāt* could <u>only</u> mean *vilayets*. Accordingly, the British argued, the resultant phrase 'lying to the west of the Vilayet of Damascus' was a clear, if implicit, exclusion of Palestine because, successive governments claimed, the Vilayet of Damascus stretched for three hundred miles southwards from Damascus to the Gulf of Aqaba.

The fundamental weakness of the government's *wilāyah* = *vilayet* interpretation can be seen from even the most cursory glance at any Ottoman Administrative map (Figure 2),[49] where a Vilayet of Damascus is not to be found; an Ottoman province does indeed stretch southward from Damascus all the way to Aqaba, namely the Vilayet of Syria, of which Damascus was the capital.

In addition, not only was the Vilayet of Damascus non-existent, the Vilayets of Homs and Hama were equally fictitious. Hence, the reference to the *wilāyah* of Damascus (in the context of the phrase 'districts of Damascus, Homs, Hama and Aleppo') must have meant the local district of Damascus, not the non-existent Ottoman Vilayet of

---

49 For the same map, see Peel Royal Commission Report (Cmd 5479), July 1937, 19 (henceforth Peel Report); Kedourie, *Labyrinth*, 91; Friedman, *Palestine. A Twice-Promised Land?*, lxxi; Antonius, *Awakening*, 176.

Damascus. Equally significantly, there is no Sanjaq of Homs: Homs is a town within the Sanjaq of Hama, so linguistically the word *wilāyāt* in the key phase did not refer either to *sanjaqs*: it could only refer to smaller town districts. Thirdly, there was indeed a Vilayet of Aleppo, but its western border was the Mediterranean coast, so in the linguistic context of the sentence, 'areas to the west of the Vilayet of Aleppo', i.e. the Mediterranean Sea, was nonsense.

It is hardly surprising, then, that for the last hundred years the Arab world and their supporters have been convinced that McMahon's letter implicitly promised the region south of today's Lebanon (roughly today's Israel/Palestine) to the Sharif. Furthermore, it was undoubtedly on the basis of this and other letters that Hussein, in June 1916, rebelled against the Ottomans, and helped the Allies to drive the former northwards during 1916–1918, towards the current Turkish–Syrian border.

Written on a Sheet of Water

Politically and militarily, the Hashimites were minor, malleable players compared to the British Empire with its formidable reach. Indeed, beyond the Hijaz, in the Ottoman Empire's other Arab provinces, the Sharif's claim to temporal leadership was far from being acknowledged. For the British, therefore, the Correspondence was primarily a temporary, wartime expedient to obtain a strategic, military edge over the Turks. At the time, all other considerations were secondary. McMahon himself believed that the letters had no binding force and would neither 'establish our right … nor bind our hands'.[50] The High Commissioner, as well as most of the British political and military leadership, including Grey, considered the growth of Arab nationalism to be insignificant, and believed that it would remain so. Even so, Lord Hardinge, the Viceroy of India, was initially averse to encouraging the Sharif's revolt because he recoiled at the thought of dividing Islam, stirring up trouble for the Caliph, or exposing the Pilgrimage to hazards. He argued that the Sharif would be regarded as a rebel in both India and Afghanistan,

---

50 Hardinge Papers, vol. 94, 356–357. McMahon to Hardinge, 4 December 1915. Cited in Kedourie, *Labyrinth*, 119–121.

and that the risk of attaching blame to Britain for embroiling the Holy Places, or the Hijaz, in the war ought not to be run.[51]

British officials in Cairo concurred with the Foreign Secretary: Gilbert Clayton wrote later, 'Whatever may be the outcome of the negotiations, it seems they have at least had the effect of preventing him from throwing in his lot on the side of our enemies.'[52] There was almost no expectation that the deliberately vague pledges described in the letters would, post-war, need to be fulfilled: they might as well have been written on water. British officials never imagined that the Correspondence (especially the Arabic texts) would ever be scrutinised. Grey told Austen Chamberlain, the Secretary of State for India, not to worry about the offers being made by Cairo as 'the whole thing was a castle in the air which would never materialise.'[53] Chamberlain was understandably worried by what he considered to be McMahon's 'disposal of Mesopotamia' in McMahon's letter of 24 October 1915. In brief, the Foreign Office did not consider that any obligation arose on Britain's part unless the Arab part of the Ottoman Empire united in rising against the Turks. They were confident that this would never happen. As Sir Reginald Wingate, Governor-General of the Sudan, told Clayton in November 1915:

> After all what harm can our acceptance of his proposals do? If the embry-onic Arab state comes to nothing, all our promises vanish and we are absolved from them – if the Arab state becomes a reality, we have quite sufficient safeguards to control it.[54]

The Sharif's reply on 5 November began by defining his attitude to the question of the frontiers. He consented to the exclusion of the Vilayet of Adana, which included the port of Mersin, but not the exclusion of 'portions of Syria lying to the west of the districts of Damascus, Homs, Hama and Aleppo', on the ground that, unlike Mersin and Adana, they were purely Arab regions; nor did he accept the exclusion of Alexandretta,

---

51 See Monroe, *Britain's Moment*, 36.

52 Clayton Papers 693/10. Clayton to Director of Military Intelligence, 3 March 1916.

53 India Office Records (L/P & S), 10/523, p.3935/1915. Cited in Kedourie, *Labyrinth*, 108.

54 Wingate to Clayton, Khartoum 15 November 1915. Cited in Elie Kedourie, *The Chatham House Version and Other Middle Eastern Studies* (London, 1970), 19.

which lay within the Vilayet of Aleppo. Regarding Iraq, he did not accept McMahon's proposal wholesale, but consented to a temporary British postwar occupation, provided that in return the government would pay a subsidy towards the financial needs of the new state. However, he accepted the reservation about those Arab Chiefs with whom Great Britain had treaty relations. The Sharif also asked for an assurance that the Arabs would not, in any event, be left alone to face the forces of Turkey and Germany; that the government would support their case in the peace negotiations, and emphasised that he must have their guarantees before he could make any active preparations for a revolt.

On 14 December, McMahon sent his third letter to the Sharif, where he expressed his satisfaction at the exclusion of the Vilayet of Adana but, significantly, shifted his ground regarding his maintenance of the reservation of northern Syria's coastal regions, from 'the region being not purely Arab' to one 'in which French interests are involved'. He vaguely informed the Sharif that the future administration of Iraq called for more detailed consideration, and gave assurances that the government did not wish to 'impel him to hasty action'. Nevertheless, McMahon continued:

> ... we deem it imperative that you should turn your endeavours to unit-
> ing the Arab peoples in our joint cause and to urging them to abstain
> from aiding our enemies in any manner whatsoever. On the success of
> your endeavours, and on the efficacy of the measures which, when the
> time comes, the Arabs will find it possible to take in aid of our cause, will
> the strength and permanence of our agreement depend.[55]

This clearly implies that in McMahon's mind there was a factor of conditionality to their potential agreement – its ultimate 'validity' would depend upon the success of the revolt. But it was left undefined who would ultimately decide what constituted 'success'. Equally signif-icant is the fact that the obligations incurred by both sides with regard to military performance were never explicitly stated in the Correspondence, although they had been discussed orally through the Sharif's messenger. And as with the High Commissioner's first two letters, it is unclear to what extent Clayton was involved in its drafting.

---

55 Antonius, *Awakening*, 424; *Correspondence* (Cmd 5957), 12.

However, on 21 December 1915, when the latter sent a copy to Wingate, the Governor-General of the Sudan, he noted only his thought that McMahon 'has made as good a job of it as possible'.[56]

Constantly pressed as the Sharif was by Constantinople to publicly declare a jihad, and to raise more troops for the defence of the motherland and of Islam, he could not afford to cement an alliance with the British and make active preparations for a revolt without specific guarantees. Moreover, without the agreement of other Arab nationalist leaders, notably those of the two secret societies, al-'Ahd and al-Fatat, he could not agree to exclude any part of Syria from the area of Arab independence. His only solution to seal the alliance with the British, as he saw it, was neither to concede, nor compromise, but to postpone the issue. Having received in December 1914 a letter from al-Faruqi, who informed the Sharif of his conversations with British officials in Cairo, the Sharif wrote to McMahon on 1 January 1916 that he was anxious to avoid disturbing French–British relations and would shelve the matter of the 'Syrian districts' reservation for the duration of hostilities. That said, he emphasised he would seize the earliest opportunity postwar to vindicate the Arab claim to the whole of Syria, and declared that it was out of the question that France or any other power should be conceded 'a single square foot of territory' in those parts. He also reiterated his resolve to initiate a revolt at the earliest moment, and indicated he would inform McMahon in due course of his requirements in arms, ammunition and supplies. It is curious that he did not ask for an answer to any of his proposals, particularly concerning the question of Syria's northern coastal regions. Indeed, the tone and the content of his letter implied that an Anglo-Arab agreement had been concluded. Was this naivety on the Sharif's part, or simply a negotiating tactic, to see how the High Commissioner would respond?

On 25 January 1916, McMahon replied, praising the Sharif in his desire not to embarrass Great Britain in its relations with France. Significantly, he did not question the Sharif's assertion that it was out of the question that France or Great Britain should or could be conceded any territory in Syria.

Two further notes were subsequently exchanged between McMahon and the Sharif, which were focused on preparations for the revolt. On 18 February 1916, the Sharif informed McMahon that a rising was

---

56 Clayton to Wingate, 21 December 1915. Wingate Papers, 135/7/174.

planned in Syria by Arab officers and men in the Turkish army under Feisal's leadership, with another at Medina led by his eldest son, Ali. The letter also listed their requirements in money, provisions and arms. In his reply on 10 March, McMahon essentially confirmed that the Sharif's proposed measures had the British government's approval. This letter to the Sharif closed the Correspondence. The frontiers issue was left in abeyance.[57] None of the later letters from McMahon to Hussein rescinded any of the pledges as written in the 24 October 1915 letter.

In the meantime, Ottoman pressure on Hussein continued to grow. In February 1916, both Djemal, the Governor of Syria, and Enver, the Ottoman Minister of War, journeyed south to Medina and pressed Hussein – unsuccessfully – to deliver the troops he had promised for the jihad. 'My greatest desire', Djemal recalled of this time 'was to do anything and everything to prevent the revolutionary tendencies displayed by Sharif Hussein from developing and to persuade him to send an auxiliary force to Palestine under the command of one of his sons.'[58] Nevertheless, on 9 June 1916, the Sharif kept his part of the bargain with the British government and revolted against Turkish authorities in the Hijaz, initially overpowering the small Turkish garrison in Mecca. The garrison at Jedda surrendered on 16 June and that of Taif on 21 September, but the garrison at Medina, with some fourteen thousand Turkish troops, held out until 10 January 1919.[59]

How was the Correspondence Interpreted by British Officials between 1915 and 1919? A Brief Survey

SIR HENRY McMAHON, HIGH COMMISSIONER IN EGYPT

On 26 October 1915, two days after sending his fateful letter to the Sharif, McMahon, in his explanatory despatch to Grey, interpreted

---

57 A.L. Tibawi, *Anglo-Arab Relations and the Question of Palestine, 1914–1921* (London, 1977), 125.

58 Djemal Pasha, *Memories of a Turkish Statesman, 1913–1919* (New York, 1922), 168. See James Barr, *Setting the Desert on Fire* (London, 2006), 22.

59 Rogan, *Fall of the Ottomans*, 396. For a useful summary of the Arab Revolt (1916–1918) and its contribution to the defeat of Turkish forces in the Hijaz and Syria, see Antonius, *Awakening*, Ch. XI–XII. See also James Barr, *Setting the Desert on Fire*; Mary C. Wilson, 'The Hashemites, the Arab Revolt, and Arab Nationalism' in Rashid Khalidi, ed., *The Origins of Arab Nationalism* (New York, 1991), 204–224.

quite clearly what regional boundaries he meant by his phrase 'west of the districts of Damascus, Homs, Hama and Aleppo'. He wrote that he was definite 'in excluding Mersina, Alexandretta and those districts on the northern coast of Syria, which cannot be said to be Arab, and where I understand that French interests have been recognised'.[60] Note, he had excluded 'those districts on the northern coast of Syria', and as any map indicates, that phrase can only refer to today's Lebanon and regions further north. Also, McMahon's completely ambiguous use of the phrase 'where Britain is free to act without detriment to the interests of her ally, France', mentioning no boundaries, was not intended to enlighten the Sharif, but to keep the way open for the French to claim those northern coastal regions of Syria, including the four towns. The Sharif was undoubtedly aware of the long-standing French connection with the Maronites and other Christian communities in and around Beirut, but had no knowledge of the Constantinople Agreement or of any Anglo-French agreements concerning the Levant.

SIR JOHN MAXWELL, GENERAL OFFICER COMMANDING, EGYPT

This interpretation can be found in a despatch, dated 1 November 1915, from Sir John Maxwell, the most senior military officer in Egypt, to the British Minister in Athens, commenting on McMahon's letter and summarising the government's agreement with Hussein. According to Maxwell, the Sharif had offered an alliance in return for British recognition of the independence of the Arab countries comprising Syria, Mesopotamia, Palestine and Arabia. Through McMahon, the government agreed with certain reservations. In Syria these involved the exclusion in favour of France of the area 'west of Damascus, Homs, Hama and Aleppo line'. It is notable that the General specifically mentioned the word 'Palestine' in the area of independence, as well as the precise definition of the excluded portion of Syria in favour of France. Maxwell's interpretation was the first of many to employ the use of the word 'line'.[61]

---

60 FO 371/2486, 163832. See Figure 6.
61 FO 882/16. G.O.C. Egypt to H.M.'s Minister, Athens, 1 November 1915.

COMMANDER DAVID HOGARTH, DIRECTOR OF
THE ARAB BUREAU, CAIRO

The third British interpretation comes from Commander David Hogarth in a memorandum headed 'The Arab Question', dated 16 April 1916. In similar fashion to Maxwell, he used the word 'line' in referring to the excluded area as lying to the 'west of the line Aleppo-Hama-Homs-Damascus'.[62] Like Maxwell some five months earlier, Hogarth understood the area in Syria excluded in favour of France to be to the west of the four towns, thus leaving Palestine well inside the areas in which Britain undertook to recognise Arab independence. Hogarth's 'common sense' interpretation, like Maxwell's before him, was based on the 24 October 1915 letter in English. A noted classicist, historian and renowned archaeologist (Keeper of the Ashmolean Museum at Oxford), Hogarth was mentor to all at the Bureau; 'our father confessor and advisor', according to T.E. Lawrence, 'who brought us all the parallels and lessons of history, of moderation and courage ... who gave us his great knowledge and careful wisdom, even in the smallest things'.[63]

THE WAR OFFICE

In a memorandum dated 1 July 1916, the General Staff, the War Office, likewise used the word 'line' in referring to the excluded area. This secret document, entitled 'The Sharif of Mecca and the Arab Movement' and written some three weeks after the outbreak of the Arab Revolt, offers the first *authoritative* British interpretation of McMahon's demand for exclusion. In the fourth paragraph the excluded areas are defined twice, once as lying 'west of the line Aleppo, Hama, Homs and Damascus', and once as 'an indefinite line drawn inland west of Damascus, Homs, Hama and Aleppo'.[64] The document was submitted to the Foreign Secretary, Sir Edward Grey, who wrote on it over his initials: 'The Dept. might have this as a secret paper.' By 'The Dept.' he meant the Foreign Office. This was the first official interpretation of the McMahon pledge, only eight months after it was made. It confirmed

---

62 FO 882/2. Hogarth to Director, Intelligence Division, the Admiralty, 16 April 1916.

63 T.E. Lawrence, *Seven Pillars of Wisdom* (London, 1935), 57–58.

64 FO 371/2773. General Staff memorandum, 1 July 1916.

the two earlier independent interpretations by General Maxwell and Commander Hogarth.

CAPTAIN WILLIAM ORMSBY-GORE MP, INTELLIGENCE OFFICER, ARAB BUREAU

The fifth British interpretation came from William Ormsby-Gore, attached as an Intelligence Officer to the Arab Bureau in Cairo. In a memorandum dated 29 November 1916, he also used the word 'line'. The memorandum was part of a lengthy dossier prepared by the Bureau, assessing the Anglo-Arab exchanges since the beginning of the war. Ormsby-Gore's assessment echoed that of Hogarth: the Sharif did not agree to exclude Alexandretta or any part of Syria; he did not agree to alienate any territory in Iraq; and he rejected any foreign sovereignty over any Arab territory. On the other hand, Britain did not set a term to its occupation of Arab territory in Iraq; did not recognise any single chief as supreme over other Arab chiefs; and did not recognise Arab independence in Syria 'west of the line Aleppo-Hama-Homs-Damascus'.[65]

Ormsby-Gore's 'line' interpretation was identical to that made by Hogarth in April, and by the General Staff in July 1916. All of these four interpretations, by Maxwell, Hogarth, the War Office and Ormsby-Gore, were based on their reading of McMahon's letter in English and his despatch of explanation two days later to Grey. They were straightforward 'military-style' assessments, untainted by later political pressures which came into play in 1920. Notably, Ormsby-Gore's interpretation was not challenged by either McMahon or his senior political officer, Gilbert Clayton.

ARNOLD TOYNBEE, POLITICAL INTELLIGENCE DEPARTMENT

The sixth British interpretation of the Correspondence emanated from Arnold Toynbee, at that time a temporary clerk in the Political Intelligence Department at the Foreign Office, who stated in an undated memorandum composed in the last week of October 1918, and circulated to senior ministers, including Foreign Secretary Arthur Balfour, and all government departments: 'With regard to

---

65 FO 882/5, 230 of the typed, unsigned text dated 29 November 1916 and marked HRG/16/65. The index in FO 882/1 shows that the author was Captain William Ormsby-Gore.

Palestine, H.M. government are committed to Sir H. McMahon's letter to the Sharif on the 24 October 1915 to its inclusion in the boundaries of Arab independence.'[66] Earlier that month Toynbee had been instructed to prepare memoranda dealing with all of the government's existing commitments in the Middle East. Toynbee's interpretation had four matching, authoritative British precedents besides that of McMahon himself: General Maxwell, Commander Hogarth, the War Office and Captain Ormsby-Gore. Thus, up to the end of the First World War these interpretations were uncontested: Palestine was indeed well to the south of the region 'west of the line of the four towns', and was thus included in the area of Arab independence.

No objections were raised to Toynbee's memorandum, which was widely distributed, to the war cabinet, to all the relevant government departments, as well as to India, Baghdad and Cairo. Balfour and Lord Robert Cecil,[67] Balfour's deputy and cousin, received personal copies, and three copies were sent to Gilbert Clayton, then Chief Political Officer to Sir Edmund Allenby, Commander-in-Chief of the Egyptian Expeditionary Force. Significantly, no government department at home or abroad, nor Balfour nor Cecil, raised any objection to Toynbee's interpretation. At the Foreign Office, Ormsby-Gore minuted that it was 'a very valuable and useful document'.[68]

LORD CURZON, CHAIRMAN OF THE WAR CABINET'S EASTERN COMMITTEE

At the war cabinet meeting on 5 December 1918, Lord Curzon stated, 'There is first the pledge to Hussein in October 1915 under which Palestine was included in the areas to which Great Britain pledges itself that they should be Arab and independent in the future.'[69] Curzon thereby provided the first postwar British interpretation of the McMahon pledge concerning Palestine. The meeting's subject was the

---

66 FO 371/3384, 586; FO 371/4368/577/480. See Kedourie, *Labyrinth*, 211.

67 In late November 1918, Cecil was appointed the head of the League of Nations section of the Foreign Office.

68 FO 371/3384.

69 CAB 27/24. See Doreen Ingrams, *Palestine Papers 1917–1922. Seeds of Conflict* (London, 1972), 48.

Arnold Toynbee CH FBA, prolific historian and philosopher of history

future of Syria and Palestine, and it was attended by Balfour, Cecil, Edwin Montagu (Secretary of State for India), Sir Henry Wilson (Chief of the Imperial General Staff), T.E. Lawrence and representatives of the Foreign Office, India Office and War Office. In the lengthy and wide-ranging discussion which followed Curzon's summary of all the wartime pledges and declarations, Curzon's interpretation of the government's 1915 pledge to Hussein concerning Palestine was not contradicted, or even commented on, by any member of the Foreign Office present.

SIR LOUIS MALLET, CIVIL SERVANT, PEACE CONFERENCE DELEGATION

Sir Louis Mallet, who was head of the Turkish section in the British delegation to the Peace Conference, provided the second authoritative postwar interpretation. Recording an interview with Herbert Samuel, who would soon become Britain's first High Commissioner to Palestine, Mallet wrote in a minute dated 30 January 1919 that 'H.M.G. were committed, by implication, to the independence of all Arab countries, excepting those areas mentioned by Sir H. McMahon from which Palestine was excluded.'[70] Though linguistically awkward, the meaning is clear: Palestine was not included in McMahon's excluded areas. This minute was submitted to Balfour, who initialled it without comment. Mallet also wrote in a memorandum dated 4 February that the excluded areas were 'a strip of country between the Mediterranean and Damascus, Homs, Hama and Aleppo'.[71]

PRIME MINISTER DAVID LLOYD GEORGE

On 19 September 1919, the Prime Minister informed Emir Feisal at a meeting at 10 Downing Street that, concerning 'the engagement entered into with King Hussein':

> Damascus, Homs, Hama and Aleppo were recognised as being within the Arab State. King Hussein had been told that the districts of Mersina and Alexandretta and portions of Syria lying to the west of that line could not be said to be purely Arab, and should be excluded from the proposed limits and boundaries of the Arab territory. The agreement entered into with the French in 1916 also provided that Damascus, Homs, Hama and Aleppo should be Arab, but that the area to the west of those towns should be subject to such direct or indirect administration or control as the French desire and as they may think fit to arrange with the Arab State or Confederation of Arab States.[72]

Lloyd George's use of the word 'line' is a further confirmation of the previous eight British interpretations of the area reserved by McMahon in the Correspondence.

THE INTERPRETATIONS IN THE CONTEXT OF
THE GREAT WAR

A more rounded analysis of the nine interpretations can only be achieved, however, by an appreciation of the progress of the war as it unfolded from the autumn of 1915, when McMahon sent his fateful

---

70 FO 608/98, 247. Mallet minute, 30 January 1919.
71 FO 608/105, 226. Mallet memorandum, 4 February 1919.
72 Underlined by the author.

'reservations' letter to the Sharif. Following the despatch of that letter to Mecca, the Foreign Office decided it was an opportune moment to inform its French allies of their contacts with the Sharif. This was potentially awkward because in 1912 Grey had declared in Parliament that Syria was within the zone of French influence, and since then the Constantinople Agreement had seen the French claim to Syria upheld. French interests in the Eastern Mediterranean region, and in particular Syria, go back many centuries – notably to the Crusades – and developed substantially in the nineteenth century with the establishment by French missionaries of schools and hospitals, orphanages and asylums. On the eve of the First World War, the Banque Ottomane represented French interests there, and business was conducted in Palestine through the Credit Lyonnais.[73] In France, *la Syrie intégrale* was openly claimed as 'the France of the Levant'.[74]

The French government were duly invited to send representatives to London to discuss the matter, and on 5 November François Georges-Picot, former French Consul-General in Beirut, arrived in London to uphold French claims, and not just to the whole of *la Syrie intégrale*. Picot, the scion of a colonialist dynasty in France – his father was a founder of the comité de l'Afrique Française – acted effectively as the advocate of the colonialist party within the Quai d'Orsay in Paris and was as dedicated a proponent of a French Syria as his government could have chosen to represent it. On 23 November, when he met Sir Arthur Nicolson, Permanent Under-Secretary for Foreign Affairs, and other members of the Foreign Office, Picot insisted that Syria was a purely French possession. No French government that surrendered that claim, he maintained, would survive a day. Four days later, Grey minuted, 'I made it clear to Picot that we have no designs on Syria and [will] promise nothing about it to anyone unless the French agree.'[75] This, a mere month after the despatch of McMahon's letter of 24 October.

After a series of fruitless meetings with Picot, who consistently upheld the French position *sans compromis*, the British designated Sir

73 See Sahar Huneidi, *The Hidden History of the Balfour Declaration* (London, 2019), 11.
74 Tibawi, *Anglo-Arab Relations*, 27.
75 FO 608/93, 5353. Minute by Grey, 27 November 1915.

Mark Sykes[76] – an advisor to the government on Middle Eastern affairs – with pencil in hand, to pore over a map with his French colleague and thrash out a mutually agreed division of the Levant and the Mesopotamian regions into French and British zones of influence and control.

Following their agreement in January 1916, and before the termination of the Correspondence between Mecca and Cairo, the two men travelled to St Petersburg and sealed the deal with the Russian Foreign Minister, Sergei Sazonov, in April/May 1916. Note that on the map (Figure 4), the Palestine region is distinguished by parallel hatching, simply because the three allies could not agree on its future, and so postponed the inevitable inter-allied squabble by agreeing to that 'special' region being controlled by an 'international administration'. Moreover, according to the agreement the only other representatives, apart from the three allies, that were to be consulted about Palestine were 'the representatives of the Shereef of Mecca'. If Palestine had been specifically excluded in McMahon's Correspondence with the Sharif, why would the British and French governments have included that particular phrase in their secret agreement? There would have been no reason to do so. While later declared by some scholars a classic example of imperial perfidy and double-dealing, others have described the agreement as standard, morally acceptable Great Power politics, and inevitable in the circumstances; still others have described it as both deceptive and inevitable. The debate continues.

Major military challenges faced the Allied Powers in 1916: the Gallipoli fiasco and the surrender of General Townsend's army of some thirteen thousand (mostly Indian Empire) troops at the end of April 1916 to the Ottomans in Mesopotamia, vividly demonstrated that Ottoman forces were far from defeated; the bear was still alive. As we shall see, as the inter-allied balance of power changed between 1916 and 1918, both the carefully crafted Constantinople Agreement of April/

---

76 Sykes was a Conservative MP and Yorkshire grandee, a man of much personal charm who had travelled extensively through parts of the Ottoman Empire between 1906 and 1913. He died in Paris of the Spanish flu in February 1919, aged thirty-nine. T.E. Lawrence later described Sykes somewhat unkindly as 'the imaginative advocate of unconvincing world-movements – a bundle of intuitions, prejudices, half-sciences' (Lawrence, *Seven Pillars of Wisdom*, 57).

Figure 4: The Sykes–Picot Agreement, 1916

May 1915 and the Sazonov–Sykes–Picot Agreement of April/May 1916 were put aside and rendered obsolete by 1920.[77]

When officials at Cairo were informed of the Sykes–Picot Agreement at the end of April 1916, they unanimously insisted that the details should not be divulged to the Sharif. McMahon himself telegraphed to London:

> Although there is nothing in arrangement agreed between France and Russia and ourselves as defined in your telegram that conflicts with any agreements made by ourselves or assurances given to Shereef and other

---

77 In Western historiography the agreement is generally referred to as the Sykes–Picot Agreement.

Arab parties, I am of opinion it would be better if possible not to divulge
details of that arrangement to Arab parties at present.

Moment has not yet arrived when we can safely do so without some
risk of possible misinterpretation by Arabs.[78]

Thus, the Sharif was deliberately kept in the dark for eighteen months
regarding the specific details of the agreement – until, as we shall see,
enlightened by the Turks. If he had been informed of it and its implications earlier, he would have, at the very least, requested the High
Commissioner to provide a satisfactory explanation.

In the spring of 1917, the arrival of a French mission in Cairo aroused
Hussein's apprehensions, and he asked Sir Reginald Wingate, who had
succeeded McMahon as High Commissioner in January 1917,[79] for
assurances as to the mission's intentions. At Wingate's suggestion, the
Foreign Office instructed Sykes to travel to Jedda to try to allay the
Sharif's anxieties as best he might, and to pave the way for the visit
which the French government wished Picot to pay him. By all accounts,
the opportunity to put the whole position frankly to Hussein was not
taken. Sykes went to Jedda in early May, saw the Sharif, and about a
fortnight later returned with Picot. On 19 May, they had the first of
two extensive audiences with him – they did not disclose in detail the
terms of the Sykes–Picot Agreement.

However, that November, when the Bolsheviks took power in
Russia, texts of the agreement were found in the Foreign Office in
St Petersburg, and passed on to the Turks. In a speech made in Beirut
on 6 December 1917, Djemal Pasha, the Governor of Syria, gave
publicity to these revelations and taunted Hussein with complic-
ity and the dismemberment and subjugation of Muslim lands.
An embarrassed Wingate then reported to the Foreign Office an
'urgent appeal' from the Sharif's son Abdullah for a definite refutation of Djemal's assertions. London's reply was typical imperial
diplomatic-speak:

---

78 FO 371/2768, 84855/938. McMahon to London, 4 May 1916.
79 McMahon was painfully surprised to learn the news – via a Reuter's telegram –
that he had been replaced by Wingate. At that moment, Lady McMahon was at sea
on her way to join him. Grafftey-Smith, *Bright Levant*, 22.

Documents found by the Bolsheviks in Petrograd Foreign Ministry do not constitute an actually concluded agreement but consist of records of provisional exchanges and conversations between Great Britain, France and Russia, which were held in the early days of the War, and before the Arab Revolt, with a view to avoiding difficulties between the Powers in the prosecution of the war with Turkey.

Whether from ignorance or from malice Djemal Pasha has distorted the original purpose of the understanding between the Powers and over-looked its stipulations regarding the consent of the populations concerned and the safeguarding of their interests. He has also ignored the fact that the subsequent outbreak and the striking success of the Arab Revolt, as well as the withdrawal of Russia, had long ago created an altogether different situation.[80]

The message, sent in Balfour's name, neither acknowledged nor denied the authenticity of the Petrograd disclosures, and deliberately evaded answering the question of whether or not the Allied Powers had concluded a secret agreement affecting the future disposal of the Arab countries. Even by diplomatic standards, it was a deliberately misleading interpretation of the nature and scope of the agreement, implying that Hussein should regard Djemal's version as another instance of Turkish intrigue. Further, the message described the Sykes–Picot Agreement as merely provisional exchanges and conver-sations, not a 'concluded agreement'. As we shall see, from 1920 successive British governments and pro-Zionist historians describe the Correspondence in similar fashion. Balfour's message also claimed misleadingly that the Sykes–Picot Agreement referred to 'the consent of the populations and the safeguarding of their interests', even though the agreement contained no such phrase.[81] By this time, of course, the British government had publicly announced the Balfour Declaration.

---

80 FO 371/4183, 131671, 2117. Minute by H.W. Young, 20 September 1919; Antonius, *Awakening*, 257.
81 For the text of the agreement, see '15 & 16 May, 1916: The Sykes-Picot Agreement', World War I Document Archive, www.gwpda.org/1916/sykespicot.html (accessed 13 January 2021).

Written on Paper

More ink has flowed describing the origins, implementation and legacy of the Balfour Declaration than over all the other pledges and agreements that the British wartime governments made concerning the Middle East. Of all the wartime pledges, it has proved the most enduring, and undoubtedly planted the seeds of the conflict which has lasted for over a century. Ostensibly an unsolicited, generous declaration by a major power to a persecuted global community, it was in fact the result of eighteen months of intense negotiations between the Zionist Organisation in London and senior British officials. Although officially it carried the signature of one man, its genesis involved scores of other individuals, including Herbert Samuel, Chaim Weizmann, Louis D. Brandeis, Lord Milner, General Jan Smuts, Leo Amery and William Ormsby-Gore. In provenance it was an Anglo-Zionist declaration.

The first 'full-dress' conference leading to the declaration took place, according to Weizmann, on 17 February 1917, at the home of his close collaborator Dr Moses Gaster, a Romanian-born scholar who was leader of the Sephardic Congregation in London. There, Sir Mark Sykes, acting in his private capacity, met a number of leading Zionists, including Herbert Samuel, Lord Rothschild and Nahum Sokolow, the Polish Secretary-General of the World Zionist Congress, and listened to their draft proposals. At the meeting Samuel emphasised, firstly, that there should be no condominium or internationalisation of Palestine – the Zionists wanted a British Protectorate – and secondly, the term 'nation' as applied to the emergent Jewish homeland in Palestine should refer to the Jewish homeland *alone*, and not to the relationship of Jews with the lands in which they lived. Weizmann added, for good measure, that 'the Jews who went to Palestine would go to constitute a Jewish nation, not to become Arabs, or Druses or Englishmen.'[82]

The declaration took the form of a letter from Arthur James Balfour, the Foreign Secretary, to a leading British Jew, Lord Rothschild:

His Majesty's Government view with favour the establishment in Palestine of a national home for the Jewish people, and will use their best endeavours to facilitate the achievement of this object, it being

---

82 Chaim Weizmann, *Trial and Error* (London, 1949), 238.

clearly understood that nothing shall be done which may prejudice the civil and religious rights of existing non-Jewish communities in Palestine, or the rights and political status enjoyed by Jews in any other country.

The letter, dated 2 November 1917, was published by *The Times* and the *Jewish Chronicle* a week later.

However ambiguous the wording of the declaration, it did clearly recognise Jewish *national* rights in Palestine, and deliberately denied any *national* rights to the majority Arab population, which was described condescendingly as 'non-Jewish communities', whose civil and religious rights should not be prejudiced by the establishment of a Jewish national home in Palestine. In fact, in 1917 there was no precedent in international law concerning the meaning of a 'national home' within a larger, defined territory or established state. Thus, it is hardly surprising, but nevertheless significant, that since 1917 no British government has ever attempted to define in strictly legal terms the meaning of 'the Jewish national home'. This issue arose on numerous occasions during the Mandate period, and notably during the St James's Conference in March 1939, when the Arab delegation pointedly asked Malcolm MacDonald, the Colonial Secretary, to define it. 'The term', he replied, 'was not capable of final definition.'[83]

Indeed, the term may never have been capable of final definition, but the interpretation put upon it at the time by the government was clearly spelled out by Lloyd George in 1937 to the Royal Commission:

... the idea was ... that a Jewish state was not to be set up immediately by the Peace Treaty without reference to the wishes of the majority of the inhabitants. On the other hand, it was contemplated that when the time arrived for according representative institutions to Palestine, if the Jews had meanwhile responded to the opportunity afforded them by the idea

---

83 FO 371/23227, 256. MacDonald to the Arab delegation, 4 March 1939. The report of the 1937 Peel Commission states: 'It is clear ... that the words "the establishment in Palestine of a national home" were the outcome of a compromise between those ministers who contemplated the ultimate establishment of a Jewish state and those who did not.' Peel Commission Report, London: HMSO, ch. II, 24.

of a National Home and had become a definite majority of the inhabitants, then Palestine would thus become a Jewish commonwealth.[84]

The former Prime Minister's statement to the Royal Commission
merits careful reading. He was factually correct regarding the government's motivation in 1917, namely, to provide the conditions
which would lead to an eventual 'Jewish commonwealth' – a euphe-
mism for a 'Jewish State', but was misleading in his claim that the
government intended at any point in time to officially consider the
wishes of the majority of the population before a Jewish state was
established.

MacDonald's twenty-two-page cabinet memorandum of 18 January
1939 echoed Lloyd George's interpretation:

> The Jews were undoubtedly led by British statesmen in 1917 and the
> immediately following years to believe that the Government would facil-
> itate their developing Palestine until, if they could secure a majority of
> the population, this people without a country would at last have a sover-
> eign state of their own.[85]

The declaration combined considerations of wartime propaganda,
imperial planning, anti-Semitic and colonial mindsets, and to some
degree biblical resonances. Although Lloyd George highlighted his
sympathy for the plight of the Jews, he was a hard-nosed imperialist,
not a born-again Christian Zionist. In reality, strategic calculations
predominated: Palestine's location on the eastern flank of the Suez
Canal (the route to India), as well as the desire to outsmart the French in
the postwar division of the bear's skin in the Levant. Another major
motivation was the need to mobilise Jewish opinion in Russia and the
USA for the flagging war effort. For the Arabs it was an immoral bill of
sale, a Great Power subterfuge. For the Zionists it was more than a great

---

84 Nevill Barbour, *Nisi Dominus. A Survey of the Palestine Controversy* (London, 1946),
66–67.
85 CP 4 (39) 'Memorandum by the Secretary of State for the Colonies. Printed for
the Cabinet', Colonial Office, 18 January 1939. This lengthy memorandum is an
excellent, wide-ranging summary of MacDonald's official thinking immediately
before the St James's Conference. Copy in Malcolm MacDonald Papers 9/10/45
(henceforth MM Papers).

event: the most powerful country in the world had formally and publicly committed itself to the Zionist cause, transforming the Zionist project from a dream into a possibility.

The Ground Must Be Theirs

To celebrate the launch of the great enterprise, an enthusiastic meeting was held on 2 December 1917 at the Covent Garden Opera House, where the speakers included Lord Robert Cecil, Sir Mark Sykes and William Ormsby-Gore, then Assistant Secretary in the war cabinet. According to Nahum Sokolow, in his speech Ormsby-Gore stated that

> he supported the Jewish claim [to Palestine] as a member of the Church of England. He felt that behind it all was the finger of Almighty God … they had in their leader in this country a man of great qualities, a statesman who had shown a skill, a determination and a patience which had endeared him to everyone. He [the speaker] had done what little he could to help forward the movement, and, in the future, if they were looking out for a friend, they could count on him as one of them.[86]

Of the Jewish speakers, Dr Moses Gaster candidly declared that what the Jews wished to obtain in Palestine was not merely a right to establish colonies, or educational, cultural or industrial institutions. They wanted to establish in Palestine an autonomous Jewish commonwealth in the fullest sense of the word. They wanted Palestine to be Palestine for the Jews, and not merely a Palestine for Jews. They wished the land again to be what it was in olden times, to be what it had been for Jews in their prayers and in their Bible – a land of Israel. 'The ground must

86 Nahum Sokolow, *History of Zionism, 1600–1918* (London, 1919), vol. II, 99–113. Five years later, Ormsby-Gore, who had just been appointed Under-Secretary of State for the Colonies, wrote that 'the Balfour Declaration in its final form was actually drafted by Col. Amery and myself.' CO 733/28. Handwritten memorandum, 24 December 1922. A cabinet memorandum (10 January 1923) states that 'the actual text [of the Declaration] was drafted by Col. L.S. (Leopold) Amery, MP.' CO 733/58.

be theirs.'[87] Not much equivocation there, more a reflection of Weizmann's and other Zionist leaders' normally private thoughts and plans.[88]

Dr Gaster's phrase 'The ground must be theirs' succinctly encapsulated both the heart of the Zionists' vision and their determination to transform Arab Palestine into a Jewish state. The manner of that transformation had been spelled out in 1896 by Theodor Herzl, the Hungarian journalist and founder of political Zionism in his book *Der Jugenstaat* (The Jewish State), and elaborated in more detail a year later in the Zionist manifesto which emerged from the First Zionist Congress in Basel, Switzerland, in 1897: the Jewish settler-colonisation of the region. For some decades thereafter, Zionists themselves used the word colonisation (*hityashvut*) to describe their project in Palestine.[89] Although the history and chief characteristics of modern political Zionism as it emerged at the end of the nineteenth century are not the focus of this study, what follows provides a brief background, essential to an understanding of the struggle for 'the ground' and power in Palestine during this period.

Political Zionism was in part the product of the religious and racial intolerance of the Europeans. It proposed a positive alternative to a centuries-old history of European anti-Semitism and pogroms.[90] According to the Australian scholar Patrick Wolfe, Herzl harnessed the conviction that Jews should have a refuge outside Europe; that the Jews constituted a European nation like others – and this meant that Europe should have a Jewish colony. 'In the annals of settler colonialism,' Wolfe wrote, 'Zionism presents an unparalleled example of deliberate,

---

87 Sokolow, *History of Zionism*, vol. II, 99–113.

88 Gaster served as Vice President of the First Zionist Congress in Basel in 1897. His residence, 'Mizpah' 193 Maida Vale in London, served as the venue for early talks between prominent Zionists and the Foreign Office in 1917. As mentioned previously, it is possible that the first draft of the Balfour Declaration was written there on 7 February 1917 in the presence of Weizmann, Sokolow, Baron Rothschild, Sykes and Samuel. Other visitors to the Gaster home included Churchill, Lenin and Freud.

89 See Nur Masalha, *The Palestine Nakba. Decolonising History, Narrating the Subaltern, Reclaiming Memory* (London, 2012), 2.

90 Pogrom: 'An organised massacre of an ethnic group, originally that of Jews in Russia or eastern Europe'. ORIGIN: Russian, 'devastation' (Oxford English Dictionary).

explicit planning. No campaign of territorial dispossession was ever waged more thoughtfully.'[91] In other words, political Zionism, an essentially Western ideology, was premised on the evacuation of Palestine by its majority native inhabitants. This conviction was expressed clearly in Herzl's diary in 1895, a year before he published his seminal work:

> We shall try to spirit the penniless population across the border by procuring employment for it in the transit countries, while denying it employment in our own country ... Both the process of expropriation and the removal of the poor must be carried out discreetly and circumspectly.[92]

Vladimir Jabotinsky, the Russian leader of the Revisionist Zionist movement, publicly expressed similar sentiments in 1923 when he wrote, 'Zionist colonisation ... can proceed and develop only under the protection of a power that is independent of the native population − behind an iron wall, which the native population cannot breach.'[93]

In the aftermath of the First World War, for Jabotinsky, Weizmann, Ben-Gurion and other Zionist leaders, only the British had the power to provide a shield of bayonets behind which the Zionists could take over Palestine. Jabotinsky and his followers called for the immediate establishment of a Jewish state; Weizmann was more cautious in his public pronouncements, but there was no difference in their ultimate

---

91 Patrick Wolfe, *Traces of History. Elementary Structures of Race* (London, 2016), 203.

92 Theodor Herzl, *Diaries*, vol. I, 88, entry for 12 June 1895. Cited in Benny Morris, *Righteous Victims. A History of the Zionist-Arab Conflict, 1881–1999* (New York, 1999), 21–22, and Khalidi, *The Hundred Years' War on Palestine*, 4. In the same study, Khalidi argues cogently that the modern history of Palestine is best understood as 'a colonial war waged against the indigenous population, by a variety of parties, to force them to relinquish their homeland to another people against their will', p. 9.

93 Vladimir Jabotinsky, 'The Iron Wall. We and the Arabs', first published in Russian in *Rassvyet*, 4 November 1923; published in English in *Jewish Herald* (South Africa), 26 November 1937. The article is available at www.marxists.de/middleast/ironwall/htm (accessed 10 May 2022). Jabotinsky (1880–1940) was the founder of the Haganah in 1920, which morphed into the Israel Defence Forces in 1948.

objective; they differed only over tactics.[94] As for Ben-Gurion, in 1929 he wrote of the need for an 'Iron Wall of [Zionist] workers' settlements surrounding every Hebrew city and town, land and human bridge that would link isolated points' and that would be capable of enforcing the doctrine of exclusive 'Hebrew labour' ('avoda 'ivrit) and 'Hebrew soil' (adama 'ivrit).[95]

According to the Palestinian intellectual Edward Said, Zionism not only accepted the racial generic concepts of European culture,

> it also banked on the fact that Palestine was actually peopled not by an advanced but by a backward people, over which it *ought* to be dominant. Thus that implicit assumption of domination led specifically to the practice of ignoring the natives for the most part as not entitled to serious consideration.[96]

Thus, in 1917, in the minds of both the British cabinet and Zionist leaders, Palestine *was* inhabited by people, but not by *a people*; natives who, for the most part, did not warrant 'serious consideration'.

Although the declaration was made public – in contrast to the Constantinople Agreement, the McMahon–Hussein Correspondence and the Sykes–Picot Agreement – it had not been discussed beyond the cabinet: Parliament had not been consulted. Neither, of course, had Palestinians (Muslims, Christians or Jews). In *The Arab Awakening* George Antonius argued that the declaration betrayed both earlier, secret British pledges regarding Palestine – to Hussein in 1915, and to the French and Russian allies in May 1916, when they had agreed that

---

94 According to Avi Shlaim, the root cause of Jabotinsky's dispute with the official Zionist leadership was twofold: his (maximalist) conception of the Jewish state, and that Zionism was not the return of the Jews to their spiritual homeland, but an offshoot or implant of Western ('superior') civilisation in the East. The Revisionist Zionist ideology was predicated on two principles: 'The first was the territorial integrity of Eretz Israel, the Land of Israel over both banks of the river Jordan ... The second was the immediate declaration of the Jewish right to political sovereignty over the whole of this area.' Shlaim, *Iron Wall*, 12.

95 See Masalha, *The Palestine Nakba*, 33.

96 Edward Said, 'Zionism from the Standpoint of its Victims', *Social Text*, no. 1 (1979), 29. As well as being an eminent academic, Said was a courageous political activist and author of the seminal work *Orientalism* (1978).

postwar Palestine would be under 'international administration'. Such contradictions and connections concerning Britain's wartime pledges have been debated by historians for decades: which officials knew what and when? In spite of increasingly abundant official records available at the UK's National Archives since the 1970s, and hundreds of books published, the truth concerning Britain's overlapping wartime pledges remains an elusive quarry. This book is limited to unearthing, if possible, the truth concerning the specific pledge to the Sharif of Mecca.

Establishing National Governments

A month to the day after *The Times* and the *Jewish Chronicle* published Balfour's letter to Lord Rothschild, Allied forces took Jerusalem. Two days later, on 11 December 1917, General Sir Edmund Allenby descended from his car outside the Jaffa Gate and entered the Holy City on foot, accompanied by his senior officers and representatives of France, Italy and the United States, including Georges-Picot, who had appeared in Cairo two weeks earlier, intent on participating in Allenby's anticipated entry into Jerusalem and determined to assert the French claim to a joint administration of Palestine with Great Britain. But Allenby objected to Picot's participation in the official entry.[97] The Foreign Office resolved the issue: Clayton and Picot, representing the Anglo-French Mission, would walk together, ten paces behind the liberator, as he walked through the Jaffa Gate – this in deliberate contrast to Kaiser Wilhelm II, who in 1898 rode into Jerusalem mounted on a splendidly decked white horse. A declaration, crafted with great care in London, was then read out successively in English, Arabic, Hebrew, French, Italian, Greek and Russian, which included:

> The object of war in the East on the part of Great Britain was the complete and final liberation of all peoples formerly oppressed by the Turks and the establishment of national governments and administrations in those countries deriving authority from the initiative and free will of those people themselves.[98]

---

97 Paris, *In Defence of Britain's Middle Eastern Empire*, 252.
98 FO 371/3384, 183683; Hansard, 21 June 1922, vol. 50, cc994–1033.

Leaflets to this effect were dropped by planes and distributed through-out the villages of Syria, including in Palestine. On 3 October 1917, Allenby had written to his wife, enclosing a copy of a leaflet dropped by the British over Palestine:

> The enclosed photo of the Sharif of Mecca – and the proclamation by him – is one of the means we have of inducing the Arabs to desert the Turks. We drop these papers – and packets of cigarettes – over the Turkish lines, from aeroplanes … A good many come in, as a result of our propaganda.[99]

The Sharif's proclamation encouraged the Arabs to desert and join the war for the freedom and independence of the Arab lands. The leaflets' appeal was clear: help us as your allies to liberate your country from Turkish rule so it may form part of the Arab kingdom under the Sharif of Mecca. It is notable that the only part of Syria which did not receive such leaflets and cigarettes was the Lebanon, another positive indication that, for the British military authorities at the time, Palestine was destined to be part of the region promised to Hussein.

Allenby's multilingual declaration of 11 December was followed by a luncheon during which Picot observed to Allenby that 'Tomorrow, my dear General, I will take the necessary steps to set up civil govern-ment in this town.' It seems the table went silent, the 'Bull' went red (Allenby, the 'Bull', was known for his formidable temper) and replied crisply, 'In the military zone the only authority is that of the Commander-in-Chief, myself.' 'But', stammered Picot, 'Sir Edward Grey …' He got no further. 'Sir Edward Grey', Allenby continued, 'referred to the civil government which will be established when I judge that the military situation permits.' And there the matter was closed – for the moment.[100]

Even before the Egyptian Expeditionary Force's assault on Beersheba two weeks previously, Clayton had convinced Allenby to establish a

---

99 Allenby Papers, 1/8/15, Allenby to Lady Allenby, 3 October 1917. Cited in Barr, *Setting the Desert on Fire*, 311; Tibawi, *Anglo-Arab Relations*, 166–167.
100 See Paris, *In Defence of Britain's Middle Eastern Empire*, 252–253. This memorable incident is gleefully recounted by T.E. Lawrence in *Seven Pillars of Wisdom* (London, 1942 edition), 464.

military administration with Colonel Alfred Parker, then Governor of the Sinai region, at its head. Clayton had foreseen that Palestine was likely to become a political hotbed as territory was liberated from the Turks, with the French, Emir Feisal, the local Syrian nationalists and the British government all determined to impose their political control, in one form or another, on the region. An initial military administration would allow political issues to be deferred until some political arrangements had been agreed. Conditions under a military administration would be governed by the Laws and Usages of War as set down in the *Manual of Military Law*, and the principles set forth in the *Manual* were based on the strict maintenance of the status quo antebellum, until conditions allowed for the establishment of a civil administration.[101]

Allenby's Jaffa Gate declaration was also notable for what it deliberately did not refer to: the Balfour Declaration, namely Lloyd George's government's pro-Zionist intentions for the future of Palestine. Although the declaration was published in the British press on Friday, 9 November 1917, it was not until May 1920, in the final days of the military administration, that the text was officially read out in Nablus by the Chief Administrator, Sir Louis Bols, who had been concerned that the announcement would awaken antagonism. Allenby had censored all mention of it in 1918. Most of the army officers in Palestine saw the declaration as an obstacle to the maintenance of law and order. Those in London saw it as the very foundation of the British presence in the country.

Palestine's ultimate fate was still unknown at the end of 1917, 'though the Balfour Declaration made its incorporation into a presumably French Syria less and less probable, even if Jerusalem were internationalised', as Storrs wrote later.[102] In fact, Palestine was to remain under British military rule until July 1920, when a civilian High Commissioner, Sir Herbert Samuel, took charge. Even so, Palestine legally remained Occupied Enemy Territory South until Turkey renounced its sovereignty over the region at the signing of the Treaty of Lausanne on 24 July 1923.

In January 1918, some two months after the Balfour Declaration, David Hogarth, then Director of the Arab Bureau, was despatched from

101 Paris, *In Defence of Britain's Middle Eastern Empire*, 264.
102 Storrs, *Orientations*, 307.

Cairo to the Hijaz to reassure Sharif Hussein concerning the British government's policy regarding the Palestinian Holy Places and Zionist colonisation. He informed Hussein, using a text specifically written by Sir Mark Sykes, that

> so far as Palestine is concerned, we are determined that no people shall be subjected to another, but in view of the fact ... [t]hat since the Jewish opinion of the world is in favour of a return of Jews to Palestine, and inasmuch as this opinion must remain a constant factor, and further, as His Majesty's Government view with favour the realisation of this aspiration, His Majesty's Government are determined that in so far as is compatible with the freedom of the existing population, both economic and political, no obstacle should be put in the way of the realisation of this ideal.[103]

This became known as the Hogarth Message of 1918, and is notable for its inclusion of the phrase 'both economic and political' in reference to the freedoms of the existing population of Palestine, a formulation which had been deliberately omitted from the Balfour Declaration and later from its legal incarnation, the Mandate document, which refers only to the 'civil and religious' rights of non-Jewish communities. The need to keep the Hashimites onside, when most of Palestine was still in Ottoman hands, was the reason why Hogarth's Message was economical with the truth. Whatever the combination of extenuating military and political circumstances, Hogarth was not entirely frank with Hussein concerning the government's *political* intentions regarding Palestine. Such was his role as the messenger – a chess piece, not the chess player – in Britain's unfolding plans for the region.

Hogarth reported to London that

> the King would not accept an independent Jewish State in Palestine, nor was I instructed to warn him that such a state was contemplated by Great Britain. He probably knows nothing of the actual or possible economy of

---

103 The Hogarth Message was published as part of *Statements made on behalf of His Majesty's Government during the year 1918 in regard to the Future Status of Certain Parts of the Ottoman Empire* (Cmd 5964), 20 March 1939. Text of Hogarth Message is also in Anglo-Arab Committee Report (Cmd 5974), 17 March 1939, Annex F, in FO 371/23231, E2166.

Palestine, and his ready assent to Jewish settlement there is not worth very much. But I think he appreciates the financial advantage of Arab co-operation with the Jews.[104]

Immediately following the publication of the Balfour Declaration, the Zionists proposed, with Sykes's backing, to send a commission to Palestine to deal with 'settlement and relief'. The Foreign Office concurred, and the multinational Zionist Commission arrived in Palestine in March 1918. It consisted of Weizmann, with Israel Sieff as secretary, and Joseph Cowen, Dr M.D. Eder and Leon Simon from Britain; Commandante Angelo Levi Bianchini from Italy; and Professor Sylvain Lévi from France. There were no representatives from America or Russia. Ormsby-Gore was attached as Liaison Political Officer.[105] Unofficially, according to Storrs, the commission's task was 'to produce certain faits accomplis creating an atmosphere favourable to the [Zionist] project, and stimulating to financial supporters, before the assembly of the Peace Conference'.[106]

As Chairman of the Zionist Commission, Weizmann, the self-confident and persuasive lobbyist par excellence, lost no time in reassuring Palestinians of Zionist intentions, informing several prominent Palestinian leaders at a dinner party in Jerusalem in March 1918 that

> Jews had never renounced their rights to Palestine; they were brother Semites, not so much 'coming' as 'returning' to the country; there was room for both to work side by side; let his hearers beware of treacherous insinuations that Zionists were seeking political power – rather let both progress together until they were ready for a joint autonomy.[107]

His listeners knew that such cautious and reassuring assertions were, according to Rashid Khalidi, 'strategic and meant to cloak the Zionists'

104 See FO 371/23229, 377.

105 By October 1918, according to Jehuda Reinharz, Ormsby-Gore had become 'an enthusiastic and unabashed supporter of Zionism'. Jehuda Reinharz, *Chaim Weizmann. The Making of a Statesman* (Oxford, 1993), 265.

106 Barbour, *Nisi Dominus*, 70.

107 Storrs, *Orientations*, 353–354. The dinner was attended by the Mayor of Jerusalem and the Mufti of Jerusalem as well as several other leading Palestinian political and religious figures.

real objectives'.[108] Weizmann was indeed a veteran lobbyist, who exuded charm whenever it suited him. Since his arrival in Britain in 1904, the Russian scientist had made a point of cultivating the friendship of parliamentarians and newspaper editors: by 1918, he was on friendly speaking terms with Lloyd George, Balfour, Churchill and half the cabinet.

However, after two months in a war-torn, devastated Palestine, Weizmann was deeply discouraged, and laid out his concerns candidly in a letter to Balfour:

> It is with a great sense of responsibility that I am attempting to write to you about the situation here and about the problems which confront the Zionist Commission ...
>
> At the head of the administration we see enlightened and honest English officials, but the rest of the administrative machinery is left intact, and all the offices are filled with Arab and Syrian employees ... We see these officials, corrupt, inefficient, regretting the good old times when baksheesh was the only means by which matters administrative could be settled ... The fairer the English regime tries to be, the more arrogant the Arab becomes ...
>
> The Administration in this form is distinctly hostile to Jews ... the Englishman at the head of affairs is fair and just [and] meticulously careful to hold the balance. But his only guide in this difficult situation is the democratic principle, which reckons with the relative numerical strength, and the brutal numbers operate against us, for there are five Arabs to one Jew ...
>
> The present state of affairs would necessarily tend towards the creation of an Arab Palestine, if there were an Arab people in Palestine. It will not in fact produce that result because the fellah is at least four centuries behind the times, and the effendi (who, by the way, is the real gainer from the present system) is dishonest, uneducated, greedy, and as unpatriotic as he is inefficient.[109]

Weizmann's proposed solution was thus predicated on the mistaken assumption that from a political point of view the Arab 'problem' did

---

108 Khalidi, *The Hundred Years' War on Palestine*, 32.
109 FO 371/3395. Weizmann to Balfour, 30 May 1918.

Chaim Weizmann, who would become Israel's first President in 1949

not exist: the Arab centre of gravity was not Palestine, but the Hijaz, the triangle formed by Mecca, Damascus and Baghdad; the problem in Palestine was merely an economic one and therefore the only relations that were necessary with the Arabs of Palestine were economic.[110] In a letter to his wife, Weizmann wrote that after explaining the Zionist point of view to the Arabs, 'we have done everything that was required of us' and they should 'take it or leave it'.[111] Throughout his life, Weizmann did not just think that as a European he was better equipped to decide for the natives what their best interests were, he also believed he 'understood' the Arab mentality, the Arab as he really was. In a memorable conversation in 1936, he informed the Colonial Secretary, Malcolm MacDonald, that Arthur Wauchope, the then High

110 Sahar Huneidi, *A Broken Trust. Herbert Samuel, Zionism and the Palestinians, 1920–1925* (London, 2001), 31–32.
111 David Vital, *Zionism: The Crucial Phase* (Oxford, 1987), 319. As Weizmann phrased it, *'c'est à prendre ou à laisser'*.

Commissioner, was too lenient towards Arabs as he did not understand
'Arab psychology'.[112]

In June 1918, the Zionist leader travelled south to Aqaba in
Transjordan to meet Feisal, and endeavoured to win his cooperation, or
at least, acquiescence, for the Zionist project in Palestine. To what
extent was the Emir charmed by the persuasive Russian,[113] who even
donned an Arab headdress for the essential photograph of the encounter? Feisal seemed to believe that Weizmann's influence might help
secure him the throne of Syria in the face of strong French opposition.
In the event, Feisal agreed to large-scale immigration of Jews into
Palestine, provided that Arab peasant and tenant farmers would have
their rights protected and would be assisted 'in forwarding their
economic development'. Although they met again and signed an agreement in January 1919 before the Peace Conference, it was a dead letter
within a few months: the French and the British were in control of the
whole region. At their second meeting, Feisal had added a codicil that
the agreement they signed was conditional upon the Arabs being
granted full independence. Weizmann later wrote that it was a lost
opportunity for mutually beneficial cooperation. According to Bernard
Wasserstein, the Zionist–Sharifian entente was a cul-de-sac rather than
a lost opportunity in the history of Palestine:

> Its chief importance lay less in its immediate political effects than in the
> material it provided in later years for Zionist propaganda. In spite of
> Feisal's final reservation, the agreement enabled the Zionists to assert that
> the recognised leader of the Arab world had been prepared, with what-
> ever stipulations, to enforce the principle of the Balfour Declaration.[114]

In Arab eyes, the main result of the entente was, as Avi Shlaim puts it,
'to identify Zionism as the ally of British imperialism in the Middle East
and as an obstacle in their own struggle for self-determination'.[115]

---

112 FO 371/20024. Record of Conversation (Weizmann and Ben-Gurion) with
Colonial Secretary, 31 August 1936. Cited in Matthew Hughes, *Britain's Pacification of
Palestine* (Cambridge, 2019), 412.
113 Weizmann took British citizenship in 1910, which he retained until 1948.
114 Bernard Wasserstein, *The British in Palestine: The Mandatory Government and the
Arab-Jewish Conflict, 1917–1929* (Oxford, 1979), 36.
115 Shlaim, *Iron Wall*, 8.

After Weizmann's return to London in the autumn of 1918, the Zionist Commission called a conference in Jaffa in December, and disregarded Weizmann's cautious approach. According to Christopher Sykes, the commission 'took upon itself the right to define and shape the needs of future Palestine'.[116] They formulated an 'Outline for the Provisional Government of Palestine': the country was to be acknowledged as 'The Jewish Homeland in whose affairs the Jewish people as a whole shall have the determining voice.' The Jewish flag was to be the national emblem and the name Palestine supressed in favour of 'Eretz Israel'.[117] The influential American Zionist Louis D. Brandeis was equally overbearing: while visiting Palestine in 1919, he simply proposed to the British Chief Administrator that every implementation of policy must receive the prior agreement of the commission.[118]

The commission soon formulated a policy to bypass the military administration: when they could not get what they wanted, they would refer the matter direct to the Zionist Organisation in London who would represent the matter direct to the Foreign Office, who would refer it once more to the administration in Palestine. A notable example of this strategy is to be found in the *Political Report of the Zionist Executive to the Twelfth Zionist Congress* (1921), which states that Major-General Sir Arthur Money (Chief Administrator, Palestine, June 1918–June 1919) had

> in a speech ... condemned the policy of creating 'separate institutions for separate communities', whether charitable or educational ... and had asked all Military Governors their opinion as to the advisability of creating mixed Government schools, for Arabs and Jews together. The Zionist Commission, it goes without saying, energetically resisted all these attempts, and it is possible that all its endeavours, as well as representations made by the London Office [of the Zionist Organisation] to the Home Government, had something to do with Major-General Money's recall from the post of Chief Administrator.[119]

116 Christopher Sykes, *Crossroads to Israel, 1917–1948* (Bloomington, 1965), 23.

117 Sykes, *Crossroads*, 23.

118 Sykes, *Crossroads*, 23.

119 *Political Report of the Zionist Executive to the Twelfth Zionist Congress* (1921), 47. See Barbour, *Nisi Dominus*, 126.

Zionist representations in London also prompted the recall some six months later of his successor, General Harry Watson, who in similar fashion adhered to Allenby's status quo antebellum policy, as required by the internationally accepted Laws of War. Once the fighting was over, Allenby's exclusive concern was to 'hand over Palestine in good condition', and in fact his military administration – between the end of 1917 and July 1920, when Sir Herbert Samuel took charge – carried out much useful 'non-political' work, alleviating the terrible famine by imports of food from Egypt, restoring the worthless currency, piping clean water to Jerusalem and creating a relatively uncorrupt administrative and judicial apparatus.[120] However, in Zionist eyes the primary concern of the British should have been to facilitate the establishment of the Jewish national home, irrespective of any Arab opposition or any other issue. So conflict between the 'non-political' military administration and the overbearing and demanding Zionist Commission was inevitable. Storrs emphatically repudiated the general accusation that the Palestine military administration was disloyal to its own government's national home policy, but he acknowledged that

> the main charge against [the military administration], more serious because it implied deliberate bad faith, was that of anti-Zionism. It cannot be denied that there were amongst us two or three officers in high positions overtly against the declared policy of His Majesty's Government. In due course these were eliminated (for only one saw fit to resign).[121]

The Zionist Commission was to remain in Palestine for three and a half years, funded by American Zionists, after which it was succeeded by the Jewish Agency. Even before it morphed into the latter, it began to function as a government for the *Yishuv*, the indigenous, Arabic-speaking Jewish community. It is significant that the latter, an economic and politically fragile minority in Palestine, increasingly had global support from which it could draw substantial political and financial strength. This support set it apart from other nationalist movements, such as in India and Ireland.

---

120 Wasserstein, *British in Palestine*, 20.
121 Storrs, *Orientations*, 376.

Final Wartime Pledge

As mentioned earlier, an Anglo-French declaration of 7 November 1918
– distributed throughout Mesopotamia, Syria, Lebanon and Palestine –
stated that the goal of the British and French governments was the
complete and final liberation of peoples oppressed by the Turks and the
setting up of national governments and administrations which should
derive their authority from the free exercise of the initiative and choice
of the indigenous population. It was a palliative gesture: there was no
intention in London or Paris of allowing the indigenous population in
the former Ottoman territories to freely choose their rulers, as evidenced
in particular by the Sykes–Picot Agreement. Moreover, the declaration
made no specific mention of Lebanon, nor of Palestine, only Syria and
Mesopotamia, but Palestine and Lebanon were seen as part of Syria at the
time. Eighteen copies were displayed in public places by Storrs, the newly
appointed Military Governor of Jerusalem, who the following day was
surprised to find a large deputation of Muslims and Christians appear in
his office to offer sincere thanks to the Allies for the declaration:

> Then they asked me formally (a) whether Palestine formed or did not
> form part of Syria, (b) whether if so Palestinians came under the
> category of those inhabitants of the liberated countries who were
> invited to choose their own future, and (c) if not, why the notices had
> ever been sent to them all. I replied to them in general terms …[122]

An embarrassed Storrs had no adequate answer to the three questions
posed. Clayton reported to London that the Arabs of Palestine took it
for granted that the declaration applied to their country as part of Syria,
and asked for confirmation. The Foreign Office replied that Palestine
was excluded, but this was for Clayton's 'private information'.[123] In the
absence of any secure agreement between Zionists and Arabs in
Palestine, Clayton began to feel that the interests of the latter should be
regarded by Britain as paramount.

Meanwhile, immediately after the Armistice was signed, on 11
November 1918, Allied troops began to occupy Constantinople.

122 Wasserstein, *British in Palestine*, 33.
123 See FO 371/3384.

Ronald Storrs, Governor of Jerusalem, 1920–1926

With Britain now in occupation of most of the Arabic-speaking provinces and a small French force stationed in Beirut, the Allies were in full control of the disposal of Ottoman territory. But would they honour the treaties and agreements they had entered into during the war?[124]

On the occasion of Clemenceau's brief visit to London at the beginning of December 1918 for a meeting of the Allied Supreme Council, Lloyd George secured the French Premier's agreement to two modifications of the 1916 Sykes–Picot Agreement: first, the transfer of Mosul (with its oilfields) from the French to the British zone of influence, and

124 See William L. Cleveland and Martin Bunton, *A History of the Modern Middle East* (Boulder, 2016) (6th ed.), 143.

second, that Palestine should come under British instead of international control. In return, Britain would give France a free hand in the
rest of Syria. According to Elizabeth Thompson, the deal 'launched the
politics of petroleum that still governs international affairs in the Middle
East'.[125]

The agreement between the two men, made on 1 December, was
oral and without any written record. It seems the Foreign Office and
even Balfour were not immediately informed, and it certainly undermined King Hussein's aspirations for a united Syria: in effect, the agreement would create two zones of foreign control along the entire Syrian
coast, British in the south and French in the north. Before December
1918, was Lloyd George aware of Britain's pledges to the Sharif? Perhaps
not. The Correspondence and other British wartime pledges concerning the Ottoman Empire were hardly of foremost concern to the Prime
Minister. Presiding over a militarily exhausted, if victorious nation, he
was preparing to go to Paris to meet the other Allied leaders to discuss a
settlement for Germany, and to negotiate the shape of a new Europe,
and to a certain extent, a new world.

---

125 Elizabeth Thompson, *How the West Stole Democracy from the Arabs. The Syrian
Congress of 1920 and the Destruction of Its Historic Liberal-Islamic Alliance* (London, 2020), 63.

2

League of Victors

1919

Between January and June 1919, Paris was at once 'the world's government, its court of appeal and parliament, the focus of its fears and hopes'.[1]
The international order had to be recreated, perhaps on a different basis;
the expectations were enormous and new economic and political ideas
filled the air. Although over thirty countries sent delegates to Paris, all
expecting to take part, the conference was inevitably dominated by the
big three, Clemenceau, Lloyd George and Woodrow Wilson, who met
for the first time on 12 January 1919. Six days later, the Peace Conference
officially opened. Clemenceau ensured that the opening took place on
the anniversary of the coronation in 1871 at Versailles of King Wilhelm
of Prussia, as Kaiser of the new German Empire.

The victors had to impose peace terms on their defeated enemies
while they still could, in particular to agree on a settlement for Germany
and to draw new lines on the map of Central Europe: Austria was on
its knees, an empire dissolved. It had no access to the sea, having lost
most of its former territory, including the German-speaking
Sudetenland and South Tyrol, Czechoslovakia and Poland, as well as
the State of Slovenes, Croats and Serbs. Bukovina and Bosnia and
Herzegovina were also gone. Across Europe, millions were on the
move and millions starving. The peacemakers also had to think of
Africa, Asia and the Middle East. Apart from the future of Germany,
the question of Russia and the fear that Bolshevik revolutions would
break out throughout Europe was to haunt the conference. The future
of the Ottoman Empire ranked as a lesser issue, especially for the

1 Margaret MacMillan, *Peacemakers. The Paris Conference of 1919 and Its Attempt to End
War* (London, 2001), 1.

American President, who had not thought through how he was going to put into effect the idealistic principles (his Fourteen Points) that he had articulated in January 1918.

For the French Premier, the elderly, intellectual '*tigre*' of French politics, the settlement with Germany was his top priority. The defeated *Boche* must never be capable of threatening France again. France wanted revenge and compensation but above all it wanted security. Wilson, aloof and scholarly, self-righteous and Bible-quoting, arrived from Washington with his vision of a League of Nations that would stabilise the new world order and prevent future wars. The defunct European system of the 'balance of powers' had helped to cause the conflict and he came across the Atlantic with the answer. Wilson arrived, said Lloyd George, like a missionary to rescue the heathen Europeans, with his little 'sermonettes' full of rather obvious remarks. Later, when asked how he thought he had done at Paris, Lloyd George replied, 'Not badly, considering I was seated between Jesus Christ and Napoleon.'

In fact, the intensely pragmatic, intuitive Lloyd George, whom Wilson found 'slippery', held a pretty good hand: Britain already had some of what it wanted, with the German fleet and the major German colonies safely in its hands, and its troops in control of most former Ottoman territories in the Middle East, including Egypt (annexed in 1914), Mesopotamia, Syria and Palestine. He understood where Britain's interests lay: its trade and its Empire, with naval dominance to protect them and a balance of power in Europe to prevent any power from challenging those interests. His Middle Eastern strategy was to direct the Americans' anti-imperialist ire against the claims presented by France and Italy, distracting the President from areas in which he might make difficulties for Britain. Maurice Hankey, British Secretary to the Peace Conference, recorded in his diary even before the conference convened that Lloyd George 'means to try and get President Wilson into German East Africa in order to ride him off Palestine'.[2] Nevertheless, like Clemenceau, the British Prime Minister was acutely aware that the United States had become Europe's banker. Together the European allies owed over $7 billion to the American government, and about half as much again to American banks. Wilson seemed to assume that the US would get its way by simply applying financial pressure.[3]

---

2 Stephen Roskill, *Hankey: Man of Secrets, vol. 2: 1919–1931* (London, 1972), 38.
3 MacMillan, *Peacemakers*, 18.

David Lloyd George, British Prime Minister, 1916–1922

For the American President, at the heart of his Fourteen Points was the creation of a League of Nations that would serve as the centrepiece of the peace settlements. If it could be brought into being, then everything else would sooner or later fall into place. A system of collective security would ideally prevent future wars. If the new borders were not quite right, the League would sort them out; it would make sure that Germany's former colonies would be run properly. There had to be some arrangement, other than annexation or colonisation, for those parts of the world not yet ready to govern themselves, and the League would act as trustee for those peoples. Lansing, the American Secretary of State, and decidedly more realistic than the President, thought it a 'calamity' that Wilson had ever hit on the phrase:

It will raise hopes which can never be realised. It will, I fear, cost thousands of lives. In the end it is bound to be discredited, to be called the

dreams of an idealist who failed to realize the danger until it was too late
to check those who attempt to put the principle into force.[4]

As for the Europeans, they had never been prepared to accept Wilson's
'utopian' Fourteen Points, declaimed from safety across the water in
January 1918, without serious modification. The French wanted repara-
tions and the British would not agree to the 'freedom of the seas' which
would prevent them from using a naval blockade as a weapon against
their enemies. Of all the ideas Wilson brought to Europe, his concept of
self-determination for small nations was perhaps the most controversial,
largely because his European allies still tended to think in terms of the
spoils of war; for many centuries, occupation, annexation, colonies and
indemnities of some sort had been taken for granted in London, Paris
and Rome. The French wanted Togoland and Cameroon and an end to
German rights in Morocco. The Italians had their eyes on parts of
Somalia. In the British Empire, South Africa wanted German South
West Africa (Namibia), Australia wanted New Guinea, and New Zealand
wanted German Samoa. The British hoped to annex German East Africa
(roughly today's Tanzania) to fill in the missing link between their colonies to the north and south. And, as we have seen, the British and the
French were still squabbling secretly to divide up the Ottoman Empire.

Wilson protested. They must not go back to the old games, parcel-
ling out helpless peoples. He would not stand, he said privately, for
'dividing the swag'. 'If the process of annexation went on,' he told the
Supreme Council, 'the League of Nations would be discredited from
the beginning.'[5] On 25 January, the Peace Conference formally
approved the setting up of a commission on the League of Nations to
draft a covenant, which Wilson insisted on chairing. Clemenceau
famously remarked that 'God himself was content with the ten
commandments. Wilson modestly inflicted fourteen points on us.' He
was not against the League; he just did not believe in it. Nevertheless, he

---

4 Robert Lansing, *The Peace Negotiations: A Personal Narrative* (Boston and New York,
1921), 97–98. At the end of 1919, a somewhat chastened Wilson told Congress,
'When I gave utterance to those words [that all nations have a right to self-
determination], I said them without the knowledge that nationalities existed, which
are coming to us day after day.' H.W.V. Temperley, ed., *A History of the Peace
Conference of Paris*, vol. 4 (London, 1920–1924), 429.
5 MacMillan, *Peacemakers*, 112.

appointed two leading experts to the commission, both lawyers. Lloyd George appointed General Jan Smuts and Lord Robert Cecil, gave them full authority and generally left them to it.

Smuts was the ideal choice. A brilliant lawyer and elegant writer, South Africa's Foreign Minister, whose imperialism equalled that of Lloyd George, had spent much of the later part of the war in London, where he sat on the small committee of the British cabinet set up to run the war.[6] Already in the previous autumn, he had put pen to paper to transform what he described as Wilson's 'rather nebulous ideas' into coherent form. His seventy-page paper, entitled 'The League of Nations. A Practical Suggestion', succinctly laid out the organisation, structure, roles and responsibilities of such a League: a general assembly of all member nations, a smaller executive council, a permanent secretariat, steps to settle international disputes and mandates (a form of temporary trusteeship) for peoples not yet ready to rule themselves. Smuts later wrote proudly to a friend, 'my paper has made an enormous impression in high circles. I see from the Cabinet Minutes that the Prime Minister called it "one of the ablest state papers he had ever read."'[7]

Wilson incorporated much of Smuts's paper into what became the Covenant of the League. Smuts's Zionist opinions – he had been won to Zionism on meeting Weizmann in June 1917 – were also evident in his paper. He wrote that

> there will be found cases where, owing chiefly to the heterogeneous character of the population and their incapacity for administrative co-operation, autonomy in any real sense would be out of the question, and the administration would have to be undertaken to a very large extent by some external authority. This would be the case, at any rate for some time to come, in Palestine, where the administrative co-operation of the Jewish minority and Arab majority would not be forthcoming.[8]

---

6 Smuts proposed that Britain should keep East Africa (Tanzania), and that South Africa must keep German South West Africa (Namibia).

7 It was published as a booklet, dated 16 December 1918. See MacMillan, *Peacemakers*, 98.

8 Jan Smuts, *The League of Nations. A Practical Suggestion* (London, 1918), 16–17.

This is a classic, if unsurprising, example of Empire-thinking. There is almost no historical evidence to suggest that the indigenous Jewish and Arab communities in Palestine would not cooperate postwar. Smuts himself had no experience of the Middle East.

On the whole, the British, realising that there was no point in antagonising the Americans by talking of adding Germany's territory, or anyone else's, to their Empire, supported the idea of mandates.[9] Initially, South Africa, Australia and New Zealand, because of their own territorial ambitions, wanted nothing to do with them. The French reacted to the whole idea with hostility and apprehension. Clemenceau exclaimed to Poincaré, the French President, 'The League of Nations guaranteeing the peace, so be it, but the League of Nations proprietor of colonies, no!' Colonies were a mark of power; they had also held what France badly needed: manpower.[10] Henri Simon, the French Minister of Colonies, preferred annexation as being 'more efficient and better for the natives'. All France wished, he declared, was to be able to continue its work of spreading civilisation in tropical Africa.

On the League Commission, Smuts and Cecil worked out a compromise proposal concerning the mandate concept which Colonel House, Wilson's chief advisor, thought could be the basis of an agreement between the US and its allies. The proposal finally saw the light of day as Article 22 of the League Covenant, which included the sentence 'The character of the mandate must differ according to the stage of the development of the people, the geographical situation of the territory, its economic conditions and other similar circumstances.' This resulted in three types of mandate: 'A' for nations, such as those in the Middle East, which were nearly ready to run their own affairs; 'B', where the mandatory power would run them; and 'C' for territories that were contiguous or close to the mandatory, which would administer the mandated territory as part of its own.[11]

---

9 MacMillan, *Peacemakers*, 108.

10 MacMillan, *Peacemakers*, 109.

11 Class A Mandates: ex-Ottoman territories; Class B Mandates: ex-German Central Africa; Class C Mandates: ex-German South West Africa and Pacific. 'C' mandates, in other words, conveniently covered South West Africa and the islands Australia and New Zealand wanted. Japan got its islands north of the equator, New Zealand and Australia their islands, France acquired Togoland and most of Cameroon, Britain a small strip of Cameroon (next to Nigeria, already a British colony) and almost the whole of German East Africa (roughly Tanzania), an area three times the size of Germany today.

For the purpose of our story, what is notable is that the two British Empire representatives on the commission drafting the League Covenant, General Smuts and Lord Robert Cecil, had both been won over to Zionism by Weizmann in the summer of 1917. Neither Mesopotamia, nor Syria, including Palestine, nor the Balfour Declaration was specifically mentioned in the draft covenant, but it was clear to all that the mandates for those territories would be 'awarded' to the British and the French. On 14 February, Wilson presented a draft of the League Covenant to a plenary session of the Peace Conference. That night, he left for the United States, confident that he had accomplished his main purpose (he returned to Paris a month later). On 28 April, a plenary session of the conference approved the covenant. Two months later, representatives of the new German government were summoned to Versailles and they signed a peace treaty with the Allies. The covenant was signed the same day, as Part 1 of the Treaty of Versailles. Historians have been arguing about the Treaty's content and legacy (too harsh or too lenient?) ever since. The covenant, together with the rest of the Treaty, came into force on 10 January 1920, signed by forty-four states, and thus the mandate system – Article 22 of the covenant – became an integral part of international law. The same Article also contained the oft-quoted, patronising phrase:

> To those colonies and territories … inhabited by peoples not yet able to
> stand by themselves under the strenuous conditions of the modern world,
> there should be applied the principle that the well-being and develop-
> ment of such peoples form a sacred trust of civilisation and that securities
> for the performance of this trust should be embodied in this Covenant.

However, between 1920 and 1948, the Palestinians, in particular, would experience little that was either sacred or trustworthy in British rule.

Palestine: Contrasting Proposals

When Feisal arrived in Paris in January 1919, as head of the Hijaz Delegation to the Peace Conference, he encountered three main influences at work in opposition to the fulfilment of Arab hopes, namely the British imperial interest in Iraq and Palestine, the French imperial interest in Syria and the Zionist national interest in Palestine (in co-ordination with Britain).

Although Feisal, representing his father, and representatives of the Zionist Organisation were both at the conference, of the two it was the latter who were much the better organised. Their delegation, some twenty-seven strong, had been in Paris since December 1918 to prepare papers for the presentation of their case, to reconstitute Palestine as a Jewish commonwealth, before the Council of Ten.[12] The initial forty-page draft, presented to the British delegation on 20 January 1919 and entitled 'Memorandum of the Zionist Organization Relating to the Reconstruction of Palestine as the Jewish National Home', pressed the notion that Palestine must be developed into a Jewish commonwealth under a British trusteeship. Among other things, it demanded the installation of a Jewish governor, the nationalisation of all absentee-owned lands and a Jewish majority on the executive and legislative councils. In deference to British objections, a shorter, anodyne second draft eliminated the demands for land expropriation and a Jewish governor, as well as a Jewish majority on the executive and legislative councils. Indeed, Weizmann and Samuel met on 30 and 31 January with Ormsby-Gore, Arnold Toynbee and Robert Cecil, all attached to the British delegation, to make sure they were in agreement before the new draft, reduced to fourteen pages and entitled 'Statement of the Zionist Organization regarding Palestine', was submitted to the British on 3 February.[13]

On 6 February, Feisal and Lawrence, both in Arab dress, appeared before the Council of Ten.

Although the tone of Feisal's speech (translated by Lawrence) was both visionary and conciliatory, its content lacked hard detail, having no talk of the Correspondence or other wartime pledges. He outlined his father's claim to all of Syria, including Palestine, and Mesopotamia as a possible future, independent, pan-Arab state. Two points in the eight-page statement he handed to the commissioners are particularly noteworthy. First, the 'privileges' (special administrative status) of

---

12 Initially, the council consisted of the big four (Wilson, Clemenceau, Lloyd George and Orlando of Italy), plus their Foreign Ministers and two Japanese delegates. In March it morphed into the Supreme Council, consisting of only the big four.

13 Reinharz, *Chaim Weizmann*, 294–296.

Emir Feisal at the Peace Conference, 1919

Lebanon which did not impair Syrian unity would be respected under a guarantee by the League of Nations. Second, he personally was prepared to accept a controlled Jewish immigration and the extension of existing Jewish colonies in Palestine, but the extreme demands made by the Zionists had greatly disturbed the people, so much so that they rejected Zionism in its entirety.[14] Near the end of his speech, the Emir said that should the members of the Supreme Council have any lingering doubts about popular consent, he invited them to send a committee of inquiry to poll Syrian Arabs.

However, Feisal's vision of a unified Arab state was the last thing the Allies wanted. His presence in Paris was an embarrassment to the French and British alike; he was holding the British to their word and getting in the way of French imperial ambitions. In fact, few Europeans took him or the Arab cause seriously, and the conference was dominated by Clemenceau and Lloyd George, men more than twice Feisal's age, who were dead set against the Wilsonian principles of self-determination.

The Zionist Mission, as it was officially called, appeared before the Council of Ten on 27 February. It was a historic occasion for the Zionists: the first opportunity to present their case before an international forum, which in and of itself represented validation of a sort. Nahum Sokolow,

---

14 FO 371/4182. Reinharz makes no mention of Emir Feisal's presentation to the big ten.

the Secretary-General of the World Zionist Congress, who described the previous eighteen centuries of Jewish suffering, was followed by Weizmann, who outlined the tragedy of the Jews in Eastern Europe. In Palestine, he claimed, five million Jews could be settled without encroaching on the legitimate interests of the present inhabitants; a million Jews in Eastern Europe were awaiting the signal to move. Their proposal: the development of an administration, under a mandatory power, which would allow for the immigration into Palestine of seventy to eighty thousand Jews annually. Menachem Ussishkin spoke in Hebrew on behalf of some three million Russian Jews, and finally the French orientalist Sylvain Lévi praised some Zionist achievements, but to the other speakers' annoyance expressed some criticism of Zionist aims. Weizmann later recalled that following the hearing, US Secretary of State Robert Lansing had called him over and asked him what he meant by a Jewish national home:

> I defined [it] to mean the creation of an administration which would arise out of the natural conditions of the country – always safeguarding the interests of non-Jews – with the hope that by Jewish immigration, Palestine would ultimately become as Jewish as England is English ... the Zionist task was indeed a difficult one, but the question was not whether Zionism was difficult, but whether it was possible [and] took as my example the outstanding success which the French had at that time made of Tunisia. What the French could do in Tunisia, I said, the Jews would be able to do in Palestine, with Jewish will, Jewish money, Jewish power and Jewish enthusiasm.[15]

Later, when Ben-Gurion asked Weizmann, 'Why didn't you demand a Jewish State in Palestine?' Weizmann replied, 'We didn't demand one because they wouldn't have given us one. We asked only for conditions which would allow us to build a Jewish state in the future. It is simply a matter of tactics.'[16] Although Sokolow, Weizmann and Ussishkin shared the same vision of a future Jewish state, of the three the latter was always more forthcoming – less tactical – in his use of language. He would later write that 'The whole of Palestine, or at least most of it, must belong to the Jewish people ... this can be achieved by three

15 Chaim Weizmann, *Trial and Error*, 305–306.
16 Norman Rose, *Chaim Weizmann. A Biography* (London, 1986), 197.

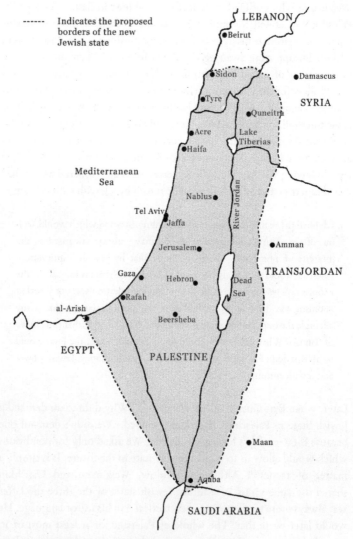

Figure 5: The World Zionist Organisation claim, 1919

means: by force, but we do not have it, governmental coercion, or purchase.'[17]

While the Supreme Council, who sat in judgment over both Feisal's and the Zionists' representations, gave no verdict, the victorious powers accepted the Balfour Declaration, a partial Zionist victory; but as no peace treaty was yet signed with Turkey (negotiations with the defeated Empire were fractious) the questions of granting Britain the Mandate for Palestine and what its borders should be were held in abeyance. It is noteworthy that at one point during the government's discussions concerning the future of Muslim Turkey, Montagu, the Secretary of State for India, declared, 'Let us not for Heaven's sake tell the Muslim what he ought to think, let us recognise what they think' – to which Balfour replied, 'I am quite unable to see why Heaven or any other Power should object to our telling the Muslim what he ought to think.'[18] Balfour clearly applied the same mind-set to the Arab former subjects of the Ottoman Empire as well. Lloyd George's outlook was equally racist. During the discussions he predicted that the competing nationalist claimants in Palestine were 'going to grow up into two troublesome chickens: the Jews virile, brave, determined, intelligent; the Arabs decadent, dishonest and producing little beyond eccentrics, influenced by the romance and silence of the desert'.[19]

When American diplomats at the Peace Conference proposed an Allied Commission to investigate popular sentiment in Greater Syria, both their French and British counterparts reluctantly greeted it with public approval. Officially called the *1919 Inter-Allied Commission on Mandates in Turkey*, it was originally meant to include French, British, Italian and American representatives. However, it ended as a two-man American investigation after the others withdrew their participation, to avoid the risk of being confronted with recommendations which would no doubt have conflicted with their policies.

In Syria, including Palestine, the populations understandably thought that their views would be taken into account by the powers. With its professed commitment to esteem public opinion, foster

17 Menachem Ussishkin, *The Ussishkin Book* (Jerusalem, 1934), 105. Cited in Wolfe, *Traces of History*, 229.

18 MacMillan, *Peacemakers*, 391.

19 Lori Allen, *A History of False Hope. Investigative Commissions in Palestine* (Stanford, 2021), 56.

representative government and respect the facts, the commission inspired optimism throughout the Middle East. Judging from newspaper accounts of the day, there was every expectation among the Arabs that the commission's findings would impact the Peace Conference and ensure the independent future of Palestine.[20] According to Antonius, when Feisal heard the news in Paris that a commission was to be appointed, he drank champagne for the first time in his life, confident that it would confirm Syrian independence under Hashimite rule.[21] Even Lord Allenby appeared to think that the commission would decide the future of the various Turkish territories, but Balfour immediately put him right: 'They will have no power to decide, but after examining all the facts of the case will tender their advice to the Council of the Principal Allied Powers, who will have to take the final decision.'[22]

The commission, led by Dr Henry C. King, President of Oberlin College, Ohio, and Charles R. Crane, an American businessman and prominent member of the Democratic Party, visited areas of Palestine, Syria, Lebanon and Anatolia, surveyed local public opinion, and reported back to conference in August 1919.[23] By all accounts, both commissioners were men of intelligence and independence and whose 'impartiality is unassailable'.[24] Among other things, they found that the Arabs of Palestine desired unity with an independent Syria, and that the Zionists' claim that they had a right to Palestine, based on an occupation two thousand years ago, 'can hardly be seriously considered'. However, Lloyd George and Clemenceau had other plans for the region, and the commission's recommendations were neither officially considered nor published. The whole report was in effect pigeonholed and ignored, although it did sour Anglo-French relations, at least temporarily, especially when Clemenceau suggested that the commission should also survey public opinion in British-occupied Mesopotamia. More

20 See Allen, *A History of False Hope*, 32, 39.

21 Antonius, *Awakening*, 288.

22 *Documents on British Foreign Policy* (DBFP), Series 1, vol. iv, no. 178. Balfour to Allenby, 31 May 1919.

23 The two commissioners were assisted by three advisors: Professor Albert H. Lybyer, Dr George R. Montgomery and Captain William Yale; and a secretary-treasurer, Captain Donald M. Brodie.

24 H. Harry Howard, *An American Inquiry in the Middle East: The King-Crane Commission* (Beirut, 1963), 236–237. Cited in Huneidi, *A Broken Trust*, 15.

fundamentally, it aroused such false hopes among various groups of Arabs that Gertrude Bell, the Arabic-speaking, influential Oriental Secretary to Percy Cox, the High Commissioner in Baghdad, denounced it as a criminal deception.[25] The commission's findings were only published in December 1922, in *Editor & Publisher*, an American monthly magazine, and although the report had no political impact on the fate of the Middle East at the time, it remains a historical reference point for Palestinians to prove the existence of their movement and potential nation-statehood in the period of Zionism's infancy.[26]

Arab aspirations were inevitably low in the pecking order of international concern after a war which had seen such a massive bloodletting in Europe. For the French, Feisal's removal from Damascus, where he was de facto ruler, was merely a matter of time. Their determination to take Syria, combined with Lloyd George's realpolitik, gave the Hashimites little chance. Britain was not going to frustrate the Middle East ambitions of France for the sake of its Arab allies, heavily dependent though they were on British money, arms and military advice. In this regard, Balfour's lengthy and oft-quoted memorandum of 11 August 1919, dealing with the future of Syria, Palestine and Iraq, deserves to be quoted at length. It reveals the mindset of one of Britain's most influential decision-makers of the era, in particular concerning the self-government of the Arab provinces and the manner in which the contradictory wartime pledges should be resolved.

In the opinion of the British Foreign Minister, the root of the trouble was in five documents: the McMahon–Hussein Correspondence, the Sykes–Picot Agreement, the Anglo-French Declaration of November 1918, the Covenant of the League of Nations that was approved in February 1919 and the directions given to the King-Crane Commission, sent out to ascertain the wishes of the people of Greater Syria. Balfour wrote that these documents were inconsistent with one another:

> In 1915 we promised the Arabs independence and the promise was unqualified, except in respect of certain territorial reservations. In 1918

---

25 Fromkin, *A Peace to End All Peace*, 397.
26 See Allen, *A History of False Hope*, 69. For the full text of the commission's recommendations, see Antonius, *Awakening*, 443–458.

the promise was by implication repeated: for no other interpretation can, I think, be placed by any unbiased reader on the phrase in the [Anglo-French] declaration about a 'national government' and 'an administration deriving its authority from the choice of the native population' ...

In our promises with regard to the frontiers of the new Arab States we do not seem to have been more fortunate than in our promises about their independence. In 1915 it was the Sharif of Mecca to whom the task of delimitation was to have been confided, nor were any restrictions placed upon his discretion in this matter, except certain reservations intended to protect French interests in Western Syria and Cilicia ...

The [1919] Covenant speaks as follows:—

'The wishes of the communities (i.e. the independent nations) must be a principal consideration in the selection of a mandatory.'

The sentiment is unimpeachable; but how is it to be carried into effect?

To simplify the argument, let us assume that two of the 'independent nations' for which mandatories have to be provided are Syria and Palestine. Take Syria first. Do we mean, in the case of Syria, to consult principally the wishes of the inhabitants? We mean nothing of the kind ... Are we going 'chiefly to consider the wishes of the inhabitants' in deciding which of these (England, America, France) is to be selected? We are going to do nothing of the kind ... England has refused, America will refuse so that whatever the inhabitants may wish, it is France they will certainly have.

The contradiction between the letter of the Covenant and the policy of the Allies is even more flagrant in the case of the 'independent nation' of Palestine than in that of the 'independent nation' of Syria. For in Palestine we do not propose even to go through the form of consulting the wishes of the present inhabitants of the country, though the American Commission has been going through the form of asking what they are. The four Great Powers are committed to Zionism. And Zionism, be it right or wrong, good or bad, is rooted in age-long traditions, in present needs, in future hopes, and far profounder import than the desires and prejudices of the 700,000 Arabs who now inhabit that ancient land.

In my opinion that is right. What I have never been able to understand is how it can be harmonised with the declaration, the Covenant, or the instructions to the Commission of Enquiry ...

Whatever be the future of Palestine, it is not now an 'independent nation,' nor is it yet on the way to become one. Whatever deference should be paid to the views of those who live there, the Powers in their selection of a mandatory do not propose, as I understand the matter, to consult them. In short, so far as Palestine is concerned, the Powers have made no statement of fact which is not admittedly wrong, and no declaration of policy which, at least in the letter, they have not always intended to violate.[27]

Such 'a tangle of hypocrisy and contradictory commitments'[28] was no mere expression of a senior decision-maker's opinions; in hindsight, it was a private statement of policy that arguably radically altered the course of history for millions of people in the Middle East.

George Kidston, a senior Foreign Office official, minuted on the memorandum:

Mr Balfour's suggestions are admirable as indicating a broad line of policy, but I doubt if he realises the difficulties of the details. Nor does he take into consideration the intense dislike of Feisal and his Arabs for a French mandate and the growing feeling of the Arabs for a union under a single mandatory … Palestine is to go to the Zionists irrespective of the wishes of the great bulk of the population, because it is historically right and politically expedient that it should do so. The idea that the carrying out of either of these programmes [the French Mandate for Syria and the British Mandate for Palestine] will entail bloodshed and military repression never seems to have occurred to him.[29]

Ten days after Balfour's memorandum, *The Times*, whose diplomatic correspondent, Aubrey Kennedy, followed closely such developments in Foreign Office thinking, published an article in which the terms of the Sykes–Picot Agreement were described as unworkable. They were, in Kennedy's judgement, 'not in harmony with engagements contracted towards the king of the Hijaz in the autumn of 1915'. When two senior members of Balfour's staff, Eric Forbes Adam and Robert Vansittart,

---

27 FO 371/4183; DBFP, Series 1, vol. iv, no. 242.

28 Khalidi, *The Hundred Years' War on Palestine*, 39.

29 FO 371/4183. Minute by George Kidston, 22 September 1919.

took exception to the article, and suggested to their minister that they correct *The Times*'s misconceptions, Balfour responded, 'It is rather dangerous to speak to *The Times* in this sense unless we can reconcile our letter to Hussein in 1915 with the S-P agreement of 1916. I cannot. Can anyone else?'[30]

The Arabs came to regard the Peace Conference as yet another betrayal by the Great Powers. Although there had been much talk, inspired by President Wilson, of a new international order based on self-determination and collective security, when all had been drafted and signed it looked singularly like just another version of the familiar old story: to the victor the spoils. On paper, the mandatory system, a 'temporary trusteeship', was not quite the same as old-style colonialism, primarily because its charter implied a time limit, and also because each mandatory power was responsible to the Permanent Mandates Commission, an international body of critics that had the right to review the power's actions once a year. Nevertheless, as the historian H.A.L. Fisher succinctly and accurately put it, the peace treaties draped 'the crudity of conquest' in 'the veil of morality'.[31] Yet, writing twenty years later, Lloyd George clearly remained irritated by claims that he had not honoured the wartime pledges to the Arabs:

> The Allies redeemed the promises made in these declarations to the full. No race has done better out of the fidelity with which the Allies redeemed their promises to the oppressed races than the Arabs ... the Palestinian Arabs fought for Turkish rule.[32]

By the autumn of 1919 the British government had decided that for economic reasons it could no longer continue to maintain an army of some 400,000 troops in the provinces of the Ottoman Empire it had conquered. In early September, Allenby was summoned to Deauville, a small town on the Normandy coast, where Lloyd George and his entourage were occasionally based during the Peace Conference, to discuss

---

30 FO 371/4183.

31 H.A.L. Fisher, *A History of Europe* (London, 1936), 1207.

32 David Lloyd George, *Memoirs of the Peace Conference* (New Haven, 1939), 491, 723–724.

the military occupation of Syria, Cilicia, Palestine and Mesopotamia, and in particular which provinces should be evacuated, meaning those for which the government did not propose to accept permanent responsibility. As a result of the four meetings that took place between 9 and 11 September, an aide-memoire was drawn up for the Prime Minister to hand to the French Premier, and eventually to Emir Feisal, which spelled out in detail the decision to withdraw British troops, in particular from the Lebanon region, and their replacement by French troops. On Saturday, 13 September, Lloyd George handed this to Monsieur Clemenceau, and two days later he communicated it to the Supreme Council in Paris, who noted it, but did not officially approve or reject it.

The Emir arrived in London on 18 September at Lloyd George's invitation, officially 'to discuss the future arrangements for Syria and Mesopotamia'. At 10 Downing Street the following morning, Feisal, who understood only a modicum of English, and two of his advisors[33] found themselves sitting opposite the Prime Minister, who was flanked by Leader of the House Bonar Law, Lord Curzon, Field Marshal Allenby and four other senior officials.[34] After informing the Emir that the government had no intention of continuing to occupy certain provinces, and that the British people were complaining of the burden of expense, the Prime Minister explained that the government had therefore decided to withdraw their troops from all these territories, except Mesopotamia and Palestine. Under Lloyd-George's predecessors, Great Britain had entered into two distinct sets of written obligations with the King of the Hijaz and with the President of the French Republic, and they were bound to respect both equally. As previously described in the survey of 1915–1919 interpretations, the Prime Minister then read out the key phrases from the English version of McMahon's 24 October 1915 letter, a copy of which he handed to the Emir, and which he described as 'the engagement entered into with King Hussein'. He continued:

---

33 Brigadier-General Haddad Pasha (Director of Public Security, Occupied Enemy Territory East), who acted as interpreter, and Sheikh Fuad el Khatib, Political Advisor to King Hussein and to Emir Feisal.

34 Colonel Cornwallis (Assistant Chief Political Officer, Egyptian Expeditionary Force), Lieutenant-Colonel Stirling (Deputy Chief Political Officer, Egyptian Expeditionary Force), Lieutenant-Colonel Sir M.P.A. Hankey (Secretary, war cabinet) and Lieutenant-Colonel L. Storr (Assistant Secretary, war cabinet).

The point about this engagement was that Damascus, Homs, Hama and Aleppo were recognised as being within the Arab State. King Hussein had been told that the districts of Mersina and Alexandretta <u>and portions of Syria lying to the west of that line</u> could not be said to be purely Arab, and should be excluded from the proposed limits and boundaries of the Arab territory. The agreement entered into with the French in 1916 also provided that Damascus, Homs, Hama and Aleppo should be Arab, <u>but that the area to the west of those towns</u> should be subject to such direct or indirect administration or control as the French desire and as they may think fit to arrange with the Arab State or Confederation of Arab States.[35]

He emphasised that the aide-memoire was a temporary, strictly military and non-political measure:

> All that they now proposed was to evacuate these territories and hand over their garrisons in accordance with the agreement entered into with King Hussein. The eventual settlement would be determined by the Treaty of Peace with Turkey.

He then assured the Emir that he had informed Clemenceau that

> the British government could not hand over Damascus, Homs, Hama and Aleppo to French troops, and that when the Field Marshal ordered his troops out of those places he would hand over the towns to the Emir Feisal to hold until the Peace Treaty finally decided their disposition. <u>West of that line</u> the Field Marshal would retire in favour of French troops, who would occupy the country until the Peace Treaty decided on its eventual disposition ... The Arab forces had redeemed the pledges they had given to Great Britain, and we should redeem our pledges.[36]

The Prime Minister's use of the word 'line' twice during this meeting can thus be added to the previous eight British interpretations of the Correspondence. Feisal, however, had no knowledge of either the

---

35 Underlined by the author.
36 DBFP, Series 1, vol. iv, no. 283. 'Notes of a meeting held at 10 Downing Street, Friday 19 September 1919'. Underlined by the author.

Lloyd George–Clemenceau verbal compact of December 1918, or of the uninterrupted British government negotiations with the Zionist Organisation, which by the end of 1919 had resulted in a detailed and provisionally agreed draft Mandate for Palestine.[37] This begs the question as to the extent to which the government deliberately kept their Arab ally in the dark between 1917 and 1922. With Balfour in Paris during the conference, Curzon was placed in charge of current affairs at the Foreign Office at home. Theoretically, there was coordination, but decisions were taken in Paris without consultation with London, which sometimes did not hear of them until much later. The Palestine policy was a case in point. Curzon only became aware of the draft mandate negotiations and their tenor months after they were initiated.

When handing the aide-memoire to the Emir, the Prime Minister emphasised that it was in no sense an agreement: it had been prepared by Field Marshal Lord Allenby, Bonar Law and himself before he ever saw Clemenceau in Paris and was not the result of negotiations with the French government behind the back of the Arab representatives. The government had decided to withdraw in such a way as would conform to the agreements made with the King of the Hijaz, as set forth in the Correspondence. He concluded by expressing the hope that the Emir would fall in with these temporary arrangements, and informing him the evacuation was scheduled to begin on 1 November.

The Emir immediately protested at this ill-disguised attempt to impose the Sykes–Picot Agreement on the region, which he declared would be 'a death sentence' to the Arab nation. Moreover, it was an unjust return to a policy of ambitious imperialism. The Arabs had fought against the Turks not with the intention of dividing the country by giving a share to the French and a portion to the British. His family could not tolerate that stain on its history and would withdraw. The McMahon Correspondence, according to the Emir, had been based on the same principles as those on which the war with Germany was fought, namely justice and the freedom of peoples, but the Sykes–Picot Agreement was based on colonisation. The Emir emphasised that the

---

37 While in Paris in July 1919, Balfour had instructed Forbes Adam and Vansittart to start official discussions with the Zionist Organisation to draft a mandate for Palestine based on the Balfour Declaration. The draft, dated 11 December 1919, is in DBFP, Series 1, vol. iv, no. 397.

evacuation of the western zone by the British troops and their replacement by French troops would lead to a rising if there was no British
administration to appeal to, and that Great Britain would be responsible
for any bloodshed that might ensue. The Prime Minister replied that 'If
bloodshed occurred, he would be very distressed, but he had inherited
two sets of engagements from his predecessors and was bound to keep
both sets.'[38]

In response, Feisal solemnly protested in the name of the Arab nation
against any change to be introduced into the prevailing form of military
administration in Syria. The status quo should remain until the final
decision of the Peace Conference as to the future form of Syria's government. After all, Lord Allenby had confirmed to him a month previously
that his military administration would continue in Syria until a final
decision by the Peace Conference was reached.[39] Not only that but the
British government, via the High Commissioner in Cairo, had informed
King Hussein that Djemal Pasha had distorted the original purpose of
the Sykes–Picot Agreement when publicising it, and omitted its stipulations regarding the consent of native populations (in fact, as previously
mentioned, the agreement contained no such stipulation). Finally, Feisal
stated that this same stipulation regarding the consent of the people was
confirmed in November 1918 by the formal declaration made conjointly
by Great Britain and France.

The Emir asked whether the government still stood by that formal
declaration and whether the opinion of the people had been taken as to
the new proposed occupation. Lloyd George made no reply. Feisal then
proposed that the whole situation should be immediately placed before
the Peace Conference, or failing that, a subcommittee of conference,
and that should it be found necessary to withdraw, why not withdraw
all European troops from Syria and leave the responsibility to the Arab

---

38 DBFP, Series 1, vol. iv, no. 283.

39 In October 1918, Allenby travelled to Damascus to reassure Feisal personally that
the installation of a French military governor of Beirut was a temporary measure.
This after Allenby, following representations from the French, had forced the Arab
governor to leave the Serail and replace the Arab flag with the French tricolour. In
protest, Feisal resigned his position as Lieutenant-General in the Allied Army. In
Damascus, Allenby had 'reminded the Amir that the Allies were in honour bound to
endeavour to reach a settlement in accordance with the wishes of the people
concerned'. See Thompson, *How the West Stole Democracy*, 18.

government who were prepared to be responsible to the Allied and Associated Powers for the interior security of the country until such time as the Peace Conference decided the future of Syria? Lloyd George demurred and politely brought the meeting to an end.

Following a second, equally fruitless meeting four days later, where both sides held to their positions,[40] both Lord Curzon and the Prime Minister wrote to the Emir in an endeavour to help him 'see reason, and if possible, to acquiesce'. Curzon attached copies of the McMahon Correspondence with his letter of 9 October, and wrote that the government's obligations to King Hussein and the French government did not conflict, but were complementary. Curzon added:

From this correspondence two things are clear. First, that the British Government are bound by their undertakings to King Hussein to recognise the establishment of an independent Arab State comprising within its borders the four towns of Damascus, Hama, Homs, and Aleppo; and second, that they made it absolutely clear to your illustrious father before the entry of Arabs into the war that they regarded France as having special rights in the area west of these four towns ... They did not communicate [the Sykes–Picot Agreement] to King Hussein, because it was in complete conformity with the undertakings they had already entered into with him.[41]

He concluded:

HMG does not see any proposal [other than the aide-memoire] which is practicable for the interim period. There is no authority of weight who believes that the people of Syria can stand alone at the present time. To attempt this solution, which you suggest, would simply be to prejudice the free and rapid progress and ultimately the independence of the Syrian and Arab peoples. Further, it is essential that until the peace is made with Turkey some first-class European Power should hold the territory to the south-east of Anatolia.[42]

---

40 See DBFP, Series 1, vol. iv, no. 309.
41 DBFP, Series 1, vol. iv, no. 309. Earl Curzon to the Emir Feisal, 9 October 1919. Underlined by the author.
42 DBFP, Series 1, vol. iv, no. 309. Earl Curzon to the Emir Feisal, 9 October 1919.

Note that Curzon here follows Toynbee and Lloyd George's 'line' interpretation and describes the reserved area as synonymous with French interests. Concerning the government's communications with the King, perhaps Curzon had not read all the previous papers relating to the Sykes–Picot Agreement, including McMahon's recommendation in May 1916 that it would be better not to divulge the details to the Sharif or any other Arab leader. According to the High Commissioner, there was 'a risk of possible misinterpretation' and 'it might be prejudicial to our present good relations.' The Foreign Office, using the unusual first-person singular, had promptly approved: 'I agree that the details of the arrangement should not be divulged.'[43]

Lloyd George wrote a day later to the Emir in more robust terms:

> It does not seem to me that the proposal you now make is practicable …
> His Majesty's Government have made up their mind that it is impossible
> for them to continue the occupation of Syria by British troops. Six months
> ago they announced to the Peace Conference and to yourself that under
> no circumstances would they accept a mandate for Syria … It is therefore
> impossible for His Majesty's Government to withdraw the proposals
> which they have made for dealing with the Syrian problem in the interim
> period until the Peace Conference can settle it.[44]

The official records of these meetings, as written by the Cabinet Secretary, indicate that they were not so much a matter of consultation with the Emir as a 'policy imposed', albeit in diplomatic discourse. The decision had been taken, and the Emir was expected to fall in line. However, even after a third and final meeting with Lloyd George and his senior officials on 13 October, the Emir still politely refused to 'see reason'. The Prime Minister, Lord Curzon and Lord Allenby subsequently urged Feisal to go to Paris and put his case to the French government. In Paris, senior government officials brushed aside all the Emir's proposals, determined as they were not to discuss politics with him until

---

43 FO 371/2768. McMahon to Foreign Office, 4 May 1916; Foreign Office to McMahon, 6 May 1916.
44 DBFP, Series 1, vol. iv, no. 313. Lloyd George to the Emir Feisal, 10 October 1919.

there was a strong contingent of French troops on the ground in and around Beirut. They merely assured him that the new French Commander in Syria, General Henri Gouraud, 'thoroughly understood Syria, and would do anything for the welfare of that country'.

In the meantime, the evacuation of British troops southwards from Cilicia went ahead on schedule; Damascus was evacuated by 26 November; and French battalions and armaments, including artillery, arrived in Beirut. Feisal left Paris in early January 1920 and returned to Syria, his honour intact, but deeply aware that his political position was almost hopeless, and his options limited. In essence, the militant Arab nationalists in Damascus were prepared to consider him their leader only as long as he could keep the French out, while the French were prepared to let him rule only if he could succeed in bringing them in.

On 7 November, Curzon instructed the British Ambassador in Paris to inform Feisal that as of 1 November the monthly subsidy of £150,000 paid by His Majesty's Government would be reduced to £75,000. Clemenceau, at a meeting at 10 Downing Street on 19 September, had agreed to pay the other half. Feisal, who had no wish to be beholden to the French, declined the offer. On the eve of his departure from Paris, the French government had finally communicated to Feisal a secret draft proposal concerning a permanent arrangement for Syria. The Emir refused to sign it, and returned to Syria with it in his pocket. On reading a copy, the British Ambassador in Paris, the Earl of Derby, wrote to Curzon that the French proposal 'establishes the whole country as a French Protectorate'.[45] As we shall see, British pragmatism and French determination soon coalesced and Feisal was expelled from Syria by French military forces in July 1920, before being installed by the British on the throne of the new state of Iraq the following summer.

As mentioned before, Feisal had no knowledge of the Lloyd George–Clemenceau verbal compact of December 1918, nor of the British government's negotiations with the Zionist Organisation throughout 1919 concerning a draft mandate for Palestine. Thus, the British simultaneously conducted separate negotiations with two rival parties concerning the future governance of the same piece of territory, then under a British military administration, without informing either competing party. This may have been considered by the government as

45 DBFP, Series 1, vol. iv, nos. 354, 402.

standard negotiating practice, but it was seen later by the Arab world as double-dealing, even treachery.

Apart from the Balfour Declaration, other wartime pledges did not figure either in Paris during the spring of 1919, or in parliamentary debates at Westminster during that year. In October 1919, Bonar Law, Conservative Leader of the House, briefly explained the government's policy regarding the occupied Turkish territories:

> While no final statement can now be made ... if the Peace Conference grants to Great Britain a Mandate for any of the territories of the ex-Turkish Empire, it is the intention of His Majesty's Government to introduce forms of administration which will give every encouragement to the growth and development of local governments and institutions.[46]

Bonar Law's statement was standard liberal-Empire speak and quite misleading because by October 1919 the government had already decided to withhold the development of any local or national representative government in Palestine. Christopher Sykes, among other writers, completely misreads British intentions when he states that Churchill offered the Palestine Arabs 'representative Government' in Palestine in 1921. According to Sykes, Churchill even 'pressed it on both parties'.[47]

Storrs's and Vickery's Arabic Drafts: A Mystery

During the autumn of 1919, with Feisal in Europe, King Hussein continued to complain to British officials in Jedda that they had not fulfilled their promises. Eventually, the acting British agent in Jedda, Colonel Charles E. Vickery, under instructions from London, which had no copies in Arabic of the Correspondence, persuaded the King to show him copies of four letters from McMahon – those of 30 August, 24 October, 14 December 1915 and of 10 March 1916 – which the agent then transcribed and sent to Cairo. Vickery was the first British official to see the Arabic versions of McMahon's letters as received by Hussein. The letters were then translated back into English, probably by Vickery

---

46 Hansard, Commons, 29 October 1919, vol. 120, cc665–666.
47 Sykes, *Crossroads*, 62.

himself, or by Storrs's successor as Oriental Secretary at the residency, Alexander Keown-Boyd, and sent to London in December 1919. However, Vickery's Arabic transcriptions were not sent. While Vickery was in Jedda, transcribing the letters, a note written by a Residency official stated, 'It will probably be wisest to say nothing more to F.O. re. the original correspondence with King Hussein, otherwise we shall have to draw attention to the fact that copies of the original Arabic versions of letters do not exist in Residency files.'[48]

It appears that shortly after Vickery's transcripts were received in Cairo, Keown-Boyd found the original Arabic drafts 'caught up on the back of a drawer in Storrs' desk'.[49] However, they too were not sent to London, which did not request copies of the Arabic texts until 1937. When the Arabic texts of McMahon's letters were required during the Palestine Conference in February 1939, copies of Vickery's 1919 English transcripts, made in 1937 at the British Embassy in Cairo, and officially certified as 'true copies' by Assistant Oriental Secretary Thomas C. Ravensdale, were supplied to the Arab delegates.[50] As will be seen later, the Vickery and Keown-Boyd translations into English were far from accurate and led to considerable embarrassment for the government. It is curious that neither Storrs's original Arabic drafts, as found by Keown-Boyd, nor Vickery's original Arabic transcripts can be found in the official records at Kew.

Writing in 1938, Storrs recollected that

much play has been made by Arab and other critics with ambiguities, mutually incompatible undertakings, and 'betrayals'; without entire justification but not without cause. Our Arabic correspondence with Mecca was prepared by Rūhi, a fair though not a profound Arabist (and a better agent than scholar); and checked, often under high pressure, by myself. I had no Deputy, Staff or office, so that during my absence on

---

48 FO 141/776, file 70/468. Note dated 28 September 1919 addressed to Owen Tweedy, signature illegible.

49 A minute (signature illegible) in FO 141/726, file 17, dated 21 February 1931, records that the draft Arabic letters were eventually found by A. Keown-Boyd 'among some rubbish left by Sir R. Storrs'.

50 A copy of Vickery's '<u>vilayets</u>' translation of the letter, entitled 'Literal Translation of original Arabic letter sent by Sir H. McMahon to King Hussein (vide copy sent by Col. Vickery)' is in FO 686/42. A Photostat copy of the letter in Arabic, sent by Ravensdale to London in 1937, is in FO 371/20807, 199.

mission the work was carried on (better perhaps) by others, but the continuity was lost. I never saw the correspondence again after leaving for
Baghdad in April 1917. It was needed in my absence and I cabled to Cairo:
'All Sharif originals ever had are in my files consult index if you pick lock
please seal up afterwards.'[51]

Storrs had left Cairo on 8 April 1917. He received the cable asking for
the keys to his private file in Basra on 2 May, en route to his new posting
in Baghdad as Political Officer, Egyptian Expeditionary Force,
Mesopotamia.[52]

According to Storrs, the letters in Arabic received by the Sharif were
drafted by Rūhi, whose quality of written Arabic seems to have been
less than professional. Moreover, we don't know which of the four
letters sent to the Sharif were actually checked by Storrs. So where does
the responsibility lie for this linguistic and political imbroglio?
According to Edwin Samuel, son of Herbert Samuel and a mandate official in Palestine for three decades, although Storrs was a good linguist,
'he pretended that he knew far more than he actually did,'[53] and as we
shall see, when Storrs was asked about the Correspondence in the late
1930s, he deliberately avoided Foreign Office enquiries about the issue.

To conclude, at the end of 1919, the Foreign Office appeared to be
satisfied with Vickery's English transliterations of the Correspondence:
the letters were not significant enough to ask Cairo for copies of the
Arabic versions, as sent to Mecca. In similar fashion, the Correspondence
and other wartime pledges concerning the fate of the Ottoman Empire
hardly figured in any of the Allied leaders' in-trays: President Wilson
was grappling, ultimately unsuccessfully, with a Senate which had no
enthusiasm for joining the League. Having suffered a severe stroke that
October, he would die in February 1924. Clemenceau was about to
resign and leave politics at the age of seventy-nine, and Lloyd George
was fully occupied with the challenges of high unemployment, rising
interest payments, increasing inflation, major troubles in Egypt and an
Irish War of Independence. Following the withdrawal of the United
States, the British government considered Anglo-French cooperation,

---

51 Storrs, *Orientations*, 161.
52 Storrs, *Orientations*, 161, 222.
53 Edwin Samuel, *A Lifetime in Jerusalem* (Chicago, 1970), 52.

however challenging, as the only workable basis for a settlement of the Turkish question, and in order to secure this cooperation it had to satisfy to a large extent the French claims in Syria. Thus, Feisal was abandoned to the French, at least temporarily. The Correspondence therefore remained off the Foreign Office and parliamentary radar for a few months, until the European Allied leaders met in San Remo the following spring to discuss the fates of Syria, Lebanon, Palestine and Iraq, and to squabble over the future control of that region's oil.

3

Detrimental to the Public Interest

1920–1924

Publication of the 'various undertakings and promises' given to the Arabs during the war appears to have been raised in Parliament for the first time on 22 March 1920, when William Ormsby-Gore, the newly elected Conservative MP for Stafford, and a supporter of the Jewish national home project, asked the Prime Minister whether the government would issue a White Paper 'setting out the various undertakings and promises given during the war by the British Government to the Arabs'. Lloyd George replied, 'It would not be desirable at the present moment to lay correspondence on the matter.'[1]

No further discussion in the Commons took place. The following month, the Allies, meeting without the USA at the Italian coastal resort of San Remo, decided to award the mandate for Syria to France, and that for Palestine to Britain. Feisal did not attend; to protest against the Allies' refusal to recognise his son as King of Syria, the Sharif temporarily broke off all ties with the Peace Conference. While at San Remo, Herbert Samuel promoted the Zionist enterprise by discussing with Lord Curzon, Cabinet Secretary Sir Maurice Hankey and Lloyd George the question of Feisal, who had been proclaimed King of Syria and Palestine at a General Syrian Congress in March. He was assured that there was no question of Feisal becoming King of a

---

1 Hansard, Commons, 22 March 1920, vol. 127, c53. 'To lay papers', meaning to lay them before the House, i.e. to make public.

united, independent Syria.[2] Samuel, along with Weizmann and Sokolow, who had both arrived unofficially and unannounced at San Remo, then consulted Balfour. As for the French, the coronation of Feisal in Damascus signified a usurpation of their claims to the region and a violation of the Sykes–Picot Agreement. At the discussions on 24 April, in a final effort to save French influence in the Holy Land, Philippe Berthelot, the Director of the Political Office at the Quai d'Orsay, argued that the Balfour Declaration 'had long been a dead letter' and that it had not guaranteed the political rights of the non-Jewish populations. His intent was less to protect Arabs in Palestine than to force Britain to respect France's claim to exclusive control of Syria.

But the British were adamant: Curzon replied that the concept of 'civil rights' in the declaration included political rights, and Francesco Nitti, the Italian Prime Minister, remarked in support of Curzon that the 'difference was one of form and not one of substance'.[3] The French and Italians also pressurised the British to grant them the right to protect their religious institutions in the Holy Land, satisfying Catholic lobbyists. That same day, Lloyd George finally decided that the military administration in Palestine should be replaced by a civilian administration and formally asked Samuel to be the first High Commissioner. Samuel's candidature had been the subject of a discussion between the Prime Minister, Weizmann and Samuel as early as December 1918, as confirmed by Aaron Aaronsohn, a colleague of Weizmann, who noted in his diary that Christmas Eve, '*Chaim me rende compte de sa visite chez Ll.G. avec Herbert Samuel. Entrevue très satisfaisante en somme. Samuel*

---

2 The Congress, meeting in Damascus and attended by some ninety deputies from today's Syria, Lebanon, Palestine/Israel and Jordan, passed a resolution on 7 March 1920 which included: 'We the members of this Congress, in our capacity as true representatives of all the Syrians in whose name we speak … have therefore unanimously proclaimed the full and absolute independence of our country Syria, including Palestine, within her natural boundaries, based on a civil, representative form of government; protection of the rights of minorities; and rejection of the claims of the Zionists to Palestine as a national homeland or place of immigration for the Jews.' Thompson, *How the West Stole Democracy*, 339, 349.

3 Jukka Nevakivi, *Britain, France and the Arab Middle East, 1914–1920* (London, 1969), 247.

accepterait de devenir le Gouverneur de la Palestine, tout en appréhendant d'être assassiné.'[4]

The choice of Samuel by Lloyd George – the arch-Zionist among Britain's interwar prime ministers (1916–1922) before Churchill – was in itself indicative of British intentions. It was not so much that Samuel was a leading member of the Anglo-Jewish elite, some of whom were anti-Zionist, but that as a cabinet minister in the previous Asquith government he had been the first British politician to broach to his colleagues the idea of the creation of a Jewish state in Palestine as early as 1915.[5] Five years later, he was to take over from Major-General Louis Bols as High Commissioner on 1 July 1920.

Following two days of talks by the Peace Conference from 24 to 26 April, where the future administration of Syria and Palestine was discussed, Curzon wrote to Lord Hardinge:

> As regards Palestine the conferment of mandate upon Great Britain is not regarded by us as inconsistent with recognition of Feisal as head of an independent Syrian State in as much as he has known throughout that British Government were pledged by Mr. Balfour's declaration to creating a national home for Jews in Palestine and this intention has been acquiesced in by him. But we cannot recognise him as King of Palestine although as mandatories we shall regard ourselves as under an obligation which will be confirmed by terms of mandate to safeguard in fullest manner interests of indigenous inhabitants of the country.[6]

From San Remo, Weizmann wrote to his wife at the end of the conference that 'Lloyd George took leave of us before his departure in a touching manner, and said, "Now you have got your start, it all depends on you."'[7]

Within Syria itself, anger and confusion attended the San Remo pronouncements. The nationalist bloc within the Arab government urged Feisal to defy the Allied Powers; more cautious voices counselled him to seek a compromise that might somehow satisfy French

---

4 Wasserstein, *The British in Palestine*, 81. [Chaim informed me of his visit to Lloyd George's with Herbert Samuel. On the whole a very satisfying interview. Samuel would accept to become the Governor of Palestine, while fearing assassination.]

5 CAB 37/123; Tibawi, *Anglo-Arab Relations*, 55.

6 DBFP, Series 1, vol. xiii, no. 243. Curzon to Lord Hardinge, 26 April 1920.

7 Weizmann letters, vol. ix, no. 317, 29 April 1920.

demands and still preserve the Syrian kingdom. General Gouraud merely continued to build up his forces in the Lebanon, in preparation for the planned occupation of Damascus. Meanwhile, neither Paris nor London recognised the legitimacy of Feisal's coronation on 6 March. From Feisal's perspective, the British pledges to his father had been sacrificed to the requirements of Allied harmony and imperial self-interest. The Arab inhabitants of the defeated Ottoman Empire had neither wished its collapse, nor to see its Arab provinces transformed into a balkanised state system beholden to European Christian powers. In Syria the government had few forces and even less materiel. According to Elizabeth Thompson:

> The Ottomans had either taken armaments with them or destroyed them in their retreat. Syrians could not equip their new army, because they were hemmed in on all sides by Allied powers that limited the import of weapons. And their dynamic military commander, Yasin al-Hashimi, had been kidnapped and transported to Palestine by the British.[8]

With newly created borders imposed upon them, the Arabs were now compelled to forge new 'national' identities as Iraqis, Syrians, Palestinians and Transjordanians.[9]

On 29 April, in his extensive report back to the House of Commons, the Prime Minister described the San Remo Conference as 'a triumph of goodwill'. His only brief reference to Palestine was that 'the mandate for Palestine has [also] been given to Great Britain, with a full recognition of the famous Balfour declaration in respect of the Jews.'[10] He mentioned no other wartime pledges or agreements. In particular, he remained tight-lipped about the agreement made at San Remo with the French, which gave the latter a quarter share in the company set up to explore for oil around Mosul. The British wanted to control both ends of a proposed pipeline between Mosul and Haifa, and this agreement signalled the start of a decade of frequently testy negotiations between

---

8 Thompson, *How the West Stole Democracy*, 206–207.

9 Like Iraq, Transjordan had no previous experience as a distinct political community. During the later Ottoman period, it was a neglected portion of the province (vilayet) of Syria, a largely desert region. In 1920, the capital Amman was scarcely more than a large village with a population of between 2,500 and 5,000.

10 Hansard, Commons, 29 April 1920, vol. 48, c1470.

the two powers – and later the USA – concerning the route as well as the control of the pipeline. Completed in 1934, it divided south-west of Mosul: one line terminated at French-controlled Tripoli in Lebanon, the other at Haifa.

Military to Civilian Administration

In the fortnight before the San Remo Conference, the first serious outbreak of violence between Arabs and Jews in Jerusalem occurred in which five Jews were killed and two hundred wounded. In essence, the causes of the riots were the Palestinians' increasing fears of Zionism, and, according to Walid Khalidi, 'their disappointment of nonfulfill-ment of promises of independence'.[11] Relations between the Zionist Commission and the military administration plunged to a new low. According to Allenby, Weizmann accused the administration of being anti-Zionist and described the riots as a pogrom, which Allenby and Bols denied. Soon afterwards, Bols, who had taken over from Major-General H.D. Watson as Chief Administrator in December 1919, despatched to Allenby an angry sixteen-page report, denouncing

> the hostile, critical, and abusive attitude of the Zionists, who ... seek not justice from the Military Occupant but that in every question in which a Jew is interested discrimination in his favour must be shown ... the Zionist Commission accuse me and my officers of anti-Zionism, the situation is intolerable ... the Zionist appears bent on committing the temporary military administration to a partialist policy before the issue of the Mandate.[12]

Bols accordingly urged the immediate abolition of the Zionist Commission. This recommendation was not received warmly in London. Five weeks later he was replaced by Herbert Samuel, whose appointment led to some discussion in Parliament, given that he was Jewish and a Zionist. On 29 June, two days before Samuel arrived in Jerusalem, Curzon felt it necessary to assure the Lords that the new

---

11 Walid Khalidi, *Before Their Diaspora* (Washington D.C., 1991), 89.
12 FO 371/5119. Bols to General Headquarters, Cairo, 25 May 1920.

High Commissioner was a 'judicially-minded and sensible and experienced man ... of singular impartiality'.[13] In the same debate, Curzon, in
spite of his misgivings about aspects of the Zionist national home
project, vigorously defended the government's Palestine policy as well
as revealing his own attitude towards Arabs, which seems to have
differed little, if at all, from that of Lord Cromer, who had governed
Egypt in the late nineteenth century:

> My Lords, what are the essential facts of the case? Palestine was conquered
> by one of the most brilliant campaigns of which we have any knowledge in
> our annals ... We found [in 1917] a country which, owing to the long and
> pestilential blight of Turkish administration, had become depopulated,
> impoverished, and relatively poor ... Whatever your views about the poten-
> tial resources of the country, there cannot be any doubt that Palestine is a
> country where there is scope for more people, for more scientific cultiva-
> tion, for the construction of more railways, for better sanitation, for affores-
> tation on a more scientific scale, and for development of all the resources of
> the country, whether great or small. Where is that development to come
> from? The Turks were quite incapable of doing it. The Arabs are equally
> incapable. There is no friend of the Arabs who will claim that they have the
> resources, wealth, or energy to do it on the scale at which, at any rate, we
> should like to see it done. It was in these circumstances that an opportunity
> was afforded to the Jews to undertake this task in their old home.[14]

Samuel had paid his first visit to Palestine in February–March 1920,
perhaps at the request of the Foreign Office, to report on financial and
administrative conditions in Palestine, and to 'advise concerning the
lines of policy to be followed in future in these respects, should a
mandate fall upon Great Britain'.[15] In effect the trip was one of reconnaissance preparatory to his new appointment. Neither the Arabs nor
the Jews were deceived by the announcement of the military government that Samuel was visiting the country solely as a great financier to

13 FO 371/5114, E7573. Hansard, Lords, 29 June 1920, vol. 40, c1031.
14 Hansard, Lords, 29 June 1920, vol. 40, cc1027–1028.
15 John Bowle, *Viscount Samuel* (London, 1957), 184. Curzon informed Parliament
on 29 June that Samuel 'went out really in a private capacity to Palestine, at the
suggestion of Lord Allenby', and that Samuel's report to Allenby on the situation
was not written for publication. See Huneidi, *A Broken Trust*, 262.

settle how the revenue of the Occupied Enemy Territory Administration (South) could be spent to the best advantage.

A letter Samuel sent to a relative a fortnight before he left for Jerusalem leaves little room for doubt concerning the depth of his commitment to Zionism:

> What is practicable in Palestine now is one thing. What the present measures will lead to – and are designed to lead to in the future – is another. For the time being there will be no Jewish state, there will be restricted immigration; there will be cautious colonisation. In five years the pace will probably be accelerated and will grow after that progressively in speed. In fifty years there may be a Jewish majority in the population. Then the Government will be predominantly Jewish, and in the generation after that there may be that which might properly be called a Jewish country with a Jewish state. It is that prospect which rightly evokes such a fine enthusiasm, and it is the hope of realising that future which makes me ready to sacrifice much in the present.[16]

Two statesmen had already expressed similar sentiments publicly. On 3 March 1919, President Wilson had announced, 'I am persuaded that the Allied nations, with the fullest concurrence of our own Government and people, are agreed that in Palestine shall be laid the foundations of a Jewish commonwealth.'[17] Later that year, General Smuts, speaking in Johannesburg, foretold an increasing stream of Jewish immigration into Palestine and 'in generations to come a great Jewish State rising there once more'.[18] The Balfour Declaration may have been deliberately ambiguous concerning a future independent Jewish state, but many statesmen of the time were less ambiguous about their aspirations for its eventual creation.

Samuel took up his position on 1 July 1920 and quickly embarked on a policy whose essence was 'to create the conditions, political, legal and … economic necessary for the Zionists themselves to carry on their work'.[19] Subtle but determined, the new High Commissioner opted for a cautious

---

16 Samuel to 'Lucy' (Franklin), 3 May 1920, House of Lords Record Office, Herbert Samuel Papers B/12/26.
17 Peel Report, ch. II, 24–25; MM Papers, 9/10/48.
18 Peel Report, ch. II, 24–25; MM Papers, 9/10/48.
19 Wasserstein, *The British in Palestine*, 87.

system of colonisation. He released Jewish and Arab activists convicted during the April riots and reopened the land registers: between 1920 and 1925 no less than ten ordinances on land-related issues were passed, the first in September 1920. These and further similar ordinances enacted throughout the 1920s and 1930s led to the increasing dispossession of Palestinian Arab tenant farmers who had clear rights under Ottoman law, but became liable to eviction by court orders under such laws. According to the American scholar Kenneth Stein:

> When ordinances dealing with land were decreed in Palestine, they inevitably incorporated Zionist opinion … [Zionists helped to draft] the Land Transfer Ordinance of 1920 and its amendments … the Zionists helped rewrite the Beisan Agreement in 1928 in order to gain legal access to these lands. In 1929 and 1933, Arab tenants were not protected by the various editions of the Protection of Cultivators Ordinances that Zionist lawyers had helped to write, and from 1931 to 1936, the Landless Arab Inquiry did not enumerate property or resettle Palestinian fellaheen on alternative land because of Zionist access to the process.[20]

Samuel also opened Palestine's gates for the first time to relatively free Jewish immigration. In August 1920, he announced a quota of 16,500 Jewish immigrants for his first year in office.[21] Between 1919 and 1923 the number of Jewish settlers doubled and the number of colonies increased to about one hundred. Hebrew was made an official language, alongside Arabic and English,[22] and the new stamps of Palestine

---

20 Kenneth W. Stein, *The Land Question in Palestine, 1917–1939* (Chapel Hill, 1985), 215. See also Huneidi, *A Broken Trust*, 211–219.

21 Khalidi, *Before Their Diaspora*, 85.

22 Norman Bentwich, writing in 1933, states that in a wartime census, some fourteen thousand of the Jewish population 'gave Hebrew as their usual language', i.e. Hebrew (recognised by the British government in 1920) was the mother tongue of about 2 percent of the wartime population of Palestine. Norman Bentwich, *Palestine* (London, 1934), 202. The mother tongue of many late-nineteenth- and early-twentieth-century European Jewish settlers in Palestine was Yiddish, a German dialect which uses some Hebrew words and is written in the Hebrew alphabet. Yiddish is more closely related to German and Slavic languages than it is to Hebrew (a Semitic language). Weizmann's mother tongue was Yiddish; he learned Russian in his teenage years. Although he became proficient in Hebrew, German, French and English, he never learned Arabic.

displayed the two Hebrew initials of the words *Eretz Israel* (Land of Israel).

In October, Samuel officially recognised the *Va'ad Leumi*, the assembly elected by the *Yishuv*, as a representative Jewish body in Palestine, whose Chairman was accorded regular access to the High Commissioner and other British officials. Yet there was no formally recognised body of Arab representatives empowered to represent the Palestinian Arabs. An Arab Executive, created at the Third Palestine Arab Congress in Haifa in December 1920, claimed to represent all Palestinians, but the British refused to accept it as a properly elected body, and never officially acknowledged its legitimacy. All this when the Jewish minority, some 10 percent of the population and still mostly Arabic-speaking, owned a mere 2 percent of the land. In Arab eyes, Palestine was an Arab land, mostly Muslim, and had been for many centuries, not a land containing two distinct national entities, as proposed by both the Zionists and the British administration. In retrospect, it is clear that this deliberate policy of 'non-recognition' of the majority's political legitimacy and subsequent constitutional paralysis was a significant factor in the outbreak of the Arab Revolt in 1936.

Although Zionists claimed that not enough provisions had been made to develop the national home, the Palestinian Arabs looked on with foreboding as Samuel's political and administrative framework was established in front of their eyes. Samuel's senior appointments in his administration reflected his ideological inclinations and speak for themselves: the Legal Department was headed by cerebral English Zionist Norman Bentwich, a nephew by marriage to the High Commissioner, who doubled the roles of Attorney General and Legal Advisor to the government. It was his duty to draft and advise the Palestine governments upon laws and proclamations, and he kept the Zionist Organisation fully informed of new ordinances while being drafted. The Immigration Department was headed by Albert Hyamson, a British Jew, between 1921 and 1934, and the equally important Lands Department by Albert Abramson, a Christian but of Jewish origin. Even the Secretariat was headed by a passionate Gentile Zionist, Wyndham Deedes. Such appointments did not go unnoticed by Arab Palestinians, who began to regard the Palestine government as 'Zionists in British uniforms'.

It was government 'of a simple "Crown Colony" type'.[23] Real power resided in a small, unpublicised executive council of officials, chaired by Samuel, with Bentwich, Deedes and the Financial Secretary, H.G. Smallwood, as members. They met at least once a week and, according to Bentwich, advised on policy as well as current affairs.[24] There was also a twenty-one-member advisory council, consisting of the High Commissioner, ten officials and ten nominated non-officials, 'of whom four were Moslem Arabs, three Christian Arabs, and three Jews'.[25] Executive and legislative power was the High Commissioner's alone. Samuel and the Colonial Office were aware of, but disregarded, the fact that the change from military to civilian administration did not alter the legal status of Palestine as an occupied enemy territory, nor did it confer any new rights on the occupying power under international law. Until Turkey, the legal sovereign, signed a peace treaty with Britain and its Allies renouncing sovereignty, neither King George V nor the High Commissioner had any legal right to alter the status quo in Palestine – that is, the new administration had no legal right to alter existing Ottoman laws, nor to introduce any new population.

The Buried Report

The Palin Commission, the first in a long line of commissions of inquiry on Palestine during the next twenty-five years, investigated the origins of the April 1920 disturbances.[26] It placed the blame for the riots squarely on the Zionist Commission and the official Zionists, 'whose impatience to achieve their ultimate goal and indiscretion are largely responsible for this unhappy state of feeling ... the Balfour Declaration was

---

23 Peel Report, ch. III, 43.

24 Huneidi, *A Broken Trust*, 104; Norman Bentwich, *My 77 Years* (London, 1962), 67.

25 Peel Report, ch. III, 43.

26 The commission had three members, Major-General Sir Philip Palin, who presided; Brigadier General E.H. Wildblood; and Lieutenant-Colonel C. Vaughan Edwards. It sat for fifty days in Palestine and interviewed some 152 witnesses. Submitted in Port Said, 1 July 1920, by coincidence, the day of Samuel's arrival in Palestine.

undoubtedly the starting point of the whole trouble'. According to the report, the Zionist Commission was gradually developing into a body 'bearing a distinct resemblance to an independent administration apparently able to control the administration, and who had access to the most secret official documents through its extremely efficient intelligence department (no documents of the administration are secret from it)'. However, the authors did not advocate a reversal of the policy of the Balfour Declaration, which they said was a *chose jugée*. Rather, the solution lay in a firm government which would be able to 'hold the scales between all parties with equal rigidity'. The report concluded with the warning that 'the situation at present obtaining in Palestine is exceedingly dangerous and demands firm and patient handling if a serious catastrophe is to be avoided.' The War Office accepted Samuel's recommendation that the report should best be forgotten. Hence it remained a secret document until decades later when it appeared in the declassified files, by which time its exposure to public scrutiny was considered to be relatively harmless, or at least manageable.[27]

Three weeks after the San Remo Conference, Major Hubert Young, Sir John Shuckburgh's deputy at the Foreign Office, penned a lengthy 'Memorandum on the Future Control of the Middle East', which revealed the government's intentions regarding the future administration of Palestine:

His Majesty's Government have declared their intention of encouraging in Palestine the formation of a National Home for the Jewish people, while ensuring that the existing rights and privileges of non-Jews should be scrupulously safeguarded. Over 80 per cent of the population are non-Jews, and hostile to the idea of a Jewish National Home. It appears from this that it is not intended to institute a representative government in Palestine, but to set up a British administration which shall make it possible for a Jewish National Home gradually to be formed there ... Mesopotamia will be provisionally independent subject to a mandate.

---

27 A complete copy of the Palin Report is in FO 371/23229, 48–129. When Lacy Baggallay of the Foreign Office was preparing the relevant papers for Lord Maugham in 1939, he found that neither the Foreign Office nor the Colonial Office files contained a copy. The War Office lent him a copy, stating that it only had the one and wished to have it returned when Baggallay had studied it. See FO 371/23229, E1920, 15 March 1939. The exact date of the declassification is unknown.

Palestine will require a greater measure of administrative control, to ensure the fulfilment of the Zionist policy of His Majesty's Government.[28]

In fact, some of the decisions taken at San Remo clearly violated certain stipulations of the Covenant of the League of Nations, at that time the only international legal instrument in play. In particular, Article 22, paragraph 4 of the covenant contained specific provisions, in the case of the Arab countries, stating that the wishes of the populations concerned were to be a principal consideration in the selection of the mandatory power. The wishes of those populations were known to the conference attendees, if only from the report of the King-Crane Commission and the resolutions of the 1919 Damascus Congress. On this issue, the Allies paid no attention to their own law.

As soon as the outcome of the San Remo Conference was communicated to Feisal, he protested to Allenby that Palestine could not be separated from Syria 'geographically, ethnographically, traditionally, economically and from the point of view of language and national desire'. He went on to say: 'There is to be found amongst correspondence between His Majesty Hussein and His Excellency Sir H. McMahon a letter in name of Great Britain, dated the 25th October, 1915, which recognised Palestine to be within Arab Empire, whose limits as therein defined are accepted by British Government.'[29]

His protests fell on deaf ears. Far from the European corridors of power, the Sharif endeavoured to negotiate with the British government, via Feisal in Damascus, for the fulfilment of the 1915 pledge, but without any of the resources of strength, military, economic or political, that were (and are) indispensable to success in diplomacy. The Sharif's only strength was the moral force inherent, as he saw it, in the justice of his case, but that by itself could hardly prevail in London or Paris.

At San Remo, France had given Britain a free hand in Iraq and Palestine and expected to have complete freedom of action in Syria, meaning Feisal's administration in Damascus was now at the mercy of French ambitions. After the conference, open conflict between Feisal

---

28 DBFP, Series 1, vol. xiii, no. 250. Memo by Major H.W. Young, 17 May 1920.
29 DBFP, Series 1, vol. xiii, no. 248. Feisal to Allenby, 13 May 1920. The English version of the fateful letter was dated 24 October, but the Arabic version, despatched two days later, may well have been dated 25 October.

and the French was postponed for a further three months, owing on the one hand to the Emir's continuous political activities in Beirut, and on the other to Gouraud's inability to act for lack of troops. The 30 May 1920 armistice between the French and the Ottoman forces led by Mustafa Kemal, however, changed the situation, enabling Gouraud to turn his army against Feisal.[30] In June, the French government told the British formally that the time for the joint Anglo-French approach to Feisal was over. On 14 July, Feisal received a written ultimatum from Gouraud: submit to a French mandate, or face the consequences.

The General threatened invasion unless Feisal accepted five conditions by 18 July: a) grant France control of the Rayak–Aleppo railroad, b) abolish military conscription and reduce the army to its size of 1 December 1919, c) accept the French Mandate, which would not involve annexation or direct administration, d) accept Syrian currency issued by the French-controlled Bank of Syria, and e) punish those guilty of hostile acts towards France. On 19 July, Feisal cabled written acceptance of Gouraud's ultimatum, but the latter was already moving his troops.[31] On 24 July, after a major skirmish at the Maysalun Pass, some sixteen miles west of Damascus, the ill-equipped remnants of the Sharifian army, supported by local irregulars from Damascus, were defeated.[32] French Empire troops, mostly Algerians and Senegalese, then entered the Syrian capital and expelled Feisal southwards through Palestine, where a distinctly embarrassed Samuel and Storrs mounted a hundred-strong guard of honour as the Emir's train passed through Lydda en route to Egypt and Europe. Storrs wrote later:

> He carried himself with dignity and the noble resignation of Islam ...
> though the tears stood in his eyes and he was wounded to the soul. The

---

30 See Nevakivi, *Britain, France and the Arab Middle East, 1914–1920*, 255.

31 See Thompson, *How the West Stole Democracy*, 272.

32 The Sharifian army was hopelessly outnumbered and outgunned. Approximately 150 Arabs were killed and another 1,500 wounded. The French claimed to have lost 42 men, with another 152 wounded and 14 missing. The size of the Arab force is estimated as at least 4,000. General Yusuf Al-'Azma, Feisal's War Minister, who led the Arab troops, was killed in action. See Philip S. Khoury, *Syria and the French Mandate. The Politics of Arab-Nationalism, 1920–1945* (London, 1987), 97–98. Even before the Battle of Maysalun, French troops had occupied Aleppo. Homs and Hama surrendered without resistance on 28 July.

Egyptian 'Sultanate' did not recognise him, and at Qantara station he awaited his train sitting on his luggage.[33]

Feisal's expulsion and flight can only be described – in truth – as a shameful stain on the history of Anglo-Arab relations. France's military occupation of the whole of Syria (excluding Palestine) was complete, and Greater Syria was divided between the two powers. The introduction of alien languages, policies, currency and even passports inevitably followed as the Europeans replaced the Ottoman Turks as the masters of the region.

In September 1920, Feisal, in temporary exile in Italy, and still a British 'ally and protégé', addressed a long memorandum to Lloyd George in which he set forth anew the Sharifian claims. According to the Emir, during the war Britain had promised to establish

> an Arab Kingdom extending from the Persian Gulf to the limits of Cilicia, including Aleppo, Hama, Homs and Damascus, up to the frontiers of Egypt, with a special administration for the vilayets of Baghdad and Basra to be decided upon with the Sharif, my father, at the end of the War.[34]

As previously mentioned, unbeknown to Feisal or his father, the Zionist Organisation and the Foreign Office had been negotiating since early 1919, in Paris and in London, the details of a mutually acceptable mandate document. Writing from the French capital in June 1920, Vansittart reported to Young that on receipt of a draft communicated to the French government:

> [Prime Minister] Millerand had nearly jumped out of his skin when [Berthelot] had showed it to him. Berthelot added that, frankly, he himself was both surprised and alarmed by it. They both think it much too judaised and judaising – full of red flags indeed. Berthelot said,

---

33 Storrs, *Orientations*, 448. The Sultanate of Egypt: the name of the short-lived protectorate that Britain imposed over Egypt between 1914 and 1922. El-Qantara is an Egyptian city near the northern end of the Suez Canal, some one hundred miles north-east of Cairo.

34 FO 371/5040, 11500/2. Feisal to Lloyd George, Cernobbio, 11 September 1920, p. 12 of memo.

however, that if we liked to run ourselves into trouble, that seemed to him our affair.[35]

A memorandum by Forbes Adam, written some six months earlier, clearly illuminates the contrasting French and British understandings of the Balfour Declaration and its implications:

> The French Government interpret the declaration as a promise to protect and somewhat extend the existing Zionist colonies (M. Berthelot repeatedly spoke of 'les colonies Sionistes existantes.') ... on the other hand, the British Government by their support of Zionism have to a much greater degree accepted the natural implications which Zionists give to the declaration of a National Home, i.e., an attempt to make Palestine a state in its natural geographical and historic frontiers and by gradual immigration and special economic facilities to turn this state into a Jewish state ... Behind British policy, therefore, is the recognition of the principle of Jewish nationality, which is the essence of Zionism and the intention to lay in the Turkish Peace Settlement the foundation for the reconstruction of a Jewish Palestine, as of an Armenia for the Armenians.[36]

By the autumn of 1920, the official records show that the government were already deeply, if not emphatically, pledged to the Zionists and their programme. The conundrum now facing the government was how to handle the Sharif's unwavering claim to Palestine – the latter was adamant in his sincere belief that the British government had promised Palestine as part of the McMahon 'compact' – without it creating a major obstacle to an Anglo-Hijazi treaty, which the government hoped would support the international legitimacy of the proposed mandate system for Palestine, and generally help stabilise the whole region in Britain's favour. To solve this conundrum, during the autumn of 1920, someone in the Foreign Office seems to have taken an Ottoman map of the Levant in one hand and McMahon's letter of 24

---

35 DBFP, Series 1, vol. xiii, no. 267. Vansittart (temporarily head, Political Section, British Peace Delegation) to Major Young, 21 June 1920.

36 DBFP, Series 1, vol. iv, no. 409. Memorandum by E.G. Forbes Adam, 30 December 1919.

October 1915 in the other, and decided to square the linguistic circle by inventing a Vilayet of Damascus.

At the time of writing, the earliest Foreign Office memorandum found in the archives that introduces a Vilayet of Damascus was written by Major Hubert Young, who had joined the Foreign Office on the recommendation of Lloyd George in early 1919.[37] The lengthy document of 29 November 1920 included:

> With regard to Palestine, a literal interpretation of Sir H. McMahon's undertaking would exclude from the areas in which His Majesty's Government were prepared to recognise the 'independence of the Arabs' only that portion of the Palestine mandatory area which lies to the west of the 'district of Damascus'. The western boundary of the 'district of Damascus' before the war was a line bisecting the lakes of Huleh and Tiberias; following the course of the Jordan; bisecting the Dead Sea; and following the Wadi Araba to the Gulf of Akaba. The southern boundary of the district of Damascus cut across the Hedjaz railway between Ma'an and Tabuk. The eastern boundary was undefined, but may be taken as identical with the edge of the desert.[38]

The official records do not reveal whether this novel solution to the government's 'districts' dilemma emanated from the mind of Young himself, or whether he was instructed to include it in his memorandum by more senior official(s). The fact is the western boundary of the 'district of Damascus' did not extend three hundred miles southward to the Gulf of Aqaba; its south-western boundary was limited to the southern suburbs of Damascus city. McMahon had not sent Arabic copies of the Correspondence to London. Young had access to the inaccurate *wilāyāt* = vilayets letter which Vickery had sent to London twelve months earlier. (As will be discussed in Chapter Five, Vickery made eleven other mistakes in his translation of the fateful letter.) Young also had access to the government's English 'districts of Damascus, Homs, Hama and Aleppo' version of the letter, sent to the Foreign Office by

---

37 See Hubert Young, *The Independent Arab* (London, 1933).

38 FO 371/5066, 14959/9. 'Foreign Office Memorandum on Possible Negotiations with the Hedjaz', 29 November 1920, paragraphs 9–12. The memorandum is printed in DBFP, Series 1, vol. xiii, no. 342. See Figure 6.

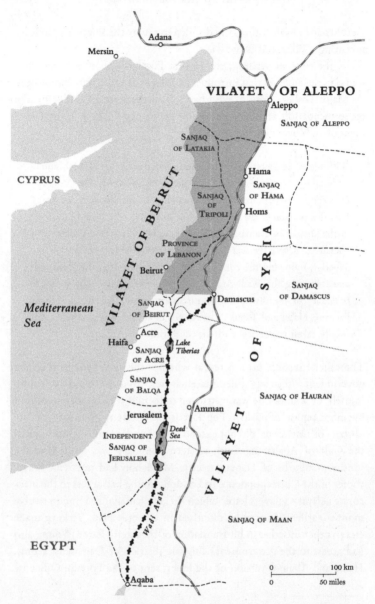

Figure 6: British interpretations of the Correspondence, 1915–1919, 'west of the line': McMahon (26 October 1915); Sir John Maxwell (1 November 1915); Commander David Hogarth (16 April 1916); General Staff, War Office (1 July 1916);

Captain W. Ormsby-Gore (29 November 1916); Arnold Toynbee (October 1918); Lord Curzon (5 December 1918, 9 October 1919); Sir Louis Mallet (30 January 1919, 4 February 1919); Lloyd George (19 September 1919). The shaded area was interpreted by all these individuals as being the area meant by the phrase 'west of the districts of Damascus, Homs, Hama and Aleppo', cited in the Correspondence, dated 24 October 1915. The thick line running from Aqaba to Damascus represents Major Hubert Young's (1920) invented, and deliberately erroneous, western boundary of the 'district of Damascus', adopted officially by Churchill in 1922. Note that the western boundary of the Vilayet of Syria extends southwards three hundred miles to Aqaba – the whole of Palestine lies to the west of the Vilayet of Syria. The most southerly district of the Vilayet of Beirut is the Sanjaq of Balqa (Nablus).

McMahon, which linguistically could only be interpreted one way, namely that districts referred to local districts, not provinces. He did not have any Arabic version of the letter. As previously mentioned, the Ottoman vilayet which extended southwards all the way to Aqaba was called the Vilayet of Syria, and included the four smaller Sanjaqs of Damascus, Hama, Hauran and Maan, a fact confirmed by examination of an Ottoman administrative map (see Figure 2).

On 2 December 1920, Feisal arrived in London, officially invited in order to discuss a projected Anglo-Hijazi treaty, about which his father was proving obstructive. The Emir was received in audience by the King two days later; Lloyd George declared in the Commons that 'No better indication could be given of the desire of the government for the Emir's continued friendship.'[39] At the same time, the French, forever suspicious of the British–Hashimite relationship ('Feisal was a British creation; Lawrence was British imperialism in Arab headgear'), were reassured by Lord Curzon that the government would not discuss with the Emir the position of Syria, which the British regarded as a *chose jugée* after the decisions of the San Remo Conference. Vansittart, in Paris, reported to Curzon that

the French are increasingly anti-Zionist. They mistrust and fear our whole policy in Palestine (incidentally they mistrust and fear our Arab policy too). They believe that we are in a direct train of making an all

39 Hansard, Commons, 6 December 1920, vol. 135, c1727.

Major Hubert Young, Assistant Secretary, Colonial Office (Middle East), 1921–1927

Jewish State, as opposed to a National Home ... [they] remain obstinately convinced that they are going to have a Bolshevik colony on their flank ... and are therefore determined that this 'Bolshevik Colony' shall be as small as possible, and conceive this necessary for their own safety ... they are at present still patting themselves on the back for having knocked out Feisal.[40]

The government's 'desire for the Emir's continued friendship', however, no longer extended to meetings with the Prime Minister. Instead, Feisal now found himself negotiating with senior Foreign Office officials. At his first meeting on 23 December with Sir John Tilley, the Assistant Secretary of State, difficulties soon surfaced when the Emir asked that 'British assurances given to his father would be fulfilled'. Tilley acknowledged that 'certain promises' had been given, and emphasised that the Arabs were free of Turkish domination and that the government were setting up an Arab government in Mesopotamia. Feisal then stated that he had brought with him certain Arabic documents, signed by High Commissioner McMahon, who had undertaken on behalf of the British

---

40 DPFP, Series 1, vol. xiii, no. 340. Vansittart (Paris) to Lord Curzon, 16 November 1920.

government 'to recognise an "Arab Kingdom".' Tilley replied that, subject to certain reservations, the British government had only promised to recognise and support the independence of the Arabs, not an 'Arab Kingdom'. Either Tilley had not studied the Correspondence or he was being dishonest: McMahon, in his letter of 14 December 1915 to the Sharif, had written 'The Government of Great Britain, as I have already informed you, are ready to give all guarantees of assistance and support within their power to this Arab Kingdom ...'[41] The following day, when Young examined the Arabic text, lent to him by the Emir, he claimed to find certain 'discrepancies' in the translation – and concluded that Feisal's version was 'inauthentic', a 'fabrication', in particular concerning the words 'Arab Kingdom' and the phrase referring to Britain's freedom to act without detriment to French interests.[42]

During a meeting at the Foreign Office on 20 January 1921, when Feisal, with T.E. Lawrence at his side translating, claimed that nothing in McMahon's correspondence with his father indicated that Palestine was excluded from Arab independence, Ronald Lindsay, the Assistant Under-Secretary of State, with Young at his side, countered that Palestine was excluded, 'lying as it did west of the Vilayet of Damascus'. The relevant passage from McMahon's letter of 24 October 1915 was then read aloud in Arabic, though the report does not disclose by whom, and Feisal continued:

> If His Majesty's Government relied upon the strict interpretation of the word 'Vilayet' as applied to Damascus, they must also interpret the word to mean the same with regard to Homs and Hama. There was not and never had been a Vilayet of Homs and Hama. While he was quite prepared to accept Mr. Lindsay's statement that it had been the original intention of His Majesty's Government to exclude Palestine, he represented that, as the Arabic stood, it would be clearly interpreted by any Arab and had been so interpreted by King Hussein, to refer to the four towns and their immediate surroundings. Palestine did not lie to the west of the four

---

41 See Appendix I, McMahon to the Sharif, 14 December 1915.

42 Major Young and Colonel Cornwallis, as well as Haddad Pasha and Rustum Haidar, attended the meeting. See Isaiah Friedman, *British Pan-Arab Policy, 1915–1922. A Critical Appraisal* (New Brunswick, 2010), 299.

towns and was therefore, in his opinion, included in the area for which
His Majesty's Government had given pledges.[43]

Feisal's argument was unanswerable, and neither Lindsay nor Major
Young attempted to query it. If Young considered that the Emir's interpretation of the key phrase was inaccurate, he would surely have made
his opinion known, but he remained silent. Lindsay, too, ignored Feisal's
explanation and quickly moved the conversation away from McMahon's
letter, to the proposed Anglo-Hijazi treaty.[44] It was a polite, but firm
imperial brush-off. According to Kedourie, 'Young's ingenious reading
of McMahon's letter was to receive official sanction, and to become the
ground on which the British government publicly justified their Zionist
policy.'[45] The day after the Lindsay–Feisal exchange, Curzon wrote that
it was too late to undertake an interpretation of 'old pledges'. Moreover,
Hussein had no right to be consulted regarding the Mandates for Iraq and
Palestine because 'he did not conquer either; we did.' Britain had taken
the Mandate for Palestine and 'whether wisely or foolishly had entered
into a bargain with the Zionists'.[46] Although he himself thought it was a
mistake, it had been passed by the cabinet and ratified at San Remo.

That January also saw Winston Churchill appointed Secretary of
State for the Colonies by Lloyd George, when the responsibility for the
future of Palestine and other Arabic-speaking mandated areas was transferred from the Foreign Office to the Colonial Office. Churchill brought
in Sir John Shuckburgh from the India Office to head the Middle East
Department, with Roland Vernon from the Treasury and Hubert
Young as joint assistant secretaries. T.E. Lawrence was attached as a
political advisor, with Colonel Richard Meinertzhagen, an ardent
Zionist, as its military expert. In March, Churchill, under considerable
pressure to reduce colonial expenditure, held a conference in Cairo with
the High Commissioners of Iraq and Palestine, and military and financial experts, largely to formalise arrangements that had been prepared in

43 FO 371/6237, 986/4.

44 FO 371/6237, 986/4.

45 Kedourie, *Labyrinth*, 237.

46 FO 371/6237, 136. Curzon's minute, 21 January 1921; Tibawi, *Anglo–Arab Relations*, 462–463.

Sir John Shuckburgh, Assistant Under-Secretary of State for the Colonies
(Middle East), 1921–1931

London for the nomination of Feisal as King of Iraq and Abdullah as
Emir of Transjordan.

From Cairo, Churchill travelled to Palestine, where, on 28 March, he
met Musa Kazim Pasha al-Husseini, the President of the Palestine Arab
Executive Committee, and five of his colleagues at Government House,
Jerusalem. There they handed him a lengthy memorandum on the situation in Palestine and a résumé of Arab demands, two of which were the
most important: the creation of a national government responsible to a
representative assembly, and the renunciation of the 'principle' of the
Jewish national home. All depended on the vital question of self-
government.[47] In his reply, Churchill declared that it was neither in his
power, nor was it his wish, to repudiate the Balfour Declaration, which
was for a national home for the Jewish people; in other words there was
no intention by the British government of allowing Palestine to become
a Jewish state. The Colonial Secretary's tactical, bland and factually
deficient assurances left the Arab leaders with all their questions unan-
swered: there was no redress; the liberator had spoken. The Cairo

---

47 CO 733/13. 'Report on the State of Palestine presented to the Right Honourable
Mr Winston Churchill P.C., M.P, by the Executive Committee of the Palestine Arab
Congress', Jerusalem, 28 March 1921.

conference thus left Palestine in limbo, under direct rule by Samuel, who had no intention of establishing any form of genuinely representative constitutional institutions. The official records confirm Samuel's approach. Following riots in Jaffa in May 1921, the cabinet met on 31 May to discuss the situation in Palestine. The minutes included: 'The development of representative institutions in Palestine was at present suspended owing to the fact that any elected body would undoubtedly prohibit further immigration of Jews.'[48]

In contrast, constitutional affairs inched forward in Iraq, where in July 1921 the provisional government decided to accept Feisal as a constitutional monarch. Wearing a full-dress military uniform rather than traditional Arab robes, Feisal was crowned King in Baghdad on 23 August 1921, ensuring institutionalised British support in the region until 1958.[49]

On 14 June 1921, Churchill had made his first speech in the Commons on Palestine since becoming Secretary of State for the Colonies. After a vague mention of the government's promises to King Hussein and those gathered around him 'for the reconstitution of the Arab nation', he continued:

> In regard to Palestine, a third promise of a very important character was made, on behalf of the Government, by my Right Hon. friend the President of the Council on 2 November 1917, that Great Britain, if successful in the War, would use her best endeavours to establish a Jewish national home in Palestine ... such were our obligations when the War came to an end ...

Thereafter followed an uncharacteristically frank admission:

> The difficulty about this promise of a national home for the Jews in Palestine is that it conflicts with our regular policy of consulting the wishes of the people in the mandated territories and of giving them representative institutions as soon as they are fit for them, which institution, in this case, they would use to veto any further immigration.[50]

---

48 CAB 23/24.
49 See Caroline Elkins, *Legacy of Violence. A History of the British Empire* (London, 2022), 172.
50 Hansard, Commons, 14 June 1921, vol. 143, cc266, 284–285.

No mention there of the Correspondence or of the Sykes–Picot Agreement – a clear indication that Lloyd George's coalition government did not regard Palestine as promised to Sharif Hussein.

On 22 August 1921, when an Arab delegation, the first of three sent to London, met with Churchill, the latter assured them that the government had made promises, and 'it would endeavour to keep those promises.' Various proposals for an 'elected' assembly in Palestine were put before the delegation. But the government were not prepared to concede a genuinely representative assembly, save one with merely advisory powers, nor a legislative assembly with substantial powers, save one with a majority of non-elected members. The delegation rejected the government's offers on the ground that the composition of the proposed assembly was insufficiently representative and its powers too narrow. When Shibli al-Jamal, the delegation's secretary, asked how the government could reconcile its guarantees under the Balfour Declaration to safeguard the rights of the people of Palestine with its current pro-Zionist policy, Churchill replied, 'No. When was that promised? Never. We promised you should not be turned off your land.'[51]

When asked to explain the term 'national home', Churchill simply responded that he could not improve on the words offered by Sir Herbert Samuel in his speech on 3 June 1921. Delivered on the occasion of the King's birthday, the High Commissioner's speech had reflected on the Jaffa riots of the previous month. Among his suggested measures to ease tension were plans for education, economic development, temporary suspension of immigration 'pending a review of the situation' and establishment of a system of municipal elections, without entering into details. Samuel had concluded with his patronising and misleading interpretation of the Balfour Declaration: the Jewish national home in Palestine would be founded

> within the limits which are fixed by the numbers and interests of the present population ... the British Government, which does indeed care for justice above all things ... [as] the trustee under the Mandate for the happiness of the people of Palestine, would never impose upon

---

51 CO 733/17.

them a policy which the people had reason to think was contrary to
their religious, their political and their economic interests. [52]

For Churchill – not a man who liked to be crossed – the matter of the
declaration was closed. He told al-Jamal bluntly that His Majesty's
Government were not prepared to change their stance:

> The British government mean to carry out the Balfour Declaration ... I
> have told you so again and again ... The Government is not a thing of
> straw ... [the declaration] contains safeguards for the Muslims, just as it
> contains clauses satisfactory to the Jews ... We have taken up our position
> before all the world, and with the support of the great victorious Powers
> gathered in Council. [53]

Finally, he suggested that they meet Weizmann to discuss the thorny
issue of immigration, but the delegates made it clear that the declaration
was at the root of all their troubles and that they had come to London
to discuss their political future – namely, constitutional development
towards self-government – with the British, not the Zionists. [54] In
Weizmann's view, the delegation were 'political blackmailers' and
'trash'. [55] Churchill, Samuel and Colonial Office officials were perfectly
aware that the success of the whole national home project depended not
only on a steady growth of Jewish immigration and settlement, but on
the maintenance of a powerless Arab opposition. Zionist objections to
the establishment of potentially self-governing institutions in Palestine
were well known at the Colonial Office. They argued that the standard
of education and political experience of the population of Palestine did
not make the experiment 'expedient or opportune'. Moreover, as the
mass of *fellahin* were illiterate and under the influence of a few *effendis*,
any representative body based on such an electorate would be unfriendly
both to British policy and the national home. [56] Without a legislative
council, Palestinian Arabs were to have no constitutional forum in

---

52 Cited in Huneidi, *A Broken Trust*, 130–131.
53 CO 733/14/38372.
54 Reinharz, *Chaim Weizmann*, 357–358; Wasserstein, *The British in Palestine*, 115.
55 Reinharz, *Chaim Weizmann*, 357–358.
56 CO 733/16/27373. S. Landman, Secretary, Zionist Organisation to Shuckburgh,
1 June 1921; CO 733/16/38128. Weizmann to Churchill, 21 July 1921.

which either to air grievances or to take gradual steps towards eventual self-government.

On 29 November, Shuckburgh chaired what turned out to be the only meeting between the delegation, led by Musa Kazim Pasha al-Husseini, and representatives of the Zionist Organisation, led by Weizmann, who merely offered to discuss the limitation of Jewish immigration and constitutional safeguards against 'Jewish political ascendancy'. For their part, the delegation stated that they would negotiate with the Zionists provided they interpreted the Balfour Declaration in an 'acceptable manner'. Further, they did not recognise the Balfour Declaration as a legitimate document. The meeting ended in total failure.

Although in Churchill's opinion the matter had been resolved and was not open for negotiation, in Palestine the army seemed to be somewhat more sympathetic to Arab aspirations. A month earlier, on 29 October 1921, General Walter N. Congreve, the Commander of the armies in Egypt and Palestine, had sent a circular to all troops stating that while 'the Army officially is supposed to have no politics', it did have sympathies, and 'in the case of Palestine these sympathies are rather obviously with the Arabs, who have hitherto appeared to the disinterested observer to have been the victims of an unjust policy forced upon them by the British Government.'[57]

In passing the circular on to Churchill, Shuckburgh noted: 'It is unfortunately the case that the army in Palestine is largely anti-Zionist and will probably remain so whatever may be said to it.' Churchill himself gloomily estimated that 90 percent of the British army in Palestine was arrayed against the Balfour Declaration policy.[58]

The British press, initially favourable to the Jewish national home policy in 1918 and 1919, had by the early 1920s become increasingly sceptical, and a movement opposed to the Balfour Declaration began to gain ground in the press and in Parliament. In October 1921, Eric Forbes Adam wrote privately to Shuckburgh on the subject of the Correspondence that

on the wording of the letter alone, I think either interpretation is possible, but I personally think the context of that particular McMahon letter

57 Martin Gilbert, *Winston S. Churchill. Companion Volume IV, Part 3: April 1921–November 1922* (London, 1977), 1659.
58 Fromkin, *A Peace to End All Peace*, 524.

shows that McMahon (a) was not thinking in terms of vilayet boundaries etc., and (b) meant, as Hogarth says, merely to refer to the Syrian area where French interests were likely to be predominant and this did not come south of the Lebanon ... Toynbee, who went into the papers, was quite sure his interpretation of the letter was right and I think his view was more or less accepted until Young wrote his memorandum.[59]

In November 1921, Shuckburgh noted that the government were 'deeply pledged to the Zionists and have always made it clear to the Arabs that there is no prospect of our wavering on this point. To waver now, in the face of renewed Arab violence, would be absolutely fatal.'[60] At the same time as Shuckburgh was maintaining his Churchillian disposition towards the Arab delegation, he was keeping Weizmann privately informed and solicited the Zionist leader's views on how the Colonial Office should respond to Arab demands. The only course of action Shuckburgh recommended was to 'find some way of repeating the story which, if it does not carry conviction, will at least compel acquiescence'. He concluded that 'The time has come to leave off arguing and announce plainly and authoritatively what we propose to do. Being Orientals, they will understand an order; and if once they realise that we mean business, may be expected to acquiesce.'[61]

On 6 January 1922, in reply to a note by the Assistant Principal of the Colonial Office which stated that 'geographically Palestine is included in the area within which Britain was to acknowledge Arab independence',[62] Shuckburgh minuted that 'although the view taken in this Office has been that Palestine was so excluded ... there is sufficient doubt in the matter to make it desirable not to drag the controversy out into the daylight.'[63]

Just as not everyone in the Colonial Office was on the same page, so it was in Parliament, where the spring and summer of 1922 witnessed a number of discussions concerning Palestine. On 15 February, Sir William Joynson-Hicks (Conservative, Twickenham), asked the Colonial Secretary whether the consent of the people of Palestine had

59 CO 733/38. Forbes Adam to Shuckburgh, 20 October 1921. Private.
60 CO 733/15. Memorandum by Shuckburgh, 7 November 1921. There had been serious disturbances in Jerusalem (April 1920), and in Jaffa (May 1921).
61 CO 733/15.
62 CO 733/8. Minute by S.M. Campbell, 6 January 1922.
63 CO 733/8. Minute by Shuckburgh, 11 January 1922.

been sought regarding the choice of Great Britain becoming the mandatory power and what the reasons were which induced His Majesty's Government to make the Balfour Declaration, and to promise the Jewish people a national home in a country 'which is already the national home of the Arabs'. In conclusion, he asked whether the government had fulfilled the pledges they had given to the Arabs through Sir Henry McMahon in 1915.[64] Churchill, however, would not be drawn. He responded, 'The hon. Baronet's questions raise points of high policy which could be dealt with more suitably in debate than by question and answer. I shall make a full statement of policy in Palestine when I present the Middle Eastern Estimates to the House.'[65]

On 9 March, Churchill made his lengthy presentation of the Eastern Estimates.[66] With regard to the Palestinian delegation's demand to grant a constitution to their country on the Iraqi model, he stated:

> I have decided to go the utmost possible length in giving them representative institutions, without falling into a position where I could not fulfil those pledges to which we are committed by the Zionist policy. I am bound to retain in the hands of the Imperial Government the power to carry out those pledges. I have, however, strongly urged the Arabs to take part in the new Elective Council and to bring their critical faculty to bear upon all questions connected with the Government of the country and with immigration.[67]

Earlier that month, Weizmann had given a revealing, but not entirely truthful, interview to *The Times*, where he described his vision for Palestine:

> We do not seek to found a Jewish State. What we want is a country in which all nations and all creeds shall have equal rights and equal tolerance. We cannot hope to rule in a country in which only one-seventh of the population at present are Jews ... By the establishment of the Jewish

64 Hansard, Commons, 15 February 1922, vol. 150, c1039.
65 Hansard, Commons, 15 February 1922, vol. 150, c1040.
66 Estimates: documents setting out each department's annual spending for approval.
67 Hansard, Commons, 9 March 1922, vol. 151, c1549. 'Elective Council', i.e. chosen by election. The contentious issue was by what system would the council be elected, and what, if any, powers it would enjoy.

National Home we mean the creation of such conditions in Palestine today as will enable us to move large numbers of Jews into the land, to settle them there, to render them self-supporting, and last but not least to establish schools, universities, and other Jewish institutions so that the country may become as quickly as possible as Jewish as England is English ... I see no reason for differences between us and the Arab non-Jewish population. There is plenty of room for us both in Palestine. It will hold five or six millions if properly developed, whereas the present population is less than 700,000. It is not likely that there will ever be an 'Arab question' in Palestine: non-Jews need not fear that they will suffer at our hands. For two thousand years we have known what it means to be strangers. We Jews know the heart of a stranger: are we likely to deal out oppression? Moreover we have never proposed that a Jewish minority should rule over the rest. Palestine will only become a Jewish self-governing commonwealth when the majority of its inhabitants are Jewish.[68]

During the same period (February–June 1922), a series of meetings between a Palestinian delegation and Churchill led to an exchange of notes which were published in June as a White Paper. It included a memorandum from the Colonial Secretary entitled 'British Policy in Palestine', written, in fact, by Samuel in collaboration with Shuckburgh, and, prior to the cabinet signing it off, approved by the Zionist Organisation. Designed first, to quell opposition to the pro-Zionist policy both in Palestine and at home, and second, to prepare for the vote on the Mandate by the League of Nations scheduled for the following month, the paper reiterated the government's commitment to the Balfour Declaration, and stated that Jews were in Palestine 'as of right and not on sufferance'. Significantly, Churchill's White Paper also launched its own interpretation of the McMahon Correspondence, asserting that

it is not the case, as has been presented by the Arab Delegation, that during the war His Majesty's Government gave an undertaking that an independent national government should be at once established in Palestine. This representation mainly rests upon a letter dated the 24th October, 1915, from Sir Henry McMahon, then His Majesty's High Commissioner in

---

68 *The Times*, 1 March 1922. See Furlonge, *Palestine Is My Country*, 81–82.

Egypt, to the Sherif of Mecca, now King Hussein of the Kingdom of the Hejaz. That letter is quoted as conveying the promise to the Sherif of Mecca to recognise and support the independence of the Arabs within the territories proposed by him. But this promise was given subject to a reservation made in the same letter, which excluded from its scope, among other territories, the portions of Syria lying to the west of the district of Damascus. This reservation has always been regarded by His Majesty's Government as covering the vilayet of Beirut and the independent Sanjak of Jerusalem. The whole of Palestine west of the Jordan was thus excluded from Sir H. McMahon's pledge.[69]

This meticulously crafted, misleading paragraph became British governments' immovable touchstone concerning the exclusion of Palestine in the Correspondence until 1939, when they finally agreed to investigate the whole matter afresh. Churchill's White Paper made no mention of McMahon's 'French reservation', but it did include the illuminating statement: 'Nevertheless, it is the intention of His Majesty's Government to foster the establishment of a full measure of self-government in Palestine. But they are of opinion that, in the special circumstances of that country, this should be accomplished by gradual stages and not suddenly.'[70]

These sentences in the White Paper are simply not true. Churchill's official biographer, Sir Martin Gilbert, a prolific, pro-Zionist scholar of the period, described the historical truth of the matter in a speech in Israel in 2011: 'The centrepiece of British mandatory policy was the withholding of representative institutions for as long as there was in Palestine an Arab majority.'[71] This deliberate 'withholding' policy was never explained to the Palestinian Arabs. Instead, for two decades they were on the receiving end of misleading, 'reassuring statements' concerning their rights.

---

69 *Palestine. Correspondence with the Palestine Arab Delegation and the Zionist Organisation* (Cmd 1700), 3 June 1922, 20. See Figure 6.

70 *Palestine. Correspondence with the Palestine Arab Delegation and the Zionist Organisation* (Cmd 1700), 3 June 1922, 20.

71 Lecture by Sir Martin Gilbert, Ben-Gurion University, 30 May 2011, 'Martin Gilbert – Sowing the Seeds of Jewish Statehood: Britain and Palestine, 1909–1922', YouTube, https://www.youtube.com/watch?v=-kub6d-ik6w (accessed 31 July 2020).

In his note of 11 April to the Arab delegation, Shuckburgh, on behalf of the Colonial Secretary, had written that the delegation appeared to have 'an incomplete acquaintance with the correspondence of 1915',[72] a somewhat ironic statement, given that in 1922 neither Shuckburgh, nor Churchill nor any other official in London had any acquaintance with any of the Correspondence in Arabic that the Sharif had received. Sir Geoffrey Furlonge, a distinguished diplomat and Arabist who spent a lifetime in the Middle East, wrote later that Churchill's exclusion of Palestine was 'geographical nonsense'.[73] More recently, it was succinctly characterised by the Oxford historian Margaret MacMillan as 'a defiance of geography'.[74]

For his part, Weizmann, as President of the Zionist Organisation, publicly gave unqualified approval to Churchill's White Paper. However, an official in the Palestine administration, Edward Keith-Roach, recorded in his diary that his doubts grew shortly afterwards, during a private conversation between Weizmann, Wyndham Deedes and himself:

> After giving a picture of the international plight of Jewry ... [and] the ever-growing anti-Semitism in Europe, [Weizmann] said: 'I accept the White Paper because when the time is ripe, I shall make it a blue paper. The Arabs must go elsewhere.'[75]

Churchill's White Paper neither convinced nor mollified the Arabs and their supporters in Britain. Less than three weeks later, on 21 June, a motion was introduced in the House of Lords by the Liberal peer Lord Islington rejecting a Mandate for Palestine that incorporated the Balfour Declaration. Islington stated that the latter directly violated the pledges made by the British in 1915 to Sharif Hussein as well as those made by General Allenby in his declaration to the Palestinian People in 1918. He urged that acceptance by the League of Nations be postponed until modifications complying with those pledges were made. The occasion

---

72 Cmd 1700, 16.

73 Furlonge, *Palestine Is My Country*, 226.

74 MacMillan, *Peacemakers* (3rd ed.), 398.

75 Edward Keith-Roach, *Pasha of Jerusalem: Memoirs of a District Commissioner under the British Mandate* (London, 1944), 96.

was notable for, among other things, Balfour's delivery of his maiden speech following his recent ennoblement to an earldom. As someone who had deliberately omitted Arab 'political rights' from his Declaration, who had insisted in private that the Palestinians could not be fully enfranchised, and who had confessed that there was a 'flagrant' inconsistency in British policy, given the promotion of degrees of self-government elsewhere in the Middle East, he felt able nonetheless to declare that 'it was impossible to imagine any political interest exercised under greater safeguards than the political interests of the Arabs in Palestine ... sentiments to the contrary being fantastic fears.'[76] His assertions would have been closer to the truth had he substituted 'Zionists' for 'Arabs'.

Balfour's speech made little impact. After a two-hour debate, the motion – rejecting the Mandate policy as it stood – was carried by a vote of sixty to twenty-nine. Churchill was not amused: with the League about to discuss the ratification of the Palestine Mandate the following month, the government could not afford to go to Geneva without the Commons' support, or at least acquiescence. At the Foreign Office, Shuckburgh's deputy, Hubert Young – the inventor of the 300-mile-long western boundary of the Damascus city district – minuted on 22 June:

> Yesterday's debate in the House of Lords will have encouraged the Arab Delegation to persist in their obstinate attitude, and unless the Lords' resolution is signally over-ruled by the House of Commons and the Council of the League of Nations, we must be prepared for trouble when the Delegation gets back to Palestine.[77]

The Arab delegation returned to Palestine that month, having rejected the White Paper, which they considered to mean that self-government would be granted only when the Jews were sufficiently numerous to benefit by it. The Zionist Organisation accepted it, hoping, as Weizmann recalled later, for 'a framework for building up a Jewish majority in Palestine, and for the eventual emergence of a Jewish State'.[78] According to Avi Shlaim, 'About the moral superiority of the Jewish claim over the Arab claim to a

---

76 Hansard, Lords, 21 June 1922, vol. 50, cc994–1033.

77 CO 733/22. Young minute, 23 June 1922.

78 Weizmann, *Trial and Error*, 361.

homeland in Palestine, he [Weizmann] never entertained any doubt.'[79] Weizmann's policy towards the Palestinian Arabs is often described as pragmatic and moderate, but it was moderate in style much more than in substance. During this period, he was prepared to accept the Arabs as partners in running Palestine through an elected council based on parity between the two communities, but he did not accept them as equal partners in negotiations on the future of the country. In his mind, such negotiations had to be conducted exclusively between Britain and the Jews.[80]

The principle of parity – equal numbers of Jews and Arabs in any potential legislative assembly, irrespective of population size – was a constant tactical demand of the Zionists from the beginning of the Mandate. During the 1920s, from Samuel's arrival in July 1920, the ordinances enacted by the administration implicitly, but not publicly, operated on the basis that two national entities existed in Palestine. During the Mandate, no British government officially supported parity, but at a secret meeting at Chequers in 1931 Prime Minister Ramsay MacDonald informed Ben-Gurion and Lewis Namier, Political Secretary of the Zionist Organisation, that he personally 'declared his full agreement principle parity between Jews and Arabs as national entities. Added in strict confidence that he himself would give such equality leaning towards Jews. Premier giving his own personal views.'[81]

With opposition in the House of Commons mounting, the government's Palestine policy appeared increasingly vulnerable. So at around 10:30 p.m. on 4 July, near the end of a five-hour debate on Colonial Estimates, Churchill shrewdly, and very briefly, slipped in the issue of the budget for Palestine, stating that he had cut the cost of maintaining Palestine from £8 million in 1920 to an estimated £2 million in 1922. It was a well-planned, finance-focused reference (hardly a discussion) to the government's Palestine policy. The Estimates vote was won at around 11:30 p.m. by a majority of 292 to 35, Palestine 'policy' being carried along in its wake. A relieved Churchill – with not a little exaggeration – immediately wrote to Samuel: 'it is now clear that the country supports His Majesty's Government in their Palestine policy.' With the Commons voting – almost inadvertently – in favour of the policy,

---

79 Shlaim, *The Iron Wall*, 6.
80 Shlaim, *The Iron Wall*, 9.
81 Namier telegram to Weizmann (in Basle), 12 July 1931 in MM Papers, 9/7/75.

the way was open for the League of Nations formally to ratify Britain's Mandate for Palestine, which was scheduled for 24 July.[82]

Second Request for Publication

A week after the Commons 'approved' the government's Palestine policy, on 11 July 1922, L'Estrange Malone (Communist Party, Leyton East) asked the Colonial Secretary whether, 'in view of the continual misinterpretations of our pledges to the Arabs, he will publish the letter of 24 October 1915, from Sir Henry McMahon to the Sharif of Mecca in full or the whole correspondence of which that letter formed one item?' 'No, Sir,' replied Churchill, 'it would not be in the public interest to publish one or all of the documents comprising the long and inconclusive correspondence that took place with the Sheriff of Mecca in 1915–1916.'[83] Later that afternoon, he informed the House that

> when I assumed responsibility for Middle Eastern affairs, I went carefully into the correspondence referred to, and my reading of it is the same as that of the Foreign Office, as was recently stated in the declaration of British policy in Palestine which has been published and laid before the House. I am quite satisfied that it was as fully the intention of His Majesty's Government to exclude Palestine from the area of Arab independence as it was to exclude the more northern coastal tracts of Syria.[84]

Churchill's statement that he had 'read the correspondence carefully' leaves little doubt concerning his personal responsibility for the maintenance of the government's misleading district = vilayet interpretation.

On 22 July 1922, just two days before the League was due to ratify the Mandate for Palestine, Balfour convened a small conference in his London house at Weizmann's request, at which the Zionist leader strongly criticised Samuel's speech in Palestine one year earlier as an abrogation of the Balfour Declaration. Also present at this meeting were Lloyd George, Churchill, Maurice Hankey and Edward Russell of the Colonial Office.

---

82 Hansard, Commons, 4 July 1922, vol. 156, cc221–343.

83 Hansard, Commons, 11 July 1922, vol. 156, c1033.

84 Hansard, Commons, 11 July 1922, vol. 156, cc1033–1034.

In response to Samuel's explanation of the Jewish national home in his speech, Balfour and Lloyd George stated that 'by the Declaration they always meant an eventual Jewish state.' Then they discussed Samuel's proposal for representative government in Palestine, and Lloyd George told Churchill that such a thing must not be allowed to happen.[85]

Two days later, the League ratified the British Mandate for Palestine, a unique document in that it provided for the preferential intrusion of a third party into a relationship between a European authority and the local population it was to administer. The Balfour Declaration was now enshrined in international law. Just as significantly, the Mandate text created a blueprint for governing structures that would deliberately ignore Palestinian Arab nationalism. According to Penny Sinanoglou, it created an ideological and physical space for Zionism 'while foreclosing any immediate prospects for Palestinian Arab political development or, more strikingly, for any kind of unitary Palestinian self-determination'.[86]

The ratification of the Mandate came at a critical moment for the Zionists. Only three months later, in October 1922, Lloyd George's pro-Zionist government resigned and a new Conservative government headed by Bonar Law was installed. However, the League's ratification did not close the debate on Palestine. The new Prime Minister was not as sympathetic to the Zionists as his predecessor, and so it appeared to the Arabs and their English supporters, headed by Lord Sydenham and Lord Islington, that new prospects might possibly open up for some sort of modification of government policy in favour of the Arabs. Nevertheless, although Lloyd George, Balfour and Churchill were out of office, senior Colonial Office officials remained largely unchanged, including Under-Secretary of State for the Colonies Ormsby-Gore,

---

85 Reinharz, *Chaim Weizmann*, 356–357. Churchill never lost his profound sympathy for the Zionist cause, in spite of Zionist militias' attacks on British troops during and immediately after the Second World War. In 1956, on the eve of the Suez Crisis, the eighty-one-year-old statesman wrote to President Eisenhower, 'I am, of course, a Zionist, and have been ever since the Balfour Declaration. I think it is a wonderful thing that this tiny colony of Jews should have become a refuge to their compatriots in all the lands where they were persecuted so cruelly, and at the same time established themselves as the most effective fighting force in the area.' Churchill to Eisenhower, 16 April 1956. Cited in Martin Gilbert, *Never Despair. Winston Churchill, 1945–1965* (London, 1988), 1191–1192.

86 Penny Sinanoglou, *Partitioning Palestine. British Policymaking at the End of Empire* (Chicago and London, 2019), 140.

Figure 7: The British and French Mandates in the Middle East, 1922

Shuckburgh, Eric Mills, Hubert Young and Colonel Meinertzhagen. Leo Amery, another Zionist supporter, was appointed Secretary of State for the Colonies in 1924.

In spite of the Mandate's ratification, the historian Arnold Toynbee maintained his initial stance concerning the Correspondence. Writing in the *The New Republic* that autumn, he concluded:

> Palestine was not excepted from the area in which the British government promised in 1915 to recognise and uphold Arab independence, and that the Balfour Declaration of 1917 was therefore incompatible with a previous commitment. To saddle [Britain] with [such] irreconcilable commitments is almost the worst crime of which the professional diplomatist is capable, for it compromises that country's reputation for straight-dealing.[87]

---

87 Arnold J. Toynbee, 'The Trouble in Palestine', *The New Republic*, vol. XXXII, no. 405 (1922), 38–40. Cited in Friedman, *Palestine. A Twice-Promised Land?*, 112.

According to Isaiah Friedman, in 1940 Toynbee told Rev Dr James Parkes, who was then working at Chatham House, that in 1918 the Foreign Office had accepted his interpretation, and that only later, 'as a result of Jewish pressure, H.M. Government changed their attitude and sought for arguments to show that the Correspondence had failed to cover Palestine.'[88]

Let Sleeping Dogs Lie

Earlier that year, on 12 March, McMahon, now retired, had written an explanatory letter concerning the Correspondence to Shuckburgh, suggesting that it be published so that the Arabs would accept once and for all the fait accompli that Palestine was excluded from the pledge to Hussein:

> It was my intention to exclude Palestine from independent Arabia, and I
> hoped that I had so worded the letter as to make this sufficiently clear for
> all practical purposes. My reasons for restricting myself to specific
> mention of Damascus, Hama, Homs and Aleppo in that connection in
> my letter were: 1) that these were places to which the Arabs attached vital
> importance and 2) that there was no place I could think of at the time of
> sufficient importance for purposes of definition further South of the
> above. It was as fully my intention to exclude Palestine as it was to
> exclude the more Northern coastal tracts of Syria.[89]

McMahon's second point, that he could think of no points of importance further south of Damascus, cannot be taken seriously. He cannot have been unaware of three towns further south, namely Dara'a, Amman and Ma'an, all of them well-known stops on the Hijaz railway line between Damascus and Medina, which opened in 1908.

The letter was forwarded to Samuel, in Jerusalem, who pressed the Colonial Office to publish it. However, Shuckburgh informed Samuel on 7 November 1922 that he was 'rather against making any further public announcements on this troublesome question', which he had always felt to

---

88 Friedman, *Palestine. A Twice-Promised Land?*, 120.
89 FO 371/7797. McMahon to Shuckburgh, 12 March 1922.

be 'one of the weakest joints in our armour'.[90] Sir Arthur Hirtzel, Deputy Under-Secretary of State in the India Office, agreed with Shuckburgh that it would be inadvisable to publish the Correspondence related to the Caliphate. 'McMahon as you know', he wrote on 12 February 1923, 'exceeded his instructions on this subject – a fact which could not of course be publicly avowed.'[91] Shuckburgh advised against publishing the letter, explaining to Samuel that the Middle East Department used the argument that Damascus, in the pledge of 1915, meant the 'Turkish Vilayet of Damascus', and that the wording of Churchill's reply to Ormsby-Gore's question in Parliament on 11 July 1922

> was drawn up with the most meticulous care and represents, I think, the best that can be said on the subject. I doubt whether anything is to be gained by further publication, and indeed it seems to me that our best policy is to let sleeping dogs lie as much as possible.[92]

Samuel was convinced, and in reply agreed that it would be 'undesirable at the present stage to reopen the controversy about the McMahon pledge by publishing Sir Henry's letter'.[93] With Samuel firmly established in Jerusalem, the Mandate officially ratified and the situation in Palestine quiescent, if fragile, the Colonial Office hoped that Britain's Palestine policy would quietly and steadily progress, unhindered by potentially embarrassing debates in the press and in Parliament.

However, the arrival in London in December 1922 of a second Arab delegation from Palestine brought the issue of Britain's wartime pledges back to centre stage. The delegates met representatives of the *Morning Post*, the *Daily Mail* and *The Times* and gave them copies of the Correspondence. The Colonial Office had expected to treat the activities of this delegation as a minor affair, to be handled quietly. What they did not expect was a four-week, sustained, frontal attack on the government's Palestine policy in a major national daily newspaper.

90 CO 733/39. Shuckburgh to Samuel, 7 Nov. 1922. Private.
91 CO 733/55, 9211.
92 CO 733/39. Shuckburgh to Samuel, 7 November 1922. Private.
93 CO 733/39. Samuel to Shuckburgh, 17 November 1922.

In January and February 1923, J.M.N. Jeffries, the *Daily Mail* correspondent, following a lengthy visit to Palestine the previous year, published a series of twenty-five articles under the heading 'The Palestine Deception'. They were detailed, deeply critical of the government's policy in Palestine, included excerpts of the Correspondence which had been hitherto not in the public domain, and provided an abundance of ready ammunition for supporters of the Arabs at Westminster. In one particularly scathing article, Jeffries focused on Churchill's invention of a Vilayet of Damascus in the June 1922 White Paper. Jeffries claimed that Churchill

> had produced as from a conjuror's tall hat a line going south from Damascus which satisfied his requirements … And the word of England, built up so painfully and lengthily by generations of Civil Servants and soldiers and merchants who have always in all parts of the world kept their word? In the waste-paper basket.[94]

Jeffries' articles were widely read and commented upon in parliamentary circles. Much to the chagrin of the government, the debate over the wartime pledges would simply not go away, and as later parliamentary debates made clear, it was the accusation of official double-dealing concerning Palestine that constituted the principal significance of Jeffries' work. Weizmann was furious. In 1949, when in office as the first President of Israel, he wrote of the *Daily Mail*'s

> virulent campaign against us. In particular a certain J.M.N. Jeffries succeeded, in a series of savage articles, in presenting a wholly distorted picture of Jewish life in Palestine. His conclusion was that the only thing to do was to annul the Balfour Declaration and scrap the whole British Palestine policy.[95]

---

94 'Inventing a Province. Vilayet of Churchill. Pledge in White Paper Basket', *Daily Mail*, 13 January 1923. See William M. Mathew, ed., *The Palestine Deception, 1915–1923. The McMahon–Hussein Correspondence, the Balfour Declaration and the Jewish National Home* (Washington D.C., 2014), 61–65.
95 Weizmann, *Trial and Error*, 351–352.

The Colonial Office pasted Jeffries' articles, excluding those parts that undermined the government's case, into its official record, and minuted that they represented 'gross misstatements'.[96]

A Broad View of the Position

On 17 February 1923, just a week after Jeffries' final missive in the *Daily Mail*, the Duke of Devonshire, a Liberal Unionist who had succeeded Churchill as Colonial Secretary the previous October, circulated a lengthy, secret memorandum entitled 'Policy in Palestine' for the consideration of the cabinet in deciding future policy. This document is worth analysing in some detail for what it reveals of government thinking some five years after the end of the war, and six months after the League of Nations had ratified Britain's Mandate for Palestine. The Duke, a former Governor-General of Canada, who had no previous experience of Middle Eastern affairs, and who lacked Churchill's ardent pro-Zionist inclinations, wrote:

> It is constantly argued by critics of the Zionist policy, that, whatever may have been the pledges given to the Jews, they are rendered null and void by prior promises made to the Arabs ... In the course of the correspondence which preceded the Arab revolt, Sir Henry McMahon ... gave an undertaking ... to the Sharif of Mecca ... that His Majesty's Government would 'recognise and support the independence of the Arabs' within certain territorial limits. The question is: Did the excluded area cover Palestine or not? The late Government [Lloyd George's Coalition] maintained that it did ... The weak point in the argument is that, on the strict wording of Sir H. McMahon's letter, the natural meaning of the phrase 'west of the district of Damascus' has to be somewhat strained in order to cover an area lying considerably to the south, as well as to the west, of the city of Damascus ...
>
> Whatever may be thought of our case ... it will probably be agreed that, on a broad view of the position, we have an effective answer to Arab criticism. What we promised was to promote Arab independence throughout a wide area. That promise we have substantially fulfilled ... The Arabs as a whole have acquired a freedom undreamed of before the

---

96 CO 733/54/2239. Minute, 18 January 1923; See Mathew, *The Palestine Deception*, 6.

war. Considering what they owe to us, they may surely let us have our way in one small area, which we do not admit to be covered by our pledges, and which in any case, for historical and other reasons, stands on a wholly different footing from the rest of the Arab countries ...

It may be too much to hope that we can ever satisfy the Palestinian Arabs; but so long as the general body of Arab opinion is not against us, the dangers arising from local dissatisfaction ought not to be serious ... The real alternative, therefore, seems to be between complete evacuation, on the one hand, and, on the other, the continuance of the policy of the late Government, as laid down in the White Paper. Within the limits of the Balfour Declaration, if that is to be maintained, there is little room for further concession to the Arabs beyond what has already been made. If we surrender the Mandate, the League of Nations may or may not succeed in finding another Mandatory. If they do not succeed, the Turks will inevitably return. Our position in that event will be an unenviable one. We shall stand for all time as the Christian Power, which, having rescued the Holy Land from the Turk, lacked the strength or the courage to guard what it had won.[97]

Three points in this memorandum stand out: first, the Duke's acknowledgement of the weakness of the government's position, in writing that 'the natural meaning' of the 'districts' phrase 'has to be somewhat strained' in order to cover an area south of the city of Damascus; second, his omission of any reference to the 'French reservations' phrase (in his mind, simply unhelpful, unimportant, or just irrelevant?); and third, his assessment of the danger of local dissatisfaction over the controversy as 'not to be serious', suggesting that although the government had a weak case, it would be able to cope with any resultant disturbances.

Jeffries' articles prompted a flurry of memoranda in the Middle East Department. Ronald Lindsay, Under-Secretary of the Foreign Office, replied to a memorandum by Shuckburgh on 19 February 1923 that 'we should not be likely to strengthen our case by publishing the McMahon letters.'[98] Two days later, Sydney Moody, a junior Colonial Office official, minuted that the reasons for not publishing the Correspondence

---

97 CAB 24/159.
98 CO 733/55. R.C. Lindsay to Shuckburgh, 19 February 1923.

'remain good'.[99] For his part, Young, now at the Colonial Office, minuted on 21 February that 'the best counterblast to arguments based on the McMahon correspondence would be the signature and publication of a Treaty with King Hussein in which he accepts our position in Palestine.'[100]

The British government had first proposed an Anglo-Hijazi treaty of friendship to Hussein in 1921, but contrary to public understanding, the government's motive for concluding a treaty was not designed to secure Hussein's rule in the Hijaz; it was to legitimise British rule in the Mandatory administrations of Palestine and Iraq. Every draft of the proposed treaty contained a clause reflecting the King's acknowledgement of the Mandates. If he, the father of the Arab nationalist movement, and descendant of the Prophet, could be induced to sign such a treaty, it would take some of the wind out of the sails of those Arab nationalists and others who opposed the pro-Zionist Mandate in Palestine. In fact, the Palestine issue appears to have been the main stumbling block over which the Anglo-Hijazi treaty of friendship with King Hussein foundered. The King genuinely believed that Palestine had been included in the promised area of Arab independence by the British government in 1915. Fundamentally a man of principle, he could not and would not surrender Palestine to the Zionists.

Between 1921 and 1924, Laurence Grafftey-Smith was Britain's Vice-Consul in Jedda. He describes in his autobiography that during this period the task of the British Agency was an invidious one:

We had to listen, dead-pan, to King Hussein's requests for the support he thought we had promised, knowing that it would be useless even to report his claims once more to our masters in London, who were weary of his asking for something they had decided not to give. We could hold out no hope to Hussein, yet we could not deny, in terms, McMahon's letter ...

Major W.E. Marshall RAMC became British Agent and Consul [in Jedda] in 1921 ... He had accompanied Lawrence and Emir Faisal in 1917 in the Arab drive north ... the F.O. still cherished the illusion that anyone who had served with Feisal must be *persona gratissima* with Faisal's royal

---

99 CO 733/57. S. Moody minute, 2 February 1923.
100 CO 733/57.

King Hussein, Sharif of Mecca (front centre), Amman, 1921. On the Sharif's right
is Musa Kazim Pasha al-Husseini, President of the Executive Committee,
Palestine National Congress.

father. It was hoped that Marshall would extract a treaty from King
Hussein; but no angel from Heaven, if holding a British passport, could
have done this.[101]

At the beginning of 1924, the High Commissioner reported to the new
Colonial Secretary, James H. Thomas, that King Hussein had made
assurances to a Palestinian delegation of his 'firm wish to continue his
endeavours for the complete independence of the Arab countries
amongst which is Palestine', that negotiations with the British had not
ended and that 'he would call for the nation's opinion prior to the

101 Grafftey-Smith, *Bright Levant*, 168.

signature of the Treaty. He would not by any means accept but that Palestine should belong to its Arab inhabitants.'[102]

The King never signed the treaty. Just as significantly, he overestimated his postwar importance to the Allies. In mid October 1924, Ibn Saud's forces captured Mecca, and forced the King to abdicate and go into exile in British-controlled Cyprus. Hashimite forces held out in Jedda and Medina until December 1925, when King Ali, Hussein's eldest son, surrendered and followed his father into exile. To his death in 1931, the former Sharif of Mecca considered Lloyd George to be 'something of an acrobat and a fox'.[103]

Detrimental to the Public Interest

Clearly encouraged and informed by Jeffries' closely documented, incisive articles, on 1 March the Conservative Lord Sydenham initiated a debate in the Lords on the wartime pledges to the Arabs. He asked the government whether they would 'lay on the Table' the Correspondence on which their predecessors based the claim that Palestine was geographically excluded from those pledges. A second Conservative peer, Lord Lamington, asked the Colonial Secretary to state 'the precise wording in which these terms or pledges were given to the Arabs'. The Duke of Devonshire, however, was too shrewd to address directly the arguments raised but, while insisting that he had 'most carefully investigated the subject', confined himself to reaffirming in broad terms his acceptance of Churchill's White Paper explanation. Following the Middle East Department's advice, he deftly avoided making available, 'much as I regret it', any of the Correspondence, on the grounds that

> it is long and inconclusive. I admit that these are not reasons why it
> should not be published, but there are very strong reasons indeed which
> show that the publication of the correspondence would be detrimental to
> the public interest. It is impossible to clear the correspondence of

---

102 CO 733/65. 'Report on the Political Situation for the Month of January, 1924', Samuel to J.H. Thomas.
103 Antonius, *Awakening*, 183.

references to a number of subjects which are quite apart from the controversy that we are discussing this afternoon, and the publication of those
other references to other subjects would, I am confident – and this is also
the opinion of my advisors – be detrimental to the public interest.[104]

When asked whether only those passages related to the pledges
concerning Palestine could be published, he cited parliamentary
custom against partial publications. As to Lord Sydenham's request that
the noble Duke at least comment on the authenticity of the numerous
passages cited in the course of the debate, the Secretary of State quite
simply ignored it.

We Are Not Responsible

A few weeks later, Lord Islington, a Liberal peer and former Governor
of New Zealand, raised the issue of the newly published Palestine
constitution, and the non-publication of the Correspondence.
Somewhat surprisingly, he was supported by Viscount Grey of
Fallodon, who as Sir Edward Grey had been Foreign Secretary in
Asquith's administration between 1905 and 1916 and under whose
instructions McMahon had carried out the Correspondence. It was a
fact of war, the Viscount reflected, that pressing circumstances led
inevitably to undertakings which might be mutually inconsistent, and
at the end of the war prove 'exceedingly embarrassing'. 'The best way
of clearing our honour in this matter', he declared, 'is officially to
publish the whole of the engagements.' Once again, the Colonial
Secretary declined, and added that it would be necessary to ask King
Hussein's consent to any publication, although without declaring that
the King's approval would be sought.[105] The weakness of the government's case was underlined when the Duke declared that the present
government 'are not responsible for any of the proceedings or pledges
that were given. It is in some ways more difficult for us to publish
information for which we are not ourselves responsible.'[106] But he

104 Hansard, Lords, 1 March 1923, vol. 53, cc226–235.
105 In December 1916, the British, French and Russian governments had officially
agreed to consider the Sharif as 'King of the Hejaz'.
106 Hansard, Lords, 27 March 1923, vol. 53, cc639–669.

would, he assured the House, keep the matter under review. On the same day the Duke noted in his diary: 'Expect we shall have to publish papers about pledges to Arabs. They are quite inconsistent, but luckily they were given by our predecessors.'[107]

A Question of Reputation ... The Honour of This Country Is Engaged

In the same debate, the Secretary of State was followed by Lord Buckmaster, a former Liberal Lord Chancellor, who could not see any reason for delaying publication of the Correspondence, given that 'what purports to be a complete copy of these Despatches has already been published in the press, and I have yet to learn that the government has repudiated these communications as inaccurate.' It seemed clear to him that a deliberate pledge had been given on the one hand, 'which had been abandoned on the other'. Speaking for the government, Lord Salisbury (Lord President of the council, and cousin of Arthur Balfour) repeated the Duke's attempt to distance himself from the Balfour Declaration policy which, he insisted, was not the policy of the government. It was the policy of the late government, to which they had succeeded. The refusal to publish the Correspondence, he indicated, was not an effort to put aside any past promises; rather, it was a question of reputation:

> ... nothing could be worse than what I may call a zig-zag administration ... To some extent at any rate you must accept the policy of your predecessors ... It cannot altogether be done, but to some extent we must pay regard to it, because the honour of this country and its consistency is engaged.

The government's *reputation*, *honour*, *consistency*: it was not, by any standards, a convincing defence either of its pro-Zionist mandate policy, or of its refusal to publish the Correspondence.[108]

---

107 Diary of the ninth Duke of Devonshire, 27 March 1923, Chatsworth MSS; See G.H. Bennett, *British Foreign Policy during the Curzon Period, 1919–24* (London, 1995), 97.
108 See Hansard, Lords, 27 March 1923, vol. 53, cc639–669.

A few weeks later, in April 1923, Shuckburgh expressed his doubts about British policy on Palestine in a private and confidential conversation with a junior official, Sydney Moody:

> We had made promises to the Arabs in the McMahon Correspondence and these conflicted or appeared to conflict with the Balfour Declaration. But this was a technical point. The Balfour Declaration did in fact conflict with our whole attitude towards the Arabs and anyhow with what ought to be the attitude of a great modern European Power towards a conquered country like Palestine ... could we, ought we, to force on the Arab population of Palestine a mass of alien immigrants mostly Russian and Polish?[109]

Shuckburgh went on to say that the McMahon promises were made during Asquith's government in 'the stress and strain' of war, and nobody in the cabinet thought 'we should have to meet these promises'. They could not foresee all those developments, and when the Balfour promise was made, 'we had not set foot in Palestine.'

Significantly, Shuckburgh told Moody:

> We should say to the Arabs and the Jews, 'look here, we have made certain promises to both of you. We have promised the Jews a national home in Palestine. We have promised the Arabs national independence. Now you must agree together. We will give you independence provided you agree on a basis of settlement about the National Home.'[110]

The Assistant Under-Secretary of State for the Colonies here explicitly acknowledged to his colleague that the British government had, via McMahon, promised the Arabs of Palestine 'national independence'.

Over the years, Shuckburgh's doubts persisted. In 1930, he acknowledged in a letter to the High Commissioner in Palestine, Sir John Chancellor:

> I have always felt that, on a strict and liberal interpretation of McMahon's famous letter of October, 1915, our case is a weak one, although I do not

---

109 Evyatar Friesel, 'British Officials on the Situation in Palestine, 1923', *Middle Eastern Studies*, vol. 23, no. 2 (1987), 200.
110 Friesel, 'British Officials', 200–201.

believe that the intention – so far as His Majesty's Government had any considered intentions in those hectic days – is open to serious doubt.[111]

Free from the Taint of Partisanship?

On 27 June 1923, Lord Islington again raised the Correspondence issue in a House of Lords debate on the government's Palestine policy.[112] He requested papers be laid on the table showing the budget accounts in Palestine for 1922, a report of the recent elections in Palestine, 'the various correspondence and Papers dealing with our engagements and commitments in Palestine; whether, in view of the recent Election having been declared void by the government and a new Advisory Council subsequently nominated by them being rejected by the Arab community, His Majesty's Government are now prepared, in the light of the present situation, to reconsider their present policy'. Following his request he opened his remarks by claiming that from the somewhat scanty and infrequent information available to the public through the press it was quite clear that the hostility of the people of Palestine to the Zionist policy in that country 'had definitely developed and hardened'. He asserted that the government's policy in Palestine was, in practical terms, 'deadlocked', and criticised both the 'Zionist-influenced' Executive Authority in Palestine and the recent disastrous election, where only a trickle of Palestinians had voted – so few, in fact, that Samuel had been forced to declare it void.

After recalling that in 1918 a proclamation had been issued in the vernacular in every village in Palestine making it clear that as far as Great Britain was concerned they would undertake to establish a system of government which was acceptable to the people of the country, he reminded the House that in the debate earlier that year, Viscount Grey had made an appeal to the Government to issue a White Paper giving all the correspondence which led up to their commitments in Palestine. He continued:

The noble Duke [Colonial Secretary] said he would have to get the assent of King Hussein and that, subject to it being not opposed to the public

---

111 Chancellor Papers, Box 16/4. Shuckburgh to Chancellor, 2 January 1930.
112 Hansard, Lords, 27 June 1923, vol. 54, cc654–682.

interest, he would do his best to issue such a White Paper. I hope that the noble Duke will be able to tell us, for the benefit of those who desire to have their doubts set at rest on this point, that such a Paper will be issued. I am credibly informed that King Hussein himself would welcome the publication of such a document, provided, of course, that matters dealing with the Sacred Places, which do not come into the controversy, were excluded from the Paper.[113]

Lord Islington was followed by Viscount Milner, a member of Lloyd George's war cabinet and a principal architect of the Balfour Declaration, who claimed that it would be a very grave matter, and would have a disastrous effect on Britain's prestige throughout the East, if the government were to allow itself to be hustled into a total reversal of policy, 'a course which a strong section of opinion in this country, supported by a vigorous agitation in the press, is trying to promote'. Surprisingly, however, he did support Islington's proposal that the Correspondence be published:

> I hold strongly that, if the documents were published, it would be proved that we had not broken faith with the Arabs ... I do not believe that the Balfour Declaration is inconsistent with any pledges which have been given to King Hussein or to anybody else. It is my conviction that when all the documents are published it will be clearly established that in all the promises which we made to King Hussein a distinct reservation was made of the country about which we are now speaking. Still, as I say, let that be decided by the documents themselves when they appear. At any rate, the Government which made the Balfour Declaration was under the impression that it was free to make it and that it was under no obligations inconsistent with it.[114]

The Viscount ended his speech with the standard government line on Palestine:

> I believe that the British Administration as conducted in Palestine today is free from the taint of any partisanship whatever and I believe that we have only to go on steadily with the policy of the Balfour Declaration as we have ourselves interpreted it in order to see great material progress in Palestine

---

113 Hansard, Lords, 27 June 1923, vol. 54, cc654–682.
114 Hansard, Lords, 27 June 1923, vol. 54, cc654–682.

and a gradual subsidence of the present agitation, the force of which it would be foolish to deny but which I believe to be largely due to artificial stimulus and, to a very great extent, to be excited from without.[115]

Contrary to the Public Interest

For the government, the Duke of Devonshire assured the House that since March he had – as he said he would – consulted his colleagues and the Foreign Office as to whether it would be possible to lay the relevant papers. However, he continued:

> I much regret to say that we have come to the conclusion, in addition to the reasons which I gave last March, that it is contrary to the public inter-est that these Papers should be laid, and I am unable to accede to the request of the noble Lord ... The Mandate is not merely a national obli-gation, it is an international obligation, and the Balfour Declaration was the basis on which we accepted from the principal Allied Powers the posi-tion of Mandatory Power in Palestine.[116]

The Duke then took the liberty of repeating two quotations from Churchill's June 1922 White Paper, explaining that it was necessary to point out that the Zionist Commission 'has not desired to possess, and does not possess, any share in the general administration of the country', and, regarding the meaning of the Jewish national home, that 'it was not the imposition of a Jewish nationality upon the inhabitants of Palestine as a whole, but the further development of the existing Jewish community.' He concluded his discourse with a sentence which can only be described as deliberately misleading:

> Again and again it has been stated that the intention from the beginning has been to make a National Home for the Jews, but every provision has been made to prevent it from becoming in any sense of the word a Jewish State or a State under Jewish domination.[117]

---

115 Hansard, Lords, 27 June 1923, vol. 54, cc654–682.
116 Hansard, Lords, 27 June 1923, vol. 54, cc654–682.
117 Hansard, Lords, 27 June 1923, vol. 54, cc654–682.

As the Zionist leaders knew full well – and as educated Palestinian Arabs correctly suspected – every policy decision implemented by the High Commissioner since July 1920 had specifically served to encourage the growth of an eventual Jewish state. Viscount Grey rounded off the debate by again calling for publication of the Correspondence. However, the Duke stuck to his brief, and simply ignored the former Foreign Secretary's request. Concerning the government's 'intentions' and 'provisions' for the future of Palestine, Lord Devonshire, Lloyd George, Balfour and Churchill, as well as Weizmann and other Zionist Organisation officials, handled the truth, whenever it suited them, equally loosely.

On the same day as the debate in the Lords, the new Prime Minister, Stanley Baldwin, appointed a high-powered cabinet committee, chaired by the Colonial Secretary, Lord Devonshire, to advise the government and enable it to make a 'prompt and final' decision about Palestine. The committee deliberated for a month and received written petitions from a number of parliamentarians. However, they would not receive the third Arab delegation, which was in London that summer. Shuckburgh informed them that the committee was not hearing oral evidence. In truth, Shuckburgh considered the delegation in no sense an official body, and believed that to allow them to appear in front of the committee 'would be giving them too much importance'. In contrast, the committee listened at length to Sir Herbert Samuel, who arrived from Palestine in late June, especially for the proceedings. Worried that the government might be wavering on the Palestine issue, Weizmann – on the alert as ever – hurriedly returned from a trip to Europe, and consulted Samuel, visited Shuckburgh the next day at the Colonial Office and wrote to both Lord Devonshire and Balfour.

In the end, it seems that Samuel's evidence finally tipped the scales in favour of the Zionists. The committee's final report, entitled 'The Future of Palestine', and dated 27 July 1923,[118] opted to maintain the national home policy. It is notable that in his evidence to the committee, the High Commissioner was quite candid about the purpose and role of the Supreme Muslim Council that he had established at the beginning of 1922, and of its head, the Mufti of Jerusalem, Haj Amin al-Husseini: it was to act as an 'intermediary between the Muslims and ourselves'. He considered it had been a success in this role, and he praised

---

118 CAB 24/161.

'the Mufti and his personal friends [who] are always active in times of political crisis ... in preventing people getting too excited and too violent'. Samuel's appointment of the Mufti, in fact, served two purposes. It initiated the friction between the latter and his cousin, Musa Kazim Pasha al-Husseini, the President of the Palestine Arab Executive Committee, and it enforced the idea that the Arab population had no national nature and consisted only of religious communities, in contrast to the Jewish 'national' community.[119] According to Ronald Hyam, the Council 'was designed to facilitate control rather than constructive change, law and order rather than effective modernisation'.[120]

The Supreme Muslim Council thus fulfilled its role for the administration as a manageable safety valve with no political power. The High Commissioner's strategy was to co-opt, rather than cooperate with, elements of the Palestinian Arab elite. The Council enjoyed considerable powers of patronage, including the right to appoint all *Qadis*, *Muftis*, and *Shari'a* and *Awqaf* officials, and in 1924 it employed a total of 1,193 persons whose salaries were paid by the government of Palestine. It wasn't until 1936 that the council acted in open defiance of the British administration, when the Mufti felt obliged to align himself with a growing popular rebellion.[121] The cabinet committee's report concluded that whether the original policy had been 'wise or unwise, it is well-nigh impossible for any government to extricate itself without a substantial sacrifice of consistency and self-respect, if not honour'.[122]

Since the San Remo Conference of April 1920, when the Mandates were assigned, British governments had exhibited considerable consistency: the pro-Zionist programme had been embodied in the Treaty of Sevres in August 1920, which was confirmed by Churchill, the Colonial Secretary, in the House of Commons in June 1921, before being reaffirmed by the government White Paper of June 1922 and reflected in the Mandate document approved by the League of Nations in July 1922. As

119 See Khalidi, *The Hundred Years' War on Palestine*, 43.

120 Ronald Hyam, *Britain's Declining Empire: The Road to Decolonisation, 1918–1968* (Cambridge, 2006), 15.

121 See Wasserstein, *The British in Palestine*, 133; Rashid Khalidi, 'The Palestinians and 1948: the underlying causes of failure', in Eugene L. Rogan and Avi Shlaim, eds, *The War for Palestine* (Cambridge, 2001), 22–23.

122 CO 733/58. Secret cabinet paper CP 351 (23), 'The Future of Palestine', 27 July 1923; Huneidi, *A Broken Trust*, 75.

Timothy Paris aptly concluded, 'When it came to the Jewish national home policy, the Lloyd George government had effectively painted all future British governments into a corner.'[123]

The Mandate for Palestine came into force on 29 September 1923.[124] At the end of that month, the Conservative government confirmed Britain's full and formal commitment to the cause of a Jewish national home. Nevertheless, doubts remained concerning the wartime pledges. When a Labour government came to power in early 1924, the new Colonial Secretary, J.H. Thomas, acting on the Middle East Department's advice, circulated a secret cabinet memorandum entitled 'Palestine', in which he noted that it had 'frequently been alleged that the Balfour Declaration was inconsistent with previous pledges given to the Arabs during the war'. However, he added that Sir Henry McMahon was 'personally' consulted in March 1922 and had 'stated definitely' that his intention had been 'to exclude Palestine' from the area of Arab independence. Nevertheless, Thomas echoed his predecessor's doubts:

> The natural meaning of the phrase 'west of the district of Damascus', has to be strained in order to cover an area lying considerably to the south as well as to the west of Damascus city … I think it is important that we should come to a decision on the question of policy at the earliest possible date. The situation in Palestine is now calm, but uncertainty is always dangerous, and if the announcement of our policy is delayed there may be a revival of agitation. My own view is that we have no alternative but to adhere to the policy carrying out the terms of the Balfour Declaration as interpreted by our predecessors. I do not underrate the difficulties, but I am satisfied that the difficulties of any alternative course could be even greater.[125]

---

123 Paris, *In Defence of Britain's Middle Eastern Empire*, 354.

124 'It was deemed advisable that the British Mandate for Palestine and the French Mandate for Syria should be put into force at the same time. Since, therefore, the promulgation of the latter was delayed by Franco-Italian discussions, it was not till September 29, 1923, that the two Mandates came into operation. In Palestine, however, the main provisions of the Mandate had already been applied; and the history of its execution may be said to have begun when in the summer of 1920 a Civil Administration was established in place of the military regime.' Peel Report, ch. III, 43.

125 CO 733/83. Secret cabinet memorandum, CP 121 (24), 19 February 1924.

On 25 February 1924, Thomas confirmed in the House of Commons that the government had decided, after careful consideration, 'to adhere to the policy of giving effect to the Balfour Declaration of 1917'.[126]

The official records of the period 1920–1924 reveal that although the pro-Zionist policy was certainly embarrassing to successive governments, they assessed that it would be much more embarrassing, indeed almost impossible, to publicly change course, and to attempt to justify that change not only in Parliament, but also at the League of Nations. Disregarding wartime pledges to Arabs was one thing, but the Zionist Organisation, it seemed, could not be ignored. Moreover, it was thought that Jewish capital and enterprise would serve Britain's strategic aims in the region. Both Parliament and government were always loath to spend money on Empire, but Jewish investment in Palestine would reduce the burden. Why not let the global Jewish community pay for this colonial adventure?

With the apparent consolidation of British power in Palestine by 1923, the Arab nationalists were plunged into despondency by the fruitlessness of their efforts in London and Jerusalem. Instead of enjoying the dignity and independence they had been led to expect, they had merely undergone a change of master. Beyond that, in order for them to be seen as legitimate representatives, Churchill and his successors demanded that they recognise the Palestine Mandate, an international legal formula designed to negate their national existence, a catch-22 dilemma which they never resolved.

Conspiracy or Contingency? Publicly Stated Aims vs. Private Intentions

Samuel's tenure in Palestine lasted five years and its long-term impact on future developments in Palestine was by any standard enormous. His personal belief and commitment to Zionism was sincerely held and undoubtedly profound. This conviction he articulated at a great rally held in the London Opera House on the second anniversary of the declaration in November 1919, where he explicitly denied that the Zionists wanted to set up a Jewish state in Palestine immediately:

---

126 Hansard, Commons, 25 February 1924, vol. 170, cc62–63.

> That ... we all fully recognise is an impracticable proposal. No responsible Zionist leader has suggested it. The immediate establishment of a complete and purely Jewish State in Palestine would mean placing a majority under the rule of a minority; it would therefore be contrary to the first principles of democracy, and would undoubtedly be disapproved by the public opinion of the world.

He explained that the real policy of the responsible leaders of Zionism was rather 'to secure the creation of conditions such that with the minimum of delay the country may become a purely self-governing Commonwealth under the auspices of an established Jewish majority'.[127]

In reality, between 1920 and 1925, Samuel successfully 'secured the creation of conditions' by arbitrarily imposing a new, complex legal framework in Palestine which would eventually establish a Jewish state with a Jewish majority, all the while continuing to proclaim, by 'reassuring statements', his 'singular impartiality'. But can the obvious gulf between Samuel's policy initiatives and his remarks designed to placate and co-opt the Palestinian Arab elite be considered a conspiracy, as has been suggested to me at an international conference on the British Mandate in Palestine? 'Conspiracy' is defined in the Oxford English Dictionary as 'a secret plan by a group to do something unlawful or harmful'. Conspiracy's bedfellow, 'deceit', is defined as 'behaviour intended to make someone believe things that are not true'. Samuel undoubtedly worked very closely with Weizmann and other leaders of the Zionist Organisation, including Sokolow and Ussishkin. As a collective they shared a clear vision of a future Jewish state, and on this they were ably supported by influential decision-makers in British governments of the period, including Lloyd George, Balfour, Churchill, Milner, Amery and Ormsby-Gore.

To my knowledge, the only British scholar who has explicitly raised even a modicum of concern about this discrepancy between publicly stated aims and private intentions is Sir Reader Bullard, a retired diplomat, who in 1951, as Director of the Institute of Commonwealth Studies at Oxford, wrote: 'If the Arabs were in fact exposed to the risk

---

127 Samuel's speech was published by the Zionist Organisation in a pamphlet, *Zionism: Its Ideals and Practical Hopes* (London, 1919).

Emir Abdullah with Sir Herbert Samuel and Winston Churchill at Government House reception, Jerusalem, 1925. Left to right: Beatrice Samuel, Emir Abdullah, Sir Herbert Samuel, Winston Churchill, Clementine Churchill.

of being outnumbered by the Jews, should this not have been made clear to them from the beginning?'[128]

As the official records show, this risk was not made clear to them at any time. It is notable, however, that although Samuel ran an ideologically 'tight ship', not all officials in his administration favoured the pro-Zionist policy of the Colonial Office, among them Ernest Richmond, an Arabic-speaking architect and the Political Secretary to Chief Secretaries Deedes and Clayton (1920–1924). Richmond was known to be in sympathy with the Arabs and had become a sort of connecting link between the administration and Arab politicians, a link which neither Samuel nor the pro-Zionist Deedes could establish. In fact, an aggrieved Richmond felt that Samuel kept him in post specifically to maintain a public counterweight to his own Zionist policies. Richmond finally quit his post in February 1924. In his letter of resignation to Samuel he wrote that he had been led

---

128 Sir Reader Bullard, *Britain and the Middle East* (London, 1951), 155.

Lord Balfour (centre) visiting the Hebrew University, Jerusalem, in 1925 with Lord Allenby (left) and Sir Herbert Samuel (right).

gradually and most reluctantly, but definitely to a conclusion that the Zionist Commission, the Middle East Department of the Colonial Office and this Administration are dominated and inspired by a spirit which I can only regard as evil, and that this spirit is, through the agencies I have mentioned, acting in a manner that is not merely unwise and impolitic but evil.[129]

In similar fashion, Sir Gilbert Clayton, Chief Secretary in Palestine from 1923 to 1925, also had serious misgivings about the development of government policy in Palestine, and there seems little doubt that Samuel had offered Clayton the post of Chief Secretary in the spring of 1923, in some measure, to disarm Arab opposition to the administration's Zionist

---

129 Richmond to Samuel, 13 March 1924. Cited in Wasserstein, *The British in Palestine*, 146.

policy.[130] Clayton disagreed with Samuel's assessment that Palestine was tranquil, and maintained that it was heading for a political and economic crisis. The Chief Secretary opposed the notion, as proposed by Meinertzhagen and others, that opposition to pro-Zionist policy was only the work of a few agitators. Nevertheless, unlike Richmond, he did not advocate the abandonment of the government's pro-Zionist policy. Instead, he recommended that some Articles of the Mandate be modified, in order to dissipate the present fear and mistrust of the Arabs. His good friend Humphrey Bowman, head of the Palestine Education Department, noted in his diary in February 1924 that Clayton 'was pretty sick of the whole thing … I doubt if he will stay long. He hates the atmosphere and is out of sympathy with [Samuel] and his eternal optimism.'[131]

Clayton also entertained misgivings about the Middle East Department. He wrote to one of his close friends that with its

mixture of Colonial Office bureaucracy and so-called expert local knowledge … [it] should never have been allowed to leave the FO which alone knows how to use it … There is an intangible 'something' behind everything, and unseen influence – something unhealthy and certainly not British, which has to be felt to be realised.[132]

Clayton's expression of an unhealthy 'unseen influence' is a reflection of the 'truth gap' that he witnessed in Palestine, and which extended beyond matters of personnel:

In general, a year in Palestine has made me regard this whole adventure with apprehension. We are pushing an alien and detested element into the very core of Islam, and the day may well come when we shall be faced with the alternatives of holding it there by the sword or abandoning it to its fate.[133]

Clayton's prediction proved correct: between 1936 and 1939 the British did, in effect, protect the position of the *Yishuv* in Palestine by the sword, and a decade later abandoned it – and the Palestinian Arabs – to

130 Huneidi, *A Broken Trust*, 109.
131 Bowman diary, 3 February 1924. Humphrey Bowman Papers, box 3B(g).
132 FO 800/156. Clayton to Walford Selby, 3 March 1924; Huneidi, *A Broken Trust*, 77.
133 Wasserstein, *The British in Palestine*, 148.

their fate. When he left Jerusalem in 1925, it is remarkable that Jew and Arab alike regarded him as a great friend, and as a forthright man of integrity. Yet it is clear that Clayton backed the Arab Revolt and their aspirations for independence in 1916 for reasons to do with 'defence of the Empire', and not because he believed the Arabs could then form a nation. His support for Arab aspirations was always 'subordinate to his fidelity to Empire'.[134] At the same time, like Ernest Richmond and some other British officials in Palestine, he spoke Arabic, had eyes and ears on the ground throughout the region, and maintained a genuine and sincere friendship with the Palestinian Arabs. According to his biographer

> even during the war years ... he found time to meet with Arabs, high and
> low, and he rarely did so for the purpose of ventilating his own views. He
> was a good listener and he possessed the ability of making the other
> believe he was convinced that what they were saying was important, even
> if it was not.[135]

Finding a Circumlocution

Many historians, and not only those of an anti-Zionist persuasion, also have little difficulty in quoting numerous conflicting Zionist statements made in the years between 1897 and 1948, in particular encouraging at one moment and denying at another the idea that the Jewish national home meant a Jewish state. The Zionist leadership never appeared to have any qualms about such mendacity: it was a necessary tactic to allay fears, on the one hand, and simultaneously to maintain party fervour, and global financial support, at that time far from extensive, on the other. In reality, in 1917 the Zionists had a very precarious hold on the two essential elements required for a state: land and population, which at the time of the First World War consisted of approximately 2 percent of Palestine and some 10 percent of the population. These were hardly very convincing figures, either morally or politically, to propose as the basis for the creation of a Jewish state, even in the sympathetic Western corridors of power. Max

---

134 Paris, *In Defence of Britain's Middle Eastern Empire*, 437.
135 Paris, *In Defence of Britain's Middle Eastern Empire*, 438.

Nordau, one of Theodor Herzl's earliest associates, related how, on his advice, the term 'Jewish national home', rather than '*Judenstaat*', was adopted in 1897 as a description of the Zionists' ultimate goal:

> I did my best to persuade the claimants of the Jewish state in Palestine that we might find a circumlocution that would express all we meant, but would say it in a way so as to avoid provoking the Turkish rulers of the coveted land ... it was equivocal, but we all understood what it meant.[136]

Zionist Congresses between 1897 and 1937 consistently made a point of denying that there was, or ever had been, any intention or desire on the part of Jews to establish a Jewish state in Palestine. The Tenth Congress, for example, held at Basle in August 1911, was opened by David Wolffsohn, the Lithuanian-born President of the World Zionist Organisation, with the following speech:

> Only those suffering from gross ignorance, or actuated by malice, could accuse us of the desire of establishing an independent Jewish kingdom. The aim of Zionism is the erection for the Jewish people of a publicly recognized, legally secured home in Palestine. Not a Jewish state, but a home in the ancient land of our forefathers, where we can live a Jewish life without oppression and persecution. What we demand is that the Jewish immigrant to Palestine be given the opportunity of naturalizing as a citizen without limitation, and that he can live unhindered in accordance with Jewish customs ... That and nothing else is our aim.[137]

In similar vein, Nahum Sokolow, Weizmann's closest collaborator, wrote in 1918:

> It has been said and is still being obstinately repeated by anti-Zionists again and again, that Zionism aims at the creation of an independent 'Jewish State'. But this is wholly fallacious. The 'Jewish State' was never a part of the Zionist programme.[138]

---

136 Sykes, *Crossroads*, 10–11.
137 *Jewish-Arab Affairs*, Jerusalem, 1931, 7–8. See Barbour, *Nisi Dominus*, 52. It is notable that the Tenth Zionist Congress included a session for the first time in Hebrew.
138 Sykes, *Crossroads*, 11.

For his part, in 1925, Weizmann told the Fourteenth Zionist Congress in Vienna:

> Palestine must be built up without violating the legitimate interests of the Arabs – not a hair of their heads shall be touched … [The Congress] has to learn the truth that Palestine is not Rhodesia and that 600,000 Arabs live there who … have exactly the same right to their homes as we have to our National Home.[139]

Weizmann clearly understood European diplomatic language and, in contrast to the Sharif, that the British concept of independence for nations like Egypt and Iraq meant ultimate British control. He knew that calling for an immediate Jewish state was not politically feasible, given international opinion of the time. Hence, from 1917 onwards, he and other Zionist leaders used the label of a 'national home' as a screen behind which they could establish a Jewish state. Weizmann's extensive correspondence with British officials throughout the Mandate period is peppered with phrases that leave no doubt as to this ultimate objective. To give just one example, in 1930 he explained in a private letter to Malcolm MacDonald that 'our work for Palestine and in Palestine has salvaged the Jewish youth of Eastern and Central Europe from the vortex of revolutionary and morally destructive forces. We have put a great ideal of national reconstruction before them.'[140]

Zionist leaders felt that the Jews' need for a country with empty spaces able to absorb future immigrants 'morally outweighed the rights of the indigenous Arabs'.[141] This point was occasionally publicly proclaimed, as when Menachem Ussishkin, one of political Zionism's founding fathers and Chairman of the Jewish National Fund, announced to journalists on 28 April 1930: 'Other inhabitants … must be transferred to some other place. We must take over the land. We have a greater and nobler ideal than preserving several hundred thousands of Arab *fellahin*.'[142] In other words, Zionists considered transfer to be a moral as well as a political and practical solution. *Plus ça change?*

---

139 Fred J. Khouri, *The Arab-Israeli Dilemma* (New York, 1985, 3rd ed.), 41.
140 MM Papers, 9/1/25. Weizmann to Malcolm MacDonald, 23 May 1930.
141 Morris, *Righteous Victims*, 140.
142 Morris, *Righteous Victims*, 141.

And what was the interpretation which the British government itself placed on the term 'Jewish national home' at the time of issue of the Balfour Declaration? As mentioned previously, Lloyd George stated to the Royal Commission some twenty years later that if the Jews responded to the opportunity afforded to them by the declaration of a national home and became a majority, then Palestine would become a Jewish commonwealth.

In similar fashion, giving evidence in secret to the same Commission, Churchill spoke of how, when he was Colonial Secretary in 1922, it had always been his view of the Jewish national home that

> if more and more Jews gather to that Home and all is worked from age to age, from generation to generation, with justice and fair consideration to those displaced and so forth, certainly it was contemplated and intended that they might in the course of time become an overwhelming Jewish State.[143]

The Arabs therefore are on strong grounds in asserting that, in spite of their many official requests for clarity, a succession of British governments from 1917 deliberately withheld from them their true intentions: to impose and maintain a legal, constitutional framework (an Iron Cage, according to Rashid Khalidi)[144] which would enable sustained Jewish immigration and land sales, and thus secure the eventual creation of a Jewish state. Did that policy amount to a conspiracy, or merely one of occasional deceit, necessitated by the imperial priorities of the period? My own conclusion is that the British–Zionist relationship and enterprise between 1916 and 1925 included so many examples of British governments' and Zionist mendacity, small and large, implicit and explicit, that there was, as Clayton remarked in 1924, an intangible and unhealthy 'something' behind everything, which suggests not only occasional deceit, but something more than a hint of conspiracy.

---

143 Peel Report, notes of evidence, 12 March 1937; Churchill Papers, 2/317. Cited in Gilbert, *Never Despair*, 455.

144 See Rashid Khalidi, *The Iron Cage. The Story of the Palestinian Struggle for Statehood* (Boston, 2006).

4

Non Possumus[1]

1924–1938

The years 1924 to 1929 in Palestine were relatively quiet. The relative tranquillity of 1924, compared to the preceding two years, was later described in the following terms by Norman Bentwich, Palestine's Zionist Attorney General:

> The people began to learn, by the '*eloquence ambiente des exemples,*' of the good intentions of the Government; and by the percolation of Jewish capital throughout the country, of the advantages to be derived from Jewish immigration. The effervescence of the two years of agitation slowly subsided; and if the Press remained as violent as ever in its denunciations of the policy, the general population acquiesced in it and in the acts of the paternal Government. They could not fail to recognise the growing material prosperity of the country; and the political leaders were brought to understand the lesson that you cannot agitate interminably for a negative.[2]

Bentwich's statement is an eloquent – and not untypical – example of the colonial and orientalist mindset of senior Mandatory officials in Palestine at that time, who consciously, and sometimes unconsciously, attempted to hug the moral and political high ground. They claimed that local political leaders lacked a true appreciation of the benefits of Jewish immigration, and clearly needed to be taught fundamental lessons concerning negotiations and governance.

---

1 Latin phrase: 'we cannot' or 'here we stand'.
2 Norman Bentwich, *England in Palestine* (London, 1932), 103.

On the contrary, the tranquillity of the period up to 1929 can also be partly explained by the drop in Jewish immigration. In the first years of the Mandate, Jewish immigration was virtually unimpeded. Between 1924 and 1927 more than 65,000 Polish Jews reached Palestine, but in 1927, as the global economic situation worsened, the Jewish Agency found itself entering a period of economic crisis: the cost of building up the national home could not be met by its productive enterprises, and in that year twice as many Jews left Palestine as reached it.[3] Nevertheless, the Jewish community continued to consolidate their settlements and develop their political, cultural and social infrastructure. By 1929, they had increased their land ownership to 4.5 percent (from 2.04 percent in 1919), and they now constituted about 17 percent of the population (compared to 10 percent in 1919).[4] A further factor which explains the relative calm up to 1929 was the absence of a Palestine-wide network to monitor land sales, which took place in an impersonal Land Registry office unseen by the majority of the Arab population, and the reluctance of some Palestinian leaders to raise an issue that would betray their own involvement in it.[5]

The British authorities became complacent and drastically reduced the garrison. During this period too, the wartime pledges disappeared off the parliamentary radar, but other mandatory issues regularly came to the fore in both Houses, in particular the Rutenberg electricity concession and the Dead Sea Salts concession; both were monopolies for the operation of key economic assets in Mandatory Palestine. As Colonial Secretary in 1922, Churchill had granted an extensive economic concession to the Russian-born engineer Pinhas Rutenberg and his Palestine Electric Corporation for the development of the water power of Palestine. This enabled the Zionists to expropriate land – even Arab-owned land – if it was needed for pumping stations and other facilities in connection with damming the River Jordan.[6] In 1930, the British government granted a concession, following several years of negotiations, to Russian-born Moshe Novomeysky and his Palestine Potash Company for the extract of potash from the Dead Sea.[7]

---

3 Martin Gilbert, *Israel. A History* (London, 1998), 55.

4 Walid Khalidi, *Palestine Reborn* (London, 1992), 32.

5 Stein, *The Land Question*, 218.

6 Gilbert, *Israel. A History*, 40.

7 Hansard, Commons, 29 January 1930, vol. 234, cc980–981. Potash contains potassium, an essential ingredient for crops and general plant health.

By the time Samuel handed over Palestine to the next High Commissioner, Field Marshal Lord Herbert Plumer, in the summer of 1925, the foundations of the British civilian administration had been firmly laid. While Samuel returned to Britain to preside over a royal commission on the coal industry, as we will see he never faltered in his deeply held Zionist convictions, nor in his belief that Palestine had not been promised to the Sharif in 1915.[8] The new High Commissioner, an elderly and distinguished soldier who had commanded British forces at Ypres and Messines, and who later served as Commander-in-Chief of the British Army of the Rhine, had no intellectual interest in Zionism and adhered rigidly to the status quo, as he found it. But the status quo in 1925 was not as it had been in 1920; now it distinctly favoured the Zionists.[9]

In autumn 1925 Musa Kazim Pasha al-Husseini led a delegation to meet the newly appointed Field Marshal. The former demanded a representative council elected by Arabs and Jews in proportion to their share in the population, as well as a national government responsible to this council. Although Plumer was not convinced, the Zionists were alarmed nevertheless, at least until they received word from their long-term parliamentary ally Ormsby-Gore (Under-Secretary of State for the Colonies) that the Colonial Secretary, Leo Amery, 'was opposed to such an attempt and that it was the last thing that Lord Plumer would think of'.[10] Amery, too, was a veteran supporter of the Zionist project for Palestine and as an assistant to Lord Milner had helped to write the final draft of the Balfour Declaration in October 1917, as mentioned previously.

In 1926 and again in 1928 the High Commissioner resisted proposals for the establishment of a legislative council, arguing that 'it would be prejudicial to the interests of the people of Palestine as a whole to attempt to introduce any form of representative government at the present time or for

---

8 Re-entering the Commons in 1929, he was the Leader of the Liberal Party (1931–1935); created Viscount in 1937; Liberal Leader in the House of Lords (1944–1955).

9 The Field Marshal was the first soldier, but not the last, to govern Palestine as High Commissioner. Military men frequently moved around the Empire and transitioned into civil administration at all levels. For many, including Plumer, 'imperial ways of thinking about the role of religion and race as they related to self-government and nationalism formed their intellectual framework.' Sinanoglou, *Partitioning Palestine*, 26.

10 Wasserstein, *The British in Palestine*, 153.

some little time to come.'[11] Indeed, no British cabinet during the 1920s would have sanctioned the establishment of a government truly representative of the Arab majority, especially not one possessing effective powers. In these circumstances there were few realistic political proposals British officials in Palestine could make to their masters in London that could have dented the imperial shield sheltering the Jewish national home.[12]

In December 1928, the Field Marshal was succeeded as High Commissioner by Sir John Chancellor, a career colonial servant with a reputation as a sound colonial administrator. However, in like fashion to Plumer, the new High Commissioner had no first-hand knowledge of Palestine (and hardly any of the Middle East) before his arrival in the country. Chancellor rapidly came to the conclusion that 'unless some steps are taken before long to associate the people more closely with the government of the country there is reason to think that political agitation against the government may assume an objectionable and even dangerous character.'[13] One of his first acts was to announce in January 1929 that he would consider the establishment of a legislative assembly. Six months later, while he was on leave in England, events occurred which persuaded him that the Balfour Declaration policy was a 'colossal blunder' involving 'grave injustice to the Arabs'.[14] In mid August, militant Zionist groups demonstrated at the Wailing Wall in Jerusalem, in reaction to which Palestinian Arabs rioted in several towns. In the resulting clashes, 133 Jews were killed and 339 wounded; 116 Palestinians were killed and 232 were wounded, almost all of the latter at the hands of the British military.[15]

The ferocity of the violence came as a colossal shock to both the Jewish community in Palestine and the Palestine administration. On 1 September, the High Commissioner issued a proclamation condemning the 'ruthless and bloodthirsty evildoers' and 'the savage murders perpetrated on defenceless members of the Jewish population'. Weizmann later recalled that he was in Wengen, Switzerland, on holiday when he first received news of the riots and he felt 'struck as by a thunderbolt'.[16]

---

11 Wasserstein, *The British in Palestine*, 152–154.

12 Wasserstein, *The British in Palestine*, 158.

13 Wasserstein, *The British in Palestine*, 157.

14 Wasserstein, *The British in Palestine*, 157.

15 Khalidi, *Before Their Diaspora*, 90.

16 Weizmann, *Trial and Error*, 410.

By all accounts, the riots and their aftermath constituted a turning point: from then on, any hopes for reconciliation between Jews and Arabs in Palestine rapidly diminished.

As in 1920 and 1921, the government decided to appoint a commission of inquiry, chaired by Sir Walter Shaw, a distinguished jurist, to investigate the causes of the disturbances.[17] The events of 1929 were too significant to be ignored, even in the context of a global empire in which outbreaks of low-level violence were not uncommon. The riots had illuminated the hollowness of the concept of a single political community in Mandatory Palestine. They also stimulated the inherent Zionist urge towards self-reliance. Just as significantly, the High Commissioner pressed the government urgently to change the direction of its policy in Palestine, and in particular to consider a modicum of constitutional reform and the establishment of a representative legislative assembly – anathema to the Zionists.

In hindsight, these disturbances can be seen as part of a wider movement whereby Asia had begun to demonstrate its opposition to European control. In 1930, Gandhi led his march to the sea for a symbolic 'making of salt', thus defying the Indian government's salt monopoly, and the following year launched his civil disobedience movement. Meanwhile, Haj Amin al-Husseini, the Mufti of Jerusalem, summoned an Islamic Congress to rally support against British policy in Palestine, and in 1932 Reza Shah, Persia's imperial monarch, unilaterally denounced the Anglo-Persian Oil Company's concession.[18] Nevertheless, Britain's iron cage in Palestine would remain unshaken until 1936.

The Shaw Commission's report was published in March 1930. It concluded that the cause of the rioting was based in Arab fears of continual Jewish immigration and land purchases, particularly resonating from a growing Arab landless class, and recommended the deletion of the Balfour Declaration from the Mandate Charter and a limitation on Jewish immigration and land purchase. The report led to the establishment of the Hope Simpson Inquiry in May 1930, which took evidence throughout Palestine between May and August 1930. The inquiry produced a very closely documented report on immigration, land

---

17 Other commission members: Sir Henry Betterton (Conservative), R. Hopkin Morris (Liberal) and Henry Snell (Labour).

18 See Monroe, *Britain's Moment*, 121.

settlement and development which supported all of Sir Walter Shaw's findings. The Jewish Agency[19] and all supporters of the Jewish national home policy in Parliament now realised, as did the Foreign and Colonial Offices, that the government's Palestine policy was again being publicly called into question, and that the Shaw Report's findings would precipitate an awkward, if not potentially damaging debate – or debates – in both Houses. However, the political landscape had changed considerably as a result of the May 1929 general election, when the Conservatives were replaced by a Labour government, once again led by Ramsay MacDonald. The new Colonial Secretary was the socialist Sidney Webb, raised to the peerage in June as Lord Passfield, and soon to be buffeted by a 'Jewish hurricane'.[20] According to Norman Rose, a parliamentary pro-Palestine group was formed on 12 November 1929 whose prime purpose was 'to act as a watch-dog for Zionist interests'.[21] An executive was elected, with Josiah Wedgwood as Chairman, and Leo Amery, Sir Herbert Samuel and James de Rothschild as members. On 9 December 1929, even before the Shaw Commission had completed its work, de Rothschild (Liberal, Isle of Ely)[22] asked Arthur Henderson, the new Foreign Secretary, whether the government had made any promises or pledges to the Arab-speaking populations of Palestine or neighbouring countries 'which invalidate in any way the Balfour Declaration of 2 November 1917, or the clauses of the Mandate for Palestine as approved by the League of Nations'.[23]

For the government, the new Under-Secretary of State for the Colonies, Dr Drummond Shiels (Labour, Edinburgh East), confirmed that the government 'have always held that there is nothing in their pledges that could invalidate the Balfour Declaration or conflict with the terms of the Mandate'. Colonel Howard-Bury (Conservative, Chelmsford), a supporter of the Palestinian Arab case, interjected:

---

19 Established in 1929 as the operative branch of the Zionist Organisation.

20 See Rose, *Chaim Weizmann*, 282.

21 Norman Rose, *The Gentile Zionists. A Study in Anglo–Zionist Diplomacy, 1929–1939* (London, 1973), 5.

22 Son of Edmond James de Rothschild of the French branch of the banking family; a distant relative to Walter Rothschild, second Baronet Rothschild, to whom the Balfour Declaration was addressed.

23 Hansard, Commons, 9 December 1929, vol. 233, cc23–24.

Is it not the case that on 24th October, 1915, Sir Henry McMahon made a declaration stating, 'I am empowered in the name of the British Government to recognise and support the independence of the Arabs within the limits of the boundaries proposed by King Hussein and that these limits included Palestine?'

Dr Shiels replied:

The pledge to which my hon. and gallant Friend referred was not made to the Palestinian Arabs, and the British Government have always taken the view that Palestine was excluded from that pledge.[24]

The leader of the 1921 British Everest reconnaissance expedition and veteran explorer of Tibet was not to be brushed aside by such general rhetoric. Two days later, he again raised the question of the wartime pledges to the Arabs, stating that it was on the assurance of the McMahon pledge that the Arabs took up arms on Britain's behalf against the Turks and that Lord Curzon in a letter to King Feisal on 9 October 1919 repeated those pledges. 'Seeing that these pledges have not up to date been carried out,' he continued, 'would [Dr Shiels] at least see that the Arabs, who form four fifths of the population of Palestine, are given a fuller share in the Government of Palestine?'

The Colonel was supported by Seymour Cocks, the newly elected Labour MP for Broxtowe, who requested the government 'to publish the correspondence between Sir Henry McMahon and King Hussein as a White Paper', to which Dr Shiels responded, 'I will consider that point.'[25] However, when Cocks again requested publication a week later, Dr Shiels crisply replied:

No, Sir. A similar question was put to the Government of the day on 11 July 1922. The reply given was that it would not be in the public interest to publish one or all of the documents comprising the long and inconclusive correspondence that took place with the Sharif of Mecca in 1915–16. The present Government see no reason to reconsider this decision.[26]

24 Hansard, Commons, 9 December 1929, vol. 233, cc23–24.
25 Hansard, Commons, 11 December 1929, vol. 233, cc447–448.
26 Hansard, Commons, 18 December 1929, vol. 233, cc1389–1390.

At the beginning of 1930, Jamal Husseini, Secretary to the Executive Committee of the Palestine Arab Congress and to the Muslim Supreme Council, came to London and eventually secured a fruitless meeting with the new Colonial Secretary; he also gave a talk in Parliament. Ahead of the latter event, a summary of Arab grievances was published and circulated to MPs. Realising this would cause more questions to be asked in the House, the Colonial Office had N.L. Mayle, a junior official, prepare a commentary on the points Husseini had raised, so that there would be material to answer the questions when they came up. In the process, Mayle started digging around the McMahon issue, as that was top of the list of the Palestinians' grievances. On 15 January 1930, Owen G.R. Williams, another junior Colonial Office official, read Mayle's commentary and minuted, 'One cannot easily escape the feeling that if Sir H. McMahon really intended to exclude "Palestine," he made a most deplorable mess of it.'[27]

A minute by Shuckburgh on Mayle's commentary was more forthright. For nearly a decade Shuckburgh had been the most senior Colonial Office figure involved in successive governments' management of the Correspondence controversy, and here he explicitly pointed to the 'districts' phrase in McMahon's 'unfortunate' letter as the government's principal reason for withholding publication:

> One point I should like to emphasise, on the matter of the pledges, I strongly urge that we should not allow ourselves to be drawn into argument about the precise meaning of this or that passage in Sir H. McMahon's unfortunate letters (e.g. whether 'vilayet' = 'district' & so forth). If we do, we are bound to get the worst of it, & shall probably make ourselves look ridiculous.
>
> There is only one safe line to take, i.e. we have always interpreted our pledges as excluding Palestine from the 'Arab' sphere: successive British Governments have taken up the same position on this point: our decision must stand, & there can be no question of reopening the question or of treating it as an arguable point.
>
> Any other line will, I am convinced, land us in endless difficulty.[28]

---

27 CO 733/178/5.
28 CO 733/178/1. Shuckburgh minute to Colonial Office colleagues, 29 January 1930. Underlined in the original.

As for McMahon's 'French reservation' in defence of the government's case, officials rarely mentioned it, either in Parliament or in internal documents, until February 1939, when it would become the 'rock' of the government's case.

On 3 April, Prime Minister MacDonald made a brief statement emphasising that the government would continue to administer Palestine in accordance with the terms of the Mandate, and that a double undertaking was involved:

> It is the firm resolve of His Majesty's Government to give effect, in equal measure, to both parts of the Declaration and to do equal justice to all sections of the populations of Palestine ... The Government is now studying the various recommendations of the Commission with a view to dealing with the immediate causes of the outbreak and to preventing a recurrence, and is in consultation with the interests concerned.[29]

However, this statement did nothing to placate the numerous parliamentary supporters of the Jewish national home policy, who considered the Shaw Commission's recommendations as a betrayal of the previous Mandate policy. Organised by Baffy Dugdale, Balfour's niece and a colleague and confidant of Weizmann and his inner circle, opposition leaders – Baldwin, Amery, Austin Chamberlain and Churchill – rallied to the Zionists. Jan Smuts protested, and from Wales, Lloyd George 'thundered the British people were not "scuttlers," whether in India or in Palestine'.[30]

---

29 Hansard, Commons, 3 April 1930, vol. 237, cc1466–1467. Ramsay MacDonald was among the first leading Labour politicians to declare in favour of Zionism. He toured Palestine in 1922, visiting Labour Zionist projects and holding discussions with Jewish labour leaders. His notes on the journey and his despatches to *Forward*, the newspaper of the Glasgow-based Independent Labour Party, do not record him meeting with Arabs. See Paul Kelemen, *The British Left and Zionism. History of a Divorce* (Manchester, 2012), 15. In 1976, his son Malcolm described his father's sympathies – at least during the 1930s – as being very friendly towards the Jews, and 'of course he wanted the Government to carry out the promise of the so-called Balfour Declaration that Palestine would become a national home for the Jews.' MM Papers, 9/10/11.

30 Rose, *Chaim Weizmann*, 282.

We Appeal to the House to Have Confidence in Our Good Intentions

It was in this febrile political atmosphere that on 9 April Cocks asked the Under-Secretary of State for the Colonies in the House whether the members of the Shaw Commission had been given the opportunity to examine an accurate copy of the Correspondence. Dr Shiels replied in the negative, adding that, 'As the Commission have pointed out, it clearly did not fall within the scope of their inquiry to examine and comment upon that correspondence.' Cocks then asked Dr Shiels whether he was aware that on page 194 of the report the commission said that 'they saw this correspondence and that it gave an inaccurate version, and that it was withdrawn on the instruction of the Commission.' He continued, 'Why should the Commission have to put up with an inaccurate version when it is within the province of His Majesty's Government to give an accurate version?' In reply, an embarrassed Dr Shiels could only point out that the commission had made it quite clear that all they were concerned with was the interpretation put upon the Correspondence, not its merits.

Clearly dissatisfied, Cocks persisted and asked whether, in view of the publication of the Shaw Report, Dr Shiels would reconsider the question of publishing the Correspondence. 'The answer is in the negative,' came the now standard reply. Cocks then continued:

> In view of general feeling among the Arab population of Palestine that this correspondence promised the Arabs their independence, will the hon. Member reconsider the question and publish the correspondence, so that we may know whether or not the Arabs were promised their independence?

But the Under-Secretary of State would not be drawn:

> This question has been before the House on many occasions and has been considered by various Governments, and it has been decided more than once that it is not desirable to publish this correspondence. I must adhere to that decision.[31]

---

31 Hansard, Commons, 9 April 1930, vol. 237, cc2147–2148.

There the matter rested until 7 May, when the equally persistent Colonel Howard-Bury asked Dr Shiels how many of the McMahon letters to Sharif Hussein had been published, how many had not been published, and whether, in view of the importance of clearing up the divergent views held, he would have the whole of this Correspondence published? Dr Shiels replied:

> I understand that none of the letters between General McMahon and the Sherif Hussein has been officially published. The second part of the question does not therefore arise. The answer to the third part of the question is in the negative.

John McShane (Labour, Walsall) asked what Dr Shiels meant by saying that they had not been officially published. If they had been unofficially published, was it possible to presume that Members of the House should have known the contents of the letters? But the Under-Secretary of State held to his 'say nothing' brief:

> I am not aware that the letters have been unofficially published, completely. There have been various extracts given from time to time, but I am not aware that the letters as a whole have been published, either officially or unofficially.[32]

That same afternoon, Cocks, clearly dissatisfied by Dr Shiels's prevarications, launched a full debate on the government's Palestine policy, and specifically called upon the government to publish certain correspondence which vitally affected the interests of the Arab population of Palestine and had a vital bearing upon the respective claims of the Zionists and the Arabs in the Holy Land. This debate is significant not for its content – it covered the usual ground – but because it precipitated a flurry of revealing memoranda about the Correspondence from worried Foreign Office and Colonial Office officials, as well as from Dr Shiels himself. After describing in detail the background to all the wartime promises, Cocks stated:

> For two reasons I plead with the Government to reconsider their decision and to publish the Correspondence. In the first place, the House will have

---

32 Hansard, Commons, 7 May 1930, vol. 238, c949.

to discuss the report of the Palestine [Shaw] Commission ... and very important matters will have to be settled with regard to the conflicting claims of Zionists and Arabs. It has been said by some that these pledges, as I have described them, conflict entirely with the Balfour Declaration. I do not say that. I do think there may be some diversity between the two documents, but it is the task of statesmanship to resolve difficulties of that nature ...

[Second], our whole position in the East, as everyone will admit, is sustained not merely by our military power but because Oriental peoples believe that on the whole we rule according to the principles of justice, but there is a feeling amongst the Arabs, a growing feeling, that we got their assistance during the War by giving certain pledges, and the War being over, we do not wish to carry out these pledges and have suppressed the correspondence. The only way to stop that feeling is for the Government to publish the correspondence so that we may know what has happened and the nature of the pledges. I ask the Government to reconsider their decision and publish this correspondence in order that the truth may be known and judgment delivered.[33]

Cocks's request to publish was supported by Colonel Howard-Bury, who added:

If we have not made these promises, as [Dr Shiels] says, and it was not most definitely laid down in that letter of Sir Henry McMahon that they were to have the Mediterranean coast up to a certain parallel, if that is not correct, surely by publishing the Correspondence, the Under-Secretary can clear himself and the Government of the charge of having broken the pledge ... We may have been wrong. We were in great danger at the time and we made pledges first to the Arabs, then to the Jews, and agreements with the French, some of them contradictory. I beg the Under-Secretary, although it is a long time ago, to publish the correspondence before we have those debates which are bound to come in regard to the future of Palestine, so that we may know exactly where we stand and the Arabs will know exactly where they stand.[34]

33 Hansard, Commons, 7 May 1930, vol. 238, cc1085–1096.
34 Hansard, Commons, 7 May 1930, vol. 238, cc1085–1096.

In reply, Dr Shiels expressed his surprise that Cocks and Colonel Howard-Bury had even raised the question of the Correspondence, and asserted that

> the present Government have taken no new or independent line in this matter ... They have merely placed themselves in the position adopted by their predecessors during the past 10 years ... The nature of these pledges was fully explained in the statement of policy published in the White Paper, Cmd. 1700 of 1922. Succeeding Governments have maintained the same attitude. I do not intend to enter into any detailed explanation of the reasons why it has always been thought inadvisable to publish the text of the McMahon correspondence. I will only say that these reasons have been held to be conclusive by successive Secretaries of State for Foreign Affairs, whatever their political views or those of the successive Administrations to which they belonged.

He concluded:

> I beg the House – and I direct my appeal to all quarters of the House without consideration of party – to accept this conclusion as a definite and final one. So far as Palestine is concerned, no object will be served by reopening the subject. The present Government take the view which all their predecessors have taken, that it has no practical bearing upon the constitutional and political aspects of the Palestine question. That question has got to be decided on broad considerations of justice and equity. To the solution of this question His Majesty's Government are now engaged in addressing themselves in the hope of achieving a settlement which may be acceptable to all concerned. We fully realise the difficulties. Our attitude is not one of easy optimism, but we are determined to find a solution if we can; and we appeal to the House to have confidence in our good intentions and to believe that it is not by raking up the controversies of the past, but by tackling the difficulties of the present and of the future, that a satisfactory conclusion will be reached.[35]

He was followed by McShane, who poured scorn on Dr Shiels's 'perfectly clear but perfectly irrelevant speech':

---

35 Hansard, Commons, 7 May 1930, vol. 238, cc1085–1096.

He [Dr Shiels] has been asked to do one of two things. He has been asked if he will be good enough to publish the McMahon correspondence, or to give a reason for the non-publication of that correspondence. He has done neither. He has asked us to engage in an article of faith which I think it is too much to ask of us. It is equivalent to asking us to shut our eyes and open our mouths and see what he will send us. One of his excuses for not publishing the correspondence was almost too ridiculous to mention. The hon. Gentleman says he wants us, in dealing with that question of Palestine, not to deal with the causes of the trouble but to look forward to the future in some sublime hope, but how by forgetting the causes we can manage to get a remedy for the causes I do not know.

Is it not perfectly true that we cannot really adequately discuss this question in the House, as it will have to be discussed, unless we know the whole of the facts? … merely to put forward, as one excellent reason why we should not press for the publication, the fact that the Duke of Devonshire and the right hon. Gentleman the Member for Carnarvon Boroughs [Lloyd George] when he was head of the Coalition, said it ought not to be published, is beside the point. Are the Labour Government going to follow in the steps of those right hon. Gentlemen? What are we doing here? … Is there any reason for us being here if we are not to take up a distinct point of view?[36]

Interventions followed – all requesting publication – from James Hudson (Labour, Huddersfield), Geoffrey Mander (Liberal, Wolverhampton East) and Gordon Lang (Labour, Oldham). The content of the debate was exceptional for two reasons: first, requests for publication came from all sides of the House, and second, not one member of the House spoke in support of Dr Shiels's plea, namely, to trust successive governments' judgment on the issue, and to 'look to the future of Palestine and not to the past'.

Childs's Memorandum

Following the debate, Dr Shiels was worried enough to ask the Foreign Office for advice about how to handle the next one, a prospect he

---

36 Hansard, Commons, 7 May 1930, vol. 238, cc1085–1096.

regarded as 'inevitable', and in particular how to better deflect from the issue of the pledges, which he assumed would be raised either in the forthcoming Colonial Office Estimates debate, or in the debate on the Shaw Commission's proposals. For the Foreign Office's consideration, Dr Shiels made three proposals: to state that the Correspondence dealt with personal questions (and was not only long, discursive and inconclusive); the government would publish the relevant passage concerning Palestine; and the government would invite all the recipients of the Correspondence to publish their versions.

Lord Monteagle, Head of the Eastern Department at the Foreign Office, forwarded these suggestions to Shuckburgh, asking for details of the issue in writing, so that the Foreign Office could consider how to advise Dr Shiels

> who is no doubt quite right in urging that this troublesome question must be cleared out of the way by some further and fuller statement when the inevitable debate about Palestine, the Shaw Commission's report etc., takes place – probably in the near future.[37]

In his note, Monteagle expressed his surprise that on 7 May no one had said a word in favour of the thesis advanced by Dr Shiels, in view of the fact that all successive governments for the previous decade had taken the same line. Two days later, Stephen Gaselee (later Sir Stephen Gaselee KCMG CBE FBA), the formidably erudite Librarian and Keeper of Foreign Office papers, sent Monteagle a brief handwritten reply:

> Please see Mr. Childs's very valuable minute annexed. I do feel that piecemeal publication is impossible: if we once begin, the whole series will be dragged out of us bit by bit. Unpleasant and difficult as it is to continue our refusal to publish what is already in the hands of one party, I think that on the whole we ought to continue in our 'Non possumus' attitude.[38]

---

37 FO 371/14495/8. Monteagle minute, 14 May 1930.
38 FO 371/14495/9. Gaselee minute, 16 May 1930. Storrs, Gaselee's contemporary at Cambridge, describes his friend as 'a Cambridge Personality': a pipe-smoking, first-class classical scholar, a bibliophile, a bibliographer, a liturgiologist who kept Siamese cats, wore his hair in a net while playing tennis, and who read, wrote and spoke Ancient Coptic (which the Copts themselves had not done for three hundred years). Storrs, *Orientations*, 14.

Gaselee's recommendations carried some weight in the Foreign Office. Appointed to his position in 1920, he presided diligently over a collection of some eighty thousand books, pamphlets, reports and manuscripts, including a number of large cabinets containing copies of UK government treaties and agreements with other powers – monarchies, republics, principalities, dukedoms and sheikhdoms – and was clearly very familiar with the background papers related to the Correspondence. The other Foreign Office official who had kept himself up to date with the Correspondence story during the 1920s was William J. Childs, considered by Lord Monteagle to be *the* expert on the subject. Childs minuted with reference to Dr Shiels's three suggestions:

Point (1) There can be no objection to telling the House that the Correspondence was long and discursive and not suited for publication. But it did not deal with 'all sorts of personal questions', for the only really personal question touched upon was that of the Caliphate for Hussein. It would also be safe to add that the correspondence was not only inconclusive but incomplete.

Point (2) Suggested publication of the relevant passage concerning Palestine.

A serious practical objection exists in giving this passage with official authority. If it is so given H.M.G. will be called upon to defend their reading of the passage word by word, and to do so will prove extremely difficult. What H.M.G. will expose themselves to if they give their authority to the passage may be seen in CMD 1700 (attached), – pages 25 and 26: the Arab arguments contained in Section 7.[39] These arguments are almost

39 *Palestine. Correspondence with the Palestine Arab Delegation and the Zionist Organisation* (Cmd 1700), June 1922. As mentioned previously, this White Paper sets out in detail both the government's policies towards Palestine and the claims of the Arab Delegation. The Arab arguments in Section 7 included: 'the word "district" and not vilayet was meant since the letter said "the districts of Damascus, Homs, Hama and Aleppo"; since Homs and Hama were districts included in the Vilayet of Syria it would have been superfluous to mention "Homs" and "Hama" specifically if the "Vilayet" of Damascus as against the "district" of Damascus were meant; the "vilayet" said to have been meant was called "Vilayet of Syria", and not "Vilayet of Damascus", as there was no Vilayet of Damascus' (pp. 25–26). There is thus no doubt whatsoever that British officials, notably Shuckburgh, Young and Churchill, knew from June 1922, if not before, of the fundamental weakness of the government's case.

irrefutable, once the accuracy of the text of the passage has been estab-lished. We may put up against the Arab arguments Sir H. McMahon's asser-tion of what his intended meaning of the passage was, but that would only be opposing the written words of the pledge by an explanatory statement made from memory seven years later.

I believe that if the official text of the relevant passage is given, it will provide the English supporters of the Arabs with such an opportunity that eventually it will be necessary to publish the whole of the corre-spondence. Besides, partial publication will give Hussein an opportunity to blackmail H.M.G. if he so desires.

Point (3) It seems to me that to invite the recipients of the letters to publish them would lead us nowhere to our advantage, but would even be in the nature of a challenge, eventually involving us in difficulties. The text of all the correspondence is already available to the supporters of the Arabs; what so far has remained uncertain is whether H.M.G. admit the correctness of the text.

The only suggestion I can make is that we should consider making, before the anticipated debate, a considered statement on the correspond-ence in which, while giving no official text, the origins of the pledge affecting Palestine might be outlined, and certain points favourable to our reading of the vital passage might be indicated.[40]

On 26 May, Shuckburgh received Childs's draft, described as 'a suggested statement in the House tracing the origin and interpretation of the phrase "districts of Damascus, Homs, Hama and Aleppo" used by Sir H. McMahon in his letter of 24 October 1915 to the Sharif of Mecca'. It included:

To make sure that the Syrian area which the Arabs deemed vital to their cause was definitely assigned to them he adopted the phrase 'the portions of Syria west of the districts of Damascus, Hama, Homs and Aleppo,' in defining what he excluded from his undertakings.

---

40 FO 371/14495. W.J. Childs's minute, 16 May 1930. Childs had written a seven-page memorandum on the subject on 17 March 1925, recounting the various demands for publication and successive governments' response to them. FO 371/10820, E2331, 232–238.

In effect, what the High Commissioner said to the Sharif in this sentence was:—'You and the Syrian Nationalists demand in Syria, as vital to your scheme, the districts of Damascus, Hama, Homs and Aleppo. His Majesty's Government accept the demand and assign these districts to you. But the portions of Syria lying to the west of the districts named must be excluded from our undertakings.'

In taking the 'district of Damascus' to represent the vilayet of Syria, His Majesty's Government have adopted the reading which, in 1915, gave the Sharif of Mecca and the Syrian nationalists the whole vilayet which would secure for them the territorial contact with Arabia that was essential to their scheme.[41]

Here, Childs deftly attempted to justify the government's interpretation of the 'district of Damascus' as representing the 'vilayet of Syria', by suggesting that McMahon used that particular 'district' phrase in order to satisfy the Syrian nationalists' (and the Sharif's) request for 'territorial contact with Arabia'. However, Childs's novel suggestion could not alter his own 'almost irrefutable' linguistic argument concerning the 'districts' phrase in the letter. In the event, although Childs's proposed 'considered statement' was never brought up in either House, his suggestion was brought forward by the government in 1939.

On 21 May 1930, Labour MP John McShane asked the Under-Secretary of State for the Colonies whether 'in view of the desire recently expressed on all sides of this House that the McMahon Correspondence should be published', he would now reconsider the question of publication. Dr Shiels replied that the matter was under consideration. Over the following ten weeks, McShane and Cocks took it in turns to request a statement on the Correspondence, asking six times in all, but to no avail.

In the meantime, the Colonial Office, now led by Labour peer Lord Passfield, decided that the most effective way of dealing with this contentious question was to produce a definitive paper, which could be considered and agreed by the cabinet, and an authoritative

41 FO 371/14495/42. 'First tentative draft, by Mr Childs, for a suggested statement in the House tracing the origin and interpretation of the phrase "districts of Damascus, Homs, Hama and Aleppo" used by Sir H McMahon in his letter of 24th October, 1915, to the Sherif of Mecca.'

statement to be read in the House. Hence, in June, Childs was charged with compiling a 'full and comprehensive' history of the Correspondence, which could then be circulated to the cabinet, signed off, and which would provide a definitive explanation for Parliament as to why it was in the highest degree undesirable to publish the McMahon Correspondence, and offer proof that the government made no pledge to include Palestine in an Arab state during the war.[42] Childs fulfilled his allotted task admirably: initially some 184 pages long, his exhaustive memorandum was then shortened to a sixty-nine page, closely argued, source-referenced printed paper.[43]

Among those to review the memorandum was the new Head of the Eastern Department in the Foreign Office, George Rendel, who had succeeded Lord Monteagle earlier that year. Like Gaselee, Rendel was a multilingual, classical scholar. A man of formidable mind, who had gained first place in the UK diplomatic entrance examination in 1913, Rendel read Childs's paper and minuted:

> In the special circumstances, there is a strong case for making a further attempt to avoid the issue of any official publication on this most difficult and invidious question. Any attempt to justify the policy of H.M.G. would, it seems to me, inevitably lead to increased ill-feeling between the Arabs and the Jews, and involve raking up the detailed history of the serious disagreements which arose between H.M.G. and the French Government in the Near East, more especially in the latter war and earlier armistice period.[44]

Childs's shortened memorandum was still comprehensive in scope. The first ten chapters described in considerable detail the history of all the relevant circumstances and events, including traditional French interests in Syria and Palestine; the Kitchener–Abdullah correspondence;

---

42 See FO 371/14495, 82. Monteagle to Oliphant, 2 August 1930.

43 FO 371/14495, 129–165. CONFIDENTIAL 13378 'MEMORANDUM on the Exclusion of Palestine from the Area assigned for Arab Independence by the McMahon-Hussein Correspondence of 1915–16 [WITH TWO MAPS]', Foreign Office, 24 October 1930.

44 FO 371/14495, E3888, 105. Rendel minute, 21 July 1930.

Russian claims;[45] the de Bunsen Report;[46] El-Faruqi's veiled ultimatum to H.M.G.;[47] the McMahon–Hussein Correspondence; the Sykes–Picot Agreement; Zionism and Palestine; the Balfour Declaration; the French occupation of Damascus; and the Mandate's establishment.

With the context of the Correspondence thus thoroughly surveyed, Childs's final chapter described the history of the various interpretations of the Correspondence, starting with that of Sir Mark Sykes in November 1915, who believed that McMahon's letter had assigned Palestine to the Arabs. Sykes had written to the War Office that he anticipated that 'the Government in Syria and Palestine will be carried on [by Arabs] on Turkish formula with local personnel.'[48]

The second interpretation described by Childs came from the *Hejaz Rising Narrative*, prepared by the Arab Bureau:

> We, for our part, have not agreed to recognise Arab independence in Syria west of the line Aleppo, Hama, Homs, Damascus, or in any other portion of the Arab area in which we are not free to act without detriment to our ally, France.[49]

Childs emphasised that both Sykes and the author of the *Narrative*,

> by ignoring the definite meaning of the word 'districts', and by substituting the idea of a line for the idea of districts, seriously perverted the meaning of the pledge ... [their] interpretations were in no way authoritative, and should not be taken at face value.[50]

---

45 Principally to Constantinople and the Straits.

46 Submitted on 30 June 1915, the report provided the guidelines for Asquith's government for negotiations with France, Italy and Russia regarding the partitioning of the Ottoman Empire.

47 El-Faruqi had hinted to British officials in Cairo in 1915 that the Arabs were 'at the parting of the ways' and would fight the French for the 'districts of Damascus, Homs, Hama and Aleppo'. See FO 371/14495, 165.

48 Sykes to the Director of Military Operations, War Office (tel. no. 20), repeated to the Foreign Office by McMahon as tel. no. 709, 21 November 1915. Childs does not give the file reference.

49 *Hejaz Rising Narrative*, vol. I, 110–112, Arab Bureau File 28 E (4). Original typescript dated 29 November 1916.

50 Childs's memorandum, 54.

Later in the memorandum, Childs states that Sykes and the *Narrative* 'unconsciously perverted the pledge'.[51]

Childs was equally unimpressed by the 1918 interpretation by Toynbee, who 'did not assess the pledge critically', but blessed and handed on the perverted reading of the pledge. However, the next examination of the pledge, according to Childs, contradicted and corrected the previous interpretations. In 1920, Major Hubert Young, on reading the Arabic text of the letter,

> saw that the Arabic of the words 'district of Damascus' had the meaning 'vilayet of Damascus'; and that, as the vilayet of which Damascus was the capital extended southward to the Gulf of Akaba, the pledge excluded Palestine from the Arab area.[52]
>
> This interpretation was adopted by His Majesty's Government, and on it they have consistently taken their stand. Major Young's reading thus brushed aside the perversion based upon imaginary lines, adopted by Sir Mark Sykes and the Arab Bureau, and restored to the pledge the meaning intended by Sir H. McMahon's use of the word 'districts.'[53]

Childs then described the Feisal–Lindsay meeting of January 1921, during which Feisal again and again 'misquoted the pledge' by the use of a 'deliberately disingenuous argument':[54]

> The vital point in His Majesty's Government's interpretation of the pledge is that the administrative 'district' of which Damascus was the capital extended southward, east of Palestine, for the whole length of Palestine. That Feisal deliberately reiterated his substitution of 'towns' for 'districts' in the interview suggested that he was fully alive to the weakness of his case.[55]

---

51 Childs's memorandum, 67.
52 Childs gives a partial source reference (E14959/9/44) for this statement. The author cannot find this document in the state papers, nor any others by Major Young, who was attached at this time to the Foreign Office.
53 Childs's memorandum, 55.
54 Childs's memorandum, 56.
55 Childs's memorandum, 56.

'Of great importance', Childs continued, was McMahon's private letter to Sir John Shuckburgh of 12 March 1922, where the High Commissioner explained the meaning he intended to convey in his letter to the Sharif. He then describes Churchill's interpretation in June of that year, where the Colonial Secretary adopted Young's interpretation.

Although Childs asserts that 'the specific (districts) reservation is absolute, and contains neither conditions nor limitations',[56] in his concluding remarks he is not so emphatic:

> The 'districts' phrase used by McMahon unfortunately lend themselves to doubt. All turn upon the meaning attached to the words 'district of Damascus' ...
>
> It must be admitted that the pledge is loosely phrased, and that inherent in the words 'districts of Damascus,' &c., is a ready invitation to interpret them as defining a line. It is only by recalling that the chief meaning of the word 'district' is 'an administrative area' that Sir H. McMahon's real intention appears. But this meaning is more clear in the Arabic text, and is powerfully supported by the history of the pledge, contained in official documents, which show how El Faroki's phrase, 'districts of Damascus,' &c., came to be adopted by Sir H. McMahon.[57]

Childs's conclusions were clearly expressed:

- First, the government were entitled to take their own and McMahon's intention into account wherever the meaning of the text was called in question.
- Second, when McMahon gave his pledge to the Sharif on 24 October 1915, he adopted al-Faroki's own phrase, 'districts of Damascus, Homs, Hama and Aleppo', using it in the same comprehensive sense that al-Faroki had done. By this phrase McMahon did *not* mean the immediate surroundings but intended to convey a broad definition of the Syrian hinterland as an area vital to the scheme of an Arab Empire or Confederation. In that sense the 'districts' he named extended from Aleppo to the Gulf of Aqaba and the confines of the Hijaz.

---

56 Childs's memorandum, 60.
57 Childs's memorandum, 66.

- Third, that view of McMahon's intended meaning of the phrase was supported by official documents of the time, including by Major Hubert Young's reading of the Arabic text as '*vilayet* of Damascus' and McMahon's personal letter of explanation to Sir John Shuckburgh in March 1922.

- Fourth, the chief cause of the pledge affecting Palestine having been misunderstood by Arabs and others lay in the 'perverted' reading adopted by Sir Mark Sykes in 1915 and the Arab Bureau in 1916.

- Fifth, if McMahon's specific 'districts' reservation did not apply to Palestine, then Palestine fell within the scope of his general reservation of French interests. This general reservation had not expired, as the Arabs contended, but was still in force. The interests of France so reserved in Palestine had to be taken as represented by the original French claim to possession of the whole of Palestine. Therefore, that reservation was sufficient by itself to exclude Palestine from the Arab area.

- Finally, from the examination of the history of McMahon's pledge of 24 October 1915, it was evident, according to Childs, that he intended the exclusion of Palestine from the pledge, and therefore His Majesty's Government's interpretation of the contested passage had been adopted on adequate grounds, and in good faith.

On 30 July, at Lord Passfield's request, and with the aid of Childs's memorandum, the cabinet discussed the Correspondence question and agreed on an official statement.[58] Two days later, when Seymour Cocks again raised the matter in the Commons, Dr Shiels read out the cabinet's carefully crafted response: the government had been impressed by the feeling shown in the House of Commons on various occasions, and especially in the debate on 7 May, and had therefore thought it necessary to re-examine this Correspondence fully in the light of the history of the period and the interpretations which had been put upon it. Dr Shiels continued:

> There are still valid reasons, entirely unconnected with the question of Palestine,[59] which render it in the highest degree undesirable in the

---

58 FO 371/14495, E4121, 111.
59 The Caliphate question, and Anglo-French wartime relations.

public interest to publish the correspondence. These reasons may be expected to retain their force for many years to come.

There are not sufficient grounds for holding that by this correspondence His Majesty's Government intended to pledge themselves, or did, in fact, pledge themselves, to the inclusion of Palestine in the projected Arab State. Sir H. McMahon has himself denied that this was his intention. The ambiguous and inconclusive nature of the correspondence may well, however, have left an impression among those who were aware of the correspondence that His Majesty's Government had such an intention.

He concluded:

The main grievance that was expressed in the [7 May] debate was that this Government had adopted a continuity of policy without themselves making a full investigation into the subject; and, in response to the request that was then made, the whole subject has been very carefully gone into again. It has taken a lot of time and trouble, and all these facts which my hon. Friend points out have been taken into consideration.[60]

All the facts may have been taken into consideration, but not all officials who read Childs's secret memorandum were entirely convinced. Cosmo Parkinson, an Assistant Secretary at the Colonial Office, minuted, 'It is an ingenious case, but I should be very sorry to have to swear that it was ingenuous.'[61]

For his part, the Colonial Secretary argued that on the strength of the evidence brought forward by Childs, the government had entered into no obligation vis-à-vis the Palestine Arabs. Nevertheless, he added in the same memorandum for the cabinet:

I have also come to the conclusion that there is much to be said on both sides and that the matter is one for the eventual judgement of the

---

60 Hansard, Commons, 1 August 1930, vol. 242, c903. P.J. Dixon, a junior official at the Foreign Office, noted later 'Let us hope that Dr Shiels' firm statement will have a quietening effect.' Dixon minute, 6 August 1930, in FO 371/14495, E4138, 112.
61 CO 733/189, 77121. The Oxford English Dictionary defines 'ingenuous' as 'innocent and unsuspecting'.

historian, and not one in which a simple, plain and convincing statement can be made.[62]

This author's judgement is plain and simple: Childs's lengthy memorandum is best described as a dodgy dossier (neither the first nor the last) written to provide official justification of the government's Palestine policy, and specifically to maintain the latter's position that Palestine was excluded from the territories promised to the Sharif.

There the matter rested until the publication of the Passfield White Paper in October 1930, the result of both the Shaw and the Hope Simpson Commissions' investigations[63] into the deeper causes of the 1929 Palestine riots, and the government's first formal statement of their policy in Palestine since the 1922 Churchill White Paper. It concluded that Jewish immigration to Palestine was taking land from the Arab tenant cultivators; sales of land to Jewish settlers should in future be restricted; and Arab unemployment levels should be a factor in considering permitted levels of Jewish immigration. Furthermore, a legislative council should be formed which would represent the majority of its population.

Zionist organisations worldwide claimed the White Paper backtracked from what they felt were commitments in the Balfour Declaration and mounted a vigorous campaign against it. It led to a six-hour debate in the Commons on 17 November 1930, initiated by Lloyd George, with lengthy interventions in support from Leo Amery, Sir Herbert Samuel, James de Rothschild[64] and Henry Snell, who all criticised the proposals to restrict immigration and establish a legislative council in Palestine. Only Colonel Howard-Bury and Rhys Morris (Liberal, Cardigan) attempted to support it, the latter the only member to raise the question of the Correspondence in the debate:

> The present Government, like the previous Government, have always declined to publish the McMahon correspondence. That does not mean that it is not published, and that you cannot obtain copies of it. If you ask

---

62 Cab 24/214. C.P.271 (30).

63 Cmd 3580 and Cmd 3686 respectively.

64 Then Chairman of the Palestine Jewish Colonisation Association.

the Foreign Office in this country for a copy of it, they will give you a
version which they themselves have prepared—excerpts—which is a
totally different thing from the full copy.[65]

MacDonald had not anticipated the full extent of the domestic political
backlash that followed the publication of the new White Paper.
Weizmann embarked on a campaign of political lobbying against the
minority Labour government, and found willing allies in the leaders of
the Conservative and Liberal parties, as well as several leading Labour
MPs. For the Conservative Opposition, the Palestine imbroglio served
as a convenient stick with which to assail the government. Lloyd George
made it clear that his fifty-nine Liberal MPs would not support Labour's
new policy for Palestine. It quickly became evident that the White
Paper stood no chance of securing a majority in the Commons and, in
fact, it was never put to the vote. If it had been voted on, and passed by
a majority – and subsequently transformed into law – it would have
significantly curtailed the further development of the Jewish national
home in Palestine. The legislative assembly proposal was defeated in the
House of Commons on the grounds of unfairness to the Zionist *colons*,
Lloyd George emphasising that the Balfour Declaration 'settled by the
Allied Powers' are the 'ruling words'.[66] Weizmann and colleagues
breathed a sigh of relief, while the Palestinian leadership's tenuous hopes
of any change in policy as a result of the Passfield White Paper turned
to despair.

Two factors had played a major role in effectively neutering the
White Paper: the strength of the pro-Zionist lobby in Parliament and
the role of Malcolm MacDonald, the newly elected National Labour
MP for Bassetlaw, and the Prime Minister's son. In his retirement,
MacDonald recalled that during the 1930s

there were a lot of representatives of the Jews, there were Jewish members
of Parliament, jolly good men, able men, [with a] passionate approach ...
the Jewish lobby, you see, were not only an able lobby, but a pleasing

---

65 Hansard, Commons, 17 November 1930, vol. 245, c158.
66 Hansard, Commons, 17 November 1930, vol. 245, cc78–79. In the same debate,
the former Prime Minister repeated the myth that the Mandate had been 'given to
our country for the government of Palestine'.

lobby ... Weizmann was a great man, and a charming man, and several of the others were remarkably able people, and they had the ears of other Cabinet members, of members of Parliament, of all sorts of important people in Britain, and so the Jewish lobby was very, very strong, in the Palace of Westminster and everywhere outside it ...

The Arab lobby was almost non-existent. In the House there wasn't any Arab member, and there was no member whose return at the next General Election depended on Arab votes in his constituency. I'm not criticising or complaining. I'm merely stating a fact. There were some very able champions of the Arab cause, but they could be counted on the fingers of two hands, and perhaps one hand.[67]

For years I felt considerable sympathy for Zionist desire to found a Jewish state in Palestine[68] ... I supported Zionism because I had only heard the Zionist case. Not aware of the Arab case [until 1938].[69]

The Zionists' campaign to reverse the Shaw Commission's recommendations doubled during the summer of 1930. In May of that year, young MacDonald was approached by Lewis Namier, Political Secretary of the Zionist Organisation, who had been one of his tutors at Oxford a decade earlier.[70] Through Namier, MacDonald was introduced to Weizmann and other Zionist officials. Weizmann turned his charm on MacDonald, and they became firm friends: by the end of 1930, Weizmann's penned notes started 'My dear Malcolm'. MacDonald later recalled, 'They put their criticisms [of the Shaw Commission's report] to me in the hope that I would pass them on to my father, or enable them to talk with my father.'[71]

---

67 MM Papers, 9/10/11. Notes from an interview with Nigel Maslin, 9 December 1976.

68 MM Papers, 9/10/30.

69 MM Papers, 9/12/12.

70 Lewis Namier (1888–1960; knighted, 1952) was born Ludwik Bernstein Niemirowski in Poland. He emigrated to Britain in 1907, studied at Balliol College, Oxford, and became a British subject, anglicising his name, in 1913. During the First World War he fought as a Private and then joined – along with Arnold Toynbee – the Political Intelligence Department of the Foreign Office. A brilliant and prolific historian, he taught at Manchester University from 1931 until 1953.

71 MM Papers, 9/10/11. Notes from an interview with Nigel Maslin, 9 December 1976.

Malcolm MacDonald, Secretary of State for the Colonies, June–November 1935
and May 1938–May 1940

Weizmann's charm worked. MacDonald arranged for the Zionist leader, and other Zionist officials, to meet the Prime Minister, and soon became a keen supporter of the national home project, as evidenced by his typed notes on Palestine to his father.[72] Weizmann and Namier sent copies of all their correspondence with the Foreign Office and Colonial Office

---

72 See, in particular, Malcolm MacDonald's 'Note on Palestine', which included: 'Lord Passfield's note to you a few days ago is not free of anti-Jewish feeling … It is not only representative Jews – as Lord Passfield suggests it is – who think that Sir John Chancellor and his administration are anti-Jew. Mr Snell, Lord Lugard, Mr John Buchan and Sir Archibald Sinclair (to name a few) are all convinced that this bias is one of the chief troubles in the situation. In these circumstances it appears to me dangerous to leave the conduct of affairs during the next two or three critical months unchecked in the hands of Lord Passfield and his Colonial Office advisors … The High Commissioner and the Colonial Office between them have shown bad judgment and made serious blunders in the last few months which have needlessly increased the difficulties of the Government. The chief amongst them was the suspension of immigration certificates and the terms of the recent White Paper … It is absurd that Lord Passfield should accept the High Commissioner's charges against the Jews and never have them thoroughly thrashed out in conference with the Jews.' MM papers, 9/1/66. Malcolm MacDonald to the Prime Minister, 29 July 1930.

officials and their replies to MacDonald. Following the publication of the
Passfield White Paper in October 1930, Weizmann and the Jewish Agency
had officially broken off relations with the government in protest. It was
MacDonald junior who played the central role in re-establishing relations
between the two parties, and it was he who unofficially facilitated the
creation of a cabinet subcommittee on 6 November 1930, consisting of
government officials, headed by Arthur Henderson, the Foreign Secretary,
and Jewish Agency officials, whose task was 'to consider the situation in
Palestine arising out of the publication of the White Paper ... and to
discuss a letter to be sent to Dr Weizmann'.[73]

This Anglo-Zionist committee met six times between December
1930 and the beginning of February 1931. Discussions were frank and
robust as the Zionist representatives insisted on trawling through every
word, phrase and paragraph of the 'offending' White Paper. In particular, the latter's proposals on future immigration and land policy were
taken to task in minute detail, which profoundly disconcerted Colonial
Office officials who were unused to having their carefully crafted ordinances questioned by European-trained, multilingual Zionist lawyers
who were equally gifted as they were in the mastery of legal phraseol-
ogy. Moreover, throughout all these discussions there was no mention
of Palestinian Arab aspirations or their political rights and no discussion
of the Correspondence, or of other British wartime pledges, apart from
the Balfour Declaration.

Weizmann asked the Jewish Agency in Palestine not to communicate
with the High Commissioner, Sir John Chancellor, concerning the
White Paper: he wanted the decision-making process in Palestine to be
subject to effective Jewish pressures in London, where Chancellor's views
could be contained, if not ignored. Weizmann's strategy succeeded:
Chancellor was outmanoeuvred.[74] The Prime Minister's lengthy letter to
Dr Weizmann, which emerged at the end of this joint enterprise, effectively reversed the White Paper's anti-Zionist proposals.[75] For Weizmann,

---

73 MM Papers, 9/8/60. MacDonald wrote later that it was 'largely as a result of my
intervention that developments started which ended in Webb [Colonial Secretary]
being persuaded to modify his policy ... [without my intervention] there would not
have been a Henderson committee of enquiry'. MM Papers, 9/12/3; 9/12/12.
74 See Stein, *The Land Question*, 125.
75 For the genesis of this extraordinarily detailed letter, see the fifty-six-page
'Summary of Discussions leading to the Prime Minister's letter of 13 February 1931
to Dr Weizmann' by L.B. Namier. MM Papers, 9/8/2.

it was an 'authoritative interpretation' of the White Paper, and to the Zionists' profound satisfaction the Prime Minister himself read it before the Commons on 13 February 1931. A delighted Weizmann penned a note to Malcolm MacDonald: 'Now that the letter is published, I thank you once more for everything. The debris are cleared away – thanks to you chiefly.'[76]

Weizmann asked MacDonald to request that his father instruct the High Commissioner in Palestine 'to meet us in a less negative spirit than they have done hitherto and that they should give us the same credit for honest intentions which the cabinet and yourself have given us'.[77] The Zionist leader was not averse to offering his suggestions to anyone, whatever their status, in pursuit of his objective. MacDonald wrote later, 'Weizmann told me (in confidence) that of course the Jews would not eventually be satisfied with Palestine alone, but would wish to expand further.'[78]

The Arabs labelled the Prime Minister's letter the 'Black Letter', regarding it as 'plain proof of the power which world Jewry could exercise in London'.[79] In essence, it confirmed that the policy of the Palestine Mandate was to continue to support Jewish immigration, and it clearly negated most of the White Paper's proposals, among them the paper's criticism of the exclusionary employment practice of the Histadrut (the General Federation of Labour), on which MacDonald wrote, 'The principle of preferential and, indeed, exclusive employment of Jewish labour by Jewish organisations is a principle which the Jewish Agency are entitled to affirm.'[80]

---

76 MM Papers 9/6/34. Weizmann to Malcolm MacDonald, 14 February 1931. Weizmann considered the word 'debris' a plural.

77 MM Papers 9/6/34. Weizmann to Malcolm MacDonald, 14 February 1931.

78 MM Papers, 9/11/1.

79 Cited in *A Survey of Palestine. Prepared in December 1945 and January 1946 for the Information of the Anglo-American Committee of Inquiry*, vol. I, 29. For a copy of the letter, see W. Laqueur, *The Israel/Arab Reader: A Documentary History of the Middle East Conflict* (London, 1969), 50–56.

80 Hansard, Commons, 13 February 1931, vol. 248, cc751–757. The *Yishuv*'s Histadrut was not a conventional trade union. It became the main state-building institution to which the World Zionist Organisation channelled funds. With the latter's patronage, it developed a range of institutions to assist the absorption of Jewish labour, including labour exchanges, banks, cooperatives, a construction company and healthcare. See Kelemen, *The British Left and Zionism*, 23.

According to Kenneth Stein, the Zionists meticulously expunged from the White Paper all implications that were potentially dangerous to their aspirations and were able 'to manipulate HMG into a focus less detrimental to the evolution of the Jewish national home and yet provide HMG with the evidence it desired to show for its concern for the Palestinian Arab fellaheen'.[81] Weizmann commented later that 'It was under MacDonald's letter to me that the change came about in the Government's attitude and in the attitude of the Palestine administration which enabled us to make the magnificent gains of the ensuing years.'[82]

In the autumn of 1931, the government replaced the High Commissioner, Sir John Chancellor, who had shown himself to be distinctly unenthusiastic about the Zionist project, with General Arthur Wauchope, who was more sympathetic to Zionist aspirations. The following January, the new High Commissioner did, nevertheless, invite George Antonius, a former senior Mandate official, to draft a constitutional proposal, which he submitted on 22 March. It was hardly radical: a legislative council of thirty-two members (nineteen popularly elected, six nominated by the High Commissioner and seven selected from the Executive Council). It would have the power to veto any laws introduced by the government and to enact legislation, subject to the High Commissioner's approval – less an advisory body to an unchecked executive and more a legislature helping to balance power.

Nevertheless, Wauchope's political advisors thought the proposal too liberal and Antonius was informed that the government intended to preclude the proposed council 'from debating any matter which conflicted with the Mandate'. When protests broke out in Jaffa, in October 1933, against the constitutional 'status quo' and increasing Jewish immigration, twenty-two demonstrators and a policeman were killed, and the nominal leader of the national movement, the octogenarian Musa Kazim Pasha al-Husseini, was beaten to the ground by baton-wielding British security forces. The High Commissioner nevertheless remained confident that the situation was quite manageable.[83] At the end of 1935, Antonius, witnessing the rising frustration of the

81 Stein, *The Land Question*, 128.
82 Weizmann, *Trial and Error*, 415.
83 See Khalidi, *The Iron Cage*, 88.

Palestinians, again urged Wauchope to introduce a scheme 'providing for an elected legislature'. Antonius's advice, which Wauchope passed on to London, remained unheeded.[84] The British government were thus fully briefed concerning the Palestinians' constitutional demands, but the bureaucratic, crown-colony-style administration in Palestine simply did not allow for constitutional change: it neither encouraged participation nor tolerated dissent.

Wauchope remained in Palestine until 1938, during which time the world witnessed the Great Depression, the coming to power of the virulently anti-Semitic National Socialist regime in Germany in January 1933 and the invasion of Abyssinia by Mussolini in October 1935. More than a decade earlier, Hitler had made his ideology, if not his intentions, clear in *Mein Kampf*; to him, Jewish culture was a spiritual pestilence, worse than the Black Death: 'In defending myself against the Jew, I am fighting for the work of the Lord.'[85] In January 1934, Poland had signed a non-aggression pact with Germany, and in September 1935 the Nuremberg Laws were passed, to protect the purity of the Aryan race. Marriage and sexual relations between Jew and German were prohibited, and Jews were stripped of citizenship and most rights and banned from employment as lawyer, doctor or journalist.[86]

Palestine thus witnessed an increasing flow of Jewish immigrants, fleeing from increasingly intolerable conditions in Germany and, to a lesser extent, in Poland and Rumania. Until the United States government imposed the quota system for immigrants in 1924, America had been the preferred destination of most Jews emigrating from Europe. However, Great Britain, the United States and most other countries refused to relax their immigration restrictions, effectively shutting their doors, and in many cases Jewish refugees had no other choice but to seek refuge in Palestine. Around 10,000 immigrants arrived in 1932; 30,000 in 1933; 42,000 in 1934 and nearly 62,000 in 1935.[87] In fact, the number of Jews who entered Palestine in 1935 was greater than the entire Jewish population of Palestine in 1917. Sometime in 1935, Ben-Gurion noted

---

84 See Susan Silsby Boyle, *Betrayal of Palestine. The Story of George Antonius* (London, 2001), 197–204.

85 Adolf Hitler, *My Struggle* [*Mein Kampf*] (New York, 1925), 60.

86 Philippe Sands, *East West Street* (London, 2016), 84.

87 Morris, *Righteous Victims*, 122.

in his diary, 'immigration at the rate of 60,000 a year means a Jewish State in all Palestine.'[88] Palestinian Arabs, of course, did not view the increasing wave of immigrants as refugees fleeing persecution, but as 'foreigners' – Germans, Poles, Russians, Ukrainians and others – who were attempting to take over their country.

According to the eminent Anglo-Lebanese scholar Albert Hourani, a new Jewish nation was emerging in Palestine in the 1930s, one that was

> consciously different from that on which it had turned its back by emigration, living through the medium of the Hebrew language, which had been revived as a language of ordinary life, separated from the Arab population by differences of culture and social customs, by the aspiration to create something totally Jewish, and by growing anxiety for the fate of the Jews in Europe, and looking to England to defend its interests until it was able to maintain itself.[89]

Slaying the Palestine Constitution

Following the MacDonald 'explanatory' letter episode, it was a further five years before Palestine was again the focus of attention in Parliament. During February and March 1936, there were three significant debates concerning the future political development of Palestine, focused almost exclusively on the controversial proposal of the government to establish a representative, democratic legislative council in Palestine (26 February, Lords; 5 March, Lords; 24 March, Commons). At the end of the latter debate, led by the devoted Zionist and heir to the chinaware fortune, Colonel Josiah Wedgwood,[90] and vigorously supported by Churchill and similar-minded members, the House rejected the government's proposal. In a letter to his daughter Camilla at the end of March, an enthusiastic Wedgwood wrote, 'I have had a successful week ... actually slain the Palestine constitution. I got Churchill and Chamberlain and Amery and Sinclair all to speak, and they did, leaving the Rt. Hon.

---

88 Cited in Shabtai Teveth, *Ben-Gurion and the Palestine Arabs: From Peace to War* (New York, 1985), 166–168. See also Khalidi, *The Hundred Years' War on Palestine*, 41.
89 Albert Hourani, *A History of the Arab Peoples* (London, 1991), 324.
90 Chairman of the Parliamentary Committee on Palestine.

J.H. Dress-shirt [Thomas] in tears.'[91] James Henry Thomas, National Labour Secretary of State for the Colonies (1935–1936), was a trade union leader of humble origins. Known as a natty dresser, he had been caricatured by the popular political cartoonist David Low as 'Lord Dress Suit'. Once again, the supporters of the Jewish national home project in the House of Commons had managed to put on hold the establishment in Palestine of any modicum of self-governing institutions.

In December 1936, Lord Lloyd, former High Commissioner in Egypt (1925–1929), and about to pay a fact-finding visit to Cairo, asked Sir Robert Vansittart (Permanent Under-Secretary of State for Foreign Affairs, 1930–1938) to be shown the Correspondence privately. This request elicited a memo from George W. Rendel, Monteagle's successor as Head of the Eastern Department, that the Foreign Office had made a rule not to show the Correspondence to former government officials, however eminent, because it was open to every sort of misconstruction, unless it was studied as a whole and in the light of a number of other confidential documents.[92] Rendel had joined the Diplomatic Service before the First World War, and by 1937 was convinced that 'if our present policy is continued, the Arabs of Palestine will ultimately become a small minority in a Jewish State.'[93] Rendel sent a forthright and revealing memorandum to Sir Lancelot Oliphant (Assistant Under-Secretary of State), written by Owen G.R. Williams, a junior Colonial Office official, which included:

> The main reasons why the correspondence should not be published are … (i) the correspondence is inconclusive and incomplete and that <u>certain crucial phrases admit of an interpretation</u> different from that put upon them by HMG and <u>entirely favourable to the Arab contention that</u>

---

91 C.V. Wedgwood, *The Last of the Radicals: The Life of Josiah Clement Wedgwood MP.* (London, 1951), 191. Josiah Wedgwood served as an officer at Gallipoli and there had become an admirer of Joseph Trumpeldor and the Zion Mule Corps; Trumpeldor, an early modern Zionist activist, had helped to found the corps, a unit of Jewish soldiers that served with the British Army in the First World War. Wedgwood met Weizmann first at a Lloyd George breakfast sometime in 1916. The historian Dame Cicely Veronica Wedgwood was Josiah Wedgwood's niece.

92 FO 371/20786, 202. Rendel to Oliphant, 22 December 1936.

93 FO 371/20805, 231. Rendel to Oliphant, 12 April 1937. In his autobiography, published twenty years later, he was still of the opinion that Palestine had been the subject of 'conflicting promises'. Rendel, *The Sword and the Olive*, 119.

Palestine should have been included in the area set aside for an independent Arab State and (ii) that the correspondence contains encouragement
of the Sherif to rebel against the Sultan Khalif of Constantinople and to
seek the Khalifate for himself with British assistance; publication of this
fact might still incense Moslem opinion in India and elsewhere which
would prove embarrassing to HMG.[94]

Not much equivocation there. As mentioned previously, Kitchener's
pre-war letter to Emir Abdullah and McMahon's first letter to the Sharif
of 30 August 1915 had dangled the prospect of British support for a
Sharifian caliphate: 'We now declare once more that the Government of
Great Britain would welcome the reversion of the caliphate to a true
Arab born of the blessed stock of the prophet.'[95] But Grey had later
instructed McMahon to not mention the question again in further
correspondence with the Sharif, and all postwar governments were
genuinely fearful that publication of the Correspondence would be
potentially embarrassing, and even, as Williams wrote, 'incense Moslem
opinion in India'.

Rattling the Iron Cage

The rejection by Parliament in the spring of 1936 of any constitutional
reform in Palestine was a significant factor in the outbreak of the Arab
Revolt. In fact, the increasing political restlessness of the country had
been reflected in the rapid formation of five new Palestinian political
parties during the period from 1932 to 1935. According to Walid
Khalidi,

a general consensus was emerging that political and diplomatic efforts
were ineffective and only an armed rebellion directed at Britain could
yield results. An early expression of this view led to the death in action
against the British, in November 1935, of a Muslim preacher and
reformer from Haifa named Izz al-Din al-Qassam, together with his

---

94 FO 371/20786, 203. Owen G.R. Williams' memorandum, December 1936.
Underlined by the author.
95 McMahon to Sharif Hussein, 30 August 1915. See Antonius, *Awakening*, 416.

comrades. Theirs was the first Palestinian guerrilla operation, and al-Qassam and his comrades became national martyrs overnight.[96]

Characteristically, the British dismissed al-Qassam as a charlatan and his followers as fanatics. Blinded by their warped understanding of Arabs, 'British officials misjudged the grassroots level of discontent into which al-Qassam had tapped.' Instead, they located the roots of Arab dissent in 'the notables' struggle for power', Arab landowners' exploitation of Arab peasants, and the opportunistic propaganda of Italy and Germany's fascist governments that besmirched the Empire's good name.[97]

The revolt had two main phases. The first lasted from May 1936 to July 1937, with a general strike that continued for the first six months of that period. In November 1935, Palestinians had watched closely events in Egypt, where anti-British demonstrations and riots had broken out; in Syria a general strike had begun in January 1936. Both movements had forced the British and French governments into a fresh round of negotiations with nationalist leaders. But concerning Palestine, the UK government appeared quite inflexible. The conclusion drawn by Palestinians was clear: in the battle for independence there was no alternative open to them other than a policy of violent confrontation.

Unrest spread to the countryside, where villagers took up arms and engaged the British security and military forces in open guerrilla warfare. The second phase of the rebellion lasted from July 1937 to the summer of 1939. Although the rebels probably never numbered more than five thousand, the bulk of the rural population supported them, and by summer 1938 much of the countryside and several major towns were in their hands. Arab casualties amounted to about five thousand killed and fifteen thousand wounded. Government services came to a virtual halt, and even portions of Jerusalem fell under rebel control.

The British Empire could not allow itself even the appearance of capitulating to popular revolt: to do so would have set a dangerous precedent in a tenuous world of imperial rule. Thus, the British adopted extreme counter-insurgency measures, including house

96 Khalidi, *Before Their Diaspora*, 87.
97 See Elkins, *Legacy of Violence*, 194, 200.

searches without warrants, night raids, preventive detention and the death penalty for possession of arms. They imposed collective punishment on towns and villages by blowing up entire residential quarters, closing schools, levying fines in kind or cash, and billeting troops at the expense of the residents. Some rebel suspects never made it as far as the courts because security forces shot them in situ, or executed them or beat them to death at Army camps or in police cells. 'Take him for a ride', as a police CID sergeant euphemistically put it when he instructed his men to assassinate a suspect.[98] According to Caroline Elkins:

> [Sometimes] during village raids, Arabs were counted off, and every fifteenth man was shot dead; women and children were killed in their sleep ... The RAF was responsible for nearly half the enemy kills during the Arab revolt; one reconnaissance alone wiped out nearly 130 Arab rebels; on other occasions, bagging a score or more was typical.[99]

On 16 June 1936, British forces blew up between 220 and 240 buildings in Jaffa – officially to improve health and sanitation, though primarily to allow military access and control. Six thousand Arabs were rendered homeless by this single act of destruction. When the British Chief Justice of Palestine, Sir Michael McDonnell (actually Irish and Roman Catholic), condemned his own government's actions, he was sacked.[100]

---

98 Matthew Hughes, *Britain's Pacification of Palestine* (Cambridge, 2019), 64–65.

99 Elkins, *Legacy of Violence*, 224, 225, 227.

100 Such collective punishments, conducted without due process, were given legal standing by a series of Emergency (Defence) Regulations passed by British authorities to combat the revolt. An estimated two thousand houses were destroyed between 1936 and 1940. See Eugene Rogan, *The Arabs. A History* (London, 2009), 258–259. The regulations were renewed in 1945, then revoked by the British as the Mandate ended. However, the newly formed Israeli State claimed that as this decision had not been published in the *Palestine Gazette* such laws were still valid. Egypt and Jordan similarly kept British laws as they were so useful for repression in Gaza and the West Bank. The Israelis layered on their own laws, such as the 'Israeli Law and Administration Ordinance of 1948', to British legislation. See Hughes, *Britain's Pacification of Palestine*, 350.

In 1938, fifty-four Palestinians were executed by hanging; fifty-five more in 1939.[101]

In a recent excellent book on Britain's suppression of the Arab Revolt, the military historian Matthew Hughes writes:

> British forces on the ground conspired with the Jews to defeat the rebels, a collaboration that suited both sides at the time. The British had been arming Jewish settlements since the early 1920s through the provision of sealed armouries that Jews supplemented with secret slick weapons caches; after 1936, the British expanded cooperation, jointly gathered intelligence with Jewish operatives, and they trained, paid for, and equipped more Jewish auxiliary police and paramilitary units that directed even more violence towards Palestinians.[102]

After the signing of the Munich Agreement in September 1938 – by Chamberlain, Hitler, Mussolini and Daladier, the French Premier, handing the Sudetenland over to Germany in the name of peace – the British were free to send more troops and police to Palestine. Once 25,000 soldiers were engaged, the inevitable outcome was secured. General Bernard Montgomery, later of El Alamein fame, banned newspaper reporters from his area of northern Palestine so that his soldiers could carry on their repressive work without inhibition. Not all security forces used excessive violence, but torture, including 'waterboarding', took place in dedicated police-run centres.[103] All forms of Arab political organisation were broken up. By the summer of 1939, as Europe edged towards war, British military force prevailed. Many of the Palestinian leadership had either been executed, imprisoned or deported. *Plus ça change.*

The initial outbreak of violence in May 1936 led, in time-honoured British fashion, to the establishment of a royal commission, charged with investigating the causes of unrest and alleged grievances 'either of Arabs or of Jews'. Chaired by Lord Robert Peel, who had served in the early 1920s as Secretary of State for India, the commission also included

---

101 See Khalidi, *Before Their Diaspora*, 189–191. An oft-forgotten aspect of politically focused historiography is the existence and the suffering of the thousands of widows and children rendered homeless and poverty-stricken during such episodes in history. The Arab Revolt (1936–1939) is a case in point.

102 Hughes, *Britain's Pacification of Palestine*, 29.

103 Hughes, *Britain's Pacification of Palestine*, 316, 318.

212 POLICY OF DECEIT

two senior colonial officials: Laurie Hammond, who had served as Governor of Assam in India in the late 1920s, and Morris Carter, who had served as Governor of Tanganyika Territory in East Africa in the early 1920s and Chairman of the Kenya Land Commission from 1932 to 1933. The committee's legal expert was Harold Morris, then President of the Industrial Court in London, and its Middle East expert Horace Rumbold, a former diplomat who had served in Cairo and Tehran. The academic on the commission was Reginald Coupland, Beit Professor of Colonial History at Oxford.

Commissions of inquiry, of course, were the standard reflex reaction of British governments to troubles of this kind throughout the Empire, as well as in Palestine. They were an imperial device, ostensibly of conflict resolution, but in reality more a pacification ploy to disperse and deflect 'troubles in the colonies' back to the peaceful realm of reasonable conversations, all the while enabling the maintenance of full colonial control. The fact that the commission would not directly address the terms of the Mandate proved to the Palestinian Arabs that once again the government were not acting in good faith. Hussein Fakhri Khalidi, Mayor of Jerusalem at the time, recorded the sense of futility that such initiatives inspired:

These commissions spend weeks and months, researching and digging up published reports, issued recommendations, government announcements and its white papers. None of the [Commission] recommendations that favoured the interests of the Arabs were implemented.[104]

The Zionists were initially hostile to the establishment of a royal commission. Weizmann in particular wanted no repetition of the breakdown of Anglo-Zionist relations which had followed the Shaw Commission of 1930. 'What', Weizmann asked Conservative Prime Minister Stanley Baldwin, 'was the commission going to investigate?' thereby implying that there was no necessity for any investigation, only a need to subdue the riots.[105] On 14 June 1936, Weizmann, his wife, Vera, and Ben-Gurion drove to the small village of Churt, in Surrey,

104 Allen, *A History of False Hope*, 95–96.
105 Minutes of an interview between Baldwin and Weizmann, 19 May 1936. Weizmann Archives, Rehovot. Cited in Rose, *The Gentile Zionists*, 125.

and the home of David Lloyd George, who had maintained a friendship with Weizmann. 'The old man', reported Ben-Gurion in his diary, 'is entirely gray, but his face is full of life. He received us most amicably … [He told us] "You don't need sympathy – you need courage, action and driving power … the Arabs are afraid Palestine will become a Hebrew state – Well, *it will* be a Hebrew state."'[106]

At the end of July, Colonial Secretary Ormsby-Gore, a long-term Zionist supporter, found himself the subject of severe criticism when in Parliament he announced that martial law had not been imposed, described the Royal Commission's very balanced terms of reference and appeared to waver on the question of an amnesty for some rebel leaders. Weizmann accused him of abdicating to the Mufti, declared that Sir Michael McDonnell was 'notoriously pro-Arab and anti-Semitic', and criticised the attempts of the Iraqi Prime Minister, General Nuri al-Said, to liaise between the government and the Palestine Arabs, efforts which had not been officially rejected by the government. Ormsby-Gore said little in reply, except that the commission would not go to Palestine until a semblance of peace had been restored to the country.[107] Nevertheless, the Zionists' tactics, but not their convictions, soon changed and they cooperated fully with the commission during its hearings.

On 1 September, the concerned and clearly irritated Colonial Secretary candidly revealed his thinking in a handwritten note to the High Commissioner concerning what he regarded as the influence of world Jewry on Britain's Palestine policy:

> Yesterday I had a very unpleasant conversation with Weizmann and Ben Gurion and additionally letters and telegrams kept flooding in from General Smuts, Lloyd George and leading American individuals, in which I was accused of wanting to betray the Jewish people, denigrate the British reputation even further, and deliver to murder and homicide. Last Sunday, Jewish demonstrations took place at different locations of the country, and our ambassador in Warsaw sends notice by telegram that he is having a most difficult time there …

---

106 Shabtai Teveth, *Ben-Gurion. The Burning Ground, 1886–1948* (Boston, 1987), 528.
107 See FO 371/23223, 18–31.

It could be true that in 1935 we let in too many Jews, maybe we did not do enough to protect the Arab farming community from losing their land and home. We may have given too little consideration to the fact that some Arabs fear being ruled by the Jews in the future. But I shall never admit that the principles of our policy were wrong. I am deeply suspicious of the Mufti and all his undertakings. I believe him to be not only anti-Jewish, but also anti-British, and a rascal.

If we try to buy peace now on the Nuri basis, we are bound to have the whole world of Jewry against us everywhere, and their sympathisers in all parties here ... firstly, British authority in Palestine has to be re-established. For that reason, it is not possible to meet half-way with the Arabs.[108]

Before the commission left London, the Arab Higher Committee, comprising all Palestinian political parties, made it clear that they would not give any testimony unless there was a suspension of Jewish immigration, a freeze on land sales to Jewish colonists, and the establishment of a legislative assembly. None of these demands was accepted.

The commission arrived in Palestine on 11 November 1936. In Jerusalem, at a public session on 25 November, Weizmann eloquently and movingly described the Zionist case to the commissioners, followed, over the next six weeks, by forty other Zionist witnesses and a dozen British officials. Some forty-seven witness sessions were held in secret, where those giving testimony were generally more candid. Weizmann, the 'star' Zionist witness, appeared five times, four of which were secret sessions. The transcripts of the public testimony were published soon afterward, but, in similar fashion to the Palin Report of 1920 (which was never officially published), the secret testimony transcripts remained classified and were only released by the UK's National Archives in March 2017, eighty years later.[109] During one such secret session, the Zionist leader insisted that Jews had no desire to dominate Palestine or to turn Arabs into hewers of wood and drawers of water. Asked three

---

108 FO 371/23233, 18–31. Ormsby-Gore to Wauchope, 1 September 1936.
109 The secret testimony is located in FO 492/19. It consists of 531 pages of densely typewritten text – a transcript of the 'real-time dialogue' of secret proceedings – and, liberated from public scrutiny, is considerably more vivid and revealing of the different parties' positions than the public testimony.

times if the Zionists aimed at a Jewish state, Weizmann replied that they did not. He instead proposed a system of parity, with equal representation for Arabs and Jews regardless of which were a majority, now or later.[110] At a further secret session, the British government official responsible for 'Migration and Statistics', Eric Mills, candidly informed the commissioners that it was the Jewish Agency, not the British government, that determined who received an immigration permit, and furthermore the British government 'was not the colonising power here, the Jewish people are the colonising power and in order to facilitate immigration you must use such organs as they have created for the purpose of colonising'.[111]

The Arab leaders boycotted the commission for all but its last few days in Palestine, when they finally agreed to participate. Speaking through a translator, the Mufti called for the abrogation of the Mandate, the end of Jewish immigration and land sales, and the sovereignty of Palestine transferred to an Arab body. Akram Zu'aytir, a lawyer, journalist and an organiser of the general strike, emphasised that

> The Palestinian Arab natural right to independence exists regardless of the Mandate character, or British promises, or President Wilson. Our right to freedom is the same as our right to life, based on our humanity, dignity, self-respect … We've spent eighteen years protesting, screaming, being in pain, writing reports, sending delegations, and meeting with Commissions of Inquiry. But it has all been without results. The government in this country ignores our rights, so the Arab has despaired of justice … that despair has led them to revolution.[112]

His plea fell on deaf ears. The commissioners appeared to be equally unimpressed with the few other Arab leaders who appeared before them. However, the final Arab advocate to appear was George Antonius,

---

110 See Oren Kessler, 'Mandate100 "A Clean Cut" for Palestine: The Peel Commission Reexamined', *fathom*, fathomjournal.org/mandate100-a-clean-cut-for-palestine-the-peel-commission-reexamined (accessed 13 December 2021).

111 Laila Parsons, 'The Secret Testimony of the Peel Commission (Part I): Underbelly of Empire', *Journal of Palestine Studies*, vol. 49, no. 1 (2019).

112 Akram Zu'aytir, *Al-Haraka al-Wataniyya al-Filastiniyya, 1935–1939: Yowmiyat Akram Zu'aytir* [The Palestinian National Movement: Diaries of Akram Zu'aytir] (Beirut, 1992), 272. Cited in Allen, *A History of False Hope*, 102.

Lebanon-born, Egypt-raised and Cambridge-educated, whose two-hour-long statement in impeccable English was, by any standards, very impressive: a factual, measured, morally laced call for natural justice.

The Jewish Agency's Political Department bugged the commission's secret sessions, placing tiny microphones in the meeting room's light fixtures. Ben-Gurion, concerned that Weizmann's approach was too accommodating to the British, particularly over the issue of immigration into Palestine, wanted to know exactly what Weizmann, as well as Sir Arthur Wauchope, was saying to the commission's members. Shabtai Teveth, Ben-Gurion's biographer, does not clarify whether Weizmann knew he was being recorded.[113] There appears to be no evidence in the official records that the commissioners or indeed the High Commissioner knew of this particular Jewish Agency tactic. Following the session on 8 January 1937, when partition was mooted for the first time, Weizmann told his Private Secretary that 'the long toil of his life was at last crowned with success. The Jewish State was at hand.'[114]

As mentioned previously, back in London in spring 1937, Lloyd George described to the commissioners what his government's pro-Zionist intentions for Palestine had been in 1917. In similar vein, Churchill told the commissioners that although the government had not committed itself in 1917 to making Palestine into a Jewish state, it certainly *had* committed itself 'to the idea that someday, somehow, far off in the future, subject to justice and economic convenience, there might be a great Jewish State there, numbered by millions, far exceeding the present inhabitants of the country'.[115]

---

113 Teveth, *Ben-Gurion. The Burning Ground*, 573–574. The Jewish Agency also bugged conversations in Hajj Amin's residence. The British even uncovered a Jewish operation tapping the central telephone switchboard. See Hughes, *Britain's Pacification of Palestine*, 254.

114 Sykes, *Crossroads*, 165. However, according to Teveth, 'There seems to be more legend than facts in these quotes ... Weizmann's life work had not been devoted to any partition-based solution.' Teveth, *Ben-Gurion. The Burning Ground*, 587.

115 FO 492/19. Churchill's Secret Testimony, 12 March 1937. Churchill was also asked whether, at the time he wrote the 1922 White Paper, when the Jewish population was 80,000, 'anyone envisaged the idea of there being by 1936, 400,000 Jews there'. Churchill said, 'Yes, certainly, I hoped for it.' When questioned about Britain's obligations to both sides, he replied that the Balfour Declaration 'is the prime and dominating pledge upon which Britain must act ... all questions of self-government in Palestine are subordinate to its discharge'.

Churchill's secret testimony is often quoted for its reference to the Palestinians as being like 'the dog in the manger' who did not have 'the final right to the manger, even though he may have lain there for a very long time'. 'The great hordes of Islam', he stated, 'had smashed [Palestine] up, turning it into a desert ... Where the Arab goes, it is often desert.'[116] Such comments epitomised in many ways the British-Empire-centred, racist mentality of the mid 1930s. Nearly a century later, that mentality has not entirely disappeared from Western political discourse, nor from Western historiography.

On 5 May 1937, Professor Reginald Coupland visited Oliphant at the Foreign Office and explained that when the commission was in Palestine the Arab witnesses had based the whole of their case upon the pledge, which according to their interpretation McMahon had given to King Hussein, that Palestine would be included in the territory to be formed into an independent Arab state or states should the Ottoman Empire be defeated. The whole of this Correspondence was available to the Arab leaders who had communicated it to the commission, and it had also been published in the Arabic press of Palestine. There was, therefore, no question of regarding it as being in any way secret or confidential. The commission, currently drafting the report, did not feel called upon to decide whether the Correspondence contained a pledge giving Palestine to the Arabs, and they did not intend to do so. Their report would merely record the fact that the government had consistently denied that the pledge covered Palestine and add an expression of regret that it had not been possible to explain this clearly to King Hussein at the time. The commission also wanted to mention the secret Anglo-French negotiations before the Correspondence, to help explain what McMahon had in mind when he wrote about Britain's ally France: a brief account of those negotiations would furnish strong support for the interpretation given by the government of the pledge. In conclusion, the professor emphasised that the commission felt that their report would be deprived of much of its authority and value if they were

---

116 FO 492/19. Churchill added that 'I do not admit, for instance, that a great wrong has been done to the Red Indians of America, or the black people of Australia. I do not admit that a wrong has been done to those people by the fact that a stronger race, a higher grade race, or at any rate, a more worldly wise race, to put it that way, has come in and taken their place. I do not admit it.' See also Nicholas Bethell, *The Palestine Triangle. The Struggle between the British, the Jews and the Arabs, 1935–48* (London, 1979), 28.

merely to describe the Correspondence in general terms and not to quote it.[117]

Writing in 1938 in *The Arab Awakening*, George Antonius, without access to the official records, expressed his puzzlement as to why in their report the commissioners examined the Balfour Declaration thoroughly, but not the Correspondence or other wartime pledges, which they stated, 'fell outside their terms of reference'.[118] This 'inequality' of examination by the commissioners 'vitiated the Report's conclusions' because it led them to accept the argument that Zionist and Arab rights in Palestine stood on an equal footing, anathema to all Arabs, who regarded the Zionist claim to Palestine as 'historically invalid and, as far as natural rights go, fictitious'.[119] In fact, the official records reveal that the commissioners did not pronounce on the Correspondence because they were divided on the issue, and the government were keen to produce a unanimous report. Professor Coupland indicated to Oliphant that

> upon this point they would be unlikely to prove unanimous … some [Commissioners] at least consider that neither King Hussein nor any intelligent reader could be blamed for supposing that the wording of the pledge contained nothing to show that Palestine was not to be included in the area of Arab independence.[120]

Coupland's conversation elicited a typed memorandum from the Foreign Secretary, Anthony Eden, to the cabinet, entitled 'Desire of

117 FO 371/20806, E2525, 140.

118 'We think it sufficient for the purpose of this Report to state that the British Government have never accepted the Arab case.' Peel Report, ch. II, 20, paragraph 8. In the report, the commissioners' comments on the Balfour Declaration included 'Lord Robert Cecil in 1917, Sir Herbert Samuel in 1919, and Mr. Winston Churchill in 1920 spoke or wrote in terms that could only mean that they contemplated the eventual establishment of a Jewish State. Leading British newspapers were equally explicit in their comments on the Declaration.' Peel Report, ch. II, 25.

119 Antonius, *Awakening*, 401–402. Antonius stated that the commissioners' misconception, that Zionists and Arabs had an equal claim to Palestine, led them to recommend a solution based on the validity of the Balfour Declaration, i.e. to divide the country between the two parties.

120 FO 371/20806, E2525, 137. 'Record of an interview between Professor Coupland and Sir L. Oliphant on 5 May, 1937'.

Royal Commission on Palestine to quote extracts from the McMahon-Hussein correspondence in their Report', which included:

> The principal reasons for the reluctance of His Majesty's Government to agree to official publication have been:—
>
> (a) The correspondence is incomplete and inconclusive and in order to make clear Sir H. McMahon's pledge and to justify HMG's interpretation of its meaning, it would be necessary to offer a great many additional explanations; furthermore any such discussion would revive old controversies which were better forgotten.
>
> (b) The correspondence, and the Kitchener-Abdullah correspondence also, shows that His Majesty's Government suggested to King Hussein that he might assume the Caliphate in place of the Ottoman Sultan, and the fact that such a suggestion was made might cause resentment among Indian Moslems. (This is a reason which few of those who press for publication are likely to have guessed and it would, of course, be impossible to give it were the question of why publication had previously been withheld ever to be pressed in the future) ...
>
> (c) The Arab leaders appear to have the whole of the correspondence in their possession, have based the whole of their case upon it, and that the meaning of the correspondence has of itself, without any official publication having taken place, become a matter of acute controversy ...
>
> The extracts which the Royal Commission propose to quote do not include the passages related to the Caliphate. On the other hand, the quotation of these passages would probably lead to a demand, which it would be difficult for His Majesty's Government to withstand, for the official publication of the whole correspondence ...
>
> [Nevertheless], I suggest that HMG should agree to the publication in the Report of the Royal Commission of any extracts from the correspondence that the Commission may desire, and should decide to accede without delay to any subsequent [Parliamentary] demand that may be made for full official publication.[121]

---

121 FO 371/20806/147. Memo by the Secretary of State (the Rt. Hon. Anthony Eden) for the cabinet, CP 149 (37), 27 May 1937. See also FO 371/20806, 140–155.

On 14 June 1937, Herbert Lacy Baggallay, First Secretary at the Foreign Office, requested that Cairo send to London their Arabic copies of the Kitchener–Abdullah Correspondence and the McMahon–Hussein Correspondence, in case it was decided to publish them as a White Paper. Cairo replied two days later that it could not find any trace of the Kitchener–Abdullah Correspondence, and that it only had Arabic texts of four letters of McMahon to Sharif Hussein, namely those of 30 August, 24 October and 14 December 1915, and of 10 March 1916. Neither was there any trace of the original Arabic texts of the Correspondence from the Sharif, but 'we do have literal translations in English.' Rendel contacted Storrs, now retired, who could shed no light on the matter and wanted nothing to do with the investigation. The Foreign Office thus assumed that the Kitchener–Abdullah Correspondence had been among those Arab Bureau files destroyed before they took possession of them in 1921; Storrs's own private correspondence had been burned in the Cyprus riots of 1931.[122]

In view of the possibility of a demand for publication, Edward R. Warner, a junior Colonial Office official, was tasked with collecting the texts of the various letters, and also the Kitchener–Abdullah Correspondence.[123] This presented him with a significant challenge:

> Unfortunately, the Arabic texts of the letters sent from the Residency were not always entirely accurate renderings of the English drafts on which they were based. To make matters worse, copies of these letters as sent in Arabic were not always retained by the Residency, or, if they were retained, were transferred at a later date, along with other documents relating to Arabian affairs, to the custody of the Arab Bureau, which was established in Cairo in 1916. The Archives of the Arab Bureau were transferred to the Foreign Office in 1921, but before this was done many files thought to be of lesser

---

122 FO 371/20807, E3284. 56. Storrs retired in 1934 on health grounds, aged fifty-three. He died in 1955.

123 FO 371/20807, E3197, 52–59. Edward R. Warner Foreign Office minute, 11 June 1937; see also FO 371/20823, E7576. Warner minute to Rendel, 24 June 1937. A copy of Warner's memorandum 'The Texts of the "Kitchener-Abdullah" and "McMahon-Hussein" Correspondence, 1914–1916: and their Sources', compiled during the autumn of 1937, can be found in FO 371/23220, E634, 261–271.

importance were destroyed, no entirely satisfactory list being kept of what was destroyed and what retained.

The position is much the same in regard to the letters received in Arabic from the Sharif Abdullah and the Sharif of Mecca. The consequence is that in some cases there are no Arabic texts extant which can definitely be said to be originals of letters received or contemporary copies of letters sent, and, in a few cases, there are no Arabic texts at all. It is not definitely known whether the Emir Abdullah of Transjordan or other family members of the late King Hussein still have in their possession any originals or copies of the Arab texts. Arabic texts have been freely published in the Middle East in the past, while partial English versions, obtained from Arab sources, were published in the 'Daily Mail' in 1923.[124]

The cabinet agreed on 29 June 1937 to the publication in the report of the Royal Commission of any extracts from the Correspondence that the Royal Commission might desire, and that they should accede without delay to any subsequent demand which might be made in Parliament for full official publication.[125]

The Royal Commission's report was published on 8 July 1937. It included a 'Palestine Partition: Provisional' map, as well as excerpts of the Correspondence, based on the English translations in the government's possession.[126] In the report, the excerpts used the word 'districts', not Vickery's '<u>vilayet</u>' translation.[127]

According to the Peel Commission, the underlying causes of the disturbances were two: the desire of the Palestinians for independence, and their 'hatred and fear of the establishment of the Jewish national home'. It recognised that a unitary state could not be created out of the contradictory obligations contained in the Balfour Declaration and went on to recommend the partition of the country into a Jewish state, a Palestinian state to be incorporated by Transjordan, and enclaves to be reserved for the Mandatory. In truth, it was

124 FO 371/23220, E634, 262–263. Foreign Office minute, dated 23 January 1939.
125 FO 371/20807, 2–4, 75.
126 For a thirty-six-page summary of the report (Cmd 5479), see FO 371/20807, 125–141. The 404-page report (including eight maps) can be found at https://palestinianmandate.files.wordpress.com/2014/04/cm-5479.pdf (accessed 31 July 2020).
127 Cmd 5479, 18.

partition with a difference. According to Norman Rose, the British-Israeli historian,

> all the vital strategic areas in Palestine were to remain in British hands under an emasculated form of the old mandate ... the Commission, in drawing up their report, seem to have been as concerned with the vulnerable nature of Britain's strategic position as with finding a viable solution to Arab-Jewish relations in Palestine.[128]

The partition scheme, according to Antonius, 'complicated the problem which it purported to solve'.[129] The Jewish State would comprise some 40 percent of Palestine at a time when their land ownership did not exceed 5.6 percent. The commission also recommended that there should be, if necessary, 'a forcible transfer of Arabs' from Arab lands allotted to the Jewish State.[130] In the proposed Jewish State there were some 225,000 Arabs; in the proposed Arab State there were only 1,250 Jews. The report was a nightmare for the Palestinians: their birthright, Palestine in its entirety, was being divided by an imperial power that proclaimed to be acting in the best interests of both communities. In fact, the commission was officially independent of the government and powerless to legislate change. Moreover, it was portrayed as impartial. But was it? At least one member was indiscreet enough himself to explain the nature of the independence he offered to the Palestinian Arabs. 'You will find', said Sir Laurie Hammond to a meeting of Jews on 5 May 1938

---

128 Rose, *The Gentile Zionists*, 87. For many British officials of the period, partition was seen as one way of reducing the costs associated with policing restive populations 'while simultaneously retaining critical imperial assets such as ports, oil pipelines, airfields, and, in the case of Palestine, symbolically loaded religious sites'. Sinanoglou, *Partitioning Palestine*, 33. Commissioner Coupland saw similarities between Palestine and Ireland, and advocated partition as a 'compromise' that 'would allow the British to keep their promise to the Jews without having to put down violent Arab uprisings and deny Palestinian self-government'. Sinanoglou, *Partitioning Palestine*, 33.
129 Antonius, *Awakening*, 402.
130 Peel Report, ch. XXII, section 10, 'Exchange of Land and Population', paragraph 43, 389–391.

Figure 8: The Peel Commission Partition Plan, 1937

that the National Home in Palestine, if you can get sufficient in that country to meet immediate requirements as a Sovereign Power, will be the first step, in my opinion, towards getting back into the rest of the country. It will take many years, but it will come.[131]

In one illuminating passage of the Peel Report, the commissioners noted that

the Jewish problem is not the least of the many problems which are disturbing international relations at this critical time and obstructing the path to peace and prosperity. If the Arabs at some sacrifice could help to solve that problem, they would earn the gratitude not of the Jews alone but of all the Western world.[132]

This phrase betrayed an anti-Semitic reluctance to open doors to Central European Jews. The British continued to act as if it were not their responsibility but that of the Palestinian Arabs to solve the Jewish Question – by giving the Jews a substantial portion of Palestine.

Delivered on 23 July, the Palestinians' statement of response to the Royal Commission's findings was as inevitable as it was unambiguous. It included:

The Arab Higher Committee bases its claim to complete independence on natural right, on the principles of the Covenant of the League of Nations and on the Promises made by the British Government to the late King Hussein. While stating that the British Government claims that Palestine was excluded from these promises, the Royal Commission has not itself confirmed this claim nor attempted to justify it.

With reference to the request of the Arab witnesses that this point should be investigated, the Commissioners have stated that they did not consider that their terms of reference required them to undertake the detailed and lengthy research among the documents of 20 years ago which would be needed for a full re-examination of this question. They

131 *Jewish Chronicle*, 13 May 1938. Cited in Barbour, *Nisi Dominus*, 181.
132 Peel Report, ch. XXIII, 395.

did not, however, hesitate to undertake a similar work with regard to the promises made to the Jews about two years later.[133]

For the Zionist leadership, partition was more a 'mixed blessing' than 'a poisoned chalice' because it was the first time the Jewish national home was officially and publicly equated with a Jewish state. According to Mearsheimer and Walt, they were sometimes willing to accept partition as a first step

> but this was a tactical manoeuvre and not their real objective. They had no intention of coexisting alongside a viable Palestinian state over the long run, as that outcome was in direct conflict with their dream of creating a Jewish state in all of Palestine.[134]

Weizmann was initially critical of the report because it potentially restricted the Zionist endeavour to take all of Palestine for the Jewish State. Ben-Gurion too publicly expressed his criticism of partition:

> The Jewish people have always regarded, and will continue to regard Palestine as a whole, as a single country which is theirs in a national sense, and will become theirs once again. No Jew will accept partition as a just and rightful solution.[135]

However, in private, he sang a different tune. On 12 July, he noted enthusiastically in his diary:

> The compulsory transfer of Arabs from the valleys of the proposed Jewish State could give us something which we never had ... We are being given an opportunity which we never dared to dream of in our

---

133 FO 371/20810, 176. The twenty-page letter was sent to the High Commissioner in Palestine, the Secretary of State for the Colonies, and the President of the Permanent Mandates Commission, Geneva. Signed by the President, Muhammad Amin Husseini, and Secretary Fuad Saba, Jerusalem, 23 July 1937.

134 John Mearsheimer and Stephen Walt, *The Israel Lobby and U.S. Foreign Policy* (New York, 2007), 93.

135 *Daily Herald*, 9 July 1937; FO 371/20808, E3966.

wildest imaginings. This is more than a state, government and sovereignty – this is national consolidation in a free homeland.[136]

According to Kenneth Stein, the interval between 1936 and 1940 was marked by 'an unmistakable Zionist conviction that a Jewish state would ultimately be established'.[137] In fact, geopolitical priorities and strategic conclusions dominated all Zionist land purchase discussions immediately prior to, during and after the outbreak of the 1936 revolt. The Jewish Agency and the Jewish National Fund did not feel morally bound to confine land purchases to within the proposed demarcation lines for the Jewish State as proposed by the Peel Report. Quite the reverse: if anything, the Zionists' thirst for land purchase increased from 1936.[138] Further, the hierarchical Arab social structure in Palestine meant the Zionists did not have to compete with an Arab middle class; instead they negotiated almost exclusively with relatively few notables and with a poor, uneducated peasantry. At the same time, the various departments of the Jewish Agency, Haganah (the paramilitary Zionist organisation which operated in Mandatory Palestine; Haganah means 'defense' in Hebrew) and the Jewish National Fund instituted a massive, detailed intelligence-gathering operation related to Palestinian society. In 1938, the British Mandatory authorities allowed the Jewish Agency to copy hundreds of thousands of official documents and practically all the official material and records existing on land registration and in tax offices relating to hundreds of Palestinian villages.[139]

By 1939, after some sixty years of colonisation, the Jewish community in Palestine owned about 6 percent of the land; however, it was definitely not a contiguous 'block' of land. Rather, the colonies formed a long, thin necklace, made up of some twenty-five separate 'beads', arranged in an N shape in the north of the country, and surrounded by Palestinian Arab-owned land – still some 94 percent of 'the ground' of Palestine. Only in the Jaffa subdistrict, which included Tel Aviv, was there a Jewish majority population; all the other fifteen subdistricts that

---

136 Morris, *Righteous Victims*, 142.
137 Stein, *The Land Question*, 221.
138 Stein, *The Land Question*, 173–211.
139 Masalha, *The Palestine Nakba*, 104.

comprised Mandatory Palestine still contained Arab majorities.[140] The Zionist colonies themselves ran north along the coast from Tel Aviv to Haifa; from there south-eastward down the Plain of Esdraelon/Marj 'ibn Amer to Beisan; and northward along the eastern finger of Galilee. Stein exaggerates when he argues that 'by 1939, and before events in Europe focused the world's attention on the Jewish condition, a geographic nucleus for a Jewish state was present in Palestine.'[141] Nevertheless, the Zionists' vision and determination to become 'masters in their own home', to incorporate all of Mandatory Palestine into a future Jewish state, remained steadfast. Ben-Gurion, the *primus inter pares* among the Zionist leaders in Palestine – and a shrewd, pragmatic, long-term planner – noted in his diary on 6 December 1937 that 'There will not be any absolute security until a Jewish state is established in Eretz-Yisrael.'[142] At a meeting of the Jewish Agency in the United States a decade later, he declared, 'We want the Land of Israel in its entirety. That was the original intention.'[143]

Partition and transfer were debated at length during the twentieth Zionist Congress, which met in Zurich in August 1937. A large minority insisted on the indivisibility of the Land of Israel and opposed the Peel Report's recommendations. However, the final vote was 299 to 160 in qualified acceptance of the Peel package. Lloyd George, then seventy-four years old, still energetic and in combative mood, joined in the public chorus of opposition to the partition plan. Writing under the headline **PALESTINE PLEDGE BROKEN BY BRITISH.** *Report Dividing Land Held Unfair to Jewish People* in the *Washington Herald* on 18 July, the former Prime Minister mentioned only one broken pledge – the Balfour Declaration.[144] St John Philby, the former Colonial Office official, Arabist and advisor to King Ibn Saud, commented in the *News Chronicle* on 9 July, 'It's a pity perhaps that the Commission has not expressed its own opinion of Mr Churchill's

---

140 See Khalidi, *Before Their Diaspora*, 239. In 1946, those same fifteen districts still contained Arab majority populations.

141 Stein, *The Land Question*, 211. Stein's maps 'Registered Land in Jewish Possession', 1930 and 1944 (209–210), clearly show that Palestine was still an overwhelmingly Arab territory.

142 Stein, *The Land Question*, 203.

143 Uri Ben-Eliezer, *The Making of Israeli Militarism* (Bloomington, 1998), 150.

144 FO 371/20810, E4375, 123.

ingenious theory that Palestine lies to the west of Damascus, Homs, Hama and Aleppo.'[145]

A five-hour debate followed in the House of Lords on 20 July 1937. Although against partition, Sir Herbert Samuel, now Viscount Samuel, praised the first part of the report, with one exception, which he termed 'a grave omission' – namely, that although the terms of reference to the commission were 'to ascertain the underlying causes of the disturbances which broke out in Palestine', the commission had decided that their terms of reference did not require them 'to undertake the detailed and lengthy research ... needed for a full re-examination of this [Correspondence] issue'. For Samuel, this was a 'fundamental point in the whole controversy'. The former High Commissioner to Palestine added:

> I had working with me [in 1923] Sir Gilbert Clayton as Chief Secretary. Sir Gilbert Clayton was a man who had been closely acquainted with this matter from the beginning, and had been with Sir Henry McMahon during the conduct of these negotiations. He was a man of the highest honour and repute ... He gave me, quite unofficially, this note dated April 12, 1923: 'I was in daily touch with Sir Henry McMahon throughout the negotiations with King Hussein, and made the preliminary drafts of all the letters. I can bear out the statement that it was never the intention that Palestine should be included in the general pledge given to the Sharif. The introductory words of Sir Henry's letter were thought at the time, perhaps erroneously, clearly to cover that point.'[146]

The viscount went on to quote a letter he had received in December 1919 from Emir Feisal, who had written of the 'perfect understanding between himself and Dr Weizmann'. He suggested that Emir Feisal would hardly have written in such terms if the Arab leadership had been

145 See FO 371/20808, E3966. After Cambridge, where he studied Oriental languages, Philby joined the Indian Civil Service in 1908, was posted to Lahore in the Punjab, and became proficient in Urdu, Punjabi, Baluchi, Persian and, later, Arabic. In late 1915, he was appointed head of the finance branch of the British Administration in Baghdad, and in late 1917 was sent to the interior of the Arabian Peninsula as head of a mission to Ibn Saud. He resigned from the Colonial Service in 1924, and in 1930 he converted to Islam.
146 Hansard, Lords, 20 July 1937, vol. 106, cc629–631.

'smarting under a sense of grievance that they had been betrayed by the British government' over Palestine. According to Samuel, Palestine had been definitely excluded from the regions promised to Hussein, and the Arabs had no legitimate grievance against the British government.

On the following day, a House of Commons debate on Peel's partition proposals was dominated by anti-partition, pro-Zionist members, led by Lloyd George and Churchill. The latter's advice to the Colonial Secretary: 'Perseverance, not partition.' Near the end of the debate, after a half-hour intervention by the pro-Zionist James de Rothschild, Anthony Crossley (Conservative, Stretford), one of the handful of pro-Arab MPs, spoke:

> Why did not Sir Henry McMahon mention a town south of Damascus if he meant to include Palestine? ... There were Deraa, Amman, Salt – even the Dead Sea – which he could have mentioned ... A revolt in the desert where there is no Turkish army is a comparatively easy operation. A revolt in Palestine with the Turkish army quartered upon the country was a hanging matter ... there were [British] aeroplanes that dropped leaflets over the Palestinian Arabs, not the Arabs of Iraq or of the Yemen or of the desert, but Palestinian Arabs – asking them to revolt against the Turks. If they did not enter into open revolt, at least the Turkish forces were depleted, at least General Allenby was received in Jerusalem as a liberator; Allah en Bey, the Officer of God who came into Jerusalem and made a proclamation upholding that the British Government, which was liberating those Arabs, would grant them self-governing institutions. They knew nothing at that date of any pledge but the McMahon pledge, and the [news of] the Balfour Declaration had not reached Jerusalem at that time.[147]

Crossley, a noted poet and publisher, and on this occasion the lone pro-Arab voice, was followed by Churchill who, after stating that 'pledges have been given on both sides', launched into an extensive history (and justification) of the Balfour Declaration without mentioning other pledges. At the end of the debate, around 12:30 a.m., Lloyd George and Churchill combined with others to push through an amendment which modified the government's partition proposal. All that the House committed itself to was the further exploration of the *possibility* of

---

147 Hansard, Commons, 21 July 1937, vol. 326, cc2323–2324.

partition, following the League's examination of the government's proposals.[148]

Casuistry and Special Pleading?

With the Correspondence issue once again in the public eye, and without consulting the Foreign Office, McMahon, now retired, decided to enter the fray. Under the headline **INDEPENDENCE OF THE ARABS. THE 'McMAHON PLEDGE'. A DEFINITE STATEMENT**, McMahon wrote in *The Times* on 23 July:

> Sir, – Many references have been made in the Palestine Royal Commission Report and in the course of the recent debates in both Houses of Parliament to the 'McMahon Pledge,' especially to that portion of the pledge which concerns Palestine and of which one interpretation has been claimed by the Jews and another by the Arabs.
>
> It has been suggested to me that continued silence on the part of the giver of that pledge may itself be misunderstood.
>
> I feel, therefore, called upon to make some statement on the subject, but I will confine myself in doing so to the point now at issue – i.e. whether that portion of Syria now known as Palestine was or was not intended to be included in the territories in which the independence of the Arabs was guaranteed in my pledge.
>
> I feel it my duty to state, and I do so definitely and emphatically, that it was not intended by me in giving this pledge to King Hussein to include Palestine in the area in which Arab independence was promised.
>
> I also had every reason to believe at the time that the fact that Palestine was not included in my pledge was well understood by King Hussein.
>
> Yours faithfully,
>
> A. HENRY McMAHON.[149]

This letter requires careful analysis. First, the *debates* referenced in the first paragraph were not over differing interpretations of the Correspondence by Arabs and Jews, but between the British

---

148 Hansard, Commons, 21 July 1937, vol. 326, cc2323–2324.
149 *The Times*, 23 July 1937. See FO 371/20810, E4294.

government and the Arabs. Secondly, McMahon's *intentions*, as referred to in paragraphs three and four, were red herrings used to avoid the fundamental question of what he actually wrote – not what he said he intended to mean. Lastly, McMahon provided no evidence whatsoever, either in this letter or elsewhere in the official records, that he ever received any verbal or written indication from King Hussein accepting the exclusion of Palestine from the area of Arab independence.

Following the publication of McMahon's letter, Edward Warner, the Colonial Office official who had collected and edited much of the Correspondence, sent George Rendel a copy of McMahon's 26 October 1915 despatch of explanation to the Foreign Office. The former High Commissioner had written:

> I have been definite in stating that Great Britain will recognise the principle of Arab independence in purely Arab territory, this being the main point on which agreement depends, but have been equally definite in excluding Mersina, Alexandretta and those districts on the <u>northern coast</u> of Syria, which cannot be said to be Arab, and where I understand that French interests have been recognised. I am <u>not aware of the extent of French claims in Syria</u>, nor of how far His Majesty's Government have agreed to recognise them. Hence, while recognizing the towns of Damascus, Hama, Homs and Aleppo as being within the circle of Arab countries, I have endeavoured to provide for possible French pretensions <u>to those places</u> by a general modification to the effect that His Majesty's Government can only give assurances in regard to those territories 'in which she can act without detriment to the interests of her ally France.'[150]

This despatch from McMahon to Grey clearly reveals his intentions. Regarding his explicit exclusion of the 'northern coast of Syria', by no stretch of the imagination could this include Palestine. As his intention was to exclude the northern coast – that is, the areas to the west of the four towns, where he understood 'French interests had been recognised' – it would, of course, have been more appropriate and more accurate to have used the word 'towns' instead of the general word 'districts'. Was this carelessness or deliberate ambiguity? More importantly, if 'towns'

---

150 FO 371/20810, E4294. McMahon to Foreign Office, 26 October 1915. Underlined by the author.

had been used, the translators would then have used a more geographi-cally specific Arabic word for towns (e.g. *mudun*), instead of *wilāyāt*. As it was, using *wilāyāt* in reference to Damascus, Homs, Hama and Aleppo in the same sentence could only mean local districts, and not <u>vilayets</u>. Boundary clarity was not, of course, McMahon's intention.

When it came to the French claims in Syria, McMahon wrote that he 'was not aware of the extent' of these claims. So did he truly expect, or should he have expected, the Sharif to have known about them? McMahon, in 1915, in 1922 and again in 1937, produced no evidence whatsoever to show that the Sharif had any knowledge of French claims, or that the French government were in contact with the Sharif. And to which places, then, did McMahon refer when he wrote 'in those places'? Did he mean 'the towns of Damascus, Homs, Hama and Aleppo', which he had just mentioned in the same sentence? Probably.

Warner commented in a minute on 13 July: 'I find this despatch very difficult to square with Sir Henry McMahon's present letter [published in *The Times*].' To which Rendel replied, 'It cannot be reconciled. All this casuistry and special pleading is a great mistake. It would be far better to recognise and admit that H.M.G. made a mistake and gave flatly contradictory promises – which is of course the fact.'[151]

Following the House of Commons' initial debate on the report, a group of eleven pro-Arab MPs wrote to the Colonial Secretary, Ormsby-Gore, concerned about the tone and pro-Zionist partiality of the debate. Commenting on this letter, Baggallay, the Foreign Office official handling the Palestine/Correspondence brief, wrote:

> The Jews have a documentary case of great strength. But the [eleven MPs] are justified in saying that the Arabs have a documentary case of great strength also. However skilfully one may construct an argument in public to show that Sir Henry McMahon's pledge did <u>not</u> include Palestine, anyone coming fresh to the problem and taking his words at their face value would have to be very perspicuous if he found in them any cause to suppose Palestine to be <u>excluded</u> from the area of Arab inde-pendence. It is the fact that both sides have a good case which makes the Palestine problem so tragic.[152]

---

151 FO 371/20810, E4294. 4. Rendel minute, 11 October 1937.
152 FO 371/20811, 225. Baggallay minute, 7 August 1937. Underlined in the original.

Baggallay's minute was initialled by Sir Lancelot Oliphant (Deputy Under-Secretary of State for Foreign Affairs), Ralph Stevenson (Legal Advisor, Foreign Office) and Lord Halifax (Secretary of State for Foreign Affairs). As previously mentioned, senior British officials were thus well aware of the weakness of their case concerning the Correspondence.

The Balfour Declaration: A Binding Obligation

In August 1937, Ormsby-Gore appeared before the Permanent Mandates Commission (PMC) in Geneva, to describe and defend the government's new 'partition' policy which, he informed the commissioners,

> transformed the Balfour Declaration from a declaration regarding the beginning of a policy into a policy of which they could see the end, namely the establishment of an independent, sovereign Jewish State, and that was certainly the conception in Lord Balfour's mind.[153]

His reply to a commissioner's question concerning Britain's previous Mandate policy is particularly revealing of the government's future intentions:

> [Ormsby-Gore] had no intention of conveying the impression that the Balfour Declaration was not still a binding obligation on both the League and the United Kingdom. Obviously, like the Mandate, it was still a binding obligation, and would remain so until replaced by an independent Jewish State. It was only if the suggested plan of partition were accepted, and eventuated in the creation of a Jewish State, that the Balfour Declaration would reach its fruition and cease to be binding.[154]

The PMC, 'very much an imperialists' club', was made up largely of European colonial officials, diplomats and lawyers. Ostensibly, the

153 Cited in Leonard Stein, *The Balfour Declaration* (London, 1961), 555.
154 Minutes (p. 182) of the 32nd Session of the Permanent Mandates Commission, July–August 1937. Cited in *Palestine Partition Commission (Woodhead) Report* (Cmd 5854), October 1938, 285.

League's oversight agent, assessing the performance of the powers' governance of the 'backward nations' for whom they were responsible, in reality it served quite a different purpose. As Lori Allen puts it:

> While proclaiming its balanced stance, it deliberately obscured a history of politics and practices facilitating Jewish colonization of Palestine, blocking democratic developments and denying Palestinians self-government.[155]

On 3 September, Churchill, still in the political wilderness, weighed in on the public debate once more. In an article in the *Jewish Chronicle* headlined **WHY I AM AGAINST PARTITION**, he wrote that partition would lead to an 'armed collision', and provided his own pro-Zionist remedy:

> a direct conference between Jews and Arabs [which] would agree for a term of years the mode of living and the settlement which, without perhaps solving the problems of the future, would afford to the present generation a measure of peace, prosperity, and happiness. It is in this direction that wise men should look and bold men march. It would be far better to persevere along the old lines. Up till three years ago they were highly successful. Palestine was being developed and enlarged. The Jews were steadily being settled in the land of their fathers. The Arabs might well be conciliated from day to day and month to month by the sense of increased well-being in which both races shared.[156]

Such 'reassuring' sentiments had been the standard rhetoric justifying the Zionist movement since 1897: Jewish immigration would benefit the indigenous people of Palestine. Here, Churchill was simply echoing the founder of political Zionism, Theodor Herzl, who wrote in 1899:

> It is their well-being, their individual wealth, which we will increase by bringing in our own ... In allowing immigration to a number of Jews bringing their intelligence, their financial acumen and their means of

155 Allen, *A History of False Hope*, 17.
156 FO 371/20813, 206.

enterprise to the country, no one can doubt that the well-being of the entire country would be the happy result.[157]

Inevitably Skating Over the Real Point?

In Amman, Emir Abdullah heard of McMahon's public statement to *The Times* in a radio broadcast and immediately sent a letter of protest to the High Commissioner of Transjordan. 'As the only living son of the king', the Emir wrote that it was only right to defend him and to state that those pledges included Palestine, and that his late father together with those in his company were firmly of that belief beyond any shadow of doubt. According to the Emir, this was confirmed by the communications between his father and Sir Henry McMahon that he had in his possession. Moreover, at that time he himself was his father's secretary and the person in charge of those discussions.

The Emir asked for the broadcast in question to be rectified by a similar broadcast

for the sake of truth and history and for the sake of loyalty to a great man, to whom, although he is removed from this world, those who remain of his family and his friends, such as ourselves, owe the duty of refuting any statement wrongly attributed to him in particular one which relates to his national honour.

After quoting extensively from the Correspondence, the Emir emphasised that

there was no doubt as to the Arab status of Palestine which fact has not been ignored by anyone and that France was not claiming the same.[158]

---

157 Letter from Theodor Herzl to Yusuf Diya Pasha al-Khalidi, 19 March 1899, reprinted in Walid Khalidi, ed., *From Haven to Conquest: Readings in Zionism and the Palestine Problem until 1948* (Beirut, 1971), 91–93. See also Khalidi, *The Hundred Years' War on Palestine*, 6–7.
158 FO 371/20813, E5306, 161. His Highness Emir Abdullah to the High Commissioner of Transjordan, 25 July 1937.

At this point in the Emir's letter, Warner commented in the margin: 'Was she [France, claiming Palestine] or not – and if so did Hussein know it? This is the whole point ... it would require some research to discover whether Hussein was aware of the French claim.'[159]

Some three weeks later, the High Commissioner wrote that His Highness was still awaiting a reply and would become restive without one. So the Colonial Secretary, who considered that the Emir's letter did not warrant a response, suggested that he be informed orally that: first, the Colonial Secretary fully appreciated His Highness's feelings in the matter and had taken note of his statement that the Emir's late father was firmly convinced that the pledges given to him included Palestine; second, he could not object if the Emir felt it necessary to make a public statement to the same effect; third, at the same time His Majesty would no doubt wish to avoid any action which might add to the difficulties of negotiating the final settlement of the Palestine question (just alike to Arabs and Jews) which the government were determined to achieve; fourth, whatever may have been the understanding of the government's intention by the Arabs (and the Royal Commission stated on this point that it was in the highest degree unfortunate that, in the exigencies of war, the British government had been unable to make their intention clear to the Sharif), the reservation in Sir Henry McMahon's letter of 24 October 1915 had always been regarded by them as excluding the whole of Palestine west of the Jordan from the territories within which a pledge was given to recognise and support the independence of the Arabs; and fifth, Ormsby-Gore, who had been himself concerned in those matters at the time, had the clearest recollection that this had been the intention of the British government in 1915.[160]

On receiving the draft at the Foreign Office, Warner commented that in 1915 the French were indeed claiming the whole of Syria, including Palestine, but he did not recollect in the papers that he had ever read any suggestion that the Sharif of Mecca was aware of this claim. Additionally, he did not see the point of including in the draft the sentence about what the Royal Commission had stated: 'it is surely

---

159 FO 371/20813, E5306, 161.

160 FO 371/20813, E5306, 166–167. Colonial Office draft to Acting High Commissioner, Mr W.D. Battershill, September 1937. Unsigned.

not intended that the Emir's attention should be called to this statement that it was unfortunate that HMG failed to make themselves
clear!'[161]

Baggallay, however, minuted a day later that the Foreign Office
should agree to the Colonial Office draft as it stood, including the statement from the Royal Commission:

> That [statement] is after all a concession to truth in a letter which inevi-
> tably has to skate over the real point, which is not whether HMG meant
> to exclude Palestine from the area of Arab Palestine, but whether they
> ever said anything to the Sherif from which he might or ought to have
> inferred that they meant to exclude it. My own impression is that they
> did not, but I dare say an extremely close study of the documents would
> show this impression to be wrong.[162]

There was never any question of broadcasting a rectifying statement.
The official records do not reveal whether the Emir was ever informed
orally of this message from the Colonial Office, or whether he issued a
public response to McMahon's statement.

Repealing the Peel Plan

Peel's partition plans only served to fan the flames of Arab rebellion.
Disturbances restarted, and on Sunday, 26 September, Lewis Andrews,
the District Commissioner of Galilee and Acre, was assassinated by
rebels on his way to prayer services at the Anglican Christ Church
in Nazareth. Andrews was the object of particular hatred among
Palestinians in the Galilee area for the repressive manner in which he
carried out government measures following the outbreak of the revolt.[163]
He left a widow and three children. His bodyguard, Peter McEwan, a
British police constable, died later in hospital. That double murder,

---

161 FO 371/20813, E5306, 154. Warner minute, 13 September 1937.
162 FO 371/20813, E5306, 155. Baggallay minute, 14 September 1937.
163 Henry Laurens, *La Question de Palestine: Une Mission sacrée de la civilisation* (Paris,
2002), 373. Andrews was buried in Jerusalem's Protestant cemetery on Mount Zion
with the epitaph 'gave his life for this land'.

accomplished in daylight, profoundly shocked the British community and provoked the Palestine government for the first time to embark on a determined offensive: summary military courts were established, mandatory death sentences for firearms offences imposed and a barbed wire fence with defensive emplacements built along part of the frontier with Lebanon and Syria. Alec Kirkbride, the Deputy Resident in Amman, was appointed to replace Andrews, which he did with great reluctance, partly because the rebels announced that any successor would be killed at the first opportunity, but mostly because

> the British personnel of the government departments were demoralized by the sudden death of their leader; the Arab civil servants sympathized openly with the rebels and the Jewish officials were more concerned in the cause of their people than in the interests of the government by which they were employed. Quite apart from these difficulties, I did not relish the prospect of working for a bureaucratic administration which was pledged to implement a policy [Lord Peel's Partition Plan] hated by the majority of the people to whom it applied.[164]

In London, the cabinet was sufficiently worried by developments in Palestine that it secretly voted against partition on 8 December 1937. Two weeks later, with no end in sight to the Arab Revolt, Rendel wrote:

> When the report of the Royal Commission on Palestine was in preparation, the question of the publication of this correspondence was revived [but] ... in the event, the question of the publication of the correspondence did not arise – chiefly as a result of an excessively misleading letter from Sir H. McMahon himself ('Times' of July 23) ...
>
> Our line in the Eastern Department has been that our pledges to the Arabs are of a much wider nature than those contained in the McMahon letter, and that our obligations to the native Arab inhabitants of Palestine rest on our avowed war aims rather than on one particular document.
>
> In these circumstances, I doubt whether the question of the publication of the McMahon correspondence will be pursued – particularly as its publication would be in the interests of the Arabs, and Jewish influence

---

164 Alec Kirkbride, *A Crackle of Thorns* (London, 1956), 99.

– which is very strong, particularly in the House of Commons – will therefore be exerted to the utmost to prevent its publication.[165]

In February 1938, the Woodhead Commission was appointed, its official object being to propose a 'detailed Partition scheme' for Palestine, including recommending the partition boundaries, and to examine the economic and financial aspects of the Peel Plan. The commission comprised Sir John Woodhead, a former civil administrator in India; Sir Alison Russell, a lawyer; Percival Waterfield and Thomas Reid, also civil servants in India. In reality, the appointment of the commission was regarded by the Colonial Office as an instrument to free Britain from its obligation to the partition plan.[166] In accordance with a decision of the cabinet, Woodhead was secretly advised that it was within the commission's authority to decide that 'no workable scheme could be produced'.[167] At the Foreign Office, Rendel did his utmost to ensure that the commission would reach the 'correct conclusion', by trying to influence the choice of personnel and placing his own memorandum before the commission as evidence.[168]

The commission conducted its investigations from April to early August 1938, and published its conclusions on 9 November 1938, after which the British government rejected the imminent partition of Palestine as involving insurmountable 'political, administrative and financial difficulties'.[169] With continuing widespread violence in Palestine, and tensions throughout Europe rapidly rising, Britain needed to 'clear the decks' – it could no longer afford to have so many troops locked up in Palestine. Hence, the government's next move:

---

165 FO 371/20823. Rendel memorandum, 23 December 1937. Kedourie's analysis of this memorandum included: 'There is no evidence that Jewish power was exerted to prevent its publication.' Kedourie, *Labyrinth*, 266.

166 Michael J. Cohen, *Palestine: Retreat from the Mandate: The Making of British Policy, 1936–1945* (London, 1978), 44–45. According to Viscount Samuel, among Palestinians the Commission was nicknamed the 'Repeal' Commission. Hansard, Lords, 8 December 1938, vol. 111, c421.

167 Itzhak Galnoor, *The Partition of Palestine: Decision Crossroads in the Zionist Movement* (New York, 1995), 53.

168 Cohen, *Palestine: Retreat from the Mandate*, 46–47.

169 *Palestine. Statement by His Majesty's Government* (Cmd 5893), November 1938, paragraph 4. See https://unispal.un.org/UNISPAL.NSF/0/4941922311B4E3C58525 6D17004BD2E2 (accessed 28 June 2019).

on 9 November 1938, the Colonial Secretary, Malcolm MacDonald
(appointed in May that year), announced in the Commons that there
would be discussions in London with both parties involved in
Palestine, to work out a compromise. On 24 November, in a seven-
hour-long debate, which finished at 11:00 p.m., MacDonald
announced the results of the Woodhead Commission: partition was
impractical, and two sovereign states 'unworkable'. He described the
government's dilemma in stark terms:

> We cannot put the Jews under the domination of the Arabs of Palestine,
> but also, unless we can remove the Arab fear that they are going to be put
> under the domination of the Jews, we shall have to face a suspicious and
> hostile people over a great area of the Near East, and we shall find that we
> have to lock up a great part of our Army in Palestine indefinitely.[170]

The official records clearly reveal that during the late 1930s British officials, both in London and in Palestine, were increasingly plagued by
doubts, if not about the morality of its imperial rule in Palestine, at least
about its financial and military cost. Writing in 1964, Hugh Mackintosh
Foot, a British officer in Palestine between 1929 and 1937, who later
became Lord Caradon and served as Minister of State at the Foreign
Office, and the UK's representative at the United Nations, considered
the situation in Palestine a classic case of 'waste and futility' because the
government offered

> no political initiative ... no hope that [the Palestinian Arabs'] most
> deep-seated fears might be removed ... The failure of British adminis-
> tration in Palestine was inevitable. The double sin had been committed
> of raising false hopes both with the Arabs and with Jews. The hopes
> were false because they were conflicting. The Arabs who fought with
> Great Britain in the first world war to throw off the yoke of the
> Turkish Empire were led to believe they were fighting for their free-
> dom ... the main responsibility was ours ... by prevarication and
> procrastination and basically by the fundamental dishonesty of our
> original double-dealing we had made disaster certain ... In 1915 we

---

170 Hansard, Commons, 24 November 1938, vol. 341, c1992.

supported King Feisal's desert rising. In 1917 we signed the Balfour Declaration.[171]

Thus, at the end of 1938, Palestine, Malcolm MacDonald's 'poisoned chalice', included not just the continuing Arab Revolt and its implications for Britain's imperial communications to the East, but also, according to Lord Caradon, the immeasurable, psychological legacy of Britain's prevarication, procrastination and original double-dealing. At the same time MacDonald, and the rest of the cabinet, had their eyes firmly fixed on developments in Germany and Czechoslovakia.

In March 1938, German troops had occupied Austria, incorporating the latter into the German Reich, and in September the signing of the Munich Agreement effectively dismembered Czechoslovakia. In Germany itself, Kristallnacht followed on 9 November. 'No foreign propagandist', observed *The Times*, 'bent upon blackening Germany before the world could outdo the tale of burnings and beatings, of blackguardly assaults on defenceless and innocent people, which disgraced that country.'[172] Ninety-one Jews were killed, and a further thirty thousand sent to the increasing number of concentration camps opened in Germany and Austria. By the beginning of 1939, Hitler's increasing pressure on the Czechoslovak government was causing mounting concern in London and Paris. From a British perspective, Palestine urgently needed to be 'pacified', one way or another, to stabilise the Middle East, and thus to release troops, in particular for Egypt's defence in case of war. But would the proposed discussions in London succeed?

171 Hugh M. Foot, *A Start in Freedom* (London, 1964), 35–36, 53. Foot, an Arabic speaker, was Assistant District Commissioner in Nablus and Galilee.
172 *The Times*, 11 November 1938.

5

Abandoning 'Vilayets'

1938–1939

In preparation for the London Conference proposed by the British government on the future of Palestine, the Foreign Office produced a position paper in December 1938 entitled 'Juridical Basis of the Arab Claim to Palestine'.[1] According to Baggallay, it was necessary 'to have the answers ready when the Arab delegations reach this country in January'. The paper, written by Foreign Office official James Y. Mackenzie, described at length the background to the Correspondence, as well as the strengths and weaknesses of the government's case. It described in detail both the principal legal arguments upon which the Arab case was founded and the legal position on all these points as seen from the government's perspective. Mackenzie recommended that if the Arabs wished to raise the Correspondence pledge issue, the government should suggest that the Arabs prepare a memorandum to which the government could in due course furnish a written reply. That would be a safe strategy to adopt as actual discussions on the topic could be embarrassing.

From this thirty-five-page, closely argued memorandum, it is perfectly clear that British officials knew that their district = vilayet contention was untenable. In fact, Mackenzie recommended that it would be unwise to rely upon it.[2] He devoted ten paragraphs to the 'districts' reservation' debate, and in particular resurrected and supported Childs's suggestion of 1930 that

---

1 FO 371/23219, 7–42.
2 FO 371/23219, 17.

the best explanation which His Majesty's Government can give of the meaning which Sir H. McMahon meant his pledge to bear is probably by a reference to the use of the phrase 'districts of Damascus, Homs, Hama and Aleppo' in certain discussions which took place in 1915 between the late Sir Gilbert Clayton, Chief Political Officer at Army Headquarters in Egypt, and Mahomed Ibn-Sherif-el-Faroki, an Arab Nationalist and former officer in the Ottoman army ...

It is thus evident that when Sir H. McMahon gave his pledge of the 24th October, 1915, to the Sherif he adopted El Faroki's own phrase in order to assure the Sharif and the Syrian Arabs that the area for which they were prepared to fight was assigned to them, and further that, in using this phrase, he used it in the same comprehensive sense as El Faroki, i.e., as one which covered the Syrian hinterland southwards to the Gulf of Akaba.

At the same time, Mackenzie acknowledged the weakness of this contention, partly because it relied exclusively on reports written by British officials. The British possessed no letter, report or any other document written in al-Faruqi's hand, supporting this contention.

Mackenzie strongly suggested that the government, having privately discarded the districts = vilayets argument, should therefore base their case primarily on McMahon's general reservation concerning French interests, however weak it might be, even if the Arabs were to argue that the Sharif of Mecca had not been aware of these inter-allied understandings or of the extent of French claims to Syria and Palestine, especially as the Sykes–Picot Agreement was not concluded until 1916 and not publicised until by the Bolsheviks at the end of 1917. Mackenzie continued:

Sir H. McMahon's letter of the 24th October, 1915, does not, it must be admitted, contain any description of the exact limits and boundaries of the French claim, but this was mainly owing to the fact that the French claim, though recognised by His Majesty's Government, had not in fact been territorially defined. The form of words chosen was, therefore, such as to cover the general claim made by the French Government, however wide it might prove to be, and the pledge was only to apply to those parts of Syria in which His Majesty's Government might eventually obtain a free hand as a result of the peace settlement.[3]

---

3 FO 371/23219, 23.

Mackenzie made two further suggestions in an effort to bolster the government's case. First, they could argue that the Sharif had some knowledge of the nature of the French claim, since in a letter of 1 January 1916 the Sharif had reserved the right to press at a later date a claim to 'what we now leave to France in Beirut and its coasts'. Second, it could also be proposed that had the Sharif been anxious to know the precise nature and extent of the French claim, it was for him to have made enquiries of either the British or the French government. Both Mackenzie's suggestions were open to question: 'Beirut and its coasts' bore no relation to the Palestine region, and Hussein had made his 'boundary' demands clear in his initial letter to McMahon of 14 July 1915, so the onus was on the latter to clarify their regional reservations concerning those demands.

Mackenzie acknowledged that concerning the Correspondence

> [i]t will therefore be seen that there are points of serious weakness in His Majesty's Government's case. In many respects the best that can be done is to maintain that in considering an agreement contained in so loosely-worded, inconclusive and incomplete a series of letters as the McMahon–Hussein correspondence, His Majesty's Government are entitled to take their own interpretation and their own avowed intentions into account, wherever the meaning of the text is ambiguous, at least as much as the interpretation and the avowed intentions of the other side.

Here, Mackenzie is once again focusing on the government's entitlement to be judged by their intentions, not by what was actually written. Malcolm MacDonald, the Colonial Secretary, was to make exactly the same 'intentions' point to the Arab delegation in February 1939. Indeed, 'intentions' had been a popular word in governments' lexicon since Churchill's use of the word in 1922: McMahon (1922, 1937), Duke of Devonshire (1923), Childs (1930) and Ormsby-Gore (1937). Mackenzie then highlighted the fact that the Arab juridical claim to Palestine was founded not only upon their interpretation of the McMahon pledge of 1915, but on the repudiation of the Balfour Declaration, on various wartime declarations made by the government, and finally on the Covenant of the League of Nations.

He concluded:

...it is sufficiently apparent from the foregoing paragraphs that so far at any rate as the McMahon–Hussein correspondence is concerned, [HMG's] counter-memorandum is likely to be dependent on a forced line of reasoning and that the case of His Majesty's Government in regard to this correspondence lacks that self-evident and decisive clarity which ought to form the basis of important international acts. Nothing in fact that can be brought forward by way of explanation of Sir H. McMahon's pledge is likely to enable His Majesty's Government to convince the world at large that the Royal Commission were wrong when they said: 'It was in the highest degree unfortunate that, in the exigencies of war, the British Government was unable to make their intention clear to the Sherif.'[4]

Commenting on Mackenzie's memorandum, Baggallay wrote:

I think it is so clearly impossible on the wording of the letter to sustain the contention that the word districts = vilayets that we should not put forward this contention ...

We are still left therefore with the question what does the word 'district' mean: and I think the best argument is that Sir H. McMahon used the same words as the Arab nationalist El Faroki had used, viz. 'districts of Damascus, Homs, Hama and Aleppo.' Therefore he meant what El Faroki had meant, and I do not think Arabs would dispute that El Faroki meant to include in the district of Damascus all the vilayet of Syria south of Damascus.

As regards the second part of the McMahon letter, namely the words 'those portions of the territories therein in which Great Britain is free to act without detriment to the interests of her ally France' ... At the time when the McMahon letter was written France was claiming the whole of Syria ... The Sykes–Picot Agreement did not come until after the McMahon correspondence was concluded. Therefore at the time that these words were written H.M.G. did not know whether she would be free to act without detriment to the interests of France in any portion of Syria and, if these words meant anything, they meant that the assurance only applied to areas in Syria with regard to which

---

4 FO 371/23219, 7–42. James Y. Mackenzie memorandum, January 1939.

H.M.G. eventually obtained a free hand as a result of the peace settlement.[5]

Baggallay sent Mackenzie's memorandum to Harold Downie, First Secretary of the Colonial Office, requesting any suggestions the Colonial Office could make. He added:

> We are taking steps to have the Arabic texts of parts of the correspondence examined afresh, with particular regard to the use of the word 'district' or 'vilayet' ... I must say that, after going into the whole question of the McMahon–Hussein correspondence again, our position in regard to this correspondence seems to me even weaker than it did before![6]

As there was no one working in the Foreign Office whose knowledge of Arabic was sufficient to deal with the question, Baggallay invited Alan Trott, Britain's Consul in Jedda, who was on leave in London, to examine the Correspondence.[7] Baggallay requested Trott to establish:

> (1) What word actually is used in the Arabic of [McMahon's letter] for 'Districts of Damascus etc.?' (2) What the real meaning of this word is when used in Arabic? (3) Whether any support for the view that it could or should have been taken to mean the 'Turkish administrative area known as the Vilayet of Syria' can be derived from the use of this word, or other words, in the Arabic of [McMahon's] letter?[8]

Neither the Foreign Office nor the Colonial Office had a complete list of the Correspondence, either in English or in Arabic – and this some

---

5 FO 371/23219, E6. Baggallay minute, 21 December 1938 and 11 January 1939. Baggallay sent eight copies of the Correspondence (based on Warner's collection of 1937) to Downie at the Colonial Office, commenting that as far as he was aware, no complete collection of the Correspondence had been made before then, and explaining that 'there are a great many points of difficulty and uncertainty connected with these texts.' FO 371/23220, E577, 159. Baggallay minute, 25 January 1939.
6 FO 371/23219, 6. Baggallay to Downie, 19 January 1939; CO 733/409/13.
7 FO 371/23220, E 515. Foreign Office minute, 19 January 1939; FO 371/23222, E870, 3 February 1939.
8 FO 371/23220, E633. 'Notes for Mr. Trott', Baggallay minute, 25 January 1939.

twenty years after the issue had first reared its head. In a further note to his colleagues six days later, Baggallay was equally pessimistic:

> Our whole case with regard to 'the districts of Damascus etc.,' is of course hopelessly weak, and I have no real hope that anything Mr Trott may discover will materially strengthen it. This is nevertheless a case in which we ought to leave no stone unturned.[9]

Trott's endeavours produced no fresh clarity. He simply confirmed that the Arabic word (*wilāyāt*) used in the letter for the word 'districts' in the phrase 'districts of Mersina and Alexandretta' was the same word as in the phrase 'districts of Damascus'. In fact, Trott translated the word into English as *viláyat*, making no comment about whether it meant a local district or a province. His conclusion:

> I fear there is no way of clearing up the various ambiguities of the Arabic text of the pledge in (8 – letter of 24/10/15). It is simply a loosely worded collection of phrases. The fact that the translator did not take very much care over what he said is also shown by the fact that he altered the order of the words Hama and Homs, putting the latter before the former.[10]

Adhering to Our Intentions?

At the Colonial Office, Downie was somewhat dismissive of Baggallay's concerns:

> Whatever apparent weaknesses there may be to our case, we should not be inclined to take the matter too tragically. The idea that the fundamental issue whether or not Palestine is to be turned into an Arab State can be decided (or even seriously affected) by a legal interpretation of the McMahon correspondence is too ridiculous to need refutation, and we doubt whether any further investigation of the Arabic texts is worthwhile.

---

9 FO 371/23220, E633. Baggallay minute, 25 January 1939.

10 FO 371/23222, E870, 51–82. Trott's 'Results of the examination of the Arabic texts of certain obscure passages', 31 January 1939.

Surely we need only concern ourselves with refuting the offensive insinuation (which constitutes the sting of the Arab case) that His Majesty's Government have been guilty of bad faith in the matter. On this point there is no reason why we should condescend to argument with the Arabs. We have always maintained that our intention was to exclude Palestine from the pledges given to the Sharif. The Royal Commission had no doubt about the genuineness of our intentions, and we must adhere to that position. Sir H. McMahon, whose evidence on the question of intention is surely vital, has gone further and has not only asserted that it was not his intention to include Palestine in the area in which Arab independence was promised, but that he had every reason to believe at the time that this fact was well known to King Hussein.

In dealing with the Arabs we need not rub in Sir H. McMahon's second assertion, and if His Majesty's Government has to accept the imputation of the Royal Commission that 'it was in the highest degree unfortunate that in the exigencies of war the British Government was unable to make their intentions clear to the Sharif,' its shoulders are broad enough to bear it.[11]

However, Baggallay remained concerned at the weakness of the British case:

I think we may agree that the legal interpretation of the McMahon pledge cannot seriously affect the fate of Palestine as things stand today.

But I am not so sure that we can agree that we need not condescend to argue with the Arabs about whether His Majesty's Government were guilty of bad faith when giving the McMahon pledge. I do not mean that we need to be in the least apologetic or refrain from refuting the accusation with vigour. But it may be necessary (if the point ever arises) to follow up our refutation with a reasoned explanation showing exactly what Sir H. McMahon was trying to say and why.

In any case Sir H. McMahon's evidence, far from being vital, is not of the slightest value whatever. In particular there is nothing in the McMahon-Hussein correspondence to bear out his statement that he had

11 FO 371/23222, E483. Stephen Luke (for Mr Downie) to Baggallay, 2 February 1939; CO 733/409/13.

every reason to believe that the Sharif knew he wanted to exclude Palestine.[12]

Baggallay's minute was also read by Sir Lancelot Oliphant (Deputy Under-Secretary of State, Foreign Office), Sir Alexander Cadogan (Permanent Under-Secretary of State, Foreign Office), R.A. 'Rab' Butler (Under-Secretary of State for Foreign Affairs) and Lord Halifax (the Foreign Secretary). Such senior officials were all well briefed on the serious weaknesses of the British case. The question was how to deal with the issue.

William E. Beckett, the Deputy Legal Advisor in the Foreign Office, shared Baggallay's concern:

> I agree. It is no doubt important to prove our good faith i.e. to refute the allegations that H.M.G. deliberately and consciously made inconsistent promises, but after all that is only half the issue. There remains the question what the McMahon letters in fact said and how the Sherif and the Arabs were entitled to read them and I am afraid on this point Sir H. McMahon's statement of his intentions and thoughts is no value at all and what the Royal (Palestine) Commission said is of very little value.[13]

Beckett here had touched the heart of the matter: whatever McMahon's intentions, there remained the question of what the McMahon letters in fact said and how the Sharif and the Arabs were entitled to read them. In international law the rules for interpreting agreements are clear: an agreement is what is agreed by both parties. In the face of the written text setting out that agreement – in this case the exchange of letters – the interpretation of one party becomes irrelevant unless it is also shared by the other. McMahon gives no evidence to support his belief in what Hussein understood, and it is clear that Hussein did not agree with McMahon's interpretation from his subsequent letters. Apart from the fact that McMahon's July 1937 letter to *The Times* is self-serving, his subjective intention is irrelevant to the common intention of the two parties to the agreement contained in the Correspondence. This is discussed in more detail in the next chapter.

---

12 FO 371/23222, E843. Baggallay minute, 4 February 1939.
13 FO 371/23222, E843. Beckett minute, 6 February 1939. Underlined in the original.

For their part, Weizmann and other Zionist leaders in Britain and the USA were mindful of the potential embarrassment to the government's pro-Zionist policy that a public discussion of the Correspondence would precipitate. For any government to allow such a discussion would be unprecedented and could, if it occurred, possibly open an uncontrollable Pandora's box in the press, in Parliament and at the League of Nations. And all this when Europe seemed to be in danger of slipping towards war, Jewish communities in Europe were being destroyed, and when a united Parliament was increasingly vital. For the government, such a public airing was out of the question.

Zionist concerns were partially revealed by the publication of a letter from a Mr Israel Cohen on 31 January 1939 in the *Manchester Guardian*. Under the headline **ARAB NATIONALISM**. *The Undertaking Given to King Hussein*, Cohen described the now-familiar pro-Zionist arguments showing that it was the intention of McMahon to exclude Palestine from the territories that were promised independence, and drawing attention to the Feisal–Weizmann agreement of 1919, which clearly showed

> by the article expressly accepting the Balfour Declaration and by other articles, that he [Feisal] regarded Palestine as excluded from the territories that were promised independence; and (2) [Feisal] submitted a memorandum to the Peace Conference on 29 January 1919, in which he stated: 'On account of its universal character I shall leave Palestine to one side for the mutual consideration of all parties concerned. With this exception, I ask for the independence of the Arab areas enumerated in the Memorandum.'[14]
>
> It may be added that according to the statement made in the House of Commons by Mr Winston Churchill, then Colonial Secretary, on July 11, 1922, it was stipulated that the undertaking given to Hussein 'applied only to those portions of the territories concerned in which Great Britain was free to act without detriment to the interest of her Allies,' and that the British Government always regarded Palestine as excluded by this proviso from the scope of the undertaking.

---

14 David Hunter Miller, *My Diary of the Peace Conference* (New York, 1924), vol. iv, 226.

In the same speech Mr Churchill mentioned that the first suggestion
that Palestine was included within the territories that were promised
independence was made by King Feisal at a conversation held in the
Foreign Office on January 20, 1921, more than five years after the conclusion of the correspondence on which the claim was based, and that when
the point of view of the Government was explained to him he 'expressed
himself as prepared to accept the statement that it had been the intention
of His Majesty's Government to exclude Palestine.' – Yours, etc.,
ISRAEL COHEN.[15]

Baggallay filed the letter with a comment:

There is nothing to show in the F-W treaty that Emir Feisal regarded
Palestine as excluded from the Arab territories that were promised independence (in 1915). What it shows was that he was prepared to accept the
fact that at that time (in 1919) Palestine should not be included in the area
of Arab independence. The conditions attached to the treaty were not
fulfilled and it was never carried out.

The same considerations apply to the memorandum of 29 January
1919.

Similarly the acceptance by the Emir Feisal of the statement of His
Majesty's Government that they intended to exclude Palestine does not
mean that he accepted their argument that they had done so.[16]

On 30 January 1939, a week before discussions on the future of Palestine
would commence at the St James's Conference, Baggallay and Baxter
had spoken with Lord Maugham, the Lord Chancellor, to ascertain his
views on Mackenzie's memorandum 'The Juridical Basis of the Arab
Claim to Palestine', which had been circulated to the cabinet[17] by

---

15 FO 371/23223, E1051. Cohen supplied his address to the *Manchester Guardian*, but
not the fact that he was the General Secretary of the UK branch of the Zionist
Organisation.
16 FO 371/23223, E1051. Baggallay minute, 6 February 1939. Also initialled by
Baxter. Baggallay's use of the word 'treaty' in his memorandum is legally incorrect;
a treaty is an agreement between two sovereign states, and Feisal and Weizmann did
not represent two sovereign states.
17 A typed copy of C.P.4 (39) [Secret. Printed for the cabinet, 18 January 1939] of
the memorandum is in FO 371/23221, 156–164.

Malcolm MacDonald. Maugham, Britain's most senior legal authority, was not a member of cabinet, but had been consulted because of the importance of the issue. Palestine was not, however, a subject with which he was familiar.[18]

Lord Maugham felt that in the memorandum the government's case could have been stated better, and significantly that the wording of the McMahon pledge was 'exceedingly vague and unsatisfactory'.[19] The Lord Chancellor, who would later describe the government's 'districts' contention as 'straw', proposed to Baggallay and Baxter two completely novel contentions that he hoped might go some way to strengthening the government's overall case. Although McMahon's intentions were 'not strictly relevant to the construction of that letter', Maugham maintained that it was permissible to take into account the whole of the surrounding circumstances when attempting to get at the true meaning of McMahon's words.

Maugham's first contention related to the importance Great Britain and France attached at the time to the ports on the Mediterranean coast. He suggested it was unthinkable that Sir Henry McMahon should have made a promise to any Arab leader which involved placing under Arab sovereignty the coast on which were situated such strategically important ports as Acre, Haifa and Jaffa. His second contention concerned the importance of Palestine to the whole world, containing as it did sites holy not only to Arabs, but also to Christians and Jews. Again, unthinkable ('inconceivable', according to the Lord Chancellor) that the Allies would, after conquering these sites from one Muslim power, hand them over without safeguards to the undisputed sovereignty of another Muslim power. No hint of either contention had ever appeared before in several hundreds of pages of official records on the Correspondence, neither those produced by numerous 'expert' Foreign Office and Colonial Office officials since 1920, nor by McMahon himself.

Despite this, Maugham proposed that on this basis the government could put forward the contention that the Sharif of Mecca, when he received the letter of 24 October 1915, must have realised that the pledge could not possibly be read as covering territory which included not

---

18 The Lord Chancellor is appointed by the sovereign, on the advice of the Prime Minister.

19 See FO 371/23222, E891, 107; CO 733/409/13.

Lord Frederic Maugham, Lord Chancellor of Great Britain, 1938–1939

only these important ports, but also the Holy Places of three religions. He also expressed the view that the McMahon pledge and the Balfour Declaration were not incompatible. In his opinion, the McMahon pledge excluded Palestine from the area of Arab independence, while the Balfour Declaration did not mean there was to be a state under Jewish sovereignty in Palestine.[20]

Following this meeting, Baggallay commented:

> With all respect [to the Lord Chancellor], I cannot see that this gets us much further.
>
> The existence of important ports on the Palestine coast, and of Holy Places revered by Christians and Jews as well as Arabs in Palestine itself, ought perhaps to have made the Sherif especially wary about making sure that His Majesty's Government had no reservations to make in regard to Palestine. But this does not seem to alter the fundamental principle

20 FO 371/23222, E891, 3 February 1939; CO 733/409/13.

that when A. tells B. he wants X. and B. tells A. in reply that he will give him X–Y, the onus on defining Y. lies on B ...

In the case of the reservation for French interests, it is possibly the case that this reservation applied to all territory to which France had a claim on October 24th, 1915, and that subsequent events were irrelevant ... But this does not get over the difficulty that it may not have been known to the Sherif that the French claimed Palestine on October 24th, 1915. The response ... that the Sherif ought to have found out does not seem to have much legal force.

If it comes to writing a legal counter-memorandum we must put the best face on things possible, and all these points may help. But I doubt if they alter the real situation.[21]

On the same day, 6 February, Oliphant noted:

With all due deference to the Lord Chancellor's views on legal points, I still feel that the then Sheriff (afterwards King Hussein) being a real backwoodsman was not called on to look out for various 'catches' in the McMahon correspondence and in the stress of war cannot be blamed for not taking the pledges *cum grano*.[22]

Oliphant's comments were read by Cadogan, Lord Halifax and 'Rab' Butler, the latter distinctly unimpressed by the Lord Chancellor's novel contention concerning Palestine's strategic importance.[23] Butler commented, 'It does not alter my view of the McMahon correspondence. There is no proof that Sir Henry McMahon was thinking of the "Ports" or "the Port".'[24]

The day before the London Conference opened, the Foreign Office received a stark message from Sir Miles Lampson, Britain's Ambassador in Cairo, who underlined the urgency of coming to an agreement with the Arab world:

---

21 FO 371/23222, E891. Baggallay minute, 6 February 1939. Underlined in the original. Beckett initialled, 'I agree.'
22 FO 371/23222, E891, 105–106; *cum grano*, i.e. with a pinch of salt.
23 Rt Hon. Richard Austen ('Rab') Butler was the government's chief spokesman on Foreign Affairs in the House of Commons.
24 FO 371/23222, E891.

From point of view of defence which so closely affects our position in Egypt I venture to urge extreme importance of its being somehow or other acceptable to Arab rulers and to Egypt. If our solution does not carry them with us then in event of hostilities we risk having to deal simultaneously with Arab rising in Palestine and Arab hostility in Iraq and Saudi Arabia … With Mediterranean and perhaps even Red Sea virtually closed at outbreak of war our position in Egypt would be very difficult.

On other hand a Palestine solution acceptable to Arabs means freeing of troops from Palestine, support of neighbouring Arab countries (with all that means to our communications) and very possibly or indeed probably trouble for Italians from Arabs in Libya.

In short there is great potential strength to be gained or lost and as seen from Egypt our whole military position in the Near East is greatly affected by success or failure of Palestine conference or by decisions which may follow.[25]

Lampson emphasised that his telegram was sent in agreement with the General Officer Commanding and had been shown to the Chief of Imperial General Staff. Indeed, it was clear to all Britain's military leaders that Britain and its Empire could not afford to go to war with the Arab world allied to Germany.[26] The Arab Revolt had not yet been extinguished and throughout the Middle East eyes were focused on Britain's brutal attempts to suppress what was considered to be a genuine – and morally right – nationalist struggle for freedom. Meanwhile, Hitler was threatening Poland and appeared to be about to swallow the rest of Czechoslovakia. London's eye was also firmly on Washington, whose support would be crucial were a European war to break out. Neutrality Acts had been passed by the US Congress in 1935, 1936 and 1937, spurred by the growth of isolationism and non-interventionism following the First World War – all in an endeavour to limit US involvement in future conflicts, and in the spring of 1939 Congress showed no inclination to repeal them.

---

25 FO 371/23222, E978. Sir Miles Lampson to Foreign Office, 6 February 1939.
26 In 1938 the Foreign Office and the Chiefs of Staff had told MacDonald that 'if the Arabs go on the other side against us, we will lose the war.' MM Papers 9/10/11, 'Notes from an interview with Nigel Maslin', 9 December 1976. See also MM Papers, 9/10/30.

Unfortunately for the thirty-eight-year-old Colonial Secretary, a successful conference on the future of Palestine looked distinctly unlikely. In fact, years later MacDonald recalled in a handwritten note that '[In 1939] I definitely believed that the St. James's Conference would not end in an Agreement, and that H.M.G. must therefore have its policy ready for quick announcement and enforcement.'[27]

In July 1937, partition had been the government's proclaimed solution, which had then been hastily withdrawn. In January 1939, with Palestine still in revolt, and as delegates from the Arab world and the Zionist Organisation prepared to come to London, MacDonald's political and military options were strictly limited, and he knew it.

---

27 MM Papers, 9/11/4.

6

Correspondence in the Conferences

1939

On Tuesday, 7 February 1939, at St James's Palace, Prime Minister Neville Chamberlain, flanked by Halifax, MacDonald, Butler and other senior officials, welcomed delegates from Egypt, Iraq, Saudi Arabia, Transjordan and Yemen, and – in a separate ceremony – those of the Jewish Agency, led by Chaim Weizmann, thus inaugurating two separate, parallel conferences to discuss the future of Palestine.[1] For the British, their unspoken top priority was 'to maintain the security of imperial lines to the East'.[2] This meant bringing the revolt to a halt because their image in the Arab/ Islamic world was suffering, and troops were needed to secure Egypt. A Foreign Office note succinctly summarised the government's dilemma:

> The British government were anxious to be fair both to the Arab majority and to the Jewish minority. Their difficulty was two-fold: they had to secure agreement in Palestine, and also to gain support for their policy in England, at Geneva and in the United States of America.[3]

Writing twenty years later, Sir George Rendel, who had been Head of the Middle East Department at the Foreign Office for most of the 1930s, recalled:

---

1 FO 371/23223, E1025, E1026. The St James's Conference is sometimes mistakenly described as a Round Table Conference: for the most part the Arab delegation refused to sit with the Jewish Agency delegation. There were very few meetings in which both sat around the same table.

2 FO 371/23225. Memorandum, unsigned (probably written by the Colonial Secretary), 27 February 1939.

3 FO 371/23227, E1729, 257. Foreign Office Note, 4 March 1939.

It proved extremely difficult to ensure that this Palestine problem was considered on its merits, or from the angle of Palestine itself. One of the most important factors in it was its bearing on Anglo-American relations. Americans could not afford to antagonize the extremely important Jewish vote in New York, Detroit, Chicago, and other cities, and therefore pressed the purely Zionist point of view on us in and out of season. There were many circles even in England which could not afford to risk Jewish hostility or even criticism, and which were therefore ready to support the extreme Zionist point of view, without perhaps understanding the Middle Eastern difficulties which stood in the way of the implementing of a purely Jewish policy. I doubt indeed whether there have been many questions where ignorance of the facts, combined no doubt with genuine idealism, has played a greater part in confusing the real issue.[4]

The Zionists wanted the Mandate to continue – that is, no constitutional development in Palestine, and unrestricted immigration and land sales; the Palestinian Arabs wanted constitutional reform, definite progress towards an independent Palestine state and prohibition on further Jewish immigration and land sales. By 1939, 29 percent of the population were Jews and they owned some 5 percent of the land area of Palestine, making up approximately 10 percent of the total cultivable land.[5]

At the initial meetings, Chamberlain, Halifax, MacDonald and Butler were surrounded by the Marquess of Dufferin and Ava (Parliamentary Under-Secretary of State, Colonial Office), Sir Cosmo Parkinson (Permanent Under-Secretary of State, Colonial Office), Sir Lancelot Oliphant, Sir John Shuckburgh and six other senior officials. In subsequent meetings, Malcolm MacDonald was the lead negotiator on the government's side. The twenty-eight Arab delegates included General Nuri al-Said (Prime Minister of Iraq), Prince Feisal (Foreign Minister of Saudi Arabia)[6] and Prince Muhammad Abdul-Moneim of Egypt. Eight Palestinian Arab delegates attended, led by Jamal Husseini. Of these delegates, some were bilingual graduates of Islamic universities or military institutes, speaking both Arabic and Turkish, but only a handful

---

4 Rendel, *The Sword and the Olive*, 121.
5 Cleveland and Bunton, *A History of the Modern Middle East*, 241.
6 Son of King Ibn Saud, founder of Saudi Arabia; unrelated to King Feisal of Iraq.

were comfortable negotiating in English, in contrast to the twenty-eight Jewish Agency delegates, of whom only a very few were not comfortable negotiating in English. Led by Weizmann, David Ben-Gurion (Chairman, Executive Committee, Jewish Agency), Moshe Shertok (Director, Political Department, Jewish Agency, Jerusalem) and Selig Brodetsky (Director, Political Department, Jewish Agency, London), the Jewish delegates were well prepared. The majority were multilingual and highly educated graduates of European universities, but more significantly for our story, none of them was an indigenous Palestinian. None had been born in Palestine, nor had any of their parents or grandparents: half of them were born either in the Russian or Austro-Hungarian empires, and only six had subsequently made their home in Palestine, including Ben-Gurion and Moshe Shertok. Most of the rest were either British or American, including the only woman delegate, Rose Jacobs, from New York. Such was the international group that was claiming Palestine as its national home, at a time when some 93 percent of the 'national home' was Arab-owned, and had been for centuries.[7]

On Wednesday, 8 February, the Prime Minister and other senior cabinet members listened to Weizmann's wide-ranging, two-hour opening speech, in which the topics covered included Jewish historic links to Palestine, Britain's solemn wartime promises confirmed by the League of Nations, the considerable Jewish achievements in Mandatory Palestine, and the prevailing mass destruction of the Jewish communities in Germany, Austria, Czechoslovakia and Hungary. According to Oliphant, it was 'a most eloquent, moving and adroit appeal'.[8]

On the wartime pledges, Weizmann stated:

It may be true that conflicting promises may have been made as far as Trans-Jordan is concerned, and it is certain that it has not been by way of compromise but by a hundred per cent settlement in favour of the Arabs. The so-called McMahon letters are constantly being quoted, but the ghost of those letters, I think, has been laid; but it does appear from time to time, and perhaps in this connection it is right to remind you of a letter

7 In similar fashion, of the thirty-seven signatories to the Declaration of Independence of the State of Israel on 14 May 1948 in Tel Aviv, only one had been born in Mandatory Palestine.
8 FO 371/23223, 84.

from Lawrence which has just been published. He says, speaking of the settlement for which Mr Churchill was responsible, '[there was] honesty before expediency in order to fulfil our promises in the letter and the spirit.' Sir Henry McMahon himself gave what I thought was a final explanation of this matter.[9]

The following day, Jamal Husseini, speaking in English, addressed the British representatives. The Arab case, he said, was one of self-evident justice. It rested on the natural right of a people to remain in undisturbed possession of their country, and on their natural desire to safeguard their national existence and ensure that it would be secured and developed in freedom and in harmony with their traditions and their ideals. It was the case of a population, who were by nature peaceful and hospitable, trying to preserve the integrity of their country and to prevent the land to which they were deeply attached from being forcibly converted into a national home for another people. He continued:

Arab opposition to [HMG's] policy initiated in Palestine manifested itself soon after the issue of the Balfour Declaration in November 1917. Until then, the Arabs had always lived at peace and on friendly terms with the numerous Jews who were in Palestine from devotional motives. It was only after the issue of the Balfour Declaration, when the Zionist Jews began to exhibit political pretensions and reveal their real intentions that Arab fears and opposition were aroused.

The policy pursued by Great Britain in Palestine since 1918 has shown that Arab fears were far from groundless. The Arabs have been denied the independence which had been promised to them in the British Government's pledge of the 24th of October, 1915, and confirmed in several subsequent pledges, in return for their share in the Allied victory. A mandate was imposed upon them of which the terms were a flagrant violation not only of the promises made to them and of their own natural rights, but also of the right to political independence which was specifically reserved to them in the Covenant of the League of Nations ...

The demands of the Palestinian Arabs may be summarised under four headings:

9 FO 371/23223, E1058. Weizmann was referring here to McMahon's letter to *The Times* of 23 July 1937.

(1) The recognition of the right of the Arabs to complete independence in their country

(2) The abandonment of the attempt to establish a Jewish National Home in Palestine

(3) The abrogation of the Mandate and of the illegalities resulting from it, and its replacement by a treaty similar to the treaty concluded between Great Britain and Iraq, creating in Palestine a sovereign Arab State

(4) The immediate cessation of all Jewish immigration and of land sales to Jews.

The Arabs are prepared to negotiate, in a conciliatory spirit, the conditions under which reasonable British interests shall be safeguarded; to approve the necessary guarantees for the preservation of, and right of access to, all Holy Places, and for the protection of all legitimate rights of the Jewish and other minorities in Palestine.[10]

Husseini's statement was perhaps only the second time that MacDonald had heard the Arab case. As he later said:

I knew there was an Arab case before 1938, but I didn't have to study it ... I hadn't heard the Arab case [before 1938] ... I had heard the Jewish case, and was friendly towards the Jews. It was only when I came into office [appointed Colonial Secretary, May 1938] and begun to be responsible that the Arab case was put to me, and I realised one had to try and find the balance or try and keep one's balance on a tight rope walk ...[11]

---

10 FO 371/23223, E1059, 9 February 1939. An Anglo-Iraqi Treaty in 1930 led to the termination of the Mandate for Iraq, and its entry into the League of Nations in 1932.

11 MM Papers, 9/10/11. Typed notes from an interview with Nigel Maslin, 9 December 1976. Sometime in 1938, MacDonald had reluctantly received Dr Izzat Tannous, Director of the Arab Centre, London, and listened to the Arab case for the first time. Unlike his predecessor at the Colonial Office, Ormsby-Gore, who had been a staunch Zionist supporter since 1917, and who knew Palestine, MacDonald had no previous experience of the Middle East, and had only been to Palestine once, in August 1938, for a two-day secret visit. He said later that he didn't see anything of the country, 'and my trip achieved nothing there, but I had good talks with the High Commissioner'. MM Papers, 9/10/11.

The Question Was One of Intention

At the next plenary session two days later, MacDonald stated:

> Jamal Effendi Husseini has also referred to the pledges of Arab inde-
> pendence given by Sir Henry McMahon in 1915. The Palestinian Arabs
> were entitled to maintain their own interpretation of these pledges; but
> His Majesty's Government had never accepted that interpretation and
> were convinced that they had fulfilled both in the letter and in the spirit
> their obligations to the Arabs. The question was one of intention, and
> surely His Majesty's Government as the authors of the pledges must be
> the best judges of what they had had in mind. There were no firmer
> friends of Arab independence than His Majesty's Government, and he
> rejected the charge of bad faith ...
>
> Palestine had for many centuries been different from any other land
> ..., a country dear to millions of people scattered all over the earth. The
> protection of the Moslem Holy Places was, he felt sure, a matter of
> supreme concern to every delegate present ... His Majesty's Government
> regarded their part in this duty as a high honour and a sacred trust which
> they would faithfully fulfil for as long as they might be associated with
> the government of Palestine.[12]

The Arab delegates were unmoved. Jamal Husseini asked whether the
United Kingdom delegation would put the McMahon documents on
the table for discussion, as that Correspondence was of the highest
importance for the Arab case. He claimed that a question of contract
was at issue and that such a question could not be discussed on the basis
of the intentions of the parties, but on the text of the documents.
Husseini's claim was legally correct. As mentioned previously, to interpret an agreement, you first study the written text and only go to the
surrounding circumstances and the intentions of individual parties
(e.g. McMahon's 1937 letter) if the meaning is not clear from the text.
Moreover, you only do that in order to establish the shared intention
of the parties. The fact that MacDonald stated 'The question was one
of intention' simply confirmed to the Arab delegates the fundamental
judicial weakness of the government's case. In conclusion, Husseini

---

12 FO 371/23223, E1147.

emphasised that the Arab case did not depend only on the interpretation of the pledges but also on the basic and natural rights of his people.

In reply, MacDonald said he would be prepared to consider with his colleagues the question of the publication of the McMahon Correspondence, but that he feared it was almost certain that the decision must be adverse. These were secret documents and subject to the rules applicable to other such documents.[13] Auni Bey Abdul-Hadi, the Sorbonne-educated Palestinian lawyer, objected: in 1919 the government had sent copies of the McMahon letters to King Feisal and it was difficult to see why they should not now be published. As Private Secretary to King Feisal he had seen these copies. He had also communicated copies of the McMahon Correspondence to the Peel Commission in 1936, and therefore it could not now be regarded as secret. However, Auni Bey emphasised that the Arab case was based primarily on their natural rights and that the McMahon pledges were only a secondary element.

Jamal Husseini then pointed out that King Hussein had published his side of the Correspondence and that there appeared to be no reason why after twenty years the British government should not publish the remainder. He thought it essential that the question of the British government's pledges should first be discussed and that the conference should then proceed to discuss the Arab claims: for independence, for the stoppage of immigration and the prohibition of land sales. George Antonius, the Secretary to the Arab delegations, added that in view of MacDonald's categorical statement that Palestine was not included in the McMahon pledge, it would be quicker in the long run to clear that point up. If this were not done, it would be continually cropping up in later discussions.

MacDonald then suggested that a paper on the pledge should be submitted by the Arab delegation to the United Kingdom delegation and that they would then consider the statement and furnish their own views as to the interpretation of the parts of the McMahon Correspondence that the government had authored.[14] After the meeting, the question of whether or not the McMahon Correspondence should be published was discussed by Colonial Office and Foreign Office representatives, and it was decided in principle that those papers should

---

13 FO 371/23223, E1147, 261.

14 FO 371/23223, E1147. Colonial Secretary's notes of third meeting between the UK and Arab delegations on 11 February 1939.

be communicated to the Arab delegates, and eventually laid before
Parliament in the form of a White Paper.

On 14 February, British officials circulated privately to the Arab
delegation English transcripts of the Correspondence (Arabic transcripts
were circulated to the delegates the following day). The Arab delegates
immediately spotted a large number of inaccuracies in the English texts,
most striking of which was in the relevant passage from McMahon's
letter of 24 October 1915. The surprised Arab delegates read:

> The two <u>vilayets</u> of Mersina and Alexandretta and portions of Syria
> lying to the west of the <u>vilayets</u> of Damascus, Homs, Hama and Aleppo
> cannot be said to be purely Arab, and should be excluded from the
> proposed limits and boundaries.[15]

They also took exception to various other passages in the English texts,
which they said were faulty translations of the Arabic originals.

Baggallay commented that the English text handed to the Arab delegates did indeed differ from that hitherto in use by successive British
governments, in particular that the word <u>vilayets</u> had been substituted
for 'districts'. He had not been party to the decision to provide the
<u>vilayets</u> version to the Arab delegates, and complained later:

> I never felt very happy about these changes myself, which I did not hear
> about until afterwards, because they meant that we were giving the Arabs
> different texts, not only from those on which H.M.G. had been working
> all these years, but also from those communicated to the Emir Feisal in
> 1919 and 1921 and to the Royal Commission (who published extracts) in
> 1937.[16]

---

15 FO 371/23223, 349. See also FO 371/23225, E1441, 96. Copies of all the
Correspondence in English, circulated to the Arab delegation on 14 February, can be
found in FO 371/23223, E1217, 339–369. Photostat copies of all the Correspondence
in Arabic, as circulated to the Arab delegation on 15 February, can be found in FO
371/23223, E1217, 311–337. For the Arabic version of the 24 October 1915 letter
circulated by HMG to the Arab delegates on 15 February, see FO 371/23223, 314.
This version is stamped as a Certified True Copy, and signed by the Assistant Oriental
Secretary, Cairo, T.C. Ravensdale, 19 June 1937.

16 FO 371/23223, E1217. Baggallay minute, 27 February 1939.

So why did the government circulate this <u>vilayets</u> version (the 1919 translation by Vickery and Keown-Boyd, with Trott's amendments), when Churchill had spoken in 1922 of the 'district of Damascus' in the Commons, and the Royal Commission in 1937 had published extracts using the word 'district'? The official records do not reveal which very senior official decided to present this misleading translation; it was certainly not Baggallay. Was this fundamentally dishonest manoeuvre executed in order to show that successive governments had been acting in good faith, even if it was 'mistaken' good faith? The official records consistently show that rebutting the accusation of bad faith was a long-standing and significant factor in British officials' thinking.

The following day, at the sixth meeting of conferences, it was agreed that an Anglo-Arab committee should be set up to consider the Correspondence, specifically to shed light on the 'meaning and intention of the correspondence'.[17] George Antonius countered MacDonald's attempt to belittle the proposed investigation as 'an honest difference of opinion'. 'The difference', Antonius said, 'is not one of points of view, but of fact.' And were they to engage in a serious study of these facts, Antonius told MacDonald, 'there could be no room for difference of opinion.'[18]

The Arab representatives on the committee were led by General Nuri al-Said, Prime Minister of Iraq (replaced after the first two meetings by Sayyid Taufiq al-Suwaidi); Abdul-Rahman Bey Azzam, Egyptian Minister in Baghdad and Jedda; two Palestinians, Auni Bey Abdul-Hadi and Musa Bey al-Alami; George Antonius, Secretary-General, Arab delegations; and, as advisor, Sir Michael McDonnell, the Chief Justice of the Supreme Court of Palestine, who was sacked after he condemned the destruction Britain wrought in Jaffa in 1936.

---

17 The Anglo-Arab Committee met four times between 23 February and 16 March. At the first meeting, the Arabs handed in a memorandum explaining generally the Arab interpretation of the Correspondence. At the second meeting, on 24 February, the Lord Chancellor handed in a memorandum explaining generally the British interpretation. At the third meeting, on 28 February, the Arabs handed in two memoranda: some legal points, expounded by Sir Michael McDonnell, and more general points provided by George Antonius. Finally, on 16 March, the Lord Chancellor handed in a memorandum commenting on the two Arab memoranda of 28 February. See Anglo-Arab Committee Report (Cmd 5974): https://unispal.un.org/DPA/DPR/unispal.nsf/0/4c4f7515dc39195185256cf7006f878c (accessed 26 April 2019).

18 FO 371/23224. Minutes of 15 February meeting. See Boyle, *Betrayal of Palestine*, 7.

MacDonald expressly asked the Lord Chancellor, Lord Frederic Maugham, to be the United Kingdom representative on this committee. A veteran barrister and judge, the seventy-two-year-old Maugham had had a distinguished career in the judiciary and was, by any standards, a 'safe pair of hands'.[19] Although the official records do not reveal MacDonald's explicit instructions to the Lord Chancellor, it is clear from the latter's statements to the committee that he had been charged not only with upholding the government's interpretation of the Correspondence, but also with appearing as accommodating as possible to the Arab contentions. It is also telling that the Colonial Secretary initially arranged for the Lord Chancellor to be the sole British representative. MacDonald did not want a repeat of the Peel Commission's private dissention over the interpretation of the Correspondence: he required an appropriate, unanimous British verdict from the committee. Maugham was to be assisted by Sir Grattan Bushe, Legal Advisor at the Colonial Office,[20] and Baggallay, who was charged with bringing the Lord Chancellor up to speed on the Correspondence and the connected pledges and undertakings.[21] In the days before the first meeting of the committee, Baggallay sent Maugham a number of notes, including:

> For reasons unconnected with Palestine (mainly the fear which has always been entertained that our encouragement of the Sharif Hussein to assume the Caliphate in opposition to the Ottoman Sultan might offend Moslem opinion in India) the McMahon-Hussein correspondence has always remained unpublished until now – or rather it has not been published

19 Maugham was called to the bar in 1890, became King's Counsel in 1913 and was knighted in 1928. He became a member of the Privy Council in 1934 and a Lord of Appeal in 1935. Neville Chamberlain appointed him Lord Chancellor in March 1938. The author W. Somerset Maugham was his younger brother.

20 Sir Henry Grattan Bushe was born in Trinidad in 1886, the son of John Scott Bushe, the Colonial Secretary of Trinidad. Called to the bar in 1909, he joined the Colonial Office in 1917, and was appointed Legal Advisor to the latter in 1931.

21 However, at the final meeting of the committee, when a joint Anglo-Arab report was signed, both Bushe and Baggallay were officially recorded as government representatives, alongside the Lord Chancellor. The report was signed by T. Swaidy, A.R. Assam, Auny Bey Abdul-Hadi, Musa Bey al-Alami, G. Antonius; Maugham, Bushe, Baggallay. FO 371/23231, 325.

officially by His Majesty's Government until now. To my mind it would have been much better if it had been officially published in full long ago.[22]

The three pledges connected with the Correspondence that Baggallay highlighted for the Lord Chancellor were the Hogarth Message, the Sykes–Picot Agreement and the Declaration to the Seven.

Declaration to the Seven

In May 1918, seven Arab notables resident in Cairo, mostly Palestinians, Lebanese and Syrians, had submitted a note to the British government. Concerned about Britain's true intentions for the region, following the publication of the Sykes–Picot Agreement and the Balfour Declaration, they asked whether it was Britain's intention that the Arabs should enjoy complete independence. On 16 June 1918, Commander David Hogarth, Director of the Arab Bureau in Cairo, conveyed to the seven a declaration, from 'His Majesty's Government', drafted by Sykes in London. According to Antonius, the declaration contained two assurances of fundamental importance:

> [One, Great Britain] would continue to work not only for the liberation of those countries from Turkish rule but also for their freedom and independence. The other, that she pledged herself that no regime would be set up in any of them that was not acceptable to their populations.[23]

Referring to the Hogarth Message and the Declaration to the Seven, Baggallay informed Maugham:

> Both these declarations are obviously embarrassing. I do not see how they can be explained away any more than any of the rest of the declarations made regarding Palestine in the years during and immediately after the War. The only thing that it seems possible to say is that all these questions were taken

---

22 FO 371/23224, 252.
23 Antonius, *Awakening*, 273. A copy of the declaration is in Antonius, *Awakening*, Appendix D, 433–434.

into account (although I doubt whether it is strictly true) when the Mandate for Palestine was conferred upon Great Britain by the League of Nations.[24]

Baggallay also sent him a typed memorandum entitled 'The Sykes–Picot Agreement of May 16, 1916; explanations given to the Sherif of Mecca',[25] which described the meetings in the Hijaz in May 1917 between Sykes, Picot and King Hussein. Baggallay concluded that

> there was nothing to show that any attempt was made to make unmistakeably clear to the Sherif (or the King as he was by then) the full extent of the reservations made by His Majesty's Government ...
>
> [The memorandum] does not, I'm afraid, aid that case very much. It is not far from the truth when Mr Antonius says that the Allies kept the Sherif in deliberate ignorance of their real intentions regarding the Arab territories. The actual truth is probably that they had no fixed intentions at all at this period, and hesitated to face the Sherif with disturbing possibilities which might not in the end materialise.[26]

Oliphant wrote 'Yes' in the margin opposite 'The actual truth ...' phrase in Baggallay's minute. According to the Palestinian historian Abdul Latif Tibawi, there is considerable evidence that Sykes and Picot did keep King Hussein in the dark concerning British and French intentions regarding the Arab territories.[27] In a note sent to Maugham, Bushe and Downie, Baggallay specified the three documents from which government instructions regarding McMahon's pledge of 24 October 1915 could be traced, and enumerated points which appeared from these documents: first, McMahon's telegram of 18 October 1915, with his general suggestions of what he might say to the Sharif on the subject of boundaries of Arab independence; second, Sir Edward Grey's telegram concurring generally with McMahon's suggestions; and third, McMahon's despatch of 26 October 1915, where he enclosed a copy of his 24 October 1915 letter to the Sharif and commented upon its terms.

24 FO 371/23224, E1357, 22 February 1939.
25 FO 371/23226, E1548, 22 February 1939.
26 FO 371/23226, E1548. Baggallay minute, 22 February 1939. Initialled also by Beckett, Baxter, Oliphant, Rab Butler and Lord Halifax.
27 For a useful discussion of this *transparency vs. perfidy* debate, see Tibawi, *Anglo-Arab Relations*, 179–186.

According to Baggallay, four points emerged from an examination of the three documents:

(*a*) Neither Palestine nor Jerusalem was mentioned at any point.

(*b*) There is nothing in the documents which is actually inconsistent with Sir H. McMahon's statement that in giving the pledge he intended to exclude Palestine from the area of Arab independence.

(*c*) There is, on the other hand, nothing which positively supports this statement.

(*d*) The most definite indication which Sir H. McMahon gives of his intentions is in paragraph 4 of his despatch of the 26th October, in which he says that he has been 'definite in excluding Mersina, Alexandretta and those districts on the northern coast of Syria which cannot be said to be Arab and where I understand that French interests have been recognised'.[28]

On 14 February 1939, the same day the government circulated its vilay-ets version of the letter to the Arab delegation, Kenneth Pickthorn (Conservative, Cambridge University) asked the Prime Minister in the Commons whether the government were prepared to publish the Correspondence as a White Paper. Following standard parliamentary procedure, the Foreign Office had asked the amenable Pickthorn, who was also President of Corpus Christi College, to raise the question in the House. It was the twenty-fifth such request for publication since 1920. Neville Chamberlain duly surprised the Commons by announcing:

Yes, Sir. A White Paper containing the correspondence is being prepared and will be issued as soon as possible. Meanwhile, for the convenience of business, copies of the letters are being placed at the disposal of the delegates to the Palestine Conference, whose proceedings are confidential.[29]

Seymour Cocks, a veteran recipient of government rebuffs on this issue, was immediately on his feet asking why, when successive British governments had always refused to publish the Correspondence on the grounds

---

28 FO 371/23226, E1549. Baggallay note, 22 February 1939.
29 Hansard, Commons, 14 February 1939, vol. 343, c1558.

of national interest, it was now in the national interest to do so. The
Prime Minister replied:

> I cannot go into the reasons why successive Governments have not thought
> it right to publish it before ... the publication was asked for by the Arab
> delegates, and it was thought desirable that it should be published in answer
> to their request. As they were going to have that information, it was thought
> desirable that the House should have it also.[30]

Two days after the government's announcement, Harold Downie, First
Secretary of the Colonial Office, wrote a confidential memorandum to
the Foreign Office:

> The documents circulated cannot necessarily be regarded as exact copies
> of the original documents. They are copies of the documents in the FO
> archives which were sent to London from Cairo, but whether the letters
> from the Sherif of Mecca are in all cases the original letters is not certain,
> nor is it certain whether the letters from Sir Henry McMahon corre-
> spond exactly with the letters actually dispatched to the Sherif.[31]

Given the Arab delegation's allegations of faulty translations, Maugham
requested to have the advice of an independent Arabic scholar who
could not be suspected by the Arabs of being subservient to the government's point of view.[32] Baggallay contacted the School of Oriental
Studies,[33] who recommended James Heyworth-Dunne, an orientalist
scholar and Senior Lecturer in Arabic. Heyworth-Dunne had studied
Arabic literature under Sir H.A.R. Gibb, and was fluent in Turkish,
Persian and Urdu, as well as Arabic. He made a preliminary study of the
texts and informed Baggallay of a number of mistakes, in particular that
wilāyāt had been incorrectly translated as <u>vilayets</u>.[34] Baggallay duly
informed Maugham of this embarrassing development on 22 February,

---

30 Hansard, Commons, 14 February 1939, vol. 343, c1558.

31 FO 371/23223, E1217, 16 February 1939.

32 FO 371/23228, 21.

33 Now known as SOAS: School of Oriental and African Studies, a constituent
college of the University of London.

34 FO 371/23225, E1441.

the day before the first meeting of the committee set up to investigate the Correspondence.

That same day, Baggallay noted, 'It seems to me to be pretty clear that no one gave Palestine a thought either one way or the other when drafting the McMahon pledge.' This produced a further comment underneath from Oliphant: 'Speaking from personal recollection of the manner in which certain matters were dealt with in 1915 I agree entirely.' Charles W. Baxter, the Head of the Eastern Department at the Foreign Office, added his own comment: 'I fear our case on the McMahon pledge gets weaker with each new investigation.'[35]

On 22 February, the Colonial Secretary reported to the cabinet on the progress of the conferences on Palestine and explained that a committee had been set up to consider the McMahon–Hussein Correspondence, and that he was grateful to the Lord Chancellor for undertaking the chairmanship. He feared, however, the probable upshot would be that the committee would report that, after investigating the matter, they were unable to reach agreement. MacDonald was also distinctly pessimistic concerning the outcome of the main conference. A day earlier, he had written to Sir Harold MacMichael, the new High Commissioner in Palestine, that 'it is unlikely that we shall get a definite agreement with either the Arab or the Jewish Delegations. We shall probably therefore have to announce on our own responsibility our Palestine policy as soon as the conference ends.'[36]

The Lord Chancellor, who was also present, explained some of the difficulties in dealing with the English texts which had been badly translated into Arabic, and for which there were sometimes more than one Arabic translation. He hoped, however, that they would be able to persuade the Arabs that 'we had acted honestly'.[37] Although the Lord Chancellor informed the cabinet committee correctly that the English text had been translated badly into Arabic, his statement that 'there was

35 FO 371/23226, E1549.

36 FO 371/23226, E1519. MacDonald to High Commissioner, 21 February 1939. MacMichael had taken over as High Commissioner in Palestine from Wauchope in March 1938. A veteran of two decades of colonial service in the Sudan, MacMichael was the only High Commissioner of Palestine who spoke Arabic. During his tenure (1938–1944), he survived seven assassination attempts by Zionist extremist groups.

37 FO 371/23225, E1466. Extracts from Cabinet Conclusions 8 (39), 22 February 1939.

more than one Arabic translation' was incorrect. The official records at Kew contain single and uncontested Arabic texts; there were differing *English* translations.

The following day, at the first meeting of the Anglo-Arab (McMahon–Hussein) committee, Maugham confined himself to making a few general comments. He made it clear that he was present as the government's representative, and not in any capacity as a judge. As Chair of the committee, and Britain's sole representative, he stated that 'we may report to the Conference that the Arab view is correct, or the government's view, or that we could not reach a common basis of agreement.' Whatever conclusions the committee might reach about the text, he hoped that he would at any rate be able to prove to the satisfaction of the Arab delegates that the government's attitude had been honourable throughout and that 'they had never wavered in the view of the interpretation of the Correspondence which they held.'[38] Was this last remark by the Lord Chancellor the main reason why the <u>vilayets</u> translation had been circulated to the Arab delegation on 14 February?

In his introductory presentation of the Arab case, Antonius reviewed the historical background, including the Sharif's initial contacts with Lord Kitchener, Britain's aims concerning Palestine at the beginning of the war, and referred to some specific inaccuracies in the English texts provided to them the previous week. He emphasised that the use of the word <u>vilayets</u> was not only a misleading rendering of the word *wilāyāt*, but also unjustified because the McMahon notes were issued from the residency in Cairo in Arabic, and that Arabic text was itself a translation from an English original. In that English original the word used in several contexts was the word 'district', as it was in the White Paper of 1922 and in the 1937 Report of the Palestine Royal Commission. He concluded by pointing out the evidence provided by the Sharif's actions in 1917–1918, and alluded in general terms to the Balfour Declaration, the Hogarth Message and the Declaration to the Seven.[39] At the end of the meeting, Maugham agreed that Antonius and Heyworth-Dunne would examine the errors in translation in the English text of the Correspondence 'which Mr Antonius had claimed to find'.

---

38 FO 371/23227, 127.
39 FO 371/23225, E1442, 101–114.

Although the Arabs refrained from any accusation of malpractice, the implications were clear. The October 1915 letter from the residency was in English, using the English word 'districts'. The English translation circulated by the government on 14 February 1939 had replaced 'districts' with <u>vilayets</u> throughout. For their part, the government could not dispute the fact that 'districts' had been used both by Churchill and in the Peel Report.

With the Lord Chancellor in the Chair, the British controlled the procedure of the committee. A detailed discussion of the complex issue, point by point, would have been distinctly embarrassing for the government. So, the procedure adopted following the introductory meeting was as follows: in the second meeting the Lord Chancellor stated the British case by reading a carefully written memorandum, drafted mostly by Baggallay. In the third meeting, the Arab delegation stated their case in two separate memoranda – one general, the other focused on the legal aspects. At each meeting, following the formal statements, considerable discussion ensued, but only the carefully crafted written statements of each side appeared as annexes in the published, joint report.

From the outset of the committee's meetings, the British contended that in order to come to a correct interpretation of the Correspondence it was necessary to take into account 'not only the words of the Correspondence itself, but all the surrounding circumstances'. In fact, during all four meetings the Lord Chancellor focused almost exclusively on the surrounding circumstances, and avoided textual analysis of the Correspondence as much as possible. On the other side, the Arab delegation maintained that 'the proper basis for a judgment on the whole question was primarily the text of the Correspondence itself.'[40] Moreover, they emphasised that they only wanted the 'truth elucidated' concerning the meaning of the Correspondence: they had no wish either to accuse the British of any duplicity or to discuss – or make any moral judgement – about the government's wartime policies.[41]

At the first meeting, Antonius had alluded to the Hogarth Message, which had never been published by the British government, but about which he had written in his book, *The Arab Awakening*, published the previous year. According to Antonius, Hogarth, in his two interviews

---

40 Anglo-Arab Committee Report (Cmd 5974), March 1939, 8.
41 Anglo-Arab Committee Report, 40.

with Sharif Hussein in Jedda in January 1918, had, on behalf of the British
government, given an explicit assurance that 'Jewish settlement in
Palestine would only be allowed in so far as it would be consistent with
the political and economic freedom of the Arab population.' Hogarth's
Message had been delivered orally, but Hussein had taken it down, and
the quotation in *The Arab Awakening* comes from Antonius's translation
of the note made by the King at that time. Antonius's contention was that
the phrase 'political and economic freedom' represented a fundamental
departure from the text of the Balfour Declaration, which only guaranteed the civil and religious rights of the Arab population. In 1937, he had
written, perhaps prophetically – and certainly with common sense:

> In that difference lay the difference between a peaceful and willing Arab-
> Jewish cooperation in Palestine and the abominable duel of the last twenty
> years. It is beyond all reasonable doubt certain that, had the Balfour
> Declaration in fact safeguarded the political and economic freedom of the
> Arabs, as Hogarth solemnly assured King Hussein it would, there would
> have been no Arab opposition, and indeed Arab welcome, to a humanitar-
> ian and judicious settlement of Jews in Palestine.[42]

At the second meeting of the committee, which took place on 24
February, the Lord Chancellor read a detailed, carefully crafted memorandum (drafted jointly with Baggallay) explaining the five principal
reasons why from 1915 the government had believed that McMahon
had excluded Palestine from the area of Arab independence. He
concluded by expressing the hope that he had convinced the committee
that the government and their predecessors were guiltless of any breach
of faith, adding that he must in any case repudiate strongly any such
charge, and appealing to the committee to remember that whatever
might have happened in the past, 'it was now necessary to take account
of the realities of the situation.'[43]

Following the Lord Chancellor's statement, there was a brief discussion, in which Maugham pointed out that 'if you define the names,
Homs etc., as the small regions around the towns, then you leave the
country westwards undefined.' To which Antonius replied, 'the

42 Antonius, *Awakening*, 268.
43 FO 371/23225, E1443, 24 February 1939; FO 371/23227, 151–166.

excluded areas were left vague as to Longitude, but <u>not</u> as to Latitude'; in other words, the extent of the region westwards was doubtful, but not southwards.[44]

Although the recorded written memorandum read out by Maugham does not discuss the Hogarth Message, the original pencil-written notes of John R. Colville, Secretary of the committee, offer a more illuminating account. These reveal that the Lord Chancellor made some remarks about the Balfour Declaration and the effect of its interpretation by the Hogarth Message.[45] Maugham also drew attention to the importance which should be attached to statements by McMahon, Sykes, Clayton and Lawrence – in their view, Palestine had not been included in the area of promised Arab independence – and then turned to Lord Grey's intervention in the House of Lords in 1923.

Colville's notes, summarising Maugham's comments, speak for themselves:

> Lord Grey's speech. Inconsistent engagements? A misunderstanding of the Balfour Declaration. He was in opposition. It was in the middle of a debate. He had entirely overstated the Balfour Decl: L. C. doesn't agree that the B. D. implies there is to be a Zionist Govt in Pal.
>
> <u>The Hogarth Statement</u>. L. C. not prepared to dispute Hogarth's assurance that Jewish settlement would only be in acc. with polit. and ec. freedom of Arab pop.
>
> 'Civil and religious rights' of Arab pop. ought to receive a liberal interp. because of the message given to Sherif by Hogarth. <u>It is reasonably clear that the Jews are not entitled to a Zionist State in Palestine</u> ... Balfour (reputation for honesty: he thought he was doing nothing contrary to pledge and he did not think Decl. wd involve a Jewish claim in Pal.).[46]

Maugham's own scribbled notes of the meeting are equally revealing:

---

44 FO 371/23225, E1484, 256. Underlined in the original.

45 FO 371/23225, E1484.

46 FO 371/23255, E1484, 256–257. Underlined in the original. 'Balfour's reputation for honesty ... did not think he was contradicting previous pledges ... that the Declaration did not mean a Jewish claim in Palestine?' All highly debatable points, but not the subject of this study.

Three things in my opinion are clear (1) Whatever may have been the Arab interpretation of the McMahon correspondence, Sir. H. did not intend it to deal with Palestine. (2) As a matter of strict legal interpretation, the reservation of French interests was sufficient to exclude Palestine from the pledge. (3) GB has never regarded herself as free to act in Palestine without reference to the rights and interests of Arabs in that land. The proclamations of Allenby, the Anglo French dec^n, the Sykes–Picot agreement, the Hogarth statements to the King Husain.

Speaking for myself, and without binding the Govt, I should have thought the Arabs would have been well advised in the present circes if they had urged that there is no very great diff^{ce} between 'civil and religious rights' in the Decl^n, and 'political and economic freedom' in the Hogarth message – and that the Arabs are entitled to rely on the latter as explaining the former and giving it a very wide meaning.[47]

Writing some thirty years later, Colville (now Sir John Colville, CB, CVO) stated that the Balfour Declaration 'promised the Jews a home' and that McMahon in his correspondence with the King of the Hijaz 'had assured the Arabs ... that when they were liberated from the rule of the Turkish Sultan, all Arabia, including Palestine, would be theirs to inhabit and govern'.[48]

Considered by his colleagues to be formidably intelligent, discreet and a talented writer – so the consummate civil servant – Colville had joined the Foreign Office straight from Oxford, whence he'd graduated with first-class honours in History. Two years later he was appointed Private Secretary to Prime Minister Neville Chamberlain, and for most of the following decade served as Private Secretary to Churchill and Attlee. In February 1939, he was a junior official at the Foreign Office under Baggallay and made meticulous notes at all four meetings of the Anglo-Arab Committee. Colville's later statement that Palestine was included in the area promised to the Sharif is thus significant and can hardly be swept aside as that of a 'sincere but misguided, guilt-ridden British official', as suggested by Friedman.[49] Colville is best known as

47 FO 371/23225, E1484, 255.
48 J.R. Colville, Man of Valour: The Life of Field-Marshal the Viscount Gort (London, 1972), 259.
49 Friedman, Palestine. A Twice-Promised Land?, xiii–xv.

the author of *The Fringes of Power. Downing Street Diaries, 1939–1955*, a 750-page tome which provides an intimate view of 10 Downing Street during Churchill's wartime premiership. The *Diaries* also reveal Colville as a discerning and balanced judge of character. Concerning Baggallay, whom he served under between 1937 and 1939, Colville wrote that the latter was 'certainly the perfect Head of a Department',[50] a far cry from Elie Kedourie's assessment of the man as incompetent and negligent over the Correspondence issue.[51]

For his part, Baggallay commented that he personally was delighted with what the Lord Chancellor said on the subject of the Balfour Declaration and the Hogarth Message. Writing about Maugham's acknowledgement that Hogarth's Message included Palestinians' rights 'both economic and political', he described the effect on all the Arab delegates as 'electrical':

> I am certain that the first part of his remarks, especially a long lecture upon the interest of the Christian world in Palestine not only upset but also bored the Arab Representatives. Their attitude completely changed, however, when he made his closing remarks. I am sure that the right thing was to admit frankly the wording of the Hogarth Message ... [It] may go a long way towards convincing the Arabs of our good faith over the question of the Arab pledges generally.[52]

The following day, Baggallay received the detailed results of Heyworth-Dunne's examination of the Arabic and English texts:

---

50 John Colville, *The Fringes of Power. Downing Street Diaries, 1939–1955* (London, 1985), 33. Herbert Lacy Baggallay (1897–1943) was educated at Rugby School and Sandhurst, served in the Rifle Brigade during the First World War, and was wounded and mentioned in despatches. He joined the Foreign Office in 1921, going on to serve as acting Head of the Eastern Department from 1939 to 1940. He died, aged forty-five, in July 1943 while in office as Counsellor, USSR. His obituary included: 'Those of his colleagues who had the great fortune to work with him will know not only that they have lost a faithful and charming friend, but that the foreign service has lost one of its most promising members whose sureness of judgment, efficiency in action, quick sympathies and uprightness of character marked him out for great things.' *The Meteor*, Rugby School, 25 October 1943, no. 892, 159.
51 Kedourie, *Labyrinth*, 126, 297.
52 FO 371/23225, E1484. 227–228.

> The following are the more obvious cases of mis-translation which Mr
> Antonius and I consider advisable to correct in your proofs. I have
> discussed these points fully with Mr Antonius and we are in complete
> agreement as to what they should be.[53]

Heyworth-Dunne's conclusions left no room for doubt:

> The term vilayet (Arabic, *wilayah*) is often wrongly used. None of the
> so-called vilayets in [that paragraph] is a vilayet except Aleppo.[54]

Then followed a list of twenty-five other mistakes in the English texts. It is
notable that Antonius and Heyworth-Dunne were in complete agreement
concerning all twenty-six mistakes. What does that indicate about the
standard of Vickery's (1919), Young's (1920) and Trott's (1939) translations?[55]

Later the same day, Heyworth-Dunne wrote a personal explanatory
note to Baggallay:

> Dear Mr Baggallay,
>   As an afterthought, the word VILAYET with a 'v' at the beginning and
> an 'et' at the end is TURKISH and means 'an administrative province'.
>   The word WILAYAH with a 'w' at the beginning and 'ah' at the end
> is ARABIC and has a much wider meaning. It can mean 'district' or 'area'
> or 'the seat of a Governor'.
>   As the documents are in Arabic, it can be argued that it has the Arabic
> meaning. Taking into consideration the 'surrounding circumstances', I
> think it has been used without discrimination. Turkish words and expres-
> sions were so commonly used at this time.
>   Yours sincerely,
>   J. Heyworth-Dunne.[56]

Was it particularly embarrassing for the government to acknowledge
that its use of <u>vilayets</u> in that key letter was an inaccurate translation?

---

53 FO 371/23226, E1571, 119. Heyworth-Dunne's typed letter to Baggallay, 25
February 1939.
54 FO 371/23225, E1441, 96.
55 FO 371/23226, E1571, 119–120.
56 FO 371/23226, E1571. Heyworth-Dunne to Baggallay, 25 February 1939.

George Antonius – trilingual, honourable and discerning

James Heyworth-Dunne, who was 'in complete agreement with Antonius concerning all twenty-six mistakes in the texts offered by the government'.

What was the Colonial Office thinking? Perhaps they calculated that although it would be mildly embarrassing to acknowledge the inaccuracy of their translation, the <u>vilayets</u> text might go some way to supporting the government's contention that they had acted in good faith since 1915. However, as mentioned previously, that contention was hard to defend.

On 28 February, Antonius, followed by Sir Michael McDonnell, the Arab delegation's Legal Advisor, presented the Arab case in great detail. So that each side's specific contentions and counter-contentions can be easily comprehended, the lengthy reports of both meetings (24 February, the Lord Chancellor's memorandum, and 28 February, the two Arab memoranda, Antonius and Sir Michael McDonnell) have been amalgamated in the sections that follow.[57]

Palestine's Global Importance

The Lord Chancellor stated that all governments of the United Kingdom from 1915 onwards had held firmly to the opinion not only that Sir Henry McMahon intended, especially by his letter of 24 October 1915, to leave the territory now known as Palestine outside the area of Arab independence, but also that the Correspondence between McMahon and the Sharif of Mecca in 1915 and 1916 could not then and 'cannot now be read as having any other meaning'. Palestine was in a unique position at the time of the Correspondence: it was 'the Holy Land of three great religions' and 'the interest of almost all the countries in the world had to be taken into account.' Thus, it would have been 'inconceivable' that McMahon would have included Palestine in the region promised to King Hussein.

The Arab delegation countered that

> not one single word of the worldwide importance of the Holy Land appears in the McMahon Correspondence. Freedom to act without detriment to the interests of France was the only condition precedent to recognition and support of Arab independence in any portion of the territory involved.[58]

---

57 The Lord Chancellor's official memorandum/statement, entitled 'The McMahon-Hussein Correspondence', is in FO 371/23225, E1484, 237–252; also in the Anglo-Arab Committee Report, Annex B, 18–26. The statements by Antonius and Sir Michael McDonnell can be found in FO 371/23226, E1605, 178–191 and FO 371/23226, E1601, 148–163; also in the Anglo-Arab Committee Report, Annexes C and D, 26–41.

58 Anglo-Arab Committee Report, 31.

Surrounding Circumstances

According to the Lord Chancellor, because the language used had given rise to controversy and speculation it was legitimate to take all the surrounding circumstances into account when attempting to reach a decision as to what the words could and should have been taken to mean. Maugham referred to the importance, for the government, of the port of Haifa, and the protection of Egypt and the Suez Canal, and claimed that as these were nowhere mentioned in the Correspondence, McMahon must have simply assumed Palestine as 'automatically and obviously' excluded from the area promised to Hussein. It would have been, according to the Lord Chancellor, 'inconceivable' for McMahon to have thought otherwise. This was the second part of Maugham's 'global importance of Palestine' contention. 'Not so', the Arabs replied: the Sharif's proposals envisaged a military alliance between Great Britain and the future independent Arab government of Palestine, and McMahon had further stipulated that European advisors and officials required in the future Arab State should be exclusively British.

The weakness of these two 'global importance of Palestine' contentions – as described in the previous chapter – proposed by the Lord Chancellor are not difficult to discern. Firstly, his claim to have inside knowledge of McMahon's mind in 1915 is far from convincing. McMahon had never expressed any such sentiments, either privately to the Foreign Office, or in his letter to *The Times* in 1937. Secondly, in the many hundreds of pages of official records between 1920 and 1939, including Shuckburgh's numerous memoranda throughout the 1920s, Childs's memorandum of 1930 and Mackenzie's memorandum of 1938, all of which critically analysed the issue in great detail, this contention had never been proposed as a defence of the British case.

Maugham then made two assertions in defence of the government's interpretation of the 'districts' phrase. First, however, he did acknowledge that the official name for the district of which Damascus was the capital was the Vilayet of Syria, and that there was no Vilayet of Homs, nor of Hama. Nevertheless, he maintained, 'It is also true that both Damascus and Aleppo were the capitals of Vilayets, and the reference to Damascus should alone have sufficed to establish Sir Henry McMahon's meaning.'[59]

The sophistry of this assertion was easily countered by the Arab delegation:

> To say that when Sir Henry wrote of the 'district of Damascus,' he meant the Ottoman Vilayet of Damascus is exactly as though one should be asked to believe that a reference to the district of Maidstone [the county town of Kent] meant the County of Kent.[60]

The Lord Chancellor's second line of defence concerning the 'districts' phrase was equally unconvincing:

> The best explanation which His Majesty's Government can give ... is that the phrase was borrowed from al-Faruqi and used in the same wide and general sense as that in which he himself used it, i.e. as one which covered the Syrian hinterland southwards to the Gulf of Aqaba.[61]

As mentioned previously, Muhammad Sharif al-Faruqi was the Iraqi Ottoman officer who deserted and turned up in Cairo in the autumn of 1915, where he was interviewed – and taken seriously – by Brigadier Gilbert Clayton and other British officials. He had met Feisal secretly in Damascus in early 1915. Although not an accredited representative either of the Sharif of Mecca or of the leaders of the Arab nationalist movement in Damascus, he was unquestionably well informed as to the views and aspirations of the Arab leaders.

The weakness of this 'borrowed from al-Faruqi' contention – as the Arab delegation pointed out – was that there was no evidence, written or otherwise, offered by the British government to back up their (erroneous?) claim that al-Faruqi held such views, only the contemporary reports of the British officials who had interviewed him. Moreover, the reports had not been made available to the Arab delegation. Nor were they subsequently offered.

---

59 Anglo-Arab Committee Report, 21.
60 Anglo-Arab Committee Report, 29.
61 Anglo-Arab Committee Report, 23.

Golden Rule of Legal Interpretation

The Lord Chancellor's attempt to defend the government's 'districts' contention cut little ice with Sir Michael McDonnell, a man with decades of judicial experience. He suggested that a reference to Map No. 1 in the report of the Royal Commission, which was a War Office map showing the pre-war Turkish administrative districts in Syria and Palestine, or to the map in Antonius's book,[62] made it perfectly easy to give a grammatical and ordinary sense to the words of the British government to which the High Commissioner of Egypt had put his signature. His analysis of Sir Henry's text was forensic:

> That which a Court of Law alone would be governed by in interpreting Sir Henry's letter of 24 October would be that which is called by a very distinguished Judge, Lord Wensleydale, the Golden Rule of legal interpretation, to the effect that in construing all written instruments, the grammatical and ordinary sense of the words is to be adhered to unless that would lead to some absurdity, or some repugnance or inconsistency with the rest of the instrument, in which case the grammatical and ordinary sense of the words might be modified so as to avoid the absurdity and inconsistency but no further …
>
> So far from being clear that Palestine was included in the reservation defined in the letter of 24 October, one can, on the contrary, only say that everything possible was done in order to indicate that it was intended to include Palestine in the area promised to the Sharif. Why, for example, speak of the districts of Damascus, Homs, Hama and Aleppo, not one of which is east of Palestine, and all of which go northward in that order away from Palestine? Why say nothing of the Sanjaks of Hauran and Maan to the west of which the whole of Palestine lies? Why not, if Palestine was to be described, speak of Lake Huleh, the River Jordan, the Lake of Tiberias and the Dead Sea as the eastern boundaries?[63]

Thus, McDonnell claimed, so far from the words in their grammatical and ordinary sense excluding Palestine, they did the exact

---

62 Antonius, *Awakening*, 248.

63 Anglo-Arab Committee Report, 27–28. For McDonnell's complete statement, see FO 371/23226, E 1601, 148–163; also in Anglo-Arab Committee Report, 26–35.

opposite, and left Palestine clearly within the area to which Arab independence was to be granted. Moreover, he pointed out that in McMahon's third letter, dated 14 December 1915, the High Commissioner explicitly referred to the regions which he wished to exclude as being the two 'Vilayets of Aleppo and Beirut'. Had he had Palestine in mind, Sir Michael contended, he would certainly have added 'and the Sanjaq of Jerusalem'. McMahon had not done so.[64]

A Perfectly Clear Reservation?

When it came to McMahon's reservation in respect of French interests, the Lord Chancellor stated that it applied 'to all territory to which France laid claim on 24 October 1915', and that referred to the whole of Syria, including Palestine. The government considered that the specific 'districts' reservation should have sufficed to exclude Palestine; however, they attached less importance to that point than to the general French interests reservation, the wording of which, in Maugham's opinion, was 'perfectly clear'. It should be noted that this contention is in contrast to Curzon, who in his October 1919 letter to Emir Feisal stated that '[HMG] regarded France as having special rights in the area west of those four towns.'[65] Perhaps the Lord Chancellor had not been shown a copy, which may have given him pause for thought.

In reply, George Antonius pointed out that the written, historical evidence proved that British statesmen, in considering the French claim to a special position in Syria (including Palestine), had already felt the necessity of opposing the French claim in so far as it related to Palestine.[66] Therefore, he contended, the reservation made by McMahon in his note of the 24 October 1915 had to be read in the light of the underlying intentions prevailing in Whitehall at the time. For

---

64 Anglo-Arab Committee Report, 13–14.
65 FO 371/20807, E3380, 100. Curzon to Feisal, 9 October 1919.
66 Extracts of the unpublished Sir Maurice de Bunsen Report (June 1915) had been circulated by the Lord Chancellor to the Arab delegation during the second meeting of the committee. See FO 371/23225, E1419. For a copy of the report, see CAB 42/3.

his part, the Lord Chancellor acknowledged that Britain in 1915 desired to restrict French claims on the Levant coast if they could find a legitimate means of doing so. Nevertheless, he maintained, 'There is a great difference between desiring an object and attaining it.'[67] Antonius pointed out that this latter assertion, although obviously true, was beside the point: the point was that the British government desired to exclude Palestine from the sphere of future French influence and were trying in the McMahon Correspondence to pave the way for the attainment of that object.[68]

To back up this latter assertion, Antonius pointed out that the government's intention to remove Palestine from French influence was borne out by the measures they took in Palestine during the war: namely, dropping thousands of leaflets in all parts of Palestine, with a message from Sharif Hussein on one side and a message from the British Command on the other, saying that the independence of the Arabs had been secured by an Anglo-Arab agreement, and asking the Arab population of Palestine to look upon the advancing British army as allies and liberators and to give them every assistance. Under the aegis of the British military authorities, recruiting offices were opened to enlist volunteers for the forces of the Arab Revolt.[69] From the end of 1917 and throughout the greater part of 1918, the attitude of the military and political officers of the British army was clearly based on the understanding that Palestine was destined to form part of the Arab territory which was to be constituted after the war on the basis of independent Arab governments in close alliance with Great Britain.[70]

The Lord Chancellor could not deny the truth concerning those measures taken by the British in Palestine in 1917–1918, and made no effort to do so. What is undoubtedly true is that McMahon's general 'French' reservation (mentioning no boundaries) had, of course, left the government at liberty to interpret as it pleased the reservation to the French and the Arabs at the end of hostilities.

---

67 Anglo-Arab Committee Report, 24.
68 Anglo-Arab Committee Report, 38.
69 Anglo-Arab Committee Report, 15–16.
70 Anglo-Arab Committee Report, 15–16.

Sharif's Gift of Clairvoyance

The Lord Chancellor asserted that the existence of French claims in October 1915 must have been known and understood 'in extreme probability if not in actual fact' by the Sharif of Mecca. In reply, Sir Michael stated there was no evidence of that, and added, 'It seems to me that the Sharif must have been endowed with a remarkable gift of clairvoyance if he understood, from the letters in question, that the Government intended to exclude Palestine from the area whose independence it guaranteed.'[71] Indeed, as mentioned previously, the Royal Commission of 1937 had stated, 'It was thus in ignorance of any other compact than the "McMahon Pledge" that in June, 1916, the Sharif declared war against the Turks.'

Intentions – Again

While admitting that the point had no legal weight on the construction of the letters, the Lord Chancellor drew to the committee's attention that McMahon and Clayton, both concerned with drafting the Correspondence, had placed it on record that the intention had been to exclude Palestine. Sir Michael replied that such intentions seemed to him to be of no consequence whatsoever:

> It was not they who were making an offer to the Sharif; it was, as Sir Henry himself states in his letter of the 24th October, the British Government. The High Commissioner in Egypt was merely the conduit pipe through which the proposals of His Majesty's Government were conveyed to the other party. Sir Gilbert merely made preliminary drafts of the letters.[72]

---

71 Anglo-Arab Committee Report, 33.
72 Anglo-Arab Committee Report, 27. A copy of McMahon's letter to Shuckburgh (12 March 1922) is in FO 371/23225, 59; Clayton's note to Sir Herbert Samuel (12 April 1923) is in FO 371/23225, E1420, 93. Baggallay commented, 'McMahon's letter to Sir John Shuckburgh in 1922 may support Sir Henry McMahon's view that he intended to exclude Palestine, but it hardly supports the view that he succeeded in doing so ... As regards Sir Gilbert Clayton's minute of December 4, 1923, the Lord Chancellor obtained the original minute in Sir Gilbert Clayton's handwriting from Lord Samuel on the morning of the second meeting of the McMahon Committee. The Lord Chancellor showed this to the members of the Committee this morning.' FO 371/23225, E1420. Baggallay minute, 27 February 1939.

Sir Michael pointed out that if any account of intentions should be made, it could only be of that person responsible for the policy, in this case Sir Edward Grey, who made it clear in the House of Lords on 27 March 1923 that 'he entertained serious doubts' as to the validity of the British government's interpretation of the scope of the pledges that he, as Foreign Secretary, had given to the Arabs in 1915.[73]

During the third meeting, the Arab delegation made three supplementary points in favour of the Arab case. First, in his letter McMahon's only stated reason for the exclusion of the portions of Syria to the west of the districts of Damascus, Homs, Hama and Aleppo, as well as the districts of Mersin and Alexandretta, was that 'they cannot be said to be purely Arab.' The Arab delegation acknowledged that the districts of Mersin and Alexandretta contained substantial Turkish minorities, and further south there were other minorities – Alawites in Latakia; Druze and Maronites in Lebanon – each living in relatively compact areas. However, they maintained, it emphatically could not be said that Palestine was an area where the population was not purely Arab: notwithstanding the presence of a number of Christian European institutions, at that time at least 95 percent of the population was Arab.[74] According to the Palestinian scholar Walid Khalidi, 'The Jewish community in Palestine (the majority of whom were non-Zionist) formed in 1919 only 9.7 per cent of the population and owned 2.04 per cent of the land.'[75]

Second, in his third letter, dated 14 December 1915, McMahon referred to the regions which he wished to exclude as being in 'the two Vilayets of Aleppo and Beirut'. Had he had Palestine in mind, claimed the Arab delegation, he would certainly have added 'and the Sanjaq of Jerusalem', a reiteration of a point already mentioned on their behalf by Sir Michael McDonnell. The fact that McMahon did not confirmed that

73 Anglo-Arab Committee Report, 15. See Hansard, Lords, 27 March 1923, vol. 53, c654.

74 Anglo-Arab Committee Report, 30–31.

75 Khalidi, *Palestine Reborn*, 21. Is the discrepancy between the Arab delegation's figure of a 95 percent Arab population and Khalidi's 90.3 percent to be explained by the delegation's inclusion of the indigenous Arabic-speaking Jewish population in its 95 percent figure?

the only portions of Syria which he proposed to reserve in favour of France were the coastal regions in the north.

Third, there was an important discrepancy between the official English text, as circulated on 14 February, and the Arabic version of McMahon's note of 14 December 1915. In speaking of the exclusion of the two vilayets of Aleppo and Beirut, he wrote 'but, as the interests of our ally France are involved *in them both*'. The words in italics occurred in the Arabic version that reached Sharif Hussein, but did not appear in the official English text. The force of these three words showed once more that McMahon had in mind to reserve only those two vilayets and that he could not have been thinking of a third province lying beyond them; the Independent Sanjaq of Jerusalem lay to the south of the Vilayet of Beirut.[76]

Maugham made no attempt to contest these three contentions. In fact, he brought forward no credible evidence, linguistic or otherwise, to substantiate the proposition that the general French reservation covered the Independent Sanjaq of Jerusalem. In sum, all the written evidence demonstrates that both of McMahon's reservations covered only Syria's northern coastal regions.

At the end of the third meeting the Lord Chancellor suggested that Baggallay and Antonius might meet privately and attempt to discover whether there was common ground upon which an agreed report could be drawn up.[77]

Unable to marshal any convincing answers to the detailed Arab contentions, the Lord Chancellor now sought to terminate the discussions. On 3 March, he instructed Baggallay to draft a letter on his behalf to the Arab delegation, reminding them that the main conference expected a report from the Anglo-Arab Committee soon, that he considered further discussion would 'lead to further counter-replies from the Arab side, and this process might continue indefinitely', and although he did not mean to reply to the points made in the two statements, this did not mean that the government accepted all that had been said on those points. His letter would politely suggest that the committee cut short its discussions, and embody in a report to the conference the points on which it was possible to record agreement. As it was, at the end of February the main conference was in full swing and would

76 FO 371/23226, E1605, 178–191.
77 FO 371/23227, 173.

probably have continued for a further two or three weeks, so had the Lord Chancellor wished to continue the discussions there would have been plenty of time to do so.

Baggallay was distinctly doubtful about the wisdom of Maugham's exit strategy, and wrote to him that if there were no further discussions, and a final, joint report was ever published, it might appear that the government had no reply to make to the two Arab statements. He proposed instead that the Lord Chancellor's letter might be transformed into a 'final statement' which could be annexed to a final joint report, if the Arabs could be persuaded to sign one. He suggested that this statement

> could be used at a final – formal – meeting of the Committee, at which nothing would happen except that this statement would be made, the draft report upon which agreement had already been reached would be adopted and signed by those concerned, and a few kind words exchanged on each side in order to conclude the proceedings. It would of course have to be arranged with the Arabs beforehand that the formal meeting <u>would</u> consist of nothing else, and for this purpose they would have to be shown the proposed statement beforehand.[78]

Maugham agreed to Baggallay's suggestion, and over the following two weeks the latter wrote a series of drafts in conjunction with Sir Grattan Bushe, all of which were closely scrutinised and amended during meetings of the Cabinet Committee on Palestine, chaired by the Prime Minister. Successive drafts were sent to Antonius, who negotiated hard. He left Baggallay in no doubt that the Arab delegation also had its red lines.[79]

Leading to the Opposite Conclusion

Although MacDonald was fully occupied directing the main conference, he kept in touch with the Lord Chancellor over the progress of

---

78 FO 371/23230, E1683/6/31. Baggallay to Lord Chancellor, 6 March 1939. Underlined in the original.

79 Baggallay's drafts can be found in FO 371/23227, E1690; FO 371/23227, E1734; FO 371/23228, E1786; FO 371/23228, E1831 and FO 371/23230, E2105. The same paragraph bears a different number in successive drafts.

the Anglo-Arab Committee's proceedings. The Colonial Secretary, embarrassed by the inaccuracy of the English texts, and what they might imply concerning the strength of the British case, asked the Attorney General, Sir Donald Somervell, to study and comment on the papers. Somervell, a well-known barrister, judge and Conservative Party politician, was, in like fashion to the Lord Chancellor, both completely new to the issue and endowed with a formidable, forensic mind.[80] He studied in particular two documents, Mackenzie's lengthy memorandum and the Lord Chancellor's statement of 24 February to the Anglo-Arab Committee.

On 27 February, the day before the third meeting of the committee, Somervell replied confidentially to MacDonald. His letter is quoted extensively here because, first, it is the observations of a disinterested very senior figure, namely the Chief Legal Advisor to the government, and second, even more significantly, it elicited a startling response from the Lord Chancellor.

Somervell informed the Colonial Secretary that he found himself in disagreement with the Lord Chancellor's contention that the Correspondence 'cannot now be read to have any other meaning' than that Palestine was excluded from the region promised to Hussein:

> First of all on the <u>mere words</u>. The argument depends on reading the words 'district of Damascus' as meaning the administrative district or vilayet of Syria … It is clear that the word vilayet is not like the word county used solely as descriptive of administrative units. I think it is therefore necessary to accept that the word 'district' was used and/or <u>would necessarily be</u> read as being <u>used</u> in its general sense …
>
> The [Lord Chancellor's] Memorandum puts in the forefront of the argument the unique position which Palestine held and holds in the world. This fact which is incapable of exaggeration seems to me on one view to lead to the opposite conclusion to that suggested in the

---

80 In 1912, Somervell had become the first chemist to be elected a Prize Fellow of All Souls College, Oxford. He was called to the bar in 1916 (*in absentia* – he was on army service in India), and appointed King's Counsel in 1929. He entered Parliament in 1931, became Solicitor General two years later and was then named Attorney General in 1936. Note: the Attorney General outranks the Solicitor General, but is still subordinate to the Lord Chancellor (Secretary of State for Justice, a cabinet-level position).

Memorandum. It is geographically difficult, I think, to regard the Holy Land as aptly described as a portion of Syria lying to the west of the district of Damascus, particularly having regard to the mention of Hama and Homs and Aleppo. If, however, this was a strip of land which had no particular interest for anyone and had no apt and obvious city or district in it to identify it it would be easier.

It is the fact that Jerusalem has the significance it has for Christians, Jews and Moslems, and other cities and places as great a significance for Christians, that it seems to me insuperably difficult to believe that anyone could possibly have used the words in the letter, and then said to himself that plainly includes Jerusalem, the Lake of Galilee and so on.

If these considerations in the Memorandum were in the mind of the writer of the letter he would surely have said, 'the one thing I must make plain is that we exclude this territory', which could have been perfectly easily described by reference to the districts, the Jordan valley or in other ways.

The uniqueness of the area as emphasised in the [Lord Chancellor's] Memo also seems to me to make the words in the letter explaining the exclusion of the portions of Syria as inept to make them include the Holy Land ...

In considering the fair meaning of the words in all the circumstances, it is, I think, very difficult to suggest that McMahon could have regarded Palestine as automatically excluded ...

I feel strongly that there is great force in saying that letters written in the circumstances in which this letter was, cannot be treated as if they were legal contracts ... but that is not the line successive British Governments have taken. I only write this to let you know my own view that the more we can avoid this issue the better, and that the more closely it is gone into, the greater I think our difficulties will appear to be.[81]

From this, it is notable that the Attorney General considered the government's districts = vilayets argument untenable, and although he agreed with Maugham that Palestine was globally important, he questioned the Lord Chancellor's use of that point, precisely because if McMahon had

---

81 FO 371/23226, E1572. Somervell to MacDonald, 27 February 1939. Underlined in the original. Read by J.R. Colville and Baxter.

intended to exclude Palestine, the latter would and should have explicitly said so, and McMahon had not.

Instead of supporting him, Somervell had simply exposed the obvious weakness of the Lord Chancellor's 'global importance of Palestine' contention. In his reply thanking Somervell for his observations, MacDonald expressed the hope that 'we may avoid any publication of our full statement', and agreed with Somervell that 'the less we publish the better.'[82] MacDonald was keen for Somervell to be up to speed on the issue, because as Attorney General and an MP, Somervell would probably be called upon in the Commons to answer future questions on the issue.

'How Pleased I Would Be'

MacDonald forwarded Somervell's letter to Maugham who, clearly displeased, if not stung, immediately put pen to paper, revealing to the Colonial Secretary for the first and only time (at least in writing) his true convictions about the British case:

My Dear MacDonald,

I could not write fully on the A. G.'s letter of 27th without some offensive observations & will therefore only say that it seems to have been written on the strange misapprehension that the Statement he criticizes represents the views of the persons who put it in – a complete error.

The letter seems to suggest a policy of admitting in full the Arab case & incidentally their view that they have been betrayed by tricky British statesmen.

Personally I should not think that wise or helpful, & should be surprised if you did.

I will conclude by saying how pleased I would be if I could hear of anyone in the Foreign Office or the Colonial Office or in the Government who could make <u>one</u> useful & helpful suggestion to assist in meeting or contesting the Arab claims.

Ever Yours, sincerely,

Maugham.[83]

---

82 CO 733/411/14. MacDonald to Somervell, 1 March 1939.
83 CO 733/411/14, 45–46. Maugham to MacDonald, 28 February 1939. Underlined in the original.

In the first paragraph, Maugham acknowledges to the Colonial Secretary that he himself, the author of the 'global importance of Palestine' contention, does not believe in its validity. As already noted, this was proposed by him as a main plank in his statement at the beginning of the second meeting of the committee. He had thought up this contention following his reading of Mackenzie's memorandum in order to bolster the government's interpretation of the Correspondence, whose weaknesses Mackenzie had so clearly spelled out. From this Somervell–Maugham episode there is thus only one tenable conclusion: the government's two most senior legal officials were in agreement that the British contentions were so weak that they would not stand scrutiny by an independent judicial inquiry, or by Parliament or public opinion.

Maugham's final sentence was a veritable *cri de coeur*.[84] Earlier that same day, he had listened to a two-hour exposé of the Arab case by Antonius and McDonnell and absolutely no one on his side of the table could suggest any convincing counter-arguments. Decades later, the Palestinian lawyer Musa Alami recounted to Geoffrey Furlonge how Sir Michael McDonnell

> had made mincemeat of the reasons originally adduced by Churchill in support of his contention that Palestine had been excluded from the area of promised independence, and the British delegates, whose attitude had changed perceptibly from self-righteousness to discomfort as the hearings proceeded, had finally felt constrained to admit that the Arab contentions 'had more force than had previously been realised' though they could not quite bring themselves to recognise that they were unanswerable.
>
> In any case ... an admission that they had been wronged twenty-two years previously, though it would have given the Palestine Arabs some moral satisfaction, would in the situation now confronting them (to which that wrong had directly led) have been rather in the nature of Dead Sea fruit.[85]

So it is hardly surprising that, as previously mentioned, Maugham then instructed Baggallay to draft a letter to the Arab delegation, politely but firmly closing down the committee without any further meetings.

---

84 Kedourie's apt phrase, *Labyrinth*, 275.
85 Furlonge, *Palestine Is My Country*, 124. Furlonge interviewed Alami in 1961.

Before this, with the committee's private discussions still ongoing, Members of Parliament had been becoming increasingly curious as to why the Correspondence had not been made available promptly, as had been promised on 14 February by the Prime Minister. On 1 March, when the Conservative Deputy Foreign Secretary, 'Rab' Butler, was asked when the White Paper containing the Correspondence would be available, he stated that the delay was due to the fact that 'certain of the Arab representatives made suggestions for alterations in the translation [and] ... as soon as the [alterations] have been agreed upon the official text will be produced.' He assured the House that the government did not wish to deprive honourable members of the opportunity of seeing copies as soon as possible. He then dug a bigger hole for the government's position by acknowledging that 'after the first official circulation had been made, members attending the Conference discovered certain inaccuracies in the translation, and, when these were discovered it was decided to present to the House of Commons an accurate version.'

This statement brought Clement Attlee, the Labour Opposition leader, to his feet:

> We now gather that there are two separate texts. The text which has been the accepted text is the one upon which, presumably, action has been taken throughout these years. It is now said that these texts were wrong and are to be altered. I want to know whether we can have both the texts, the one on which policy has been formed hitherto, and also the correct text?

This prompted a further, startling revelation by Butler:

> I think the right hon. Gentleman may appreciate the point better if it is understood that the original action was taken upon Arabic texts, and when the English translation of the Arabic texts was examined certain of the delegates found that it was inaccurate. It is in the interests of accuracy that this should be put right.[86]

When a surprised Attlee asked whether there had or had not been an authorised translation of those Arabic texts into English, Butler would

---

86 Hansard, Commons, 1 March 1939, vol. 344, cc1247–1249.

only confirm that the Arabic texts were in the government's possession and that they had made their own translation. The increasingly embarrassed minister was then put on the spot by the Liberal leader, Sir Archibald Sinclair:

> Is the right hon. Member trying to persuade the House that the Cabinet have taken action on Arabic texts? Surely the documents which we were promised are the documents which were before the Government and on which the Government have taken action? Those were the documents which the Prime Minister promised. Surely we should have these documents now, and if there are any errors in the translations they can be put right.[87]

Butler could only reply that he would at once consider that point with the Prime Minister.

Baggallay commented later:

> Just at the time I was talking to Mr Antonius ... Mr Butler was having a very difficult time in the House of Commons over the question of the publication of the correspondence. As a result of the attitude of the House, it was decided that the White Paper should be produced at the shortest possible notice, and that the White Paper should indicate the differences between the original text and text agreed to by Mr Antonius and Mr Heyworth-Dunne.[88]

The following day, Thursday, 2 March, the Lord Chancellor reported back to the cabinet that the Correspondence 'was extremely unsatisfactory'. He informed them that, subject to one point,

> it was very difficult to contend that the letter of the 24th October, 1915, contained any specific exclusion of Palestine. At the same time, he thought it would be very undesirable to abandon the view which we had maintained consistently for twenty years, more especially since the Arabs were suspicious people and appeared to regard all our actions as dishonest.[89]

---

87 Hansard, Commons, 1 March 1939, vol. 344, c1249.
88 FO 371/23226, E1587, 140. Baggallay minute, 1 March 1939.
89 FO 371/23227, E1686.

The one point to which he referred was that the letter did exclude those territories for which the French had made a claim – namely all of Syria, which at the time included Palestine. Therefore, according to the Lord Chancellor, it was possible for the government to maintain that, since they had reserved territories claimed by the French, they had not given any undertaking in 1915 to the Arabs in regard to Palestine. The Arabs had argued that since there was no evidence whatsoever that King Hussein had any knowledge of French claims to Palestine in 1915, he would have been given to understand that Palestine was not among those territories so excluded. Furthermore, as the French claim to Palestine had not then been upheld, it followed that the Arab claim to Palestine held good.

Maugham proposed two answers to this argument. First, it did not follow that if the French relinquished their claim to Palestine, the Arab claim to Palestine was thereby established, and second, the French had, in fact, relinquished their claim to Palestine in favour of the establishment of a British Mandate over that territory, but only on the understanding that if the government abandoned the Mandate, the French might claim they had certain interests which must be safeguarded.[90] The cabinet simply noted the Lord Chancellor's statement.

Publication, at last

The Correspondence was officially published as a White Paper during the first week of March 1939, and included a map, 'Pre-war Administrative Districts comprised in Syria and Palestine'.[91] It begins with an explanatory note:

> The correspondence of which an English text follows was exchanged in Arabic.
>
> The English text is based upon the original drafts in English of the letters sent by Sir Henry McMahon and the contemporary translations

---

90 FO 371/23227, E1686.
91 The same map as in the Report of the Royal Commission on Palestine (1937). https://upload.wikimedia.org/wikipedia/commons/7/75/Correspondence_between_Sir_Henry_McMahon_and_the_Sherif_Hussein_of_Mecca_Cmd_5957. pdf (accessed 27 November 2019).

into English of the letters received by Sir Henry McMahon. The language of some of the original drafts or contemporary translations has, however, been modified in certain places where the language has been criticised on the ground that it does not reproduce accurately the Arabic of the actual correspondence and the criticism has been found on examination to be justified.

The text printed in the following pages is the revised text which results from these modifications. Except where otherwise stated, the foot-notes indicate the text as it stood before the modifications were introduced.

His Majesty's Government have been advised in this matter by Mr. J. Heyworth-Dunne, Senior Lecturer in Arabic at the School of Oriental Studies, University of London.[92]

When one examines the text of McMahon's letter of 24 October 1915, on pages 7–8 of the White Paper, the key paragraph reads, correctly:

> The two districts of Mersina and Alexandretta and portions of Syria lying to the west of the districts of Damascus, Homs, Hama and Aleppo cannot be said to be purely Arab, and should be excluded from the limits demanded.

However, the footnote at the bottom of the page, which is supposed to indicate the text as it stood before the modifications were introduced, is incorrect. It reads:

> Former reading: The districts of Mersina and Alexandretta and the portions of Syria lying to the west of the districts of Damascus, Homs, Hama and Aleppo cannot be said to be purely Arab and should be excluded from the proposed limits and boundaries.[93]

The former reading actually stated '<u>vilayets</u> of Damascus', not 'districts of Damascus'. The government appears here to have lied by omission: there was no indication that the text before revision read vilayets. Thus, parliamentarians and others who read the White Paper were not

---

92 FO 371/23227, 356.
93 FO 371/23227, 359.

informed of that crucial change. All the other less consequential changes to the fateful letter, as agreed by Antonius and Heyworth-Dunne, were noted, but not vilayets. It is hard to believe that a genuine mistake occurred. The official records do not reveal which very senior official. or officials, decided on the wording of that key footnote. Nor is it known how the Arab delegation reacted to the publication of the Correspondence, but the omission of that key footnote change would not have reassured them of British good faith.

In the same 24 October 1915 letter, McMahon had written: 'With regard to the *vilayets* of Baghdad and Basra'. This use of *vilayets* by McMahon clearly shows that in 1915 he (or whoever drafted the letters for him to sign) knew the word *vilayet*, and knew that Baghdad and Basra should be so described, as compared to the district of Damascus. In the letter sent to King Hussein, the words '*vilayets* of Baghdad and Basra' were translated by the same Arabic word *wilāyah* (in its dual plural form, *wilāyatāni*) as the *wilāyah* (in plural form, *wilāyāt*) of Damascus, Homs, Hama and Aleppo, earlier in the same letter. Baghdad and Basra were indeed both vilayets. Damascus, Homs and Hama were not vilayets.[94] Finally, it should be noted that the Correspondence as published in the White Paper, and in particular that of the fateful 24 October 1915 letter, agrees with Antonius's translation, as published in *The Arab Awakening* in 1938 – an implicit, if unavowed, acknowledgement by the government of its inaccurate vilayets interpretation.

The publication of the Correspondence White Paper caused little stir. At the beginning of March 1939, all eyes in Parliament and the press were turned towards Berlin and Prague. On 15 March, Hitler's forces invaded and occupied what remained of Czechoslovakia. Two weeks later, Britain pledged its support to Poland in the event of an invasion. On 27 April, the Military Training Act introduced conscription. The elaboration of Palestine policy, which was finally announced in May, was conducted in the context of an increasing threat of a global war.

---

94 A photostat copy of the 24 October 1915 letter in Arabic is in FO 371/23223, E1217.

7

Anglo–Arab Report

1939

When the St James's Conference established the Anglo-Arab Committee in mid February 1939, to study the Correspondence, it was expected that the latter would in due course report on its official findings, and the government were keen to produce a joint report. The dilemma for the British was how to persuade the Arabs to sign one. Baggallay prepared a provisional draft which he sent to the Lord Chancellor, Sir Grattan Bushe and Harold Downie, for their comments. Following a meeting with Antonius, who raised various criticisms of it, Baggallay minuted that the successful production of a joint report turned on two issues, namely whether the government, first, admitted that the Arabs had a strong case, and second, accepted the importance of certain subsequent pledges, especially the Hogarth Message. Baggallay thought that the Arabs would not sign up to a joint report unless those two points were accepted.

Both Baggallay and Bushe thought it appropriate that some sort of admission should be made that the Arab case was strong. According to Bushe, only such an admission would restore the Arabs' confidence in the good faith of the government. The question of the Hogarth Message was equally important to the Arab delegation, who believed that the government were bound by it. Moreover, the message argu-ably contradicted the Balfour Declaration, which had preceded it. The Arab delegation emphasised that they regarded the findings of the committee as a test of the government's good faith.

According to Baggallay, 'the Arabs presented a very strong case' at the third meeting of the committee on 28 February, and in consequence drew up a further draft report.[1] This was discussed at the beginning of March at a meeting attended by Maugham, MacDonald, Butler, Somervell, Bushe and Baggallay, during which the Colonial Secretary expressed his reluctance to insert the Hogarth Message into the draft for two main reasons: first, that if the committee attempted to express an opinion on matters that could only be thoroughly investigated if many other factors were taken into account, it would expose itself to criticism, 'above all from the Jews'.[2] Second, a reference to the Hogarth Message would unduly encourage the Arabs. But in Baggallay's mind there was no getting away from the fact that the Hogarth Message was very relevant to the questions considered by the committee, and the Lord Chancellor had freely admitted this. Baggallay doubted that the government would succeed in getting a joint report without a reference to the later pledges, and that, he thought, 'would be a pity'.[3]

Although there was some divergence of legal opinion between the Lord Chancellor and the Attorney General, who thought the government's case over the Correspondence far weaker than the Lord Chancellor did, the meeting ended with an agreement to submit the draft report, including the Hogarth Message, to the Cabinet Committee on Palestine.

Having read the draft, Baxter noted on the same day:

> I think that we must be honest over this. The Arabs have got a very much stronger case than many people have thought. And we shall have to admit this to some extent when explaining the position to Parliament and the public. Most people do not realise that the Arabs have a strong case at all.[4]

At the seventh meeting of the Cabinet Committee on Palestine, held on 6 March, the draft report was again scrutinised. Present were Neville Chamberlain, Sir John Simon (Chancellor of the Exchequer), Halifax, Butler, MacDonald, Maugham, Baggallay and five other senior

---

1 FO 371/23227, E1734. Minute by Baggallay, 2 March 1939.
2 FO 371/23227, E1734. Minute by Baggallay, 2 March 1939.
3 FO 371/23227, E1734. Baggallay minute, 2 March 1939.
4 FO 371/23227, E1734. Baxter minute, 2 March 1939.

officials.[5] The Lord Chancellor informed the committee in some detail of the proceedings of the Anglo-Arab Committee, including a frank description of the strengths and weaknesses of both sides' contentions. He stated that he thought the 'districts' reservation was perhaps a weak position, but it was one that had for years been stoutly maintained, particularly by Churchill when Secretary of State for the Colonies. On the other hand, the more general 'French interests' reservation was a substantially stronger position and no one had ever suggested that it could be surrendered.

Maugham's opinion was that the Balfour Declaration was a promise to the Jews of a national home in Palestine, and that promise had been implemented. However, the declaration did not, and could not, mean the establishment in Palestine of a Jewish state, because that would have been in direct conflict with the government's promise to the Arabs that their rights should be preserved. He emphasised that the Hogarth Message was all important as it clearly indicated that it was not the government's intention to establish a Jewish state in Palestine but that the government were determined that in Palestine no people should be subject to another, and that they favoured a return of Jews to Palestine 'in so far as is compatible with the freedom of the existing population, both economic and political'. In January 1918, Commander Hogarth had been sent to Sharif Hussein with a message which, according to Maugham, had pacified the Sharif, and it was contended by the Arabs that the government were bound by its terms.

MacDonald stated his agreement with the Lord Chancellor's views and expressed his gratitude for the assistance which the Lord Chancellor had given in acting as British representative on the Anglo-Arab Committee and in the preparation of the draft report. He acknowledged that near the end of the report certain concessions had been made to the Arab point of view, which went somewhat further towards admitting the Arab case than he had originally envisaged. Further to this, he pointed out that the government's argument, now founded on the reservation in respect of French interests, would be a novelty to the general public as attention had not up to the present been drawn to it.

5 FO 371/23228, E1784, 35–57. For Baggallay's draft, see FO 371/23228, 72. The committee also reviewed at length the negotiations with the Arab delegation and the Jewish Agency, particularly concerning possible constitutional reform in Palestine.

His concern was that the government might now give the impression that having been defeated in argument over the 'specific reservation' they were changing their ground and instead relying on the general 'French interests' reservation.

In reply, Maugham stated that with regard to the 'specific' reservation much confusion had resulted from the fact that the word 'vilayet' meant in Turkish a definite administrative division of the Ottoman Empire, whereas the Arabic word from which it was derived '*wilāyah*' had a different meaning:

> We now knew that in the McMahon–Hussein correspondence the expression had been used in its Arabic sense and we could quite legitimately plead that the misunderstanding which has arisen was due to confusion arising from the interpretation of an Arabic expression.[6]

Maugham and the government could plead this point, but not, according to this author, with integrity. There had been no long-term misunderstanding: Maugham had read Mackenzie's memorandum and knew that British officials were aware from 1916 onwards that 'districts' did not mean vilayets.

The cabinet committee briefly discussed the question of how best the Hogarth Message and other important unpublished documents considered by the Anglo-Arab Committee should be published. MacDonald suggested that it might make an undesirable impression on the House of Commons and the public if so important a statement as the Hogarth Message were made public for the first time as an annex to the report of the committee, so it was decided that the Hogarth Message should be published as a White Paper following a suitable question in the Commons.

When Baggallay handed Antonius an amended draft of the report on 7 March, which included the Hogarth Message, Antonius pointed out that they had no independent means of judging whether or not the message which Hogarth had been instructed to deliver was in fact delivered in the form intended. He asked whether the Foreign Office could furnish them with anything in the nature of a report from Hogarth that would allay these concerns and also indicate the reactions of King Hussein. Antonius thought it unlikely that the King would have received so important a message without making some comment upon it.

This request was distinctly problematic for the government because Hogarth's report included:

> <u>Settlement of Jews in Palestine and common cause among Arabs, Jews and Armenians in Syria</u>.
>
> The King would not accept an independent Jewish State in Palestine, nor was I instructed to warn him that such a state was contemplated by Great Britain.[7]

Baggallay commented that this quote in Hogarth's report was 'not very fortunately expressed', i.e. where Hogarth had written that he was not instructed to tell King Hussein that a Jewish state was contemplated in Palestine, and that he did not do so. Baggallay thought it tended to show that Hogarth knew the government contemplated a Jewish state and that they had withheld that information from the King.

Baggallay suggested it might be possible to take the line with the Arab delegation that the report dealt with a great number of confidential matters in addition to that of the message itself, and that what was an essentially confidential report from one of His Majesty's representatives abroad to his government was not suitable for general publication. Still, to refuse all information about what King Hussein replied seemed to Baggallay to be out of the question. Neither the Jews nor the Arabs were likely to let matters stand and they would keep pressing, possibly through Members of Parliament, for more information. In the circumstances by far the best thing seemed to be to make public a fair and adequate summary of what Hogarth had reported. Baggallay considered any other course was likely to create a mystery where none really existed and with the example of the McMahon Correspondence before them 'it seems far best to give information straight away and not let the facts be dragged from us piecemeal'.[8]

---

7 See FO 371/23229, 377. Baggallay minute, 8 March 1939; FO 882/7, 240. Hogarth's diary on 'Interviews with King Hussein', 8–14 January 1918. Underlined in the original.
8 FO 371/23230, E2023, Baggallay minute, 14 March 1939.

On 9 March, Baggallay met the Lord Chancellor, the Colonial Secretary, Rab Butler and Sir Grattan Bushe to discuss the draft report. The meeting agreed that enough of the report by Commander Hogarth might be given to the Arabs to show that the message was actually delivered, but that the bit about King Hussein refusing to have a Jewish state need not be included.[9] Later that same evening they decided that, in fact, it would be 'undesirable' to give the Arabs only part of Commander Hogarth's report, since sooner or later the whole might somehow or other become public property, with the result that the government might appear to have been trying to conceal something.[10]

The next day, Baggallay informed Antonius that, as a matter of principle, they could not give him Commander Hogarth's report on his conversation about the message with King Hussein, but could reassure him that the message had been delivered as originally intended. Antonius responded that the Arab delegation felt considerable doubt as to whether King Hussein had swallowed the whole of it without any reservation. If the delegation was to agree to attach the text of the government's instructions to Commander Hogarth as an annex to a report to which they had put their signatures, they would in effect be admitting that these instructions were not merely instructions, but also the terms of an agreement reached between King Hussein and Commander Hogarth. Unless they could be given some indication (not necessarily the actual

---

9 FO 371/23229, E2022, 369. Baggallay minute, 9 March 1939. Baggallay drafted a summary paragraph of Hogarth's report, in which the embarrassing phrase was suitably amended, and which might be included in the joint report. The paragraph read: 'As regards the third paragraph, the King had seemed quite prepared for this and had agreed enthusiastically, saying he welcomed Jews to all Arab lands. Commander Hogarth had explained that His Majesty's Government's resolve safeguarded the existing local population. Commander Hogarth had furthermore gained the impression that the King would not accept a Jewish State in Palestine but that he appreciated the financial advantage of Arab co-operation with the Jews.' FO 371/23230, 275.

10 FO 371/23229, 249. Baggallay continued: 'Furthermore, there is, on general principles, considerable objection to making public reports received by His Majesty's Government from their Representatives abroad, save in exceptional circumstances.' FO 371/23229, E1968, 249–250. On 9 March, at an informal meeting with Chaim Weizmann and Moshe Shertok, MacDonald handed over a copy of the Hogarth Message and informed them that it would be shortly published as a White Paper. See FO 371/23228, E1874, 256.

words of Commander Hogarth's report) of what King Hussein said, they would have to make it clear that they did not accept the message as representing any kind of agreement between King Hussein and Commander Hogarth. The Jewish Agency similarly asked for information about King Hussein's reply.[11]

Two days later, MacDonald came round to the view that, 'in the circumstances', the Hogarth Message should be published 'practically in full'. So, on 13 March, the House of Commons was informed that the text of the Hogarth Message, and of the Declaration to the Seven, would be published in a White Paper at an early date.[12]

Intentions – Again

For the government, it was particularly important to try to induce the Arabs to recognise specifically the consistent sincerity of British intentions to exclude Palestine, both at the time of the Correspondence and thereafter. Paragraphs thirteen and fourteen of Baggallay's first draft report demonstrate the government's proposed formula in this regard:

> 13. The nearest approach to common ground which they have been able to make in relation to the point of legal interpretation is that they agree that the language used in the correspondence is often vague and unprecise and that if one side were to admit that Sir Henry McMahon had failed to make it clear to the Sherif of Mecca that Palestine was to be excluded from the area of Arab independence, the other side would

---

11 FO 371/23230, 8. Shertok's written request to MacDonald, 13 March, included 'according to our information, in a conversation which Commander Hogarth had with Sharif Hussein on the occasion of the delivery of the message which it is now proposed to publish, the Sherif expressed himself as in agreement with His Majesty's Government's policy with regard to Palestine, including the return of the Jews to that country. We presume that there must be a contemporary record of that conversation, and if so, we would suggest that it should also be published.'

12 *Statements made on behalf of His Majesty's Government during the year 1918 in regard to the Future Status of Certain Parts of the Ottoman Empire* (Cmd 5964), 20 March 1939. FO 371/23230, E2023.

equally have to admit that the Sherif of Mecca had failed to make it clear to Sir Henry McMahon that Palestine was to be included in that area.[13]

However, this paragraph was quite unacceptable to the Arabs, who stated in reply that the Sharif had made the boundaries quite clear in his first letter.

14. The Arab representatives accept the assurance of the United Kingdom representatives that in the correspondence Sir Henry McMahon intended to exclude Palestine from the area of Arab independence, and that His Majesty's Government have acted in the belief that Palestine was so excluded until later events began to show that there was some misunderstanding.[14]

This paragraph was equally unacceptable to the Arabs, who believed that McMahon intended to include Palestine in the area of Arab independence: there had been no 'misunderstanding'.

Conversely, paragraph fifteen of Baggallay's draft included this startling admission:

15. The United Kingdom representative has, moreover, informed the Arab representatives that the Arab contentions, as explained to the committee, regarding the interpretation of the correspondence, and especially their contentions relating to the meaning of the phrase 'portions of Syria lying to the west of the districts of Damascus, Hama, Homs and Aleppo,' have far greater force than has appeared hitherto, and that so far as the words just quoted at any rate are concerned the Sherif could not reasonably have inferred that Palestine was to be excluded from the area of Arab independence.[15]

The last four lines of this paragraph, underlined by the author, could not be clearer. Baggallay hoped that this admission would induce the Arabs to accept the previous two paragraphs – as well as others that the Arabs were reluctant to accept. In the final, joint report, in deference to

13 FO 371/23227, E1690, 118. Also in FO 371/23230, E2103.
14 FO 371/23227, E1690, 119.
15 FO 371/23227, E1734, 279–280.

Arab wishes, paragraphs thirteen and fourteen were omitted, but in return for that omission the British insisted on inserting the paragraph describing McMahon's letter and Clayton's note, which put on record their intention to exclude Palestine from the pledge. More significantly, the underlined portion of paragraph fifteen was also omitted. Baggallay's superiors simply could not allow such a frank admission, which would have crossed the Lord Chancellor's red line that 'on a proper construction of the Correspondence, Palestine was excluded from the area of Arab independence.'

The Anglo-Arab Report was signed at the final meeting of the committee on 16 March 1939, and consists of a joint statement, followed by ten annexes.[16] The twenty-two-paragraph statement was signed by Taufiq al-Suwaidi, Abdul-Rahman Bey Azzam, Auni Bey Abdul-Hadi, Musa Bey al-Alami and George Antonius for the Arab delegation; and by Lord Maugham, Sir Grattan Bushe and H. Lacy Baggallay for the government. Paragraphs twelve to fifteen summarise the cases of both sides. Paragraphs sixteen to eighteen elucidate the heart of the unresolved debate:

16. Both the Arab and the United Kingdom representatives have tried (as they hope with success) to understand the point of view of the other

16 Proof copy of the Anglo-Arab Committee Report (Cmd 5974) is in FO 371/23231, E2166. The report was adopted officially by the main conference on 17 March (see FO 371/23231, E2108) and published on 21 March, a day after the Hogarth White Paper. The report included ten annexes: A) 'Memorandum on British Pledges to the Arabs' (handed in by the Arab representatives at the first meeting on February 23rd); B) 'The McMahon-Husain Correspondence' (handed in by the United Kingdom representatives at the second meeting on February 24th); C) 'Statement by Sir Michael McDonnell on certain legal points arising out of the Lord Chancellor's statement at the Second Meeting of the Committee on February 24th' (handed in by the Arab representatives at the third meeting on 28 February); D) 'Observations arising out of the Lord Chancellor's statement on 24th February, 1939' (handed in by the Arab representatives at the third meeting on February 28th); E) 'Statement by the Lord Chancellor' (handed in by the United Kingdom representatives at the fourth meeting on March 16th); F) The Hogarth Message of January, 1918; G) The Declaration to the Seven of June, 1918; H) Sir Edmund Allenby's assurance to the Amir Faisal of October, 1918; I) The Anglo-French Declaration of November 7th, 1918; J) Extract from the report of a [UK Government] Committee presided over by Sir Maurice de Bunsen, June 1915.

party, but they have been unable to reach agreement upon an interpretation of the Correspondence, and they feel obliged to report to the conference accordingly.

17. The United Kingdom representatives have, however, informed the Arab representatives that the Arab contentions, as explained to the committee, regarding the interpretation of the Correspondence, and especially their contentions relating to the meaning of the phrase 'portions of Syria lying to the west of the districts of Damascus, Hama, Homs and Aleppo', have greater force than has appeared hitherto.

18. Furthermore, the United Kingdom representatives have informed the Arab representatives that they agree that Palestine was included in the area claimed by the Sharif of Mecca in his letter of the 14th July, 1915, and that unless Palestine was excluded from that area later in the Correspondence it must be regarded as having been included in the area in which Great Britain was to recognise and support the independence of the Arabs. They maintain that on a proper construction of the Correspondence Palestine was in fact excluded. But they agree that the language in which its exclusion was expressed was not so specific and unmistakable as it was thought to be at the time.[17]

At the committee's concluding meeting, the Lord Chancellor's final memorandum included:

The Correspondence as a whole, and particularly the reservation in respect of French interests in Sir Henry McMahon's letter of the 24th October, 1915, not only did exclude Palestine, but should have been understood to do so, having in view the unique position of Palestine.[18]

Note his final 'justification' for Palestine's exclusion – 'the unique position of Palestine' – a contention that had been convincingly countered by Sir Michael McDonnell in the previous meeting. Also, the official records demonstrate conclusively that Maugham knew his contention – that Palestine was excluded – was a lie.[19]

Paragraph twenty of the report includes:

---

17 Anglo-Arab Committee Report, 9.
18 FO 371/23230, E2052, 172, paragraph 9.
19 The Oxford English Dictionary defines a lie as a 'deliberately false statement'.

> ... it has seemed necessary to His Majesty's Government in the United
> Kingdom, in the interests of clarity, to make public the terms of the
> whole message which Commander Hogarth was instructed to deliver
> and of the report which he furnished upon his visit (See Annex F).

Annex F contains the Hogarth Message, including the phrase 'political and economic freedom', but inexplicably omits the report referred to, 'which he furnished upon his visit'.[20] Was that omission 'in the interests of clarity' – or a deliberate cover-up? One can only surmise that it would have been distinctly embarrassing for Hogarth's comments concerning British intentions to create a Jewish state in Palestine to have been the object of parliamentary or press debate.

The following day, 17 March, witnessed the final main conference meeting of the British government and the Arab delegations. When the Colonial Secretary suggested that the report of the Anglo-Arab Committee be adopted by the conference, Antonius dissented and remarked that no Arabic translation had yet been made, the report had only been signed the previous day, and there had not been much time for the delegations to study it. When he suggested, however, that one session of the conference should be devoted to it, the Colonial Secretary disagreed: the question had been examined very thoroughly, it was a unanimous report and the gist of it was that the Arab and British delegates agreed to differ except on one or two points. If further discussion took place, there would probably be nothing to be added on the British side or on the part of other delegations who had been represented on the committee. He acknowledged, nevertheless, that no delegation would wish to be committed without a chance of studying the report. However, after further exchanges the proposal that the report should be adopted was put to the conference and accepted unanimously. Antonius asked that it should be recorded in the minutes that he dissented from the decision to adopt the report without discussion. He didn't expect the British to accept fully the Arab case – he knew them too well for that – but a 'moral victory' would provide some vindication of their twenty-two-year struggle with the British on the issue.

Following the adoption of the report, all the Arab delegations (Iraqi, Egyptian, Saudi Arabian, Transjordanian, Yemeni and Palestinian) made

---

20 See FO 371/23231, 343–344; Anglo-Arab Committee Report, 43–44.

definitive statements rejecting the British proposals concerning the future of Palestine. MacDonald and his colleagues were dismayed, but not surprised.[21] Three days earlier, the Zionist delegation had also rejected MacDonald's final proposals. Weizmann was particularly critical of the government's 'u-turn' and told MacDonald that their proposals would 'crystallise' and 'kill the National Home', that the government were 'ushering in a period of violence' in Palestine and that the responsibility for that bloodshed would be on the heads of those who were framing the government's policy.[22] He accused MacDonald of treachery:

> He had betrayed them … and created theories to justify the betrayal … Everything had been prejudged … three months ago … [he] never mentioned that an independent state was in his mind … [his] strategic arguments were so much bunk.[23]

Weizmann refused to cooperate further with MacDonald, or to attend the final meeting between the government and the Zionist delegation on 15 March. Following both parties' rejection of the government's final proposals on the future of Palestine, the latter was now forced to draft a statement of policy on its future unilaterally.

Without Removing the Bails

Reading the Anglo-Arab Report some eighty years later – and given the context of the British government's foreign policy priorities at the time – it is hard not to conclude that, for the government, the Anglo-Arab Committee was primarily a concessionary tactic, a minor element in a dangerously unpredictable global game then being played out between Britain, the Arab world, the Jewish Agency and the League: placate the Arabs, reject any 'bad faith' implications (hold the moral high ground, accept no political culpability), implicitly abandon the 'districts'

21 FO 371/23231, E2108.
22 See FO 371/23230, E2024. MacDonald note of his conversation with Weizmann on 14 March 1939.
23 Dugdale Diaries, Rehovot. Cited in Rose, *The Gentile Zionists*, 193.

reservation if need be, maintain the 'French interests' reservation, and confidently wrap it up with the 'smoke and mirrors' phrase 'On a proper construction of the Correspondence, Palestine was in fact excluded.' As mentioned in the Introduction, the government's position was best summed up by MacDonald himself: 'We have let the ball touch one stump without removing the bails.'[24]

The report was undoubtedly a meticulously drafted, imperial fudge designed to bury the Correspondence issue once and for all. Without exception, all the senior officials involved in the issue – Halifax, MacDonald, Maugham, Somervell, Butler, Oliphant, Rendel, Bushe, Baxter, Beckett, Baggallay and Colville – considered that the British case concerning the Correspondence was deeply flawed. But uphold it they did – through parliamentary rhetoric or silence.

Baggallay candidly noted that during the committee's proceedings the government had used the argument that certain phrases were obscure and could be interpreted in different ways. But the government could not admit that the whole Correspondence was so hopelessly confused and muddled that no one could legitimately say that Palestine was either excluded or included in the area of Arab independence. If they had gone that far, given that the Lord Chancellor had admitted the onus of exclusion lay with them, it would have meant the Arab contentions were right. Baggallay continued, 'If nothing but my own personal feelings were involved, I should probably be willing to go as far even as this, although it might not, admittedly, be politic at this late date.'[25]

The final eleven words of this quote, underlined by the author, were crossed out thoroughly in ink by Oliphant, Deputy Under-Secretary of State, who placed a full stop after the word 'this' – and wrote in the margin alongside 'and I'. It is noteworthy that this minute was initialled without comment by Baggallay's three superiors at the Foreign Office, Charles W. Baxter (Head of the Eastern Department), Sir H. William Malkin (Senior Legal Advisor) and Sir Lancelot Oliphant (Deputy Under-Secretary of State for Foreign Affairs, Middle East).

---

24 FO 371/23231, E2166, 319. Baggallay minute, 18 March 1939.

25 FO 371/23231, E2166, 319. Baggallay minute, 18 March 1939. The author is grateful to Dr Lucia Pereira Pardo, Senior Conservation Scientist of the National Archives, Kew, for her assistance in revealing, for the first time since 1939, the crossed-out text, by the use of a multi-spectral imaging machine.

Straw, Tricky and Cast-Iron

On 18 March, Baggallay commented:

> It is fairly clear to those who read between the lines that the UK Representatives abandoned the argument that the words 'district of Damascus' mean 'the administrative area known as the Vilayet of Syria' upon which Mr Winston Churchill relied in the White Paper of 1922 and which has been the main plank of the British case until now. The Lord Chancellor has called the British case on this point 'straw' and Mr MacDonald has called it 'tricky.' Both adjectives are thoroughly deserved.
>
> On the other hand, mainly on the Lord Chancellor's advice, H.M.G. have, through their Representatives, laid great stress in this report upon the 'French reservation' argument. The Lord Chancellor has called this argument 'cast-iron,' although he has also qualified it by saying that it holds good 'on a strictly legal interpretation.'
>
> In my own mind I am fairly satisfied that whatever may be the proper legal construction of the language used in regard to French interests (and I rather think that the Attorney-General and some other legal experts do not entirely share the Lord Chancellor's convictions) both Sir H. McMahon and the Sharif must have meant that H.M.G. would carry out their promise to the Arabs in any territory in which French claims were found not to have prevailed when a final territorial settlement had been reached.

Beckett, the Second Legal Advisor to the Foreign Office, added, 'I have always thought that this was what it meant.'[26]

On 22 March, under the headline **PROMISES TO THE ARABS. A BRITISH ADMISSION**, *The Times* published a brief summary of the report's conclusions:

> The British representatives on the British and Arab Committee … have agreed that the language in which the exclusion of Palestine from the area in which Britain was to recognise Arab independence 'was not so specific and unmistakable as it was thought to be at the time.' The British

---

26 FO 371/23231, E2166.

and Arab representatives, however, have been unable to reach agreement
upon an interpretation of the correspondence …

The article concluded without further commentary by quoting in full
what it described as the report's 'salient passages', namely, paragraphs
sixteen through eighteen.[27]

A lengthy, ostensibly balanced commentary appeared in the paper
the next day. It spelled out in considerable detail the British government's arguments, notably the 'surrounding circumstances', Palestine's
unique position, its proximity to Egypt and the Suez Canal, and Feisal's
silence concerning Palestine at Versailles, but omitted all the arguments
favourable to the Arab side, apart from the fact that the latter 'had
adhered to a legalistic interpretation of the Correspondence'. It
concluded:

> It is certainly strange that the Arab Delegation to the Peace Conference
> led by EMIR FEISAL, as he then was, and including two of the Arab
> representatives who have been taking part in the proceedings of the
> LORD CHANCELLOR'S Committee, should have made no demand
> for Palestine before the Council of Five at Versailles, if they were then
> persuaded of the justice of the Arab claim to that region.[28]

So faithful a rendering of the Foreign Office's position, one could be
forgiven for wondering whether it had been drafted by Baggallay
himself.

In the same edition, The Times published a letter from Chaim
Weizmann, in which he wrote:

> The United Kingdom representatives on the committee … having given
> full weight to all the considerations advanced in support of the Arab case,
> declined to accept the construction of the McMahon undertaking so long
> and so assiduously contended for on the Arab side.

His letter contained two further comments: first, the Jewish delegation
were not consulted, and had no opportunity of offering their comments

---

27 'Interpreting the McMahon Letters', The Times, 22 March 1939.
28 The Times, 23 March 1939.

on those documents, or of producing others, of which the existence and relevance were acknowledged in the report; and second, the report did not contain the 'highly relevant' fact that no demand was made at the Peace Conference by the Arab delegation, headed by the Emir Feisal, for the fulfilment of the promise alleged to have been contained in the McMahon–Hussein Correspondence – on the contrary, the Arab delegation, in their statement before the Council of Five, expressly excluded Palestine from their demand for the independence of the Arab territories.[29]

After reading Weizmann's letter, Baggallay commented:

> The short answer to Dr Weizmann's points is, I think (a) The Committee was set up to consider British pledges to the Arabs during the war – primarily the McMahon correspondence, but also any subsequent declarations which threw light upon the meaning or intention of that correspondence. They were not set up to consider the discussions which took place between His Majesty's Government and the Arabs, or any other parties, during the Peace Conference or subsequently. (b) In any case, what the Emir Feisal and other Arabs may have said at the Peace Conference cannot throw any light on the meaning of the pledges given by His Majesty's Government. Moreover, it does not follow that, because the Emir Feisal agreed to exclude Palestine from his demands at certain stages of the post-War negotiations, he did not regard Palestine as probably included in the area of independence promised to the Arabs during the War.[30]

Five days later, in the same newspaper, under the headline **THE MCMAHON-HUSSEIN CORRESPONDENCE**, Issat Tannous, the Director of the Arab Centre in London, replied to Dr Weizmann's assertions:

> First, even supposing the Emir Feisal to have 'excluded Palestine' in his speech at Versailles, which Dr Weizmann fantastically asserts he did, this act of his would only have become valid after ratification of it by his father, King Hussein, whose envoy he was at the Peace Conference. But

29 *The Times*, 23 March 1939. See FO 371/23231, E2230.
30 FO 371/23231, E2230.

King Hussein, as Dr Weizmann should be aware, refused to ratify the Treaty of Versailles for the very reason that it was concluded without Arab independence being guaranteed in the manner and within the limits, including Palestine, which he demanded.

Secondly, the Emir Feisal and his companions at the Peace Conference in point of fact never 'excluded Palestine from their demand for the independence of the Arab territories.' What Feisal did, when speaking at the Peace Conference early in February 1919, was to adjourn discussion of Palestine because of the interests involved in the Holy Places, a very different thing from Dr Weizmann's version. The Emir Feisal envisaged a future meeting between all parties concerned with the purpose of settling this matter. It could have been settled then, as it could be settled now, entirely within the orbit of an independent Palestine, ruled by its own people.[31]

A few weeks later, *The Times* published a repost to Dr Tannous from Leonard Stein, President of the Anglo-Jewish Association, who ended his letter with: 'The whole idea of seeking to construe the McMahon correspondence so as to bring Palestine within the area of Arab independence was, in fact, a mere afterthought.'[32]

Following this exchange, the issue of the Correspondence disappeared temporarily from public gaze, but not entirely from Whitehall's. In Palestine, the revolt was not yet fully extinguished (at least twenty thousand British troops, plus the RAF were still involved). Moreover, the British government had announced the previous December that if the conference on Palestine did not produce a successful agreement, they would announce unilaterally their own policy; the onus was now on the government to do so. However, by mid March 1939, there were bigger challenges to tackle than the embarrassing failure of the Palestine Conference: the day before the Anglo-Arab Report was signed, Hitler's troops had invaded Czechoslovakia.

It was a further two months before the government issued the fateful White Paper on Palestine. The delay was due partly to a series of semi-official discussions that it continued with the Arab delegations, following the official end of the conferences on 17 March, and to the

---

31 *The Times*, 28 March 1939. See FO 371/23231, E2230.
32 *The Times*, 15 April 1939; FO 371/23231, E2230, 388.

growing uncertainty of the international situation. The government still hoped to extract from the Arab leaders a declaration of general approval of their policy. Although the talks collapsed, and no declaration was issued by any Arab government, the government's primary objective, to keep the Arab world onside, worked – at least for the moment.

In the process of drafting the policy statement, the only point on which the Foreign Office and the Colonial Office did not see eye to eye was the paragraph concerning the Correspondence. The Colonial Secretary was keen to maintain paragraph nine of the draft (as of 27 April) in its entirety:

> 9 His Majesty's Government regret the misunderstandings which have arisen owing to the lack of precision in the language used in the correspondence, and the difference of opinion which still exists. For their part they can only adhere to the view that the whole of Palestine west of Jordan was excluded from Sir Henry McMahon's pledge, <u>and they therefore cannot recognise the claim, based upon the McMahon correspondence, that Palestine should be converted into an independent Arab State</u>.[33]

However, Lord Halifax – as well as Butler, Oliphant and Baxter – was keen to omit the final phrase (underlined by the author), and pointed out that the phrase was bound to give rise to controversy: the Correspondence had been dealt with, so far as was possible, by the Anglo-Arab Committee, and it would be well to let that difficult and embarrassing question alone. They all felt it would be impossible to deal adequately with the Arab claim under the McMahon Correspondence in half a short sentence in the White Paper. Baxter suggested that in the next cabinet meeting on Palestine, the Foreign Secretary could take the approach that the whole McMahon controversy, in which the government's case was 'none too strong', was dealt with once and for all by the Anglo-Arab Committee – their report had been published and nothing more should be done. Such a

---

33 FO 371/23233, E2783. *PALESTINE. Statement of Policy. Presented by the Secretary of State for the Colonies to Parliament by Command of His Majesty.* MOST SECRET. FIRST PROOF (twelve-page booklet), 163, paragraph 9.

sentence in the White Paper might, he wrote, 're-open the whole of that troublesome controversy'; better to regard it as 'dead and buried'.[34]

MacDonald held his ground at the next cabinet meeting on 8 May, and argued that the draft policy statement contained much that would be satisfactory to the Arabs and unsatisfactory to the Jews, and that such a reference would be one of the comparatively few which would be pleasing to the latter. He felt omission of that phrase would render the policy statement unbalanced, and that just as in the preceding paragraphs the government had disposed of the contention that Palestine should become a Jewish state, so in paragraph seven (previously paragraph nine) they should make it clear that, in their view, Palestine should not become an Arab state.

At the end of the discussion, the Prime Minister suggested, and the committee agreed, that the last three lines of the paragraph should be amended to read 'and they cannot agree that the McMahon correspondence forms a just basis for the claim that Palestine should be converted into an Arab State.'[35]

MacDonald's views prevailed. In the White Paper, issued on 17 May, the concluding sentence of paragraph four stated, 'His Majesty's Government therefore now declare unequivocally that it is not part of their policy that Palestine should become a Jewish State.'[36] And, to provide 'balance' à la MacDonald, the concluding sentence of paragraph seven stated: 'They therefore cannot agree that the McMahon correspondence forms a just basis for the claim that Palestine should be converted into an Arab State.'[37]

Three days before publication, Weizmann had reluctantly accepted an invitation by Malcolm MacDonald to meet at the latter's home in Essex. It signalled the bitter end of a genuine friendship, a final encounter which neither ever forgot. In a recorded interview in 1976, MacDonald recalled:

34 FO 371/23235, E3488, 9. Baxter minute, 6 May 1939.
35 FO 371/23234, E3439. Conclusion of the Cabinet Committee on Palestine, 8 May 1939.
36 *Palestine. Statement of Policy* (Cmd 6019), May 1939, 4. Copy in FO 371/23235, E3681.
37 Cmd 6019, 5.

We talked, just the two of us together ... and I don't think this should be in our public recording: nobody's ever been nastier to me than he was in our discussion, but I understood completely. He said to me, 'Malcolm' (my father had died fairly recently), and Weizmann knew how devoted I was to my father, he said, 'Malcolm, if your father knew that you were doing this, he would turn in his grave, he would hate you.' This, needless to say, hurt me a lot and he knew ... but I understood, and my affection for him never died ... he was very cruel, and he wasn't by nature a cruel man, he was sensitive, friendly, charming ... I told him, as I had before, that we were doing our best to carry out the Balfour Declaration, and to be faithful to it, but that we could not afford to lose the support of the Arabs, and it was in the long-term interests of the Jews themselves, the survival of his creation, the Jewish National Home ... My first aim was Britain's survival; my second, to preserve the Jewish National Home. To achieve those aims we <u>had</u> to placate the Arabs. If we lost the war, as the FO and Chiefs of Staff said we probably would if the Arabs were against us, there would be no National Home for the Jews. I told him, 'Look, you hate me, so do the Arabs. They are furious ... that there's immigration going on, with more Jews coming in, and [Jews] have accused me of being a hypocrite and a coward.'[38]

At that point it appears Weizmann interrupted icily, as it is reported that he said, 'I have never called you a coward.'[39] The furious Zionist leader challenged the government to bring the matter to the Hague Court. He pitied the Prime Minister, 'the innocent victim of specious advisers', and claimed the Jewish Agency was being spied upon, 'their letters ... opened and their telephone tapped'.[40] When he came out of the house, he was trembling with anger, and he told his secretary and driver, Yeheskiel Sacharoff, that now, for the first time, he believed that the English were double-faced and perfidious. 'That he could do this, he

---

38 MM Papers, 9/10/11. 'Notes from an interview with Nigel Maslin', 9 December 1976. The word '<u>had</u>' underlined in the original. At the same interview, when questioned about the Correspondence, MacDonald had to be reminded what it was, in stark contrast to his vivid memory of his final, distressing encounter with Weizmann.

39 Bethell, *The Palestine Triangle*, 67.

40 Rose, *The Gentile Zionists*, 203–204.

who made me believe he was a friend!'[41] Above all else, the meeting personified the total collapse in relations between the government and the Jewish Agency. Henceforth, MacDonald was *persona non grata* with the Zionists.

MacDonald's White Paper provided for limits to Jewish immigration (75,000 over five years) and land purchase, and indicated there would be progress towards developing self-governing institutions and, after a transitional period of ten years, the independence of the country. The Arabs were assured that after the immigration of the following five years, the Jewish community would not number more than a third of the total population and that no further immigration would take place without their consent.

The White Paper's rejection by other Zionist leaders was as unequivocal as it was predictable. The Director of the Zionist Executive, Ben-Gurion, said of the document, 'a more evil, foolish and short-sighted policy could not be imagined.'[42] Two months later, at the twenty-first Zionist Congress in Geneva, he declared, 'For us the White Paper neither exists nor can exist. We must behave as if we were the State in Palestine until we actually become the State in Palestine.'[43]

The Arab rejection of the White Paper was less predictable, given that it undoubtedly represented a major reversal of British policy. According to some accounts, a majority of members of the Arab Higher Committee, the primary representative body for Palestinians during the Mandate, approved it. However, the committee's founder, Haj Amin al-Husseini, the Mufti of Jerusalem, stood firm in rejecting it. Some more recent Palestinian scholars consider the Arab reaction a missed opportunity. 'Zionist opposition may have doomed the White Paper from the very start,' Yezid Sayigh has written, 'but the Palestinians had, through their own reactions, lost the opportunity to enter the mandatory administration at higher levels and prepare for their own

---

41 Sykes, *Crossroads*, 195.

42 Cited in Tom Segev, *One Palestine, Complete. Jews and Arabs under the British Mandate* (New York, 1999), 440, from Ben-Gurion, *Memoires* (in Hebrew) (Tel Aviv, 1971), Am Oved, vol. VI, 200 ff.

43 *Judische Welt Rundschau* [Jewish World Review], 25 August 1939. Cited in Barbour, *Nisi Dominus*, 206.

post-colonial state.'[44] For the Arabs, continued Jewish immigration was a major issue, as well as the government's insistence that independence would only be granted when there was cooperation between Arabs and Jews. The Arabs believed correctly that the Zionists would never cooperate in the establishment of an independent Palestinian state with an Arab majority. In this regard, MacDonald's draft notes written in 1976 in preparation for an interview, reveal his largely unspoken attitude in 1939 to an eventual independent state:

> [In 1939] we did not propose to hand over to Arab majority rule unless the Jews agreed. The Jews could veto an independent state with an Arab majority. I wanted to save the Jewish National Home if war broke out. In 1938–39 my Zionist sympathies were not eroded. I maintained them. But my hopes of being able to satisfy the Zionists' requests adequately eroded …[45]
>
> [In 1939] I made clear to Weizmann and Ben Gurion my fears of result of war for us and for Jews if Arabs opposed us. I told Ben Gurion Jewish State should come slowly over generations.[46]

According to George Rendel, the White Paper approached the problem primarily from the point of view of Palestine:

> It did not attempt to suggest any alternative solution to the quite distinct, but now perhaps equally urgent problem of what could be done to find a refuge for the unfortunate persecuted Jews of Germany and Central Europe – who were anyhow far too numerous ever to be accommodated in a small area of the Middle East … The increasing violence of the horrible persecution of the Jews by the Nazis had by now swung public opinion solidly to the Zionist cause. The United States threw its whole weight into the scale on the same side, and it became clear that we should lose much American support in our impending conflict with Germany if we continued to treat the Palestine problem as a local Middle Eastern issue.

---

44 Yezid Sayigh, *Armed Struggle and the Search for a State: The Palestinian National Movement, 1949–1993* (Oxford, 1997), 7.
45 MM Papers, 9/12/6–8. MacDonald's draft interview notes (*c.* 1976) included, in relation to the Zionist case, 'If ancient historical connections established rights, Italians would have right to England.' MM Papers, 9/10/37.
46 MM Papers, 9/10/39.

Thus, although the 1939 White Paper remained the basis of our official policy during the war, that policy was abandoned as soon as the war was over, and I do not think that its sponsors were ever forgiven.[47]

On 22 May, MacDonald moved that the House of Commons approve the government's policy relating to Palestine as set out in the White Paper. Referring to the Correspondence, he stated:

> Physically this country could force upon the Arabs of Palestine any kind of Jewish National Home that it liked. But we could not do that with any moral justification, for we are bound to the Arabs also by a pledge in this matter. I am not referring to any of the contents of the celebrated McMahon Correspondence. We do not recognise any claim to Palestine based upon that exchange of letters. But there is a later promise [Hogarth Message] ... the proposals of His Majesty's Government are conceived in a spirit of absolute impartiality between Jews and Arabs, and we believe that they are consistent with the obligations which we have undertaken to both people.[48]

His statement cut no ice with Thomas Williams (Labour, Don Valley), a veteran supporter of the Jewish national home policy, who maintained that the proposals in the White Paper were inconsistent with the spirit and letter of the Mandate and that, if his reading of the White Paper was correct, the Colonial Secretary had 'destroyed the very basis of the Balfour Declaration'.[49] He was followed by Anthony Crossley, one of the few long-time supporters of the Arab case in the House, who noted that in the Anglo-Arab Committee's report the government had departed some way from their original view of the McMahon Correspondence. If the government wanted to decide on the rights and wrongs of that Correspondence, they ought to submit it to a purely judicial tribunal – which the Arabs were willing to do.[50] A studious silence emanated from the front bench in response to that suggestion.

---

47 Rendel, *The Sword and the Olive*, 123.
48 Hansard, Commons, 22 May 1939, vol. 347, cc1941, 1954.
49 Hansard, Commons, 22 May 1939, vol. 347, c1955.
50 Hansard, Commons, 22 May 1939, vol. 347, c1972.

The following day, after a second lengthy and acrimonious debate in the Commons, the White Paper was approved by 268 votes to 179, with 110 MPs abstaining.[51] Herbert Morrison (Labour, Hackney South) and Churchill made particularly strong speeches denouncing the White Paper. Years later, MacDonald remembered 'having one hell of an argument' in the lobby of the House of Commons with Churchill (in 1976, MacDonald didn't specify whether it occurred in 1938 or 1939). 'He told me I was crazy to help the Arabs, because they were a backward people who ate nothing but camel dung.'[52] During a parallel debate in the Lords, Viscount Samuel spelled out at length why the White Paper should be rejected. Referring to the Correspondence he repeated the government's (and Weizmann's) oft-repeated contentions, namely 'intentions' and 'Feisal's silence at Versailles':

> Now His Majesty's Government have declared categorically that Palestine was not included. To my mind that is undoubtedly the case, and is proved not merely by the wording of the document itself, which as I have said is obscure, but by two other facts. One is the fact that the British negotiator, Sir Henry McMahon, and his colleague Sir Gilbert Clayton, have both declared in terms since that date, that Palestine was not included, and that it was so understood by the Arab leaders; and the word of those men of honour is not to be doubted.

This is simply untrue. Neither McMahon nor Clayton had ever declared, publicly or privately, that Palestine was not included in the area assigned for Arab independence, only that the government had intended it to be so excluded. Quite a different matter. The viscount continued:

> The second is that at the Conference in Paris after the War, when the future fate of Palestine had to be determined, the Arab delegation there, led by the Emir Feisal, who had taken a leading part in the Arab revolt,

51 Hansard, Commons, 23 May 1939, vol. 347, c2194.
52 Bethell, *The Palestine Triangle*, 44. When preparing his book in 1976, Bethell had interviewed MacDonald about events in 1938 and 1939, including the latter's aforementioned spat with Churchill.

never once suggested that Palestine had been allotted to the Arabs by virtue of the McMahon letters.[53]

Two days earlier, the *New York Herald Tribune* had published a major article headlined **Viscount Samuel Brands White Paper Unfair to Jews.** *Denies Plan for Arab State Breaks Promise to Either Side, but Warns That Immigration Ban Will Kill Zionist National Home.* Referring to the wartime pledges, Samuel had written:

> It is constantly said that the troubles in Palestine originated in the British government, during the war, having given contradictory pledges – promising Palestine to the Arabs in 1915 in Sir Henry McMahon's formal undertaking as to future Arab domains, and promising it also to the Jews in the Balfour Declaration two years later.
>
> The White Paper points out once more that there is no truth to either part of that contention. It repeats categorically that the McMahon letter excluded Palestine west of the Jordan from the promise to the Arabs. The reasons are overwhelming for accepting that view of the disputed passage. And it recalls yet again that the Balfour Declaration promised no more than that a Jewish national home might be established in Palestine and said nothing about a Jewish state.[54]

Yet in December 1945 he stated in the House of Lords:

> It is true that the Balfour Declaration contemplated that the maximum Jewish immigration into Palestine should be encouraged and it is quite true that it was foreseen by the statesmen who promoted that Declaration that if there were to be large Jewish immigration into Palestine, and if the whole enterprise were successful, in course of time the country would come to have a mainly Jewish population and would then become a Jewish State. At that time, or not long after, forecasts of that kind were made by many people, by Mr. Lloyd George, Mr. Winston Churchill and General Smuts, as he then was. Incidentally, I myself said much the same.

---

53 Hansard, Lords, 23 May 1939, vol. 113, cc98–99.
54 *New York Herald Tribune*, 21 May 1939. See FO 371/23236, E3947.

What was promised, so far as promises are concerned, was not a Jewish State, but the opportunity to bring about conditions which might in time make a Jewish State possible.[55]

A few weeks after the publication of the White Paper, Antonius met with the British Ambassador to Cairo, Sir Miles Lampson, and explained to him exactly why the Palestinians distrusted the government's proposal for independence. First, there was no assurance of Palestinian independence after the transition period. Second, a genuine promise of independence would not have made a distinction between Arab states and a Palestinian state. British insistence that neither Jews nor Arabs should dominate Palestine was interpreted in Arab circles as an espousal in disguise of the Zionist slogan of parity and as robbing the promise relating to independence of all value, the argument being that if neither side was to be dominant, there could be no room for the constitutional exercise of majority rights. Finally, all the 'verbal tributes to Arab rights' appeared to be no more than 'the old wolf in a new lamb's clothing', because even after a review of the McMahon Correspondence, the government continued to reject its wartime pledge to support Palestinian independence. This was particularly serious, Antonius emphasised, because 'the belief that Palestine was included in the pledges to the Sharif Hussein is deeply rooted in the Arab mind.'

He suggested to the Ambassador that the government publish a declaration that 'they regard themselves as having fulfilled their obligation to the Jews.'[56] Although Lampson forwarded Antonius's remarks to Butler in the Foreign Office, the government decided there would be no further official clarifications or explanation of the statement of policy. Lampson was instructed to avoid controversy and to put Antonius off 'with some vague oral reply'.[57]

Thus it was that in the summer of 1939 the Correspondence debate was rendered 'dead and buried', no longer an embarrassing political

---

55 Hansard, Lords, 10 December 1945, vol. 138, c496.

56 FO 371/23237, E4420. Antonius to Lampson, 3 June 1939. See Boyle, *Betrayal of Palestine*, 271.

57 FO 371/23239. J. Bennett (British Embassy, Alexandria) to Baggallay, 8 August 1939.

issue, but merely a footnote in the history of Britain's presence in Palestine.[58] That same September, the European empires went to war for six years. However, after the Second World War, the war of words over the Correspondence eventually re-emerged, mostly within academia, and has continued intermittently to this day, fuelled partly by the still unresolved war for Palestine. It is to the history of that discussion we will now turn.

---

58 Nevertheless, it is notable that in 1947 Arab leaders at the fledgling United Nations attempted (unsuccessfully) to refer the Correspondence – as part of the 'case for Palestine' for an advisory opinion by the International Court of Justice. See Kattan, *From Coexistence to Conquest*, xix, 150.

8

Discordant Historiography

1938–

In the spring of 1931, George Antonius met with Hussein ibn Ali in Amman, just a few months before the latter's death. The seventy-eight-year-old former Sharif of Mecca, who had been in exile in Cyprus since his abdication and then expulsion from the Hijaz by Ibn Saud in 1924, granted him access to copies of the original Correspondence that he had received from McMahon, which Antonius carefully copied out and translated. Seven years later, he published them in his seminal work, *The Arab Awakening*, the first time complete versions of the Correspondence had been published in English.[1] According to Antonius, by 1938, the terms of the Correspondence were known throughout the Arab world, extracts had from time to time been officially published in Mecca by Sharif Hussein himself, several of the letters had appeared verbatim and in full in Arabic books and newspapers, and Chapter 2 of the 1937 Peel Commission Report had reproduced the whole of the 24 October 1915 letter in English.[2]

Antonius's was the first major work in English by an Arab scholar to tell the story of the modern renaissance of the Arabs, and the book still stands as a classic. Antonius surveys in turn the origins of the Arab national movement in the nineteenth and early twentieth centuries, the frustration of that movement by the ambitions of Western imperialism and the Arabs' struggles since the Great War to free themselves from

---

1 Antonius's Appendix A (413–427) contains the first eight letters exchanged. *Correspondence* (Cmd 5957), reproduced in Appendix I in this book, includes all ten letters.

2 Antonius, *Awakening*, 180–181.

Western control. Chapter Nine, entitled 'GREAT BRITAIN'S
PLEDGE: 1915', describes the process of the Correspondence and the
main provisions of what Antonius calls the 'compact', including its
territorial implications.

Born in Lebanon, Antonius was for some time a senior official in the
Education Department of the British Mandate administration in
Palestine, a negotiator on behalf of the Palestinian leadership with the
British, and an official of an American foundation in the Middle East. He
was also the first Arab historian to challenge the British version of the
events that took place during the First World War. Antonius was critical
of the Balfour Declaration and later wrote that the Sykes–Picot
Agreement was 'a startling piece of double dealing', a 'by-product of
greed at its worst'.[3]

Some scholars have been sharply, and in my view, unduly, critical of
Antonius's scholarship, including Elie Kedourie, who described his work
as 'untrustworthy' and at times 'misleading', 'exaggerated', 'misconceived' and even 'impertinent'.[4] Isaiah Friedman is equally critical:

> It was not the promotion of truth that dominated his writings. His
> primary object was to shame and stigmatize the British in order to create
> in them a feeling of guilt and thereby ease the Arabs' task of wresting
> Palestine from the shackles of the British mandate.[5]

Yet, according to Antonius's biographer, Susan Silsby Boyle, he was a
brilliant and honourable scholar, diplomat and cultured Arab nationalist.[6] 'He became an influential authority', wrote Albert Hourani, 'on
the tragic implications of the inequality of relations between the Arab
world and the West.'[7] And another Oxford scholar, Derek Hopwood,
remarked that

> as Antonius' life demonstrates so clearly, morality finds it difficult to
> combat immorality in practical politics. He tried hard but failed … with

---

3 Antonius, *Awakening*, 248.

4 Kedourie, *Labyrinth*, ch. 10.

5 Friedman, *Palestine. A Twice-Promised Land?*, 163.

6 Boyle, *Betrayal of Palestine*, xiii–xv.

7 Albert Hourani, *The Emergence of the Modern Middle East* (London, 1990), 197–199.

inner conviction he fought and lost a moral battle in an immoral world, and perhaps failure in such a way is nobler than success.[8]

The Arab Awakening had a significant impact in policy circles when it appeared, and had a considerable influence on the academic study of the Middle East during the following decades. Although some of Antonius's findings have been superseded by more recent research, his book remains essential reading for any scholar who wishes to grapple effectively with the subject.

A year after its publication, J.M.N. Jeffries' *Palestine. The Reality* appeared. But for the outbreak of the Second World War, it would have contributed significantly to the ongoing public debate at that time concerning the future of Palestine. As it was, it had little influence because almost all the print was destroyed in the Blitz, and until 2017, when it was reprinted, very few copies were available. Jeffries' 750-page work was the first anti-Zionist critique of British mandatory policy between 1920 and 1939 by a British scholar. A work of advocacy, written with a journalist's skill, wit and occasional sarcasm, it provides a detailed account of the slow, deliberate dispossession of the Palestinian Arabs during that period, and the concomitant growth of the Zionist 'state within a state'. Concerning the 1915 pledge, he wrote:

> There was no mention of [Palestine's] exclusion. We gave our word that on its soil the Arabs should be free of all foreign control save such as they chose of their own will … For this reason today [1939] more than twenty years after this Anglo-Arab treaty was concluded, the treaty remains of tremendous importance to Palestine.[9]

For Jeffries, it was the Balfour Declaration, 'a calmly planned piece of deception', and its implementation that turned Palestine into a powder keg, and where the 'sacred trust of civilisation' was betrayed.[10] Although neither Antonius nor Jeffries had access to the interwar official records, Antonius's book is strengthened by his judicious use of footnotes, which are absent in Jeffries' tome. These two men were the main contributors

---

8 Review by Derek Hopwood, *Journal of Islamic Studies*, vol. 15, no. 2 (2004), 259.
9 Jeffries, *Palestine*, 81, 91.
10 Jeffries, *Palestine*, 180; ch. 13.

to the historiography of the Correspondence before the Second World War, and both wholeheartedly subscribed to the Arab interpretation of it.

Following the declassification of large amounts of the UK's official records in the 1960s, the first detailed examination of the Correspondence appeared in the *Journal of Contemporary History* in 1970.[11] Penned by Isaiah Friedman, the article aroused some controversy and led to an exchange with Arnold Toynbee in a subsequent issue. Friedman confidently asserted that 'the matter was now finally resolved', a big call to make for any scholar: McMahon had no intention to include Palestine in the area assigned to the Sharif, and did not do so, although Friedman did acknowledge that the 'so-called pledge' could have been expressed with greater clarity.[12] 'Textual examination of the correspondence alone', he suggested, 'will not lead us far.'[13] He wrote that the letter was (1) composed in haste; (2) despatched without the Secretary of State's approval; (3) the Foreign Office was unhappy, the India Office furious; (4) the cabinet did not endorse it; (5) it was a provisional preliminary to a final settlement to be ironed out after the cessation of hostilities; and (6) it was merely an expression of intent and goodwill, not a treaty. Moreover, the pledge was conditional upon the Arabs rising and expelling the Turks from the region, which did not happen; it was compatible with the subsequent Sykes–Picot Agreement and the Balfour Declaration; the claim that Palestine was a twice-promised land was a myth; and from the point of view of international law the Correspondence had no validity.[14]

What, in fact, constitutes a treaty? Although during the nineteenth century and at the turn of the twentieth century, treaties could only be concluded between states, these included, as Victor Kattan has pointed out, those concluded between the British government and Arab Sheikhs.[15] In the years 1820, 1835, 1853, 1861 and 1868, as well as in later years, successive British governments concluded a number of treaties

---

11 The journal was edited by Walter Laqueur and George L. Mosse.

12 'McMahon's ambiguous wording in his fatal letter ... left a loophole for future assertions that the British pledge extended also to Palestine.' Friedman, *Journal of Contemporary History*, vol. 5, no. 2 (1970), 108.

13 Friedman, *Journal of Contemporary History*, vol. 5, no. 2 (1970), 84.

14 Friedman, *Journal of Contemporary History*, vol. 5, no. 2 (1970), 83–122.

15 See Kattan, *From Coexistence to Conquest*, ch. 4.

with the Sheikhs of Bahrain, Abu Dhabi, Qatar, Sharjah and Dubai over acts of piracy in the Gulf. Not once did Britain claim that these agreements were not binding because the Sheikhs did not have the capacity to enter into binding obligations with Britain. According to Kattan, during the First World War there was no particular form through which British Foreign Office diplomats were required to conclude international agreements: it was the common intention of the parties, not the form through which it was expressed, that was important (e.g. the Sykes–Picot Agreement was an exchange of notes between Edward Grey, Britain's Foreign Minister, and Paul Cambon, the French Ambassador to London).[16]

Furthermore, in all the discussions which took place in later years over the terms of the Correspondence, the British government never advanced the argument that it was not binding because Hussein did not have the capacity to enter into a legal relationship with them. And, as mentioned before, in the text of the Correspondence reference was made to 'Britain's existing treaties with Arab chiefs'. The British dealt with the Sheikh of Bahrain, for example, as the representative of the State of Bahrain. Why would McMahon have mentioned these treaties if he did not think his government were entering into a legal relationship with the Sharif? Thus, Friedman's contentions concerning the Correspondence's lack of validity in international law are unconvincing.

Although Friedman consistently proposed in his three books (1973, 2000 and 2010) that both of McMahon's reservations ('districts' and 'French') were sound, it is notable that his interpretation of the word *wilāyah* appears to be less consistent. In 1970 he wrote, 'in vernacular Arabic it [*wilāyah*] stands for "environs", a narrower meaning than district or the Turkish vilayet.'[17] However, thirty years later he wrote, 'For any Arab, there was only one meaning of wilāya, a large administrative district, equivalent to a Turkish *vilayet*.'[18] To compound the confusion, he later wrote, 'The claim that "district" meant "vicinity" or "neighbourhood" was a bogus claim.'[19]

16 See Kattan, *From Coexistence to Conquest*, 102.
17 Friedman, *Journal of Contemporary History*, vol. 5, no. 4 (1970), 198.
18 Friedman, *Palestine. A Twice-Promised Land?*, 40.
19 Friedman, *Palestine. A Twice-Promised Land?*, 50.

In his response to Friedman's 1970 article, Toynbee, now in his eighty-first year, stuck to the thesis he had maintained for half a century:

> I do not think that Young's or Childs's or Mr Friedman's interpretation of McMahon's use of the word 'wilayahs' is tenable. After studying Mr Friedman's paper and writing these notes, I am inclined to think that the drafting of this letter was, not disingenuous, but hopelessly muddle-headed. Incompetence is not excusable in transacting serious and responsible public business[20] ... The consequences of interpreting McMahon's 'wilayahs' as meaning 'Ottoman provinces' are so disconcerting that it was – and, to my mind, still is – difficult to believe that McMahon was intending to use the word in this sense in his letter. This interpretation would force on us a choice between the two following alternative conclusions: (i) First alternative: McMahon was completely ignorant of Ottoman administrative geography. He did not know that the Ottoman vilayet of Aleppo extended westward to the coast, and he did not know that there were no Ottoman vilayets of Homs and Hama. It seems to me incredible that McMahon can have been as ill-informed as this, and that he would not have taken care to inform himself correctly when he was writing a letter in which he was making very serious commitments on HMG's account.
>
> (ii) Second alternative: McMahon was properly acquainted with Ottoman administrative geography, and was using the word 'wilayahs' equivocally. Apropos of Damascus, he was using it to mean 'Ottoman provinces'; apropos of Homs and Hama, and Aleppo, he was using it to mean 'environs.' This equivocation would have been disingenuous, impolitic, and pointless. I could not, and still cannot, believe that McMahon behaved so irresponsibly.[21]

Toynbee acknowledged that although the Correspondence did not result in a treaty, such a pledge could be morally valid, even if it did not have the force of law; the letter was not a dead letter and he disagreed that the controversy had no more than an academic interest. In fact, he concluded, 'McMahon's letter of 24 October 1915 struck some of the

---

20 Toynbee, *Journal of Contemporary History*, vol. 5, no. 4 (1970), 193.
21 Toynbee, *Journal of Contemporary History*, vol. 5, no. 4 (1970), 188–189.

sparks that have set ablaze the present conflagration in the Middle East.'[22] As pointed out earlier, legal obligations can be contained in an agreement which takes any form – and there is no reason why they could not be contained in an exchange of letters as, indeed, they frequently are.

Friedman's immediate response to Toynbee's article made no mention of the latter's 'wilayahs' arguments; they were simply ignored.[23] Instead, Friedman focused on criticising Hogarth's 'line' interpretation, maintained that Ormsby-Gore was unaware of the 'line' error of Hogarth and claimed that the 'districts' phrase of McMahon originated with al-Faruqi, who certainly 'did not intend a narrow interpretation [of the word "districts"]'.[24]

Friedman was emphatic that the record of the British government in the whole matter was clean. It was 'downright false as it was absurd' to imply the British government had made contradictory commitments: one to the Arabs and one to the Jews.[25] It was not McMahon's letter of 24 October 1915, he stated, that complicated Anglo-Arab-Jewish relations, 'but the myth that was built up around it'.[26] McMahon's letter, he wrote, 'was not a legal, but political, nonbinding document ... and considering the way it had been extracted, was devoid of a moral base essential to any contract, private or public'.[27]

This article was reprinted in full as Chapter Six of his book *The Question of Palestine, 1914–1918*, published in 1973. Both Friedman's and Toynbee's articles (and Friedman's reply to Toynbee) make up the fifty-page preamble to his next book, *Palestine. A Twice-Promised Land?* published in 2000. According to Friedman, Toynbee did the opposite of what he claimed: 'Far from demythologizing history, [Toynbee] was consciously, or unconsciously, creating new myths – notably the myth of the "twice-Promised Land."'[28]

---

22 Toynbee, *Journal of Contemporary History*, vol. 5, no. 4 (1970), 193.
23 In the same October 1970 issue Friedman was given 'an extra bite of the cherry' by the *Journal of Contemporary History*'s editors.
24 Friedman, *Journal of Contemporary History*, vol. 5, no. 4 (1970), 198.
25 Friedman, *Palestine. A Twice-Promised Land?*, 85.
26 Friedman, *Journal of Contemporary History*, vol. 5, no. 4 (1970), 201.
27 Friedman, *Palestine. A Twice-Promised Land?*, xvi, 50.
28 Friedman, *Palestine. A Twice-Promised Land?*, 121.

In fact, the first four chapters of this book are a clear attempt to demolish Toynbee's reputation as a historian of the Middle East,[29] concluding that 'the ultimate test of a historian is how genuine is his search for truth', and that Toynbee had failed that test.[30] Given Toynbee had died twenty-five years earlier and could not reply, Friedman's questioning of Toynbee's integrity, and not simply his scholarship, was both unwarranted and inappropriate.

In the introduction to his last book, *British Pan-Arab Policy, 1915–1922*,[31] Friedman suggested that Hussein's revolt against Turkey was not in consequence of British promises:

> Hussein's prime concern was his own physical survival; this was the only way of saving himself and his family from the Turkish gallows. It was completely devoid of struggle for liberation and Arab independence as erroneously portrayed in historiography.[32]

He repeated first, his conviction that the chief reason for Britain's official secrecy concerned the Caliphate, and that Hussein continued during the 1920s, 'to live in his make-believe world, indulging in his grandiose imperial dream'.[33] Second, that Rūhi's translation conveyed precisely McMahon's intention to exclude Palestine, as well as western Syria, from the deal with Hussein:

> Ruhi's language was even stronger than McMahon's term 'district,' for *wilā yā*, as shown already, denotes a large administrative unit, and, in the case of Damascus, refers to the whole area east of the River Jordan southwards to Akaba.[34]

Third, it was Feisal, in January 1921, 'who laid the foundation of the myth that Palestine had been promised to the Arabs first'.[35]

---

29 In particular ch. 3, 'Toynbee *versus* Toynbee' and ch. 4 'Pro-Arab or Pro-Zionist?'.
30 Friedman, *Palestine. A Twice-Promised Land?*, 122.
31 Isaiah Friedman, *British Pan-Arab Policy* (New Brunswick, 2010).
32 Friedman, *British Pan-Arab Policy*, 2–3.
33 Friedman, *British Pan-Arab Policy*, 31.
34 Friedman, *British Pan-Arab Policy*, 254.
35 Friedman, *British Pan-Arab Policy*, 280.

Friedman's ideological inclinations are revealed – sympathetically – in one reviewer's comments:

> Friedman's book furnishes chapter and verse to discredit the Antonius thesis and confirms that British policy during World War I was carefully and systematically formulated to award Palestine to the Jews without prejudicing the rights of other citizens therein ... it also confirms the legitimacy, in international law, of the designation of Palestine as a Jewish homeland.[36]

Friedman's suggestion that the principle of self-determination did not apply to the Middle East because of a 'prevailing backwardness, heterogeneity, and historical absence of democracy'[37] is more in tune with the questionable assumptions of early-twentieth-century orientalist scholars and imperial policymakers than current scholarship. It also blithely ignores Article 22 of the Covenant of the League of Nations.[38]

In 1976, three years after the publication of Friedman's first book on the subject, Elie Kedourie produced his landmark study *In the Anglo-Arab Labyrinth. The McMahon–Husayn Correspondence and Its Interpretations, 1914–1939.* As outlined in the Introduction, Kedourie claimed that: the British did not betray the Arabs; no firm commitments were made to Hussein regarding territorial boundaries; Palestine was definitely excluded from the so-called 'pledge' to the Sharif; British commitments were conditional upon an uprising, which Hussein 'proved impotent to accomplish'; no treaty was involved; and McMahon's letters were merely a series of statements of intention regarding future policy.

Kedourie's assertion that '[The] Sykes–Picot agreement was worded precisely so as not to conflict – rather so as exactly to fit in – with

---

36 Book review by Shlomo Slonim, Professor Emeritus, Hebrew University of Jerusalem, *Israel Affairs*, vol. 11, no. 3 (2005), 567–569.
37 Friedman, *British Pan-Arab Policy*, 195.
38 Article 22 included: 'Certain communities formerly belonging to the Turkish Empire have reached a stage of development where their existence as independent nations can be provisionally recognized subject to the rendering of administrative advice and assistance by a Mandatory until such time as they are able to stand alone.'

[Britain's] pledges to the Arabs'[39] simply does not fit with the facts as revealed in the official records. Neither does his claim that the Hogarth Message 'is no more than a reiteration of the Balfour Declaration, adds nothing to, and detracts nothing from, it'.[40] Kedourie's claim that Britain did not betray the Arabs is highly debatable and, I would argue, morally and politically untenable.

He presented an extensive and fascinating complexity of evidence from the UK's official records, as well as other primary and secondary sources. For Kedourie, there is no key to the labyrinth: it was created by the obscure nature and circumstance of the Correspondence itself, and by McMahon's 'loose and misleading'[41] language. Kedourie leads readers into and through the labyrinth, but rarely out of it: they are too often left to themselves to draw conclusions.

Ideologically, he appears thoroughly supportive of the concept and ideals of the British Empire, yet is very severe on British officials who carried out imperial policy, particularly concerning Palestine. The British were not wicked, but feeble and inept in their dealings with what he designates as the unreliable Arabs. In the late 1930s, British governments' placation of the Arabs was 'muddled and profitless'.[42] 'There was also', he continued, 'a great deal of ignorance and self-deception on the part of [McMahon] and of his subordinates',[43] and particular criticism is reserved for Lacy Baggallay who, as Secretary to the Anglo-Arab Committee in 1939,

> had, with culpable negligence, failed to inform himself about the original significance of these documents, and failed in his duty to put the facts before the Lord Chancellor, the colonial secretary, the cabinet committee

---

39 Kedourie, *Labyrinth*, 312. As described earlier, the 1916 Sykes–Picot Agreement divided the Arab provinces of the Ottoman Empire between the two European powers, in flat disregard of McMahon's 1915 pledge to the Sharif that (roughly) the same region would become independent, subject to certain conditions.

40 Kedourie, *Labyrinth*, 284. As acknowledged by the government in 1939, the 1918 Hogarth Message cited the economic and political rights of the Arabs in Palestine; the 1917 Balfour Declaration deliberately omitted the whole concept of those rights for Palestine's indigenous population.

41 Kedourie, *Labyrinth*, 258.

42 Kedourie, *Labyrinth*, 297.

43 Kedourie, *Labyrinth*, 126.

on Palestine, and the cabinet who, at one time or another, had to consider
what should be said to the Arabs, or included in the committee's report.[44]

In truth, a close reading of the relevant and numerous official records
shows Baggallay in quite a different light: as intelligent, hard-working,
thoroughly competent and having mastered the relevant papers.

Concerning the fateful letter, Kedourie declared that McMahon's
reservations meant that at most only the four towns were promised to
Hussein:

> [The] exchanges between Cairo and the foreign office in October 1915
> conclusively show that McMahon had in mind to offer nothing more
> than the four towns for which he understood Faruqi to be asking, that
> it is for this offer that he sought and received Grey's approval, and that
> the actual terms of McMahon's letter to the Sharif where he spoke of
> 'portions of Syria lying to the west of the districts of Damascus,
> Homs, Hama and Aleppo' had never been authorized by Grey ...
> McMahon's language was so qualified that it meant almost nothing,
> and from his words it was equally easy to infer the exclusion, as well as
> the inclusion, of any territory whatever. This, in fact, was McMahon's
> object, as Baggallay could have easily ascertained from the
> documents.[45]

But would the Sharif, however unfamiliar with negotiating with a
Western imperial government, really have thrown caution to the winds,
committed treason and risked all for the sake of four towns only?

In contrast to Friedman, however, Kedourie suggested that
McMahon's word 'districts' in the letter was 'mistranslated' into *wilāyāt*,
and that a more appropriate word would have been *mudun* (towns): since
Homs and Hama were never vilayets, the conjunction of the four place
names in the same sentence meant that *wilāyāt* could not have meant
vilayets. Young's interpretation in 1920, according to Kedourie,
'depended on the illegitimate assumption that in speaking of the district
of Damascus, McMahon meant the *vilayet* of Damascus ... But this was

44 Kedourie, *Labyrinth*, 126, 297.
45 Kedourie, *Labyrinth*, 261, 268. See also Kedourie, *International Journal of Middle East Studies*, vol. 10, no. 3 (1979), 420–426.

an untenable argument.'[46] In his description of the Lindsay–Feisal encounter of January 1921, he wrote that Lindsay 'tried to counter Feisal's claim with the lame argument about boundaries which Young had invented and Feisal had no difficulty in showing up its absurdity'.[47] Curiously, Kedourie does not take his analysis to its logical conclusion by asking himself 'what is the implication of Young's invention?' The only logical answer to that question is that Palestine in the text was included in the area assigned to the Sharif. Kedourie's complete silence on this point is telling.

Kedourie is equally critical of the Peel commissioners 'who contented themselves with reiterating the absurd, and easily rebutted, argument invented by Young and advanced by Churchill in 1922 that Palestine was excluded from McMahon's pledge because it was "to the west of the district of Damascus."'[48] His thesis that Palestine was excluded from the area of Arab independence rests primarily on McMahon's 'explicit proviso' concerning French interests in Palestine,[49] and he criticises Toynbee for having disregarded this reservation. Furthermore, he omits to explain that the British later acknowledged that Hussein did not know in 1915 of French interests in Palestine. Even more significantly, his brief description of the four meetings of the Anglo-Arab Committee in February and March 1939 does little justice to their undoubted significance:

> The exchange began with an memorandum by Antonius, the strongest point of which was the argument – really unanswerable – that by the word 'districts', which Ruhi had translated as *wilayat*, McMahon could not possibly have meant *vilayets*, and that therefore the British case as expounded by Young and the Palestine white paper of 1922 was untenable. For the rest it abounded in red herrings, debating points and in inaccurate but plausible assertions about the history of British policy. Antonius could easily have been dealt with if the officials had known what their files contained, and if they had not been bemused, on the one hand, by *The Arab Awakening*, and determined, on the other, to get rid of

---

46 Kedourie, *Labyrinth*, 237.
47 Kedourie, *Labyrinth*, 241.
48 Kedourie, *Labyrinth*, 263.
49 Kedourie, *Labyrinth*, 210.

the Zionist embarrassment ... In reply to the lord chancellor, Antonius and Sir Michael McDonnell put in two counter memoranda with a wealth of ingenious argumentation and a profusion of legal references, which however were either misconceived or irrelevant, and which it would be tedious to review in any detail.[50]

Here, Kedourie's final phrase is unfair. By any standard – legal, political or moral – Antonius's and Sir Michael McDonnell's arguments are very persuasive. The phrases 'red herrings' and 'tedious to review' reflect Kedourie's deliberately minimalist use of the scores of documents in the official records detailing the committee's discussions, as described in Chapter Five. Tellingly, in contrast to his underuse of the extensive records of the committee's proceedings, Kedourie then spends ten pages analysing the subsequent negotiations concerning the drafting of the joint Anglo-Arab Report.[51] For his part, Friedman briefly mentions the existence of the committee in the preamble to *Palestine. A Twice-Promised Land?* but omits any reference whatsoever to its proceedings. Thus, it is no surprise that neither 'Anglo-Arab committee' nor 'McMahon committee' features in the index of that work.

The third scholar to have made a very thorough study of the UK's official records provided a radically different perspective to that of Friedman and Kedourie. Abdul Latif Tibawi's closely documented tome *Anglo-Arab Relations and the Question of Palestine, 1914–1921*, published in 1977, could just as appropriately have been entitled 'Anglo-Arab-Zionist Relations', as it also describes those relations as they developed before and during the First World War, particularly the negotiations that led to the publication of the Balfour Declaration. Chapter Three, 'The Husain-McMahon Correspondence', and Chapter Four, 'Perfidious Albion?', cover much the same ground as Antonius, but in greater detail, and with the advantage of the author's extensive study of the official records. According to Tibawi, Palestine was undoubtedly included in the area promised to the Sharif. Throughout his narrative the old shadow of British dishonour persists, with Tibawi repeating the charge of betrayal just as forcefully as Kedourie

---

50 Kedourie, *Labyrinth*, 300–301.
51 Kedourie, *Labyrinth*, 298–308.

implicitly and Friedman explicitly absolved the British of the same. For example, in his epilogue Tibawi points to Samuel's speech on 3 June 1921 to the Palestinians, where the High Commissioner declared that the British government would never impose upon the people of Palestine a policy 'which they could have reason to think was contrary to their religious, their political or their economic interests'. Tibawi called such discourse 'hypocritical nonsense' and asked rhetorically, 'What was his autocratic administration other than exacting taxation without any form of representation?'[52]

Since the Second World War, apart from the three aforementioned authors who dealt with the Correspondence in detail, scores of other well-established scholars of the Middle East have commented briefly on it. The following examples demonstrate the variety of approaches taken on the subject:

- Sir Reader Bullard (1951): 'The writer believes, for reasons already given, that Palestine was excluded from the area of Arab independence, but many Englishmen whose opinions are entitled to great respect reject this view and hold the Arabs to be right.'[53]
- Leonard Stein (1961): '... if the question is whether the British Government had committed itself in 1915 to leaving Palestine under Arab control, the answer seems clearly to be that there was no such commitment.'[54]
- Elizabeth Monroe (1963): 'The McMahon letter, by contrast [to the Sykes–Picot Agreement], was unclear about Palestine, for the ambiguous reference to areas west of the "vilayet" of Damascus might have included Palestine, or it might not.'[55]
- Peter Mansfield (1981): 'This correspondence is of cardinal importance because it became the subsequent basis of Arab nationalist charges against Britain of betrayal. The debate continues to this day

---

52 Tibawi, *Anglo-Arab Relations*, 497. See also Huneidi, *A Broken Trust*, 131.
53 Bullard, *Britain and the Middle East*, 154. Sir Reader William Bullard had a diplomatic career between 1920 and 1946, including positions in the Colonial Office, Russia, Iraq and Saudi Arabia; he served as Ambassador to Iran from 1942 to 1946.
54 Stein, *The Balfour Declaration*, 269.
55 Monroe, *Britain's Moment*, 33.

and will never be resolved because of the deliberately imprecise style in which the letters were written.'[56]

- Albert Hourani (1991): 'Whether anything was actually promised, and if so what, and whether the *sharif*'s revolt played a significant part in the allied victory, are matters of dispute, but what is clear is that for the first time the claim that those who spoke Arabic constituted a nation and should have a state had been to some extent accepted by a great power.'[57]

- Benny Morris (1999): 'The Arabs argued that, as Palestine was not to the west but to the southwest of Damascus, and as it had not been explicitly excluded, it was to be part of the Arab state. On balance it appears that they were right.'[58]

- Tom Segev (1999): 'Later, the question would arise about whether Palestine was included in [McMahon's] promise. Apparently it was, but the letter's wording was vague, perhaps deliberately so, either to mislead the Arabs or out of carelessness.'[59]

- Avi Shlaim (2000): 'Britain's public promise to the Jews could not be reconciled either with its earlier promise to Hussein, the sharif of Mecca, ... or with the secret Sykes-Picot agreement of 1916.'[60]

- Margaret MacMillan (2003): 'McMahon, in what has remained a highly controversial correspondence with the sharif, promised that, if the Arabs rose against the Turks, they would have British assistance, and, more importantly, their independence ... The boundaries between the exempted territories and the rest were not made clear. The British later argued, in defiance of geography, that Palestine also lay west of the Aleppo-Damascus line ... In 1915 the details of what was an exchange of promises, not a firm treaty, did not matter that much.'[61]

- James Barr (2006): 'Exactly what McMahon promised in his letters to Husein has never satisfactorily been made clear, just as McMahon intended ... By [1939], the British, recognising that basing their case

56 Peter Mansfield, *The Arabs* (London, 1981), 192.

57 Hourani, *A History of the Arab Peoples*, 317.

58 Morris, *Righteous Victims*, 69.

59 Segev, *One Palestine, Complete*, 46.

60 Shlaim, *The Iron Wall*, 7.

61 MacMillan, *Peacemakers*, 398–399.

on McMahon's words was fruitless, had resorted to defending their argument that Palestine had not been included through a description of the context.'[62]

- Karl Sabbagh (2006): 'It is difficult to know precisely what Britain promised Hussein. The documents involved – memos, letters, translations, telegrams – are contradictory and confusing ... So some kind of promise was made to Hussein if he agreed to help Britain fight the Turks, but it was sufficiently vague for the British to say after the war that Palestine was excluded.'[63]

- Ilan Pappe (2008): 'In ambiguous language, each promise contradicted the other two. The first associated the future of Palestine with that of an Arab Hashemite kingdom in the Arab world; the second proposed placing Palestine under Anglo-French colonial rule; and the last envisaged it as a future Jewish state.'[64]

- Victor Kattan (2009): 'It is abundantly clear from both the actual text of the Hussein-McMahon correspondence, and from the correspondence between Grey and McMahon, that Palestine was not excluded from the territory promised to Hussein in which he was to create his "Arab Caliphate of Islam."'[65]

- Eugene Rogan (2009): 'Moreover, the Sykes-Picot Agreement respected neither the spirit nor the letter of the Husayn-McMahon correspondence.'[66]

- Jonathan Schneer (2010): 'I have no intention of entering, let alone attempting to settle [the argument over the meaning of *wilāyāt* in the Correspondence].'[67]

- John McHugo (2013): 'The promises made to Hussein were inconsistent with the slightly later Sykes-Picot agreement with France ... Historians still discuss the extent of the commitments Britain made to the Sharif Hussein, the degree of inconsistency between these and the secret agreement with France, and precisely what the Balfour Declaration meant.'[68]

---

62 Barr, *Setting the Desert on Fire*, 312–313.

63 Karl Sabbagh, *Palestine. A Personal History* (London, 2006), 99–100.

64 Ilan Pappe, *A History of Modern Palestine* (Cambridge, 2008), 68.

65 Kattan, *From Coexistence to Conquest*, 46.

66 Rogan, *The Arabs*, 190.

67 Schneer, *The Balfour Declaration*, 66.

68 John McHugo, *A Concise History of the Arabs* (London, 2013), 113–114.

- Sean McMeekin (2015): 'Then there were the ill-fated negotiations between Hussein and Sir Henry McMahon … over the future disposition of Palestine, Syria, and Mesopotamia, in which McMahon so elegantly sidestepped making direct promises that diplomatic historians (and some politicians) still argue today about who, exactly, the British promised would get to rule each area after the war.'[69]

- Timothy J. Paris (2016): 'This issue [Palestine's inclusion or exclusion], which would engender decades of argument, ill will and scholarly debate, cannot be resolved because of the more general reservations concerning French interests.'[70]

- Bernard Regan (2017): 'Britain avoided [making] any firm commitments … Following their own agenda, the British were to ignore the promises contained in the McMahon–Hussein correspondence which Arab leaders believed expressed an undertaking to support the right of self-determination for Arab lands.'[71]

- Ian Black (2017): 'The truth [concerning Britain's wartime pledges] remains buried in imprecise definitions, misunderstandings and duplicity.'[72]

- Gardner Thompson (2019): 'Different parties have, unsurprisingly, accorded the McMahon letter different levels of significance. This controversy will continue.'[73]

- Rashid Khalidi (2020): '… for decades, British officials disingenuously but steadfastly maintained that Palestine had been excluded from wartime promises of Arab independence.'[74]

- Elizabeth Thompson (2020): 'In October 1915 McMahon responded in the affirmative, with the exception of territories along the Syrian-Lebanese coast claimed by the French and in southern Iraq and along the Persian Gulf occupied by the British and their clients … The alliance was sealed in March 1916, but the vague wording of

---

69 McMeekin, *The Ottoman Endgame*, 303–304.

70 Paris, *In Defence of Britain's Middle Eastern Empire*, 132.

71 Regan, *The Balfour Declaration*, 46, 91.

72 Black, *Enemies and Neighbours*, 14.

73 Gardner Thompson, *Legacy of Empire* (London, 2019), 65.

74 Khalidi, *The Hundred Years' War on Palestine*, 37.

McMahon's promises, unknown to Faisal in 1918, would haunt British-Arab negotiations at war's end.'[75]

- Lori Allen (2021): 'It was implied in the correspondence exchanged during 1915–1916 that Palestine was included in the promise.'[76]

75 Thompson, *How the West Stole Democracy*, 6–7.
76 Allen, *A History of False Hope*, 65.

Conclusions

Steadfastly Disingenuous

The UK's official records between 1920 and 1939 confirm that successive cabinets were reluctant to publish the McMahon–Hussein Correspondence because, first, neither the 'districts' reservation nor the even vaguer 'French interests' reservation in McMahon's 24 October 1915 letter could be successfully defended in Parliament; second, the references in Kitchener's and McMahon's letters to the Caliphate would, they feared, disturb the Muslim subjects of the Empire, particularly in India; and third, no government during the 1920s and 1930s wished to resurrect memories of Anglo-French rivalry for control of the region which publication of the Correspondence might produce. But all the Foreign Office and Colonial Office evidence suggests that the second and third considerations were of secondary importance. The principal reason why successive British governments refused to publish throughout this interwar period was without question the serious weakness of McMahon's reservations concerning Palestine.

After an exhaustive examination of the official records available at the time of writing in 2022, I think that Toynbee comes closest to the truth when he indicated in his 1970 article that to publish, post-1920, would have been very embarrassing for any government, with their eyes not only on Parliament and public opinion, but also on Britain's position vis-à-vis France, the United States, the Empire and the fledgling League of Nations. Toynbee does not explain his assertion in detail, but by pointing out that Young's (1920) and Churchill's (1922), in his opinion erroneous, 'districts' interpretations were put forward later than all previous 'west of the line of the four towns' interpretations, including his own (1918), he appears to indicate that by the early 1920s, all other wartime pledges, agreements and declarations concerning Palestine had to be put aside, one way or another, if they were not fully in line with pro-Zionist policy of successive governments.

Toynbee's thesis is supported by the eminent American scholar C. Ernest Dawn, who argues that the post-1920 British interpretation of the 'districts' phrase 'is virtually impossible on both linguistic and documentary grounds. Linguistic and logical considerations are decisive ... the later official exegesis is highly suspect ... intrinsically self-serving, by its very nature subject to serious question'.[1] Like Toynbee, Dawn also points out that Young's exegesis was advanced after the Palestine Mandate had been assigned to Britain and the Mandate had been challenged by the Arabs.

All the written evidence I have discovered in the official records points in that direction, to the integrity of Toynbee's and Dawn's arguments, although it must be said that on this major question I'm in the position of an observer who has watched smoke emerging uninterrupted for twenty-four hours from all windows of a building, and yet is unable to produce a photograph of the flames. Nevertheless, I have become convinced of the *factual* existence of a fire. Thus, although I have not found a single document by any British official which states that successive governments' refusal to publish was motivated explicitly by their desire to maintain a pro-Zionist policy, I have found no evidence in the official records that points to any other motive.

Moreover, although the official records enable much of the story to be coherently described, there are still some evidential gaps where the dots do not quite join up, concerning the origins and discussions surrounding Young's 1920 'corrective' interpretation, which was immediately taken up by the Foreign Office, and where there appear to be no written instructions to Childs in 1930 to produce his 'monumental' (Rendel's word) 184-page memorandum. Nevertheless, I think we can reasonably make the following deductions.

The 1920 Young episode remains a particularly multi-layered mystery. In his 1930 memorandum, Childs writes that Young studied the Arabic text of McMahon's 24 October 1915 letter to the Sharif 'and saw that the Arabic of the words "district of Damascus" had the meaning "vilayet of Damascus"; and that, as the vilayet of which Damascus

1 C. Ernest Dawn, *From Ottomanism to Arabism*, 93.

was the capital extended southward to the Gulf of Akaba, the pledge excluded Palestine from the Arab area'.[2]

Childs, who did not read Arabic, stated that Young was a 'competent Arabist' and, as we have seen, the government adopted his translation without reserve – Churchill adopted it in 1922 and it remained successive governments' official interpretation until 1939. However, in February 1939, Heyworth-Dunne and Antonius were unanimous in concluding that *wilāyāt* had been erroneously translated as <u>vilayets</u>. The Lord Chancellor did not question Heyworth-Dunne's competence, his conclusions or his independence; neither did Antonius or anyone else.[3]

What is particularly curious, apart from the question of Young's (in)competence in translating written Arabic, is the apparent lack of any state papers written by Young himself which herald this discovery, nor any written commentary on the matter by other Foreign Office officials, either junior or senior to Young. What is more, there appears to be no trace of any of Young's memoranda or minutes of the period, apart from his 'Foreign Office Memorandum on Possible Negotiations with the Hedjaz', where he erroneously defines the western boundary of the District of Damascus as reaching as far south as Aqaba.[4] If the Foreign Office were already in possession of an Arabic version of the letter, there is no trace of it. During the First World War, certain papers from foreign posts were lost, burned or destroyed, but this episode is postwar and London-centred, so the likelihood of files having being mislaid is small. Equally curious, of course, is the case of both Storrs's original Arabic drafts (1915–1916), later found by Keown-Boyd, and Vickery's original Arabic texts (1919), none of which can be found in the UK's National Archives, and which do not ever seem to have been sent to London.

In January 1921, there was undoubtedly an Arabic version of the letter available at the memorable Feisal–Lindsay encounter, with Lawrence and Young in attendance, where the relevant 'districts' paragraph was read out in Arabic and commented upon by Feisal. In the

2 See FO 371/14495, 129–165. CONFIDENTIAL 13378 'MEMORANDUM on the Exclusion of Palestine from the Area assigned for Arab Independence by the McMahon-Hussein Correspondence of 1915–16 [WITH TWO MAPS]', Foreign Office, 24 October 1930.

3 Heyworth-Dunne received an honorarium of £50 from the government for his translation work.

4 FO 371/5066, 14959. Young memorandum, 29 November 1920.

report of the meeting, probably written by Young, there is no mention
of the latter questioning Feisal's interpretation or offering any remark.
Why? Did Feisal or Lawrence then allow Young to peruse the letter? If
so, as a competent Arabist he would have immediately deduced that in
the 'districts' phrase *wilāyāt* meant 'local districts' and not vilayets.
Moreover, he would almost certainly have previously studied Vickery's
English vilayets translation sent to London in 1919, and spotted Vickery's
errors.

Until I can find documentary evidence to the contrary, I remain
unconvinced that Young had access to an Arabic copy of the letter when
he wrote his 'corrective' interpretation of it in November 1920. Did he
base his interpretation on McMahon's English 'districts' letter (as sent to
the Foreign Office on 26 October 1915) and/or Vickery's English vilayets translation of the Arabic letter that Vickery had copied in Jedda in
1919 directly from the King's original? Whatever its provenance,
Young's interpretation was critically important, as was the decision by
his superiors at the Foreign Office, and later the Colonial Office, as
expressed in Churchill's 1922 White Paper, to adopt it as government
policy. Young's interpretation in 1920 remains the first written evidence
of the government's reinterpretation of the 1915–1916 Correspondence.
From the government's perspective, it brushed aside any legitimacy to a
future claim to Palestine by King Hussein. Furthermore, it laid the
foundations of Britain's broken promise over Palestine, although in his
defence it must be said that Young – a senior official (Shuckburgh's
deputy) – did not decide policy, or indeed changes in policy. Like
Hogarth, he was a chess piece, not the chess player, in Whitehall and
Downing Street's postwar game of colonial acquisition in the Middle
East.

The written evidence clearly reveals three things. First, that Lloyd
George's government in November 1917 committed itself to the policy
of a Jewish national home in Palestine, and promoted that policy vigorously until October 1922, when the coalition government fell, by which
time the Mandate for Palestine was enshrined in the international law of
the day. Second, the lobbying power of the Zionist Organisation on
successive governments was consistently much stronger during this
decisive period than that of any pro-Arab group or Arab delegation.
Finally, the extensive Hansard records throughout the period testify to
the importance in Parliament of a very substantial measure of support

for a publicly announced policy such as the Jewish national home project: the government's (and thus the Empire's) honour, reputation, prestige and ultimately stability were involved.

Any shift of policy would have indicated weakness on the part of the government, whose self-image as a morally sound, globally civilising enterprise had been somewhat shaken, but not fundamentally called into question, by the horrors of the war. Furthermore, acknowledgement of senior officials' mistakes was extremely rare, and normally 'could not be countenanced'. Hence, on the McMahon pledge, the *non possumus* attitude that prevailed between 1920 and 1939. Unsurprisingly, Childs's lengthy dodgy dossier, written for the cabinet in 1930, simply confirmed previous governments' interpretations of the Correspondence.

Leaving aside all the 'extenuating and surrounding circumstances', 'avowed intentions', professions of 'good faith' and the sophistry of numerous circumlocutions, as well as the phrase 'Yes, but on the other hand', so beloved of diplomats, politicians and historians, the facts that emerge from a close scrutiny of the Arabic and English texts of the Correspondence (as officially agreed in 1939) and of the official records between 1915 and 1939 are as follows.

Linguistically, the Arabic text of McMahon's fateful letter of 24 October 1915 unambiguously includes the Palestine region in the area promised to the Sharif of Mecca. The latter was fully entitled to read the 'districts' (*wilāyāt*) phrase as including the Palestine region in the area of Arab independence promised to him by the High Commissioner.

McMahon's two reservations in this letter were – to a degree – deliberately ambiguously phrased. If he had intended to be precise as to the limits of his reserved area, he would have used the phrase 'west of the four towns', not 'west of the four districts'. Storrs and Rūhi would or should then have written an Arabic word for 'towns', such as *mudun*, and not *wilāyāt*. Alternatively, if McMahon had intended to exclude Palestine, and wished to be specific, he would have used the phrase 'west of the Vilayet of Syria'. But boundary clarity was not McMahon's intention, nor Storrs's. Yet the letters were precise about mentions of Aden, the sheikhdoms in the Persian Gulf, and the Vilayets of Basra and Baghdad. Did McMahon, Storrs, Rūhi, Clayton write what they thought would be just enough to get the Sharif to accept their terms and launch a revolt against the Ottomans?

Concerning the regions he reserved, McMahon made his intentions clear in his explanatory despatch to the Foreign Office on 26 October 1915. In relation to the 'districts' phrase, he wrote of the 'northern coasts of Syria', in other words the Lebanon region. Linguistically, this point brooks no alternative interpretation: those were his words.

The text of the letter is not *that* ambiguous. The Sharif was perfectly correct to conclude that *wilāyāt* meant local districts in that particular phrase, and not *vilayets* (provinces). Any other interpretation is linguistically untenable. Feisal's assertion of that point in his interview at the Foreign Office on 20 January 1921 was equally correct.

From 1916 onwards, British officials correctly interpreted the 'districts' reservation phrase as meaning the area 'west of the four towns' – the Lebanon region.

In the Correspondence, the Sharif did not agree at any point to leave 'Beirut and its coasts', or indeed any other part of Greater Syria out of the area he initially requested. He merely agreed to postpone the discussion about the future of 'Beirut and its coasts' until the end of hostilities. In a similar vein, at the 1919 Peace Conference, Feisal merely agreed to postpone the issue of Palestine to later discussions. Both father and son consistently maintained their claim for Arab independence for the region, including Palestine, based on McMahon's pledge, later Allied pledges – and then Article 22 of the Covenant of the League.

In the official notes exchanged between Churchill and the Arab delegation in 1922,[5] the latter clearly exposed the fallacy of the British claim that 'districts' meant *vilayets*. The official records reveal that Sir John Shuckburgh and other senior Colonial Office and Foreign Office officials were perfectly aware of this from that time, if not before.

British interpretations changed in 1920. That cannot have been achieved without considerable discussion in the Foreign Office, which would normally have produced a number of memoranda and minutes. Yet, there is a definite and uncharacteristic scarcity of official records on this and surrounding issues between the autumn of 1920 and the summer of 1921. This begs the question as to whether some relevant documents remain classified.

---

5 *Palestine. Correspondence with the Palestine Arab Delegation and the Zionist Organisation* (Cmd 1700), 3 June 1922.

Young's, and later Churchill's, invented 'district of Damascus' reservation remained the official bedrock of British policy until it was abandoned in 1939 by the Lord Chancellor, who relied on a novel contention, 'the unique position of Palestine', and the deliberately ambiguous 'French interests' reservation in McMahon's letter to maintain the government's case during his discussions with the Arab delegation. Maugham himself described the 'districts' reservation as 'straw', thereby privately undermining Churchill's 1922 White Paper interpretation, and brought forward the 'unique position of Palestine' contention to bolster the British case, while acknowledging privately to MacDonald that it was a hollow ploy. By any standard, it was a deceitful stratagem.

The Sharif faithfully fulfilled his side of the pledge, and British postwar governments never suggested he had not done so. Most Arabs declined to join him when he revolted in June 1916, but he and his sons, particularly Abdullah and Feisal and their troops, did the best they could in the circumstances to assist the Allied war effort and defeat the Turks. Lord Curzon and General Allenby, as well as other senior British officials, stated as such, privately and publicly. For example, on 9 October 1919, Curzon wrote to Emir Feisal:

> His Majesty's Government recognise gladly and fully the indispensable assistance rendered to the Allied cause by King Hussein and yourself, and by the valiant Arab troops under your command. The courage and activity of Your Highness's troops were an essential element in the campaign which led to the overthrow of Turkish despotism.[6]

Allenby reminded Curzon in 1920 that

> I think it may be fairly said that each [Sharif of Mecca, Ibn Saud and the Idrisi], according to his capacity, rendered real and effective assistance at a time when the result of the war still hung in the balance and, by so doing, brought to nought the plans for a Jihad, diverted or rendered innocuous large Turkish forces, and greatly facilitated our task in keeping open to traffic the Red Sea.[7]

6 FO 371/20807, E3380, 101.
7 DBFP, Series 1, vol. xiii, no. 253. Allenby to Curzon, 28 May 1920.

McMahon never stated – neither privately to Shuckburgh in 1922, nor in his letter to *The Times* on 23 July 1937 – that he had excluded Palestine in his pledge to the Sharif, only that he had intended to do so. Where McMahon was misleading (according to Rendel, and I concur) was to express in his letter to *The Times* that 'I also had every reason to believe at the time that the fact that Palestine was not included in my pledge was well understood by King Hussein.' McMahon never supplied any evidence, written or anecdotal, to back up this assertion. In fact, no British official has ever produced any evidence indicating that in 1915 the Sharif knew of French claims either to Syria (i.e. Greater Syria, which included Palestine) or specifically to the Palestine region. McMahon's assertion in this matter is manifestly self-serving.

In February 1939, it was a dishonest manoeuvre for the government to circulate to the Arab delegation the inaccurate <u>vilayets</u> version of the letter that Vickery produced in 1919. Given the twenty-six mistakes in this translation, Antonius's and Heyworth-Dunne's unanimous conclusions concerning its validity can hardly be contested.

It was equally dishonest for the government to state, in the explanatory note at the beginning of the Correspondence White Paper,[8] that footnotes indicated the former, inaccurate renderings of the Correspondence, and then to omit the crucial footnote (no. 9, p. 8) regarding the change from <u>vilayet</u> to 'district'. This omission would hardly have gone unnoticed by the Arab delegation.

The 1915 Constantinople Agreement between Britain, France and Russia was a secret inter-state treaty, as was the 1916 Sykes–Picot Agreement. The 1915 pledge to Hussein, the 1917 pledge to the Zionist Organisation and the later relevant messages and declarations – the Hogarth Message, Anglo-French Declaration and Declaration to the Seven – were not, in judicial terms, inter-state treaties. Nevertheless, they were all pledges, with their own debatable degrees of logic, morality, and military and political implications. It is both significant and ironic that while the exchange of letters with the Sharif contained legal obligations, the Balfour Declaration itself did not. The latter only became a legal text when it was incorporated into the Palestine Mandate.

---

8 *Correspondence* (Cmd 5957), 2.

The issue of whether the Sharif of Mecca had any moral, religious or political authority to represent the Palestinians, or indeed to represent any of the other regions that he claimed beyond the Hijaz, is a valid and closely related topic of debate, but has not been the focus of this book. Concerning political authority, he did not, save to the extent that the peoples of the other regions granted him such authority, if they did so at all. In a similar vein, a discussion concerning Britain's moral and political right in 1917 to propose on the future of a small slice of an enemy's empire, although undoubtedly of interest to some historians and international lawyers, has been left aside. Nevertheless, this book confirms definitively that Palestine was a twice-promised land. Britain's contradictory wartime pledges – one denied (a broken promise), the other fulfilled – far from being a minor footnote in its chequered imperial history, unquestionably laid the foundations of the conflict for control of Palestine, which remains unresolved more than a century later.

To conclude, in the heat of war Asquith's government promised the Sharif of Mecca an independent Arab state, including the Palestine region, and two years later Lloyd George's government promised the Palestine region to the global Jewish community. For their own imperial reasons, after the First World War, successive British governments kept their pledge to the Jewish community and reneged on their earlier pledge to the Sharif through denial, fact-deficient rhetoric and silence. Since the 1939 Anglo-Arab Report, which in the light of all the written evidence can be best described as a whitewash, no British government has reviewed the case, and MacDonald's 'bails and stumps', shrewdly but not honourably defended by the Lord Chancellor, have remained firmly in place, quite undisturbed by occasional academic debate.

Throughout their history, the British have rarely been coy in calling other nations to account. Memories may fade, but the significance of an official acknowledgement of the truth of past events in a nation's imperial history does not diminish with the passing of time. To heal the wounds of history anywhere requires acknowledgement of error and the willingness of all parties to be held to account for the policies they pursued. In the Middle East, where such wounds have festered for so long, a British government's acknowledgement, however late in the day, of the truth concerning the pledge given by a predecessor to the Sharif of Mecca in 1915 would surely be welcomed.

Epilogue

In Search of Change

> *History, despite its wrenching pain, cannot be unlived,*
> *but if faced with courage, need not be lived again*
> Maya Angelou

Since 1939, no British government has examined its predecessors' contradictory promises, including the 'broken promise' of the McMahon–Hussein Correspondence, which led inexorably to a hundred years of warfare in Palestine. Instead, governments of all parties have consistently favoured policies on Palestine which have been politically convenient domestically, which have not reflected reality on the ground, and which have not acknowledged one iota of responsibility for the destruction of Palestinian society in 1948.

In the ensuing years, pogroms, dispossession and exile have been the Palestinians' lot. During the eighteenth and nineteenth centuries, the indigenous peoples of North America had little, if any, power to resist the European settler government in Washington D.C. So far, the indigenous Palestinians have endured a not dissimilar history. The myth of two peoples in an equal fight, engaged in a 'conflict' of 'right against right', still lingers in Western corridors of power, as well as in the media, and prevents the possibility of constructive negotiations. According to Mearsheimer and Walt, 'In addition to Israel's commitment to maintaining its Jewish identity and its refusal to grant de jure equality for non-Jews,' the 2.08 million Palestinian citizens of Israel 'are de facto treated as second-class citizens'.[1]

Since 1967, a succession of governments in London, their eyes firmly fixed on trade, oil and regional security, have shown no desire to hold

---

[1] Mearsheimer and Walt, *The Israel Lobby*, 88.

their ally, a self-proclaimed liberal democracy, to account for its un-Jewish, colonising, oppressive policies, which therefore remain consequence-free. At the time of writing in April 2024, Israel's barbaric 'starve and bomb' military campaign in Gaza, and 'pogrom' policy in the West Bank, following Hamas's terror attack on 7 October 2023, is not a conventional war, but a colonial-style ethnic-cleansing operation. Over 30,000 Palestinians have been killed, including 13,000 children.[2]

Some of Israel's rhetoric is dehumanising. There is no 'parity of esteem', an essential ingredient for successful negotiations towards some sort of pragmatic, reasonably just, long-term solution. At the United Nations, the UK government willingly follows the US's oil- and empire-focused policy, abstaining, Pontius Pilate-like, on current proposals for an immediate ceasefire. This is indefensible and inhumane.

All the parties involved endeavour to hug the moral high ground. Is it unduly naive to hope that if the British government gave a lead, all might inch forward cautiously towards a settlement on the basis of 'acknowledgement' of their own past and present mistakes, rather than constantly proclaiming, from the summits of their self-made moral mountains, the sins of the 'Other'? What is certain is that the citizens of Israel will have neither security nor peace while the Palestinian people continue to be denied both.

The moral and political imperative for change is clear. Some examples in recent history demonstrate that what is unthinkable today can become reality tomorrow, when the high priests of scepticism and real-politik are confounded, and a new political dispensation emerges. South Africa and Northern Ireland come to mind, whose present political arrangements are considerably better than they were previously. Could 'acknowledgement', unimaginable at present, and the establishment of 'parity of esteem', where all parties would be involved in negotiations, be two of the initial stepping stones towards a potential new dispensation for the region, or must the war for Palestine continue for a further century?

---

2 'Anatomy of a Genocide: Report of the Special Rapporteur on the situation of human rights in the Palestinian territories occupied since 1967' (advance unedited version), UN Human Rights Council, 25 March 2024, A/HRC/55/73, available at www.ohchr.org/en/documents/country-reports/ahrc5573-report-special-rapporteur-situation-human-rights-palestinian (accessed 4 April 2024).

Acknowledgements

Over the past decade, the theme of this book was discussed with many friends. I owe a particular debt of friendship and gratitude to Roger and Monica Spooner, who first suggested I investigate the contentious and unresolved issue of the Correspondence.

A number of friends read early drafts. I am especially thankful to Philip Boobbyer, Mary Embleton, Tim Llewellyn, John McHugo, John Metson, Geoffrey Nash, Bernard Regan, Abdel Razzaq Takriti and Andrew Whitley, who provided information, constructive criticism and constant encouragement for a project which seemed a moral and political minefield. Numerous conversations with Geoffrey Nash helped me to stay focused and to avoid my worst meanderings. Mary Embleton was equally generous with her academic expertise. She and John Metson later read and improved the entire manuscript, applying their extensive knowledge and formidable editing skills. Nevertheless, for the remaining infelicities of style I alone am responsible.

My thanks go to the staff of the National Archives at Kew for their cooperation, and in particular to Dr Lucia Pereira Pardo, Senior Conservation Scientist, for her assistance in revealing the hidden text of a 1939 Foreign Office memorandum, using a multi-spectral imaging machine.

I also wish to thank the Oxford Middle East Centre's archivist, Debbi Usher, for her support in my research in the archives' collection of British Mandate officials' private papers; the staff of the Barker Research Library at the University of Durham for permission to consult the Malcolm MacDonald papers, a particularly rich trove of information; to Dorothea Skelton-Foord for her translations from the German Press, and to Peter Goodwin, for his professional archival and website research, compiling the relevant photographs. The photograph of James Heyworth-Dunne was kindly offered to me by his family.

To Novin Doostdar and all the team at Oneworld, many thanks for taking on this manuscript, and in particular to Jonathan Bentley-Smith and David Inglesfield for their intelligent, imaginative and meticulous copyediting.

My family have borne the brunt of my increasing obsession with this topic over the past decade. My wife, Alison, has been a constant source of strength and inspiration during this long journey towards publication, as have our children, Patrick, Teresa and Anthony. I owe them an immeasurable debt.

Such conclusions as I have drawn are entirely my own.

Appendix I

The McMahon–Hussein Correspondence (Cmd 5957)

Author's Note

What follows is a verbatim reproduction of the Correspondence 'Presented by the Secretary of State for Foreign Affairs to Parliament by Command of His Majesty' and published by His Majesty's Stationery Office in 1939. For the avoidance of doubt, the footnotes are a part of the said publication; none are additions of this author. Only the page numbers in the contents have been altered.

Miscellaneous No. 3 (1939)

CORRESPONDENCE
BETWEEN
SIR HENRY McMAHON
G.C.M.G., G.C.V.O., K.C.I.E., C.S.I.
HIS MAJESTY'S HIGH COMMISSIONER AT CAIRO
AND
THE SHERIF HUSSEIN OF MECCA
July 1915—March 1916
[WITH A MAP]

*Presented by the Secretary of State for Foreign Affairs
to Parliament by Command of His Majesty*

LONDON

PRINTED AND PUBLISHED BY HIS MAJESTY'S
STATIONERY OFFICE

To be purchased directly from H.M. STATIONERY OFFICE
at the following addresses:

York House, Kingsway, London, W.C.2;

120 George Street, Edinburgh 2;

26 York Street, Manchester 1; 1 St. Andrew's Crescent, Cardiff;

80 Chichester Street, Belfast;

or through any bookseller

1939

Price 4d. net

Cmd. 5957

CONTENTS.

APPENDIX.—Map of Pre-war Turkish Administrative Districts comprised in Syria and Palestine.

EXPLANATORY NOTE.

The correspondence of which an English text follows was exchanged in Arabic.

This English text is based upon the original drafts in English of the letters sent by Sir Henry McMahon and the contemporary translations into English of the letters received by Sir Henry McMahon.

The language of some of the original drafts or contemporary translations has, however, been modified in certain places where the language has been criticised on the ground that it does not reproduce accurately the Arabic of the actual correspondence and the criticism has been found on examination to be justified.

The text printed in the following pages is the revised text which results from these modifications. Except where otherwise stated, the foot-notes indicate the text as it stood before the modifications were introduced.

His Majesty's Government have been advised in this matter by Mr. J. Heyworth-Dunne, Senior Lecturer in Arabic at the School of Oriental Studies, University of London.

CORRESPONDENCE BETWEEN SIR HENRY McMAHON, G.C.M.G., G.C.V.O., K.C.I.E., C.S.I., HIS MAJESTY'S HIGH COMMISSIONER AT CAIRO, AND THE SHERIF HUSSEIN OF MECCA [WITH A MAP].

July 1915–March 1916.

No. 1.

Translation of a letter from the Sherif of Mecca to Sir Henry McMahon, His Majesty's High Commissioner at Cairo.([1])

([1]) Undated and unsigned, but enclosed in an unsigned personal letter dated 2nd Ramadan, 1333 (14th July, 1915), from the Sherif to Mr. Storrs.

To his Honour: *July* 14, 1915.

WHEREAS the whole of the Arab nation without any exception have decided in these last years to live, and to accomplish their freedom, and grasp the reins of their administration both in theory and practice; and whereas they have found and felt that it is to the interest of the Government of Great Britain to support them and aid them to the attainment of their firm and lawful intentions (which are based upon the maintenance of the honour and dignity of their life) without any ulterior motives whatsoever unconnected with this object;

And whereas it is to their (the Arabs') interest also to prefer the assistance of the Government of Great Britain in consideration of their geographical position and economic interests, and also of the attitude of the above-mentioned Government, which is known to both nations and therefore need not be emphasised;

For these reasons the Arab nation see fit to limit themselves, as time is short, to asking the Government of Great Britain, if it should think fit, for the approval, through her deputy or representative, of the following fundamental propositions, leaving out all things considered secondary in comparison with these, so that it may prepare all means necessary for attaining this noble purpose, until such time as it finds occasion for making the actual negotiations:—

Firstly.—England to acknowledge the independence of the Arab countries, bounded on the north by Mersina and Adana up to the 37° of latitude, on which degree fall Birijik, Urfa, Mardin, Midiat. (²)Jezirat (Ibn 'Umar), Amadia,(²) up to the border of Persia; on the east by the borders of Persia up to the Gulf of Basra; on the south by the Indian Ocean, with the exception of the position of Aden to remain as it is; on the west by the Red Sea, the Mediterranean Sea up to Mersina. England to approve of the proclamation of an Arab Khalifate of Islam.

Secondly.—The Arab Government of the Sherif to acknowledge that England shall have the preference in all economic enterprises in the Arab countries whenever conditions of enterprises are otherwise equal.

Thirdly.—For the security of this Arab independence and the certainty of such preference of economic enterprises, both high

---

(²)—(²) Former reading: "Amadia Island (Jezireh)."

contracting parties to offer mutual assistance, to the best ability of their military and naval forces, to face any foreign Power which may attack either party. Peace not to be decided without agreement of both parties.

Fourthly.—If one of the parties enters upon an aggressive conflict, the other party to assume a neutral attitude, and in case of such party wishing the other to join forces, both to meet and discuss the conditions.

Fifthly.—England to acknowledge the abolition of foreign privileges in the Arab countries, and to assist the Government of the Sherif in an International Convention for confirming such abolition.

Sixthly.—Articles 3 and 4 of this treaty to remain in vigour for fifteen years, and, if either wishes it to be renewed, one year's notice before lapse of treaty to be given.

Consequently, and as the whole of the Arab nation have (praise be to God) agreed and united for the attainment, at all costs and finally, of this noble object, they beg the Government of Great Britain to answer them positively or negatively in a period of thirty days after receiving this intimation; and if this period should lapse before they receive an answer, they reserve to themselves complete freedom of action. Moreover, we (the Sherif's family) will consider ourselves free in word and deed from the bonds of our previous declaration which we made through Ali Effendi.

No. 2.

Translation of a letter from Sir H. McMahon, His Majesty's High Commissioner at Cairo, to the Sherif of Mecca.

To his Highness the Sherif Hussein.   *August* 30, 1915.
(After compliments and salutations.)

WE have the honour to thank you for your frank expressions of the sincerity of your feeling towards England. We rejoice, moreover, that your Highness and your people are of one opinion—that Arab interests are English interests and English Arab. To this intent we confirm to you the terms of Lord Kitchener's message, which reached you by the hand of Ali Effendi, and in which was stated clearly our desire for the independence of Arabia and its inhabitants, together with our approval of the Arab Khalifate when it should be proclaimed. We declare once more that His Majesty's Government would welcome the resumption of the Khalifate by an Arab of true race. With regard to the questions of (³)limits and boundaries,(³) it would appear to be premature to consume our time in discussing such details in the heat of war, and while, in many portions of them, the Turk is up to now in effective occupation; especially as we have learned, with surprise and regret, that some of the Arabs in those very parts, far from assisting us, are neglecting this their supreme opportunity and are lending their arms to the German and the Turk, to the new despoiler and the old oppressor.

Nevertheless, we are ready to send your Highness for the Holy Cities and the noble Arabs the charitable offerings of Egypt so soon as your Highness shall inform us how and where they should be delivered. We are, moreover, arranging for this your messenger to be admitted and helped on any journey he may make to ourselves.

Friendly reassurances. Salutations!

(Signed)
A. H. McMAHON.

No. 3.
Translation of a letter from the Sherif of Mecca to Sir H. McMahon, His Majesty's High Commissioner at Cairo.

September 9, 1915.

To His Excellency the Most Exalted, the Most Eminent—the British High Commissioner in Egypt; may God grant him Success.

WITH great cheerfulness and delight I received your letter dated the 19th Shawal, 1333 (the 30th August, 1915), and have given it great consideration and regard, in spite of the impression I received from it of ambiguity and its tone of coldness and hesitation with regard to our essential point.

It is necessary to make clear to your Excellency our sincerity towards the illustrious British Empire and our confession of preference for it in all cases and matters and under all forms and circumstances. The real interests of the followers of our religion necessitate this.

(³)—(³) Former reading: "Limits, frontiers and boundaries."

Nevertheless, your Excellency will pardon me and permit me to say clearly that the coolness and hesitation which you have displayed in the question of the limits and boundaries by saying that the discussion of these at present is of no use and is a loss of time, and that they are still in the hands of the Government which is ruling them, &c., might be taken to infer an estrangement or something of the sort.

([4])As the limits and boundaries demanded are not those of one person whom we should satisfy and with whom we should discuss them after the war is over, but our peoples have seen that the life of their new proposal is bound at least by these limits and their word is united on this.

Therefore, they have found it necessary first to discuss this point with the Power in whom they now have their confidence and trust as a final appeal, viz., the illustrious British Empire.([4])

([5])Their reason for this union and confidence is mutual interest, the necessity of regulating territorial divisions and the feelings of their inhabitants, so that they may know how to base their future and life, so not to meet her (England?) or any of her Allies in opposition to their resolution which would produce a contrary issue, which God forbid.([5])

([6])For the object is, honourable Minister, the truth which is established on a basis which guarantees the essential sources of life in future.

Yet within these limits they have not included places inhabited by a foreign race. It is a vain show of words and titles.

May God have mercy on the Khalifate and comfort Moslems in it.([6])

([4])—([4]) It has been suggested that a better translation of this passage would be: "As the limits and boundaries demanded are not those of one individual whose claim might well await the conclusion of the war, but are those of our people who have decided that those frontiers are as a minimum vitally necessary to their new life, and whose resolution is final on this point. Therefore, they have decided to discuss this point in the first resort with the Power in which they now have their confidence and trust and whom they regard as their ultimate appeal, namely, the Illustrious British Empire."

([5])—([5]) It has been suggested that a better translation of this passage would be: "Their reason for this aim and confidence is the reciprocity of interests, the necessity of regulating territorial divisions and the wishes of the populations concerned, so that they may know how to base their future life and avoid finding Great Britain or any of her allies in opposition to or in conflict with their wishes, which God forbid!"

([6])—([6]) It has been suggested that a better translation of this passage would be: "For our aim, O respected Minister, is to ensure that the conditions which are essential to our future shall be secured on a foundation of reality, and not on highly decorated phrases and titles. As for the Caliphate, God have mercy on its soul and comfort the Moslems for their loss."

I am confident that your Excellency will not doubt that it is not I personally who am demanding of these limits which include only our race, but that they are all proposals of the people, who, in short, believe that they are necessary for economic life.

Is this not right, your Excellency the Minister?

In a word, your high Excellency, we are firm in our sincerity and declaring our preference for loyalty towards you, whether you are satisfied with us, as has been said, or angry.

With reference to your remark in your letter above mentioned that some of our people are still doing their utmost in promoting the interests of Turkey, your goodness (lit. "perfectness") would not permit you to make this an excuse for the tone of coldness and hesitation with regard to our demands, demands which I cannot admit that you, as a man of sound opinion, will deny to be necessary for our existence; nay, they are the essential essence of our life, material and moral.

Up to the present moment I am myself with all my might carrying out in my country all things in conformity with the Islamic Law, all things which tend to benefit the rest of the Kingdom, and I shall continue to do so until it pleases God to order otherwise.

In order to reassure your Excellency I can declare that the whole country, together with those who you say are submitting themselves to Turco-German orders, are all waiting the result of these negotiations, which are dependent only on your refusal or acceptance of the question of the limits and on your declaration of safeguarding their religion first and then the rest of rights from any harm or danger.

Whatever the illustrious Government of Great Britain finds conformable to its policy on this subject, communicate it to us and specify to us the course we should follow.

In all cases it is only God's will which shall be executed, and it is God who is the real factor in everything.

With regard to our demand for grain for the natives, and the moneys ("surras") known to the Wakfs' Ministry and all other articles sent here with pilgrims' caravans, high Excellency, my intention in this matter is to confirm your proclamations to the whole world, and especially to the Moslem world, that your antagonism is confined only to the party which has usurped the rights of the Khalifate in which are included the rights of all Moslems.

Moreover the said grain is from the special Wakfs and has nothing to do with politics.

If you think it should be, let the grain of the two years be transported in a special steamer to Jedda in an official manner, in the name of all the natives as usual, and the captain of the steamer or the special "Mamur" detailed as usual every year to hand it over on his arrival at the port will send to the Governor of Jedda asking for the Mamur of the grain at Jedda or a responsible official to take over the grain and give the necessary receipt signed by the said Mamur, that is the Mamur of the grain himself. He should make it a condition that he would (? not) accept any receipt but that signed by this Mamur.

Let the captain of the steamer or the "Mamur" (detailed with the grain) be instructed that if he finds anything contrary to this arrangement he should warn them that he will return home with the cargo. Thereupon the Mamur and the special committee detailed with him, which is known as the committee of the grain for the natives, will take over the grain in the proper form.

Please accept my best regards and salutations.

If you choose to send a reply to this, please send it with the bearer.

29th Shawal, 1333.

No. 4.

Translation of a letter from Sir H. McMahon, His Majesty's High Commissioner at Cairo, to the Sherif of Mecca.

October 24, 1915.

I HAVE received your letter of the 29th Shawal, 1333, with much pleasure and your expressions of friendliness and sincerity have given me the greatest satisfaction.

I regret that you should have received from my last letter[7] the impression that I regarded the question of the limits and boundaries with coldness and hesitation; such was not the case, but it appeared to me [8]that the time had not yet come when that question could be discussed in a conclusive manner.[8]

I have realised, however, from your last letter that you regard this question as one of vital and urgent importance. I have, therefore, lost no

---

[7] No. 2.

[8]—[8] Former reading: "that the moment had not yet arrived when they could be most profitably discussed."

time in informing the Government of Great Britain of the contents of your letter, and it is with great pleasure that I communicate to you on their behalf the following statement, which I am confident you will receive with satisfaction:—

(⁹)The two districts of Mersina and Alexandretta and portions of Syria lying to the west of the districts of Damascus, Homs, Hama and Aleppo cannot be said to be purely Arab, and should be excluded from the limits demanded.

With the above modification, and without prejudice to our existing treaties with Arab chiefs, we accept those limits.

As for those regions lying within those frontiers wherein Great Britain is free to act without detriment to the interests of her ally, France, I am empowered in the name of the Government of Great Britain to give the following assurances and make the following reply to your letter:—

(1) Subject to the above modifications, Great Britain is prepared to recognise and support the independence of the Arabs in all the regions within the limits demanded by the Sherif of Mecca.(⁹)

(2) Great Britain will guarantee the Holy Places against all external aggression and will recognise their inviolability.

(3) When the situation admits, Great Britain will give to the Arabs her advice and will assist them to establish what may appear to be the most suitable forms of government in those various territories.

(⁹)—(⁹) Former reading: "The districts of Mersina and Alexandretta and the portions of Syria lying to the west of the districts of Damascus, Homs, Hama and Aleppo cannot be said to be purely Arab, and should be excluded from the proposed limits and boundaries. With the above modification, and without prejudice to our existing treaties with Arab chiefs, we accept these limits and boundaries, and, in regard to those portions of the territories therein in which Great Britain is free to act without detriment to the interests of her ally, France, I am empowered, in the name of the Government of Great Britain, to give you the following assurances and make the following reply to your letter:—

Subject to the above modifications, Great Britain is prepared to recognise and support the independence of the Arabs within the territories included in the limits and boundaries proposed by the Sherif of Mecca."

(4) On the other hand, it is understood that the Arabs have decided to seek the advice and guidance of Great Britain only, and that such European advisers and officials as may be required for the formation of a sound form of administration will be British.

(5) With regard to the *vilayets* of Bagdad and Basra, the Arabs will recognise that the established position and interests of Great Britain necessitate ([10])special administrative arrangements([10]) in order to secure these territories from foreign aggression, to promote the welfare of the local populations and to safeguard our mutual economic interests.

I am convinced that this declaration will assure you beyond all possible doubt of the sympathy of Great Britain towards the aspirations of ([11])her friends([11]) the Arabs and will result in a firm and lasting alliance, the immediate results of which will be the expulsion of the Turks from the Arab countries and the freeing of the Arab peoples from the Turkish yoke, which for so many years has pressed heavily upon them.

I have confined myself in this letter to the more vital and important questions, and if there are any other matters dealt with in your letters which I have omitted to mention, we may discuss them at some convenient date in the future.

It was with very great relief and satisfaction that I heard of the safe arrival of the Holy Carpet and the accompanying offerings which, thanks to the clearness of your directions and the excellence of your arrangements, were landed without trouble or mishap in spite of the dangers and difficulties occasioned by the present sad war. May God soon bring a lasting peace and freedom to all peoples!

I am sending this letter by the hand of your trusted and excellent messenger, Sheikh Mohammed Ibn Arif Ibn Uraifan, and he will inform you of the various matters of interest, but of less vital importance, which I have not mentioned in this letter.

(Compliments.)

(Signed)
A. HENRY McMAHON.

([10])—([10]) Former reading: "special measures of administrative control."

([11])—([11]) Former reading: "her traditional friends."

No. 5.

Translation of a letter from the Sherif of Mecca to Sir H. McMahon, His Majesty's High Commissioner at Cairo.

November 5, 1915.

(In the name of God, the Merciful, the Compassionate!)
To his Excellency the most exalted and eminent Minister who is endowed with the highest authority and soundness of opinion. May God guide him to do His Will!

I RECEIVED with great pleasure your honoured letter, dated the 15th Zil Hijja([12]) (the 24th October, 1915), to which I beg to answer as follows:—

1. In order to facilitate an agreement and to render a service to Islam, and at the same time to avoid all that may cause Islam troubles and hardships—seeing moreover that we have great consideration for the distinguished qualities and dispositions of the Government of Great Britain—we renounce our insistence on the inclusion of the *vilayets* of Mersina and Adana in the Arab Kingdom. But the two *vilayets* of Aleppo and Beirut and their sea coasts are purely Arab *vilayets*, and there is no difference between a Moslem and a Christian Arab: they are both descendants of one forefather.
    We Moslems will follow the footsteps of the Commander of the Faithful Omar ibn Khattab, and other Khalifs succeeding him, who ordained in the laws of the Moslem Faith that Moslems should treat the Christians as they treat themselves. He, Omar, declared with reference to Christians: "They will have the same privileges and submit to the same duties as ourselves." They will thus enjoy their civic rights in as much as it accords with the general interests of the whole nation.
2. As the Iraqi *vilayets* are parts of the pure Arab Kingdom, and were in fact the seat of its Government in the time of Ali ibn Abu Talib, and in the time of all the Khalifs who succeeded him; and as in them began the civilisation of the Arabs, and as their towns were the first towns built in Islam where the Arab power became so great; therefore they are greatly valued by all Arabs far and near, and their traditions cannot be forgotten by them. Consequently, we cannot satisfy

---

([12]) No. 4.

the Arab nations or make them submit to give us such a title to nobility. But in order to render an accord easy, and taking into consideration the assurances mentioned in the fifth article of your letter to keep and guard our mutual interests in that country as they are one and the same, for all these reasons we might agree to leave under the British administration for a short time those districts now occupied by the British troops without the rights of either party being prejudiced thereby (especially those of the Arab nation; which interests are to it economic and vital), and against a suitable sum paid as compensation to the Arab Kingdom for the period of occupation, in order to meet the expenses which every new kingdom is bound to support; at the same time respecting your agreements with the Sheikhs of those districts, and especially those which are essential.

3. In your desire to hasten the movement we see not only advantages, but grounds of apprehension. The first of these grounds is the fear of the blame of the Moslems of the opposite party (as has already happened in the past), who would declare that we have revolted against Islam and ruined its forces. The second is that, standing in the face of Turkey which is supported by all the forces of Germany, we do not know what Great Britain and her Allies would do if one of the *Entente* Powers were weakened and obliged to make peace. We fear that the Arab nation will then be left alone in the face of Turkey together with her allies, but we would not at all mind if we were to face the Turks alone. Therefore it is necessary to take these points into consideration in order to avoid a peace being concluded in which the parties concerned may decide the fate of our people as if we had taken part in the war without making good our claims to official consideration.

4. The Arab nation has a strong belief that after this war is over the Turks under German influence will direct their efforts to provoke the Arabs and violate their rights, both material and moral, to wipe out their nobility and honour and reduce them to utter submission as they are determined to ruin them entirely. The reasons for the slowness shown in our action have already been stated.

5. When the Arabs know the Government of Great Britain is their ally who will not leave them to themselves at the conclusion of peace in the face of Turkey and Germany, and that she will support and will effectively defend them, then to enter the war at once will, no doubt, be in conformity with the general interest of the Arabs.

6. Our letter dated the 29th Shauâl, 1333([13]) (the 9th September, 1915), saves us the trouble of repeating our opinions as to articles 3 and 4 of your honoured last letter regarding administration, Government advisers and officials, especially as you have declared, exalted Minister, that you will not interfere with internal affairs.

7. The arrival of a clear and definite answer as soon as possible to the above proposals is expected. We have done our utmost in making concessions in order to come to an agreement satisfying both parties. We know that our lot in this war will be either a success, which will guarantee to the Arabs a life becoming their past history, or destruction in the attempt to attain their objects. Had it not been for the determination which I see in the Arabs for the attainment of their objects, I would have preferred to seclude myself on one of the heights of a mountain, but they, the Arabs, have insisted that I should guide the movement to this end.

May God keep you safe and victorious, as we devoutly hope and desire.
27th Zil Hijja, 1333.

No. 6.
Translation of a letter from Sir H. McMahon, His Majesty's High Commissioner at Cairo, to the Sherif of Mecca.

To Sherif Hussein: *December* 14, 1915.
(After customary greetings and acknowledgment of previous letter.)

I AM gratified to observe that you agree to the exclusion of the ([14])districts of Mersina and Adana from boundaries of the Arab territories.

I also note with great pleasure and satisfaction your assurances that the Arabs are determined to act in conformity with the precepts laid down by Omar Ibn Khattab and the early Khalifs, which secure the rights and privileges of all religions alike.

In stating that the Arabs are ready to recognise and respect all our treaties with Arab chiefs, it is, of course, understood that this will apply

([13]) No. 3.
([14]) Former reading: "vilayets."

to all territories included in the Arab Kingdom, as the Government of Great Britain cannot repudiate engagements which already exist.

With regard to the *vilayets* of Aleppo and Beirut, the Government of Great Britain have ([15])fully understood and([15]) taken careful note of your observations, but, as the interests of our ally, France, are involved ([16])in them both,([16]) the question will require careful consideration and a further communication on the subject will be addressed to you in due course.

The Government of Great Britain, as I have already informed you, are ready to give all guarantees of assistance and support within their power to the Arab Kingdom, but their interests demand, as you yourself have recognised, a friendly and stable administration in the *vilayet* of Bagdad, and the adequate safeguarding of these interests calls for a much fuller and more detailed consideration than the present situation and the urgency of these negotiations permit.

We fully appreciate your desire for caution, and have no wish to urge you to hasty action, which might jeopardise the eventual success of your projects, but, in the meantime, it is most essential that you should spare no effort to attach all the Arab peoples to our united cause and urge them to afford no assistance to our enemies.

It is on the success of these efforts and on the more active measures which the Arabs may hereafter take in support of our cause, when the time for action comes, that the permanence and strength of our agreement must depend.

Under these circumstances I am further directed by the Government of Great Britain to inform you that you may rest assured that Great Britain has no intention of concluding any peace in terms of which the freedom of the Arab peoples from German and Turkish domination does not form an essential condition.

As an earnest of our intentions, and in order to aid you in your efforts in our joint cause, I am sending you by your trustworthy messenger a sum of twenty thousand pounds.

(Customary ending.)

(Signed)
H. McMAHON.

([15])—([15]) The former reading omitted these words.
([16])—([16]) The former reading omitted these words.

No. 7.

Translation of a letter from the Sherif of Mecca to Sir H. McMahon, His Majesty's High Commissioner at Cairo.

January 1, 1916.

(In the name of God, the Merciful, the Compassionate!)

To his Excellency the eminent, energetic and magnanimous Minister.

WE received from the bearer your letter, dated the 9th Safar (the 14th December, 1915), with great respect and honour, and I have understood its contents, which caused me the greatest pleasure and satisfaction, as it removed that which had made me uneasy.

Your honour will have realised, after the arrival of Mohammed (Faroki) Sherif and his interview with you, that all our procedure up to the present was of no personal inclination or the like, which would have been wholly unintelligible, but that everything was the result of the decisions and desires of our peoples, and that we are but transmitters and executants of such decisions and desires in the position they (our people) have pressed upon us.

These truths are, in my opinion, very important and deserve your honour's special attention and consideration.

With regard to what had been stated in your honoured communication concerning El Iraq as to the matter of compensation for the period of occupation, we, in order to strengthen the confidence of Great Britain in our attitude and in our words and actions, really and veritably, and in order to give her evidence of our certainty and assurance in trusting her glorious Government, leave the determination of the amount to the perception of her wisdom and justice.

As regards the northern parts and their coasts, we have already stated in our previous letter what were the utmost possible modifications, and all this was only done so to fulfil those aspirations whose attainment is desired by the will of the Blessed and Supreme God. It is this same feeling and desire which impelled us to avoid what may possibly injure the alliance of Great Britain and France and the agreement made between them during the present wars and calamities; yet we find it our duty that the eminent minister should be sure that, at the first opportunity after this war is finished, we shall ask you (what we avert our eyes from to-day) for what we now leave to France in Beirut and its coasts.

I do not find it necessary to draw your attention to the fact that our plan is of greater security to the interests and ([17])protection of the rights of Great Britain than it is to us, and will necessarily be so whatever may happen, so that Great Britain may finally ([18])see her friends([18]) in that contentment and advancement which she is endeavouring to establish for them now, especially as her Allies being neighbours to us will be the germ of difficulties and discussion with which there will be ([19])no peaceful conditions([19]). In addition to which the citizens([20]) of Beirut will decidedly never accept such dismemberment,([21]) and they may oblige us to undertake new measures which may exercise Great Britain, certainly not less than her present troubles, because of our belief and certainty ([22])in the reciprocity and indeed the identity of our interests,([22]) which is the only cause that caused us never to care to negotiate with any other Power but you. Consequently, it is impossible to allow any derogation that gives France, or any other Power, a span of land in those regions.

I declare this, and I have a strong belief, which the living will inherit from the dead, in the declarations which you gave in the conclusion of your honoured letter. Therefore, the honourable and eminent Minister should believe and be sure, together with Great Britain, that we still remain firm to our resolution which Storrs learnt from us two years ago, for which we await the opportunity suitable to our situation, especially in view of that action the time of which has now come near and which destiny drives towards us with great haste and clearness, so that we and those who are of our opinion may have reasons for such action against any criticisms or responsibilities imposed upon us in future.

Your expression "we do not want to push you to any hasty action which might jeopardise the success of your aim" does not need any more explanation except what we may ask for, when necessary, such as arms, ammunition, &c.

([17]) Former reading: "presumption."
([18])—([18]) Former reading: "see all her own peoples."
([19])—([19]) Former reading: "no peace of mind."
([20]) Former reading: "people."
([21]) Former reading: "isolations."
([22])—([22]) Former reading: "in the reciprocity of our interests."

I deem this sufficient, as I have occupied much of your Honour's time. I beg to offer you my great veneration and respect.

25th Safar, 1334.

No. 8.

Translation of a letter from Sir H. McMahon, His Majesty's High Commissioner at Cairo, to the Sherif of Mecca.

(After customary greetings.)   *January 25, 1916.*

WE have received with great pleasure and satisfaction your letter of the 25th Safar (the 1st January([23])) at the hands of your trusty messenger, who has also transmitted to us your verbal messages.

We fully realise and entirely appreciate the motives which guide you in this important question, and we know well that you are acting entirely in the interests of the Arab peoples and with no thought beyond their welfare.

We take note of your remarks concerning the *vilayet* of Bagdad, and will take the question into careful consideration when the enemy has been defeated and the time for peaceful settlement arrives.

As regards the northern parts, we note with satisfaction your desire to avoid anything which might possibly injure the alliance of Great Britain and France. It is, as you know, our fixed determination that nothing shall be permitted to interfere in the slightest degree with our united prosecution of this war to a victorious conclusion. Moreover, when the victory has been won, the friendship of Great Britain and France will become yet more firm and enduring, cemented by the blood of Englishmen and Frenchmen who have died side by side fighting for the cause of right and liberty.

In this great cause Arabia is now associated, and God grant that the result of our mutual efforts and co-operation will bind us in a lasting friendship to the mutual welfare and happiness of us all.

We are greatly pleased to hear of the action you are taking to win all the Arabs over to our joint cause, and to dissuade them from giving any assistance to our enemies, and we leave it to your discretion to seize the most favourable moment for further and more decided measures.

([23]) No. 7.

You will doubtless inform us by the bearer of this letter of any manner in which we can assist you and your requests will always receive our immediate consideration.

You will have heard how El Sayed Ahmed el Sherif el Senussi has been beguiled by evil advice into hostile action, and it will be a great grief to you to know that he has been so far forgetful of the interests of the Arabs as to throw in his lot with our enemies. Misfortune has now overtaken him, and we trust that this will show him his error and lead him to peace for the sake of his poor misguided followers.

We are sending this letter by the hand of your good messenger, who will also bring to you all our news.

With salaams.

(Signed)
H. McMAHON.

No. 9.
Translation of a letter from the Sherif of Mecca to Sir H. McMahon, His Majesty's High Commissioner at Cairo.

February 18, 1916.

(In the name of the Merciful, the Compassionate!)

To the most noble His Excellency the High Commissioner. May God protect him.

(After compliments and respects.)

WE received your Excellency's letter dated 25th Rabi El Awal, and its contents filled us with the utmost pleasure and satisfaction at the attainment of the required understanding and the intimacy desired. I ask God to make easy our purposes and prosper our endeavours. Your Excellency will understand the work that is being done, and the reasons for it from the following:—

Firstly.—We had informed your Excellency that we had sent one of our sons to Syria to command the operations deemed necessary there. We have received a detailed report from him stating that the tyrannies of the Government there have not left of the persons upon whom they could depend, whether of the different ranks of soldiers or of others, save only a few, and those of secondary importance; and that he is awaiting the arrival of the forces announced from different places, especially from the people of the country and the surrounding Arab regions as Aleppo and the south of Mosul, whose total is calculated at not less than 100,000, by their estimate; and he intends, if the majority of the forces mentioned are Arab, to begin the movement by them; and, if otherwise, that is, of the Turks or others, he will observe their advance to the Canal, and when they begin to fight, his movements upon them will be different to what they expect.

Secondly.—We purposed sending our eldest son to Medina with sufficient forces to strengthen his brother (who is) in Syria, and with every possibility of occupying the railway line, or carrying out such operations as circumstances may admit. This is the beginning of the principal movement, and we are satisfied in its beginning with what we had levied as guards to keep the interior of the country quiet; they are of the people of Hejaz only, for many reasons, which it would take too long to set forth; chiefly the difficulties in the way of providing their necessities with secrecy and speed (although this precaution was not necessary) and to make it easy to bring reinforcements when needed; this is the summary of what you wished to understand. In my opinion it is sufficient, and it is to be taken as a foundation and a standard as to our actions in the face of all changes and unforeseen events which the sequence of events may show. It remains for us to state what we need at present:—

Firstly.—The amount of £50,000 in gold for the monthly pay of the troops levied, and other things the necessity of which needs no explanation. We beg you to send it with all possible haste.

Secondly.—20,000 sacks of rice, 15,000 sacks of flour, 3,000 sacks of barley, 150 sacks of coffee, 150 sacks of sugar, 5,000 rifles of the modern pattern and the necessary ammunition, and 100 boxes of the two sample cartridges (enclosed) and of Martini-Henry cartridges and "Aza," that is those of the rifles of the factory of St. Etienne in France, for the use of those two kinds of rifles of our tribes; it would not be amiss to send 500 boxes of both kinds.

Thirdly.—We think it better that the place of deposit of all these things should be Port Sudan.

Fourthly.—As the above provisions and munitions are not needed until the beginning of the movement (of which we will inform you officially), they should remain at the above place, and when we need them we will inform the Governor there of the place to which they may be conveyed, and of the intermediaries who will carry orders for receiving them.

Fifthly.—The money required should be sent at once to the Governor of Port Sudan, and a confidential agent will be sent by us to receive it, either all at once, or in two instalments, according as he is able, and this (ﻍ) is the (secret) sign to be recognised for accepting the man.

Sixthly.—Our envoy who will receive the money will be sent to Port Sudan in three weeks' time, that is to say, he will be there on the 5th Jamad Awal (9th March) with a letter from us addressed to Al Khawaga Elias Effendi, saying that he (Elias) will pay him, in accordance with the letter, the rent of our properties, and the signature will be clear in our name, but we will instruct him to ask for the Governor of the place, whom you will apprise of this person's arrival. After perusal of the letter, the money should be given to him on condition that no discussion whatever is to be made with him of any question concerning us. We beg you most emphatically not to tell him anything, keeping this affair secret, and he should be treated apparently as if he were nothing out of the way.

Let it not be thought that our appointment of another man results from lack of confidence in the bearer; it is only to avoid waste of time, for we are appointing him to a task elsewhere. At the same time we beg you not to embark or send him in a steamer, or officially, the means already arranged being sufficient.

Seventhly.—Our representative, bearer of the present letter, has been definitely instructed to ensure the arrival of this, and I think that his mission this time is finished since the condition of things is known both in general and in detail, and there is no need for sending anyone else. In case of need for sending information, it will come from us; yet as our next representative will reach you after three weeks, you may prepare instructions for him to take back. Yet let him be treated simply in appearance.

Eighthly.—Let the British Government consider this military expenditure in accordance with the books which will be furnished it, explaining how the money has been spent.

To conclude, my best and numberless salutations beyond all increase.

14 *Rabi al Akhar*, 1334.

No. 10.

Translation of a letter from Sir H. McMahon, His Majesty's High Commissioner at Cairo, to the Sherif of Mecca.

(After customary greetings.)   *March* 10, 1916.

WE have received your letter of the 14th Rabi el Akhar[24] (the 18th February), duly delivered by your trusted messenger.

We are grateful to note the active measures which you propose to take. We consider them the most suitable in the existing circumstances, and they have the approval of His Majesty's Government. I am pleased to be able to inform you that His Majesty's Government have approved of meeting your requests, and that which you asked to be sent with all haste is being despatched with your messenger, who is also the bearer of this letter.

The remainder will be collected as quickly as possible and will be deposited at Port Sudan, where it will remain until we hear from you officially of the beginning of the movement and of the places to which they may be conveyed and the intermediaries who will carry out the orders for receiving them.

The necessary instructions, as set forth in your letter, have been issued to the Governor at Port Sudan, and he will arrange everything in accordance with your wishes.

Your representative who brought your last letter has been duly facilitated in his journey to Jeizan, and every assistance has been given him in his mission, which we trust will be crowned with good results.

We have arranged that, on completion, he will be brought to Port Sudan, whence he will proceed by the safest means to join you and report the results of his work.

We take the opportunity, in sending this letter, to explain to you a matter which might otherwise not have been clear to you, and which might have given rise to misunderstanding. There are various Turkish posts and small garrisons along the coasts of Arabia who are hostile to us, and who are said to be planning injury to our naval interests in the Red Sea. We may, therefore, find it necessary to take hostile measures against these posts and garrisons, but we have issued strict instructions that every care must be taken by our ships to differentiate between the

---

[24] No. 9.

hostile Turkish garrisons and the innocent Arab inhabitants, towards whom we entertain such friendly feelings.

We give you notice of this matter in case distorted and false reports may reach you of the reasons for any action which we may be obliged to take.

We have heard rumours that our mutual enemies are endeavouring to construct boats for the purpose of laying mines in the Red Sea, and of otherwise injuring our interests there, and we beg of you that you will give us early information should you receive any confirmation of such reports.

We have heard that Ibn Rashid has been selling large quantities of camels to the Turks, which are being sent up to Damascus.

We hope that you will be able to use your influence with him in order that he may cease from this practice and, if he still persists, that you will be able to arrange for the Arabs who lie between him and Syria to seize the camels as they pass, a procedure which will be to our mutual advantage.

I am glad to be able to inform you that those misguided Arabs under Sayed Ahmed el Senussi, who have fallen victims to the wiles of Turkish and German intriguers, are now beginning to see the error of their ways, and are coming in to us in large numbers, asking for forgiveness and friendship.

We have severely defeated the forces which these intriguers had collected against us, and the eyes of the Arabs are now becoming open to the deceit which has been practised upon them.

The capture of Erzerum, and the defeats sustained by the Turks in the Caucasus, are having a great effect in our favour, and are greatly helping the cause for which we are both working.

We ask God to prosper your endeavours and to further the work which you have taken in hand.

In conclusion, we beg you to accept our warmest salutations and expressions of friendship.

(Signed)
A. H. McMAHON.

6 Jamad Awwal, 1334.

Appendix II

McMahon's 24 October 1915 Letter to Sharif Hussein

The Letter in English

No. 4.

Translation of a letter from Sir H. McMahon, His Majesty's High Commissioner at Cairo, to the Sherif of Mecca.

October 24, 1915.

I HAVE received your letter of the 29th Shawal, 1333, with much pleasure and your expressions of friendliness and sincerity have given me the greatest satisfaction.

I regret that you should have received from my last letter([7]) the impression that I regarded the question of the limits and boundaries with coldness and hesitation; such was not the case, but it appeared to me ([8])that the time had not yet come when that question could be discussed in a conclusive manner.([8])

([7]) No. 2.

([8])—([8]) Former reading: "that the moment had not yet arrived when they could be most profitably discussed."

I have realised, however, from your last letter that you regard this question as one of vital and urgent importance. I have, therefore, lost no time in informing the Government of Great Britain of the contents of your letter, and it is with great pleasure that I communicate to you on their behalf the following statement, which I am confident you will receive with satisfaction :—

([9])The two districts of Mersina and Alexandretta and portions of Syria lying to the west of the districts of Damascus, Homs, Hama and Aleppo cannot be said to be purely Arab, and should be excluded from the limits demanded.

With the above modification, and without prejudice to our existing treaties with Arab chiefs, we accept those limits.

As for those regions lying within those frontiers wherein Great Britain is free to act without detriment to the interests of her ally, France, I am empowered in the name of the Government of Great Britain to give the following assurances and make the following reply to your letter :—

(1) Subject to the above modifications, Great Britain is prepared to recognise and support the independence of the Arabs in all the regions within the limits demanded by the Sherif of Mecca.([9])

(2) Great Britain will guarantee the Holy Places against all external aggression and will recognise their inviolability.

(3) When the situation admits, Great Britain will give to the Arabs her advice and will assist them to establish what may appear to be the most suitable forms of government in those various territories.

(4) On the other hand, it is understood that the Arabs have decided to seek the advice and guidance of Great Britain only, and that such European advisers and officials as may be required for the formation of a sound form of administration will be British.

(5) With regard to the *vilayets* of Bagdad and Basra, the Arabs will recognise that the established position and interests of Great Britain necessitate ([10])special administrative arrangements([10]) in order to secure these territories from foreign aggression, to promote the welfare of the local populations and to safeguard our mutual economic interests.

([9])—([9]) Former reading: "The districts of Mersina and Alexandretta and the portions of Syria lying to the west of the districts of Damascus, Homs, Hama and Aleppo cannot be said to be purely Arab, and should be excluded from the proposed limits and boundaries. With the above modification, and without prejudice to our existing treaties with Arab chiefs, we accept these limits and boundaries, and, in regard to those portions of the territories therein in which Great Britain is free to act without detriment to the interests of her ally, France, I am empowered, in the name of the Government of Great Britain, to give you the following assurances and make the following reply to your letter : —

Subject to the above modifications, Great Britain is prepared to recognise and support the independence of the Arabs within the territories included in the limits and boundaries proposed by the Sherif of Mecca."

([10])—([10]) Former reading: "special measures of administrative control."

I am convinced that this declaration will assure you beyond all possible doubt of the sympathy of Great Britain towards the aspirations of ([11])her friends([11]) the Arabs and will result in a firm and lasting alliance, the immediate results of which will be the expulsion of the Turks from the Arab countries and the freeing of the Arab peoples from the Turkish yoke, which for so many years has pressed heavily upon them.

I have confined myself in this letter to the more vital and important questions, and if there are any other matters dealt with in your letters which I have omitted to mention, we may discuss them at some convenient date in the future.

It was with very great relief and satisfaction that I heard of the safe arrival of the Holy Carpet and the accompanying offerings which, thanks to the clearness of your directions and the excellence of your arrangements, were landed without trouble or mishap in spite of the dangers and difficulties occasioned by the present sad war. May God soon bring a lasting peace and freedom to all peoples!

I am sending this letter by the hand of your trusted and excellent messenger, Sheikh Mohammed Ibn Arif Ibn Uraifan, and he will inform you of the various matters of interest, but of less vital importance, which I have not mentioned in this letter.

(Compliments.)

(Signed)   A. HENRY McMAHON.

(11)—(11) Former reading: "her traditional friends."

The Letter in Arabic

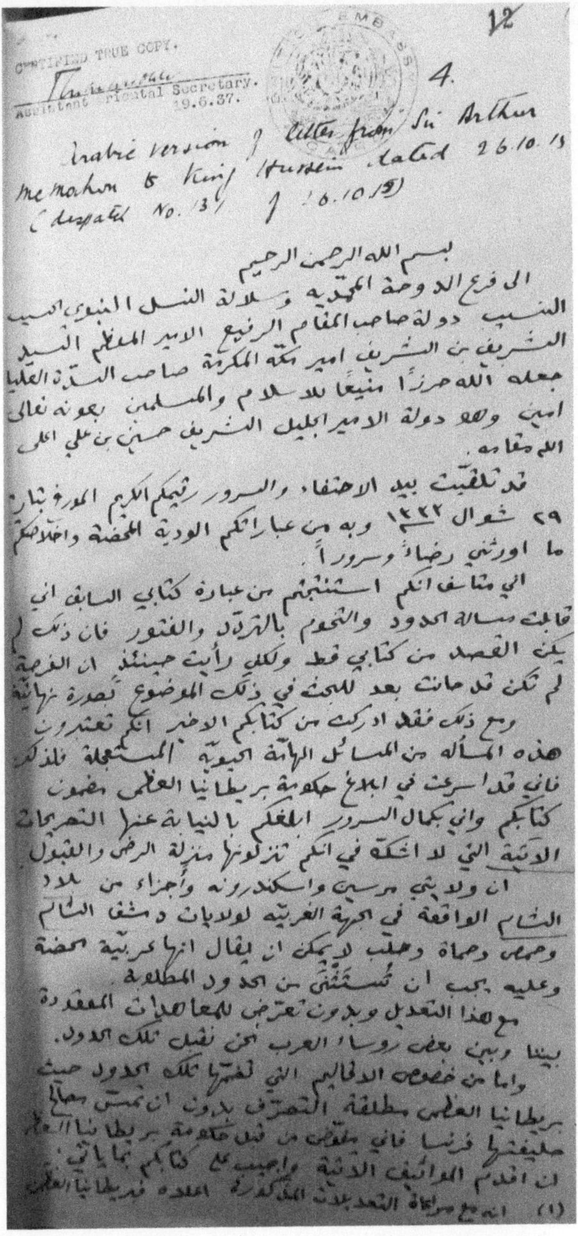

CERTIFIED TRUE COPY.
Assistant Oriental Secretary.
19.6.37.

12

4.

Arabic version of letter from Sir Arthur McMahon to King Hussein dated 26.10.15 (despatch No. 131 of 26.10.15)

بسم الله الرحمن الرحيم

الى فرع الدوحة المحمديه وسلالة النسل النبوي الحسيب
النسيب دولة صاحب المقام الرفيع الامير المعظم السيد
الشريف بن الشريف امير مكة المكرمة صاحب السدة العليا
جعله الله حرزاً منيعاً للاسلام والمسلمين بعونه تعالى
امين وهو دولة الامير الجليل الشريف حسين بن علي اعلى
الله مقامه.

قد تلقيت بيد الاحتفاء والسرور رقيمكم الكريم المؤرخ بتاريخ
٢٩ شوال ١٣٣٣ وبه من عباراتكم الودية المحضة واخلاصكم
ما اورثني رضاءً وسروراً.

اني متأسف انكم استنتجتم من عبارة كتابي السابق اني
قابلت مسألة الحدود والتخوم بالتردد والفتور فان ذلك لم
يكن القصد من كتابي قط ولكني رأيت حينئذ ان الفرصة
لم تكن قد حانت بعد للبحث في ذلك الموضوع بصورة نهائية
ومع ذلك فقد ادركت من كتابكم الاخير انكم تعتبرون
هذه المسألة من المسائل الهامة الحيوية المستعجلة فلذلك
فاني قد اسرعت في ابلاغ حكومة بريطانيا العظمى مضمون
كتابكم واني بكمال السرور ابلغكم بالنيابة عنها التصريحات
الآتية التي لا اشك في انكم تتلقونها بمنزلة الرضى والقبول

ان ولايتي مرسين واسكندرونه واجزاء من بلاد
الشام الواقعة في الجهة الغربية لولايات دمشق الشام
وحمص وحماة وحلب لا يمكن ان يقال انها عربية محضة
وعليه يجب ان تستثنى من الحدود المطلوبة

مع هذا التعديل وبدون تعرض للمعاهدات المعقودة
بيننا وبين بعض رؤساء العرب نحن نقبل تلك الحدود.

واما من خصوص الاقاليم التي تضمها تلك الحدود حيث
بريطانيا العظمى مطلقة التصرف بدون ان تمس مصالح
حليفتها فرنسا فاني مفوض من قبل حكومة بريطانيا العظمى
ان اقدم المواثيق الآتية واجيب على كتابكم بما يأتي:
(١) انه مع مراعاة التعديلات المذكورة اعلاه فبريطانيا العظمى

مستعدة بأن تعترف باستقلال العرب وتوثق ذلك الاستقلال
في جميع الاقاليم الداخلة في الحدود التي يطلبها دولة شريف
مكة

(٢) ان بريطانيا العظمى تضمن الاماكن المقدسة من كل اعتداء
خارجي وتعترف بوجوب منع التعدى عليها

(٣) وعندما تسمح الظروف تقدم بريطانيا العظمى العرب
بما تجد وتساعدهم على ايجاد هيئات حامية سلامة لتلك
الاقاليم المختلفة

(٤) هذا وان المفهوم ان العرب قد قرروا طلب نصائح وارشادات
بريطانيا العظمى وحدها وان المستشارين والموظفين الاوربيلوين
اللازمين لتشكيل هيئة ادارية قويمة يكونون من الانكليز

(٥) اما من خصوص ولايتي بغداد والبصرة فان العرب
تعترف ان مركز ومصالح بريطانيا العظمى المطردة هناك تستلزم
اتخاذ تدابير ادارية خصوصية لوقاية هذه الاقاليم من الاعتداء
الاجنبي ولزيادة خير سكانها وحماية مصالحنا الاقتصادية المتبادلة

واني متيقن ان لهذا التصريح يؤكد لدولتكم بدون ادنى
ارتياب ميل بريطانيا العظمى نحو جانب اصدقائها العرب ونشرحي
بعقد حالفة دائمة ثابتة بعزم ويكون من نتائجها المستعجلة
طرد الاتراك من بلاد العرب وتحرير الشعوب العربية من نير
الاتراك الذي اثقل كاهلهم السنين الطوال

ولقد اقتصرت في كتابي هذا على المسائل الحيوية ذات
الاهمية الكبرى وان كان هناك مسائل في خطابكم
لم تذكر هنا فسنعود الى اللجنة فيها في وقت مناسب
في المستقبل

ولقد تلقيت بمزيد السرور والرضى خبر وصول الكسوة
الشريفه وبما جاء من الصدقات بالسلامة وانا ببعض
ارشاداتكم السامية وتدابيركم المحكمة قد انزلت الى البر بلا
تعب ولاضرر ونجا من الاخطار والمصاعب التي تعترها
هذه حرب المحزنة ونرجو الله سبحانه وتعالى ان يعجل
الصلح الدائم والكرتة لدخل العالم

ابريل خطابي لهذا مع رسول النبيل الامين الشيخ
حمد بن عارف بن عريفات وسيعرض على سماعكم

بعض المسائل المعلقة التي هي من الدرجة الثانية من الاهمية
ولم اذكرها في كتابي هذا .

وفي الختام ان دولة الشريف ذا الحب المنيف
والامير الجليل كامل نجيب وخالص مودتي واعرب عن
تمنيه له ولبنيه افراد اسرته الكريمة اجنيا من ذي
احلال ان يوفقنا جميعا لما فيه خير العالم وصلاح الشعوب
ان بيده مفاتيح الامر والغيب يحركها كيف يشا،
ونساله تعالى حسن الختام والسلام

تحريرا في يوم الاثنين ١٥ ذي الحجة ١٣٢٢

نائب جلالة الملك   عبد الاكرم الشريف بعاليه برق الله
السير ارثر مكماهون

Selected Bibliography

Primary Sources

The British Library, India Office (L/P & S)
Cabinet Office (CAB)
Colonial Office (CO)
Foreign Office (FO)
Middle East Centre, St Antony's College, Oxford (Private papers: George Antonius, Norman Bentwich, Wyndham Deedes, Hubert Young)
The National Archives (United Kingdom)
Sudan Archive, University of Durham (Private papers: Gilbert Clayton, Malcolm MacDonald, Reginald Wingate)

Secondary Sources

Allen, L., *A History of False Hope. Investigative Commissions in Palestine*, Stanford: Stanford University Press, 2021
Antonius, G., *The Arab Awakening*, Beirut: Librairie du Liban, 1938
Asquith, H.H., *Letters of the Earl of Asquith and Oxford to a friend, 1915–1922*, London: Geoffrey Bles, 1933
Barr, J., *Setting the Desert on Fire*, London: Bloomsbury, 2006
_____, *A Line in the Sand. Britain, France and the Struggle for the Mastery of the Middle East*, London: Simon & Schuster, 2011
Ben-Ami, S., *Scars of War, Wounds of Peace: The Israel-Arab Tragedy*, London: Weidenfeld & Nicolson, 2005
Bennett, G.H., *British Foreign Policy during the Curzon Period, 1919–24*, London: Palgrave Macmillan, 1995

Bethell, N., *The Palestine Triangle. The Struggle between the British, the Jews and the Arabs, 1935–48*, London: Andre Deutsch, 1979

Black, I., *Enemies and Neighbours. Arabs and Jews in Palestine and Israel, 1917–2017*, London: Allen Lane, 2017

Boyle, S.S., *Betrayal of Palestine. The Story of George Antonius*, New York: Perseus, 2001

Caplan, N., *Palestine Jewry and the Arab Question, 1917–1925*, London: Frank Cass, 1978

Cohen, M.J., *The Origins and Evolution of the Arab–Zionist Conflict*, Los Angeles: California University Press, 1987

Colville, J.R., *Man of Valour. The Life of Field Marshal the Viscount Gort*, London: Collins, 1972

Dawn, C.E., *From Ottomanism to Arabism. Essays on the Origins of Arab Nationalism*, Urbana: University of Illinois Press, 1973

Djemal Pasha, *Memories of a Turkish Statesman, 1913–1919*, New York: Arno Press, 1973

Documents on British Foreign Policy, 1919–1939, First Series, Vols. IV, XIII, HMSO, 1963

Elkins, C., *Legacy of Violence. A History of the British Empire*, London: The Bodley Head, 2022

Ferguson, N., *Empire. How Britain Made the Modern World*, London: Penguin, 2004

Friedman, I., *The Question of Palestine, 1914–1918. British-Jewish-Arab Relations*, London: Routledge & Kegan Paul, 1973

———, *Palestine. A Twice-Promised Land? The British, the Arabs & Zionism, 1915–1920*, London: Transaction Publishers, 2000

———, *British Pan-Arab Policy, 1915–1922, A Critical Appraisal*, London: Transaction Publishers, 2010

Fromkin, D., *A Peace to End All Peace: Creating the Modern Middle East, 1914–1922*, London: Penguin, 1991

Gilbert, M., *Winston S. Churchill. Companion Volume IV, Part 3: April 1921–November 1922*, London: Heinemann, 1977

———, *Exile and Return. The Emergence of Jewish Statehood*, London: Weidenfeld and Nicolson, 1978

Haycraft, T., *Palestine. Disturbances in May, 1921. Reports of the Commission of Inquiry with Correspondence Relating Thereto* (Cmd 1540), HMSO, October 1921

Hope Simpson, J., *Palestine. Report on Immigration, Land Settlement and Development* (Cmd 3686), HMSO, October 1930

Hourani, A., *A History of the Arab Peoples*, London: Faber & Faber, 1991

Hughes, M., *Britain's Pacification of Palestine. The British Army, the Colonial State, and the Arab Revolt, 1936–1939*, Cambridge: Cambridge University Press, 2019

Huneidi, S., *A Broken Trust. Herbert Samuel, Zionism and the Palestinians, 1920–1925*, London: I.B. Tauris, 2001

_____, *The Hidden History of the Balfour Declaration*, New York and London: Or Books, 2019

Hyam, R., *Britain's Declining Empire: The Road to Decolonisation, 1918–1968*, Cambridge: Cambridge University Press, 2006

Ingrams, D., *Palestine Papers. 1917–1922: Seeds of Conflict*, London: Eland, 1972

Jeffries, J.M.N., *Palestine. The Reality*, London: Longmans, Green & Co., 1939. Reprinted, Skyscraper, 2017

_____, *The Palestine Deception, 1915–1923. The McMahon–Hussein Correspondence, the Balfour Declaration and the Jewish National Home*, ed. William M. Mathew, Washington D.C.: Institute for Palestine Studies, 2014

Kattan, V., *From Coexistence to Conquest: International Law and the Origins of the Arab-Israeli Conflict, 1891–1949*, London: Pluto Press, 2009

Kedourie, E., *The Chatham House Version and Other Middle Eastern Studies*, London: Weidenfeld and Nicolson, 1970

_____, *In the Anglo-Arab Labyrinth. The McMahon–Husayn Correspondence and Its Interpretations, 1914–1939*, Cambridge: Cambridge University Press, 1976

Keith-Roach, E., *Pasha of Jerusalem. Memoirs of a District Commissioner under the British Mandate*, London: Radcliffe Press, 1994

Kelemen, P., *The British Left and Zionism. History of a Divorce*, Manchester and New York: Manchester University Press, 2012

Khalidi, R., *The Iron Cage. The Story of the Palestinian Struggle for Statehood*, Boston: Beacon Press, 2007

_____, *The Hundred Years' War on Palestine. A History of Settler Colonial Conquest and Resistance*, London: Profile Books, 2020

Khalidi, W., *From Haven to Conquest: Readings in Zionism and the Palestine Problem until 1948*, Washington D.C.: Institute for Palestine Studies, 1987

_____, *Palestine Reborn*, London: I.B. Tauris, 1992

Klieman, A.S., *Foundations of British Policy in the Arab World: The Cairo Conference of 1921*, London: John Hopkins Press, 1970

Laqueur, W., and B. Rubin, eds, *The Israel–Arab Reader. A Documentary History of the Middle East Conflict*, New York: Facts on File, 1985

MacMillan, M., *Peacemakers. The Paris Conference of 1919 and Its Attempt to End War*, London: John Murray, 2001

Mansfield, P., *A History of the Middle East*, London: Penguin, 1992

Masalha, N., *The Palestine Nakba. Decolonising History, Narrating the Subaltern, Reclaiming Memory*, London and New York: Zed Books, 2012

McHugo, J., *A Concise History of the Arabs*, London: Saqi, 2016

McMahon–Hussein, *Correspondence between Sir Henry McMahon, G.C.M.G., G.C.V.O., K.C.I.E., C.S.I., His Majesty's High Commissioner at Cairo, and the Sherif Hussein of Mecca, July 1915–March 1916 [with a map]* (Cmd 5957), HMSO, March 1939

McMeekin, S., *The Ottoman Endgame: War, Revolution and the Making of the Modern Middle East, 1908–1923*, London: Allen Lane, 2015

Mearsheimer, J.J., and S.M. Walt, *The Israel Lobby and U.S. Foreign Policy*, New York: Farrar, Straus and Giroux, 2007

Mearsheimer, J.J., *Why Leaders Lie. The Truth about Lying in International Politics*, Oxford: Oxford University Press, 2011

Monroe, E., *Britain's Moment in the Middle East, 1914–1956*, London: Methuen, 1963

Morris, B., *Righteous Victims. A History of the Zionist-Arab Conflict, 1881–1999*, New York: Alfred A. Knopf, 1999

Palin, P., 'Report of the Court of Inquiry convened by order of H.E. the High Commissioner and Commander-in-Chief, dated the 12th day of April, 1920' [Palin Report], August 1920

Pappe, I., *A History of Modern Palestine*, Cambridge: Cambridge University Press, 2004

Parsons, L., *The Commander. Fawzi Al-Qawuqji and the Fight for Arab Independence, 1914–1948*, London: Saqi, 2016

_____, 'The Secret Testimony of the Peel Commission (Part I): Underbelly of Empire', *Journal of Palestine Studies* 49, 1 (2019), 7–24

_____, 'The Secret Testimony of the Peel Commission (Part II): Partition', *Journal of Palestine Studies* 49, 2 (2020), 8–25

Peel, W., *Palestine Royal Commission Report* [Peel Report] (Cmd 5479), HMSO, July 1937

Porath, Y., *The Emergence of the Palestinian Arab National Movement, 1918–1929*, London: Frank Cass, 1974

_____, *The Palestinian Arab National Movement, 1929–1939. From Riots to Rebellion*, London: Frank Cass, 1977

Regan, B., *The Balfour Declaration. Empire, the Mandate and Resistance in Palestine*, London: Verso, 2017

Reid, W., *Empire of Sand. How Britain Made the Middle East*, Edinburgh: Birlinn, 2011

Reinharz, J., *Chaim Weizmann: The Making of a Statesman*, Oxford: Oxford University Press, 1993

Rendel, G.W., *The Sword and the Olive. Recollections of Diplomacy and the Foreign Service, 1913–1954*, London: John Murray, 1957

Rogan, E., *The Arabs. A History*, London: Allen Lane, 2009

_____, *The Fall of the Ottomans. The Great War in the Middle East, 1914–1920*, London: Allen Lane, 2015

Rose, N.A., *The Gentile Zionists. A Study in Anglo-Zionist Diplomacy, 1929–1939*, London: Frank Cass, 1973

_____, *Chaim Weizmann. A Biography*, London: Weidenfeld and Nicolson, 1986

Sabbagh, K., *Palestine. A Personal History*, London: Grove Atlantic, 2006

Said, E.W., 'Zionism from the Standpoint of its Victims', *Social Text* 1 (1979), 7–58

_____, *The Question of Palestine*, New York: Vintage, 1992

Samuel, H., *Memoirs*, London: Cresset Press, 1945

Sanders, R., *The High Walls of Jerusalem. A History of the Balfour Declaration and the Birth of the British Mandate for Palestine*, New York: Holt, Rinehart and Winston, 1983

Sayigh, Y., *Armed Struggle and the Search for a State: The Palestinian National Movement, 1949–1993*, Oxford: Oxford University Press, 1997

Schneer, J., *The Balfour Declaration. The Origins of the Arab-Israeli Conflict*, London: Bloomsbury, 2010

Segev, T., *One Palestine, Complete. Jews and Arabs under the British Mandate*, New York: Metropolitan, 1999

Shaw, W., Report of the *Commission on the Palestine Disturbances of August, 1929* [Shaw Report] (Cmd 3530), HMSO, March 1930

Shepherd, N., *Ploughing Sand: British Rule in Palestine, 1917–1948*, New Brunswick: Rutgers University Press, 2000

Sherman, A.J., *Mandate Days. British Lives in Palestine, 1918–1948*, London: Thames & Hudson, 1997

Shlaim, A., *The Iron Wall. Israel and the Arab World*, London: Allen Lane, 2000

Sinanoglou, P., *Partitioning Palestine. British Policymaking at the End of Empire*, Chicago and London: Chicago University Press, 2019

Stein, K., *The Land Question in Palestine, 1917–1939*, Chapel Hill and London: University of North Carolina Press, 1985

Stein, L., *The Balfour Declaration*, London: Valentine, Mitchell and Co., 1961

Storrs, R., *Orientations*, London: Ivor Nicholson & Watson Ltd., 1939

Sykes, C., *Crossroads to Israel, 1917–1948*, Bloomington: Indiana University Press, 1965

Teveth, S., *Ben-Gurion. The Burning Ground, 1886–1948*, Boston: Houghton Mifflin Co., 1987

Thompson, E.F., *How the West Stole Democracy from the Arabs. The Syrian Congress of 1920 and the Destruction of Its Historic Liberal-Islamic Alliance*, London: Grove Press, 2020

Thompson, G., *Legacy of Empire. Britain, Zionism and the Creation of Israel*, London: Saqi, 2019

Tibawi, A.L., *Anglo-Arab Relations and the Question of Palestine, 1914–1921*, London: Luzac & Co., 1977

Ulrichsen, K.C., *The Logistics and Politics of the British Campaigns in the Middle East, 1914–22*, Basingstoke: Palgrave Macmillan, 2011

———, *The First World War in the Middle East*, London: Hurst & Co., 2014

Wasserstein, B., *The British in Palestine: The Mandatory Government and the Arab-Jewish Conflict, 1917–1929*, Oxford: Blackwell, 1991

Wedgwood, C.V., *The Last of the Radicals: The Life of Josiah Clement Wedgwood MP.*, London: Jonathan Cape, 1951

Weizmann, C., *Trial and Error*, London: Hamish Hamilton, 1949

Westrate, B., *The Arab Bureau. British Policy in the Middle East, 1916–1920*, University Park: Pennsylvania State University Press, 1992

Wolfe, P., *Traces of History. Elementary Structures of Race*, London and New York: Verso, 2016

Young, H., *The Independent Arab*, London: John Murray, 1933

Zu'aytir, A., *Al-Haraka al-Wataniyya al-Filastiniyya, 1935–1939: Yowmiyat Akram Zu'aytir* [The Palestinian National Movement: Diaries of Akram Zu'aytir], Beirut: Institute of Palestine Studies, 1992

Index

References to images are in *italics*.